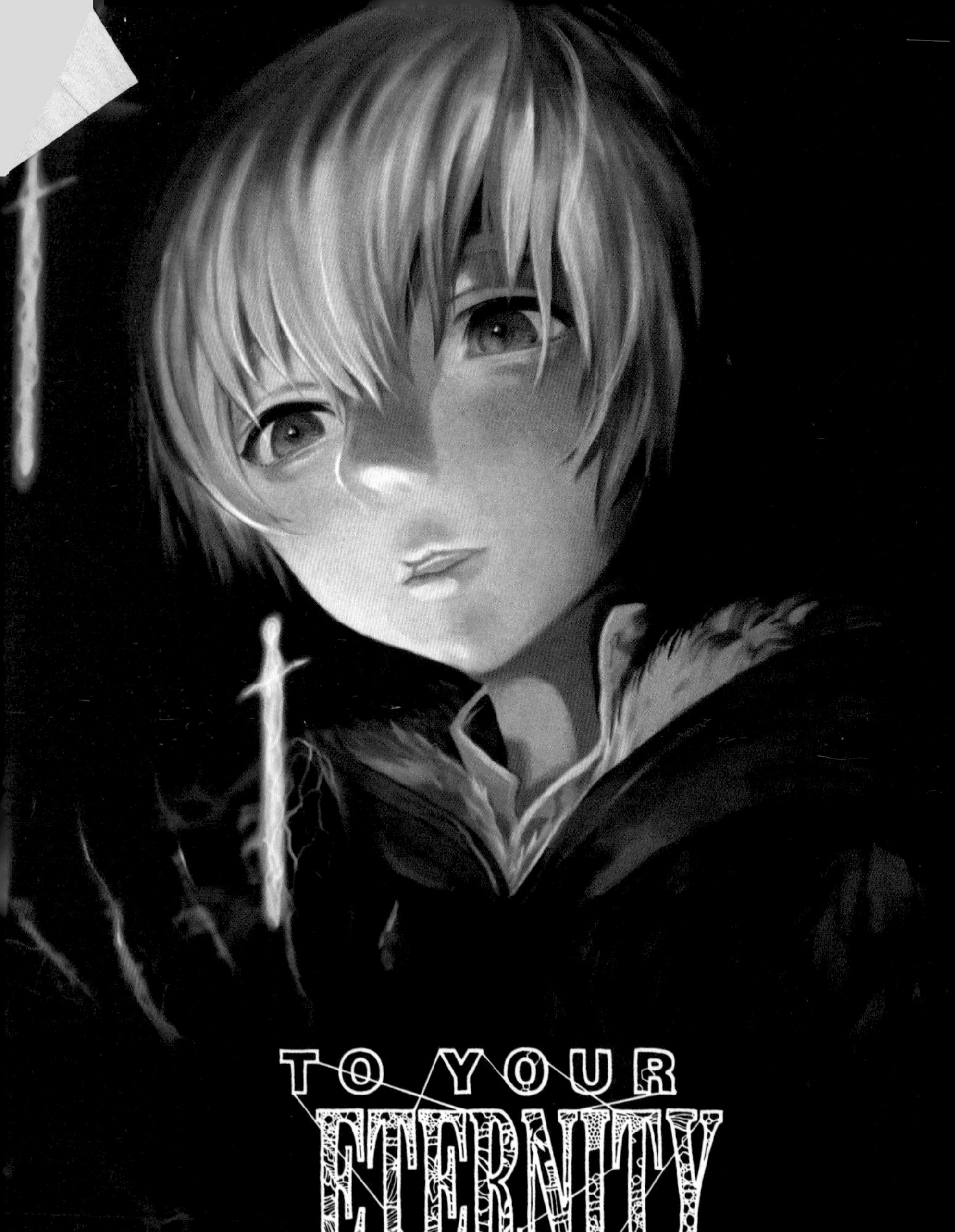

TO YOUR ETERNITY

YOSHITOKI OIMA

3

CONTENTS

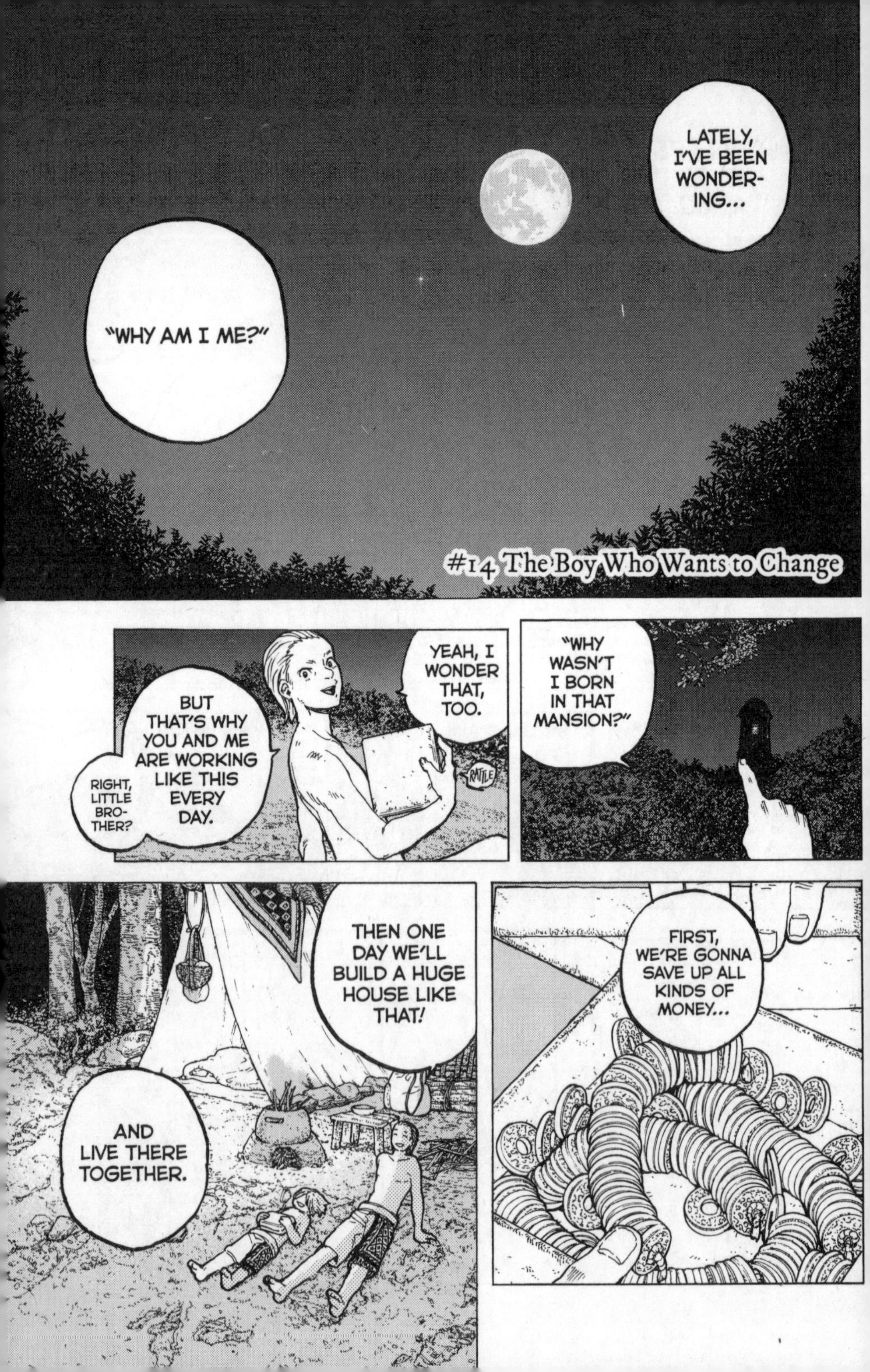
LATELY, I'VE BEEN WONDER-ING...
"WHY AM I ME?"
#14 The Boy Who Wants to Change
"WHY WASN'T I BORN IN THAT MANSION?"
YEAH, I WONDER THAT, TOO.
RATTLE
BUT THAT'S WHY YOU AND ME ARE WORKING LIKE THIS EVERY DAY.
RIGHT, LITTLE BRO-THER?
FIRST, WE'RE GONNA SAVE UP ALL KINDS OF MONEY...
THEN ONE DAY WE'LL BUILD A HUGE HOUSE LIKE THAT!
AND LIVE THERE TOGETHER.

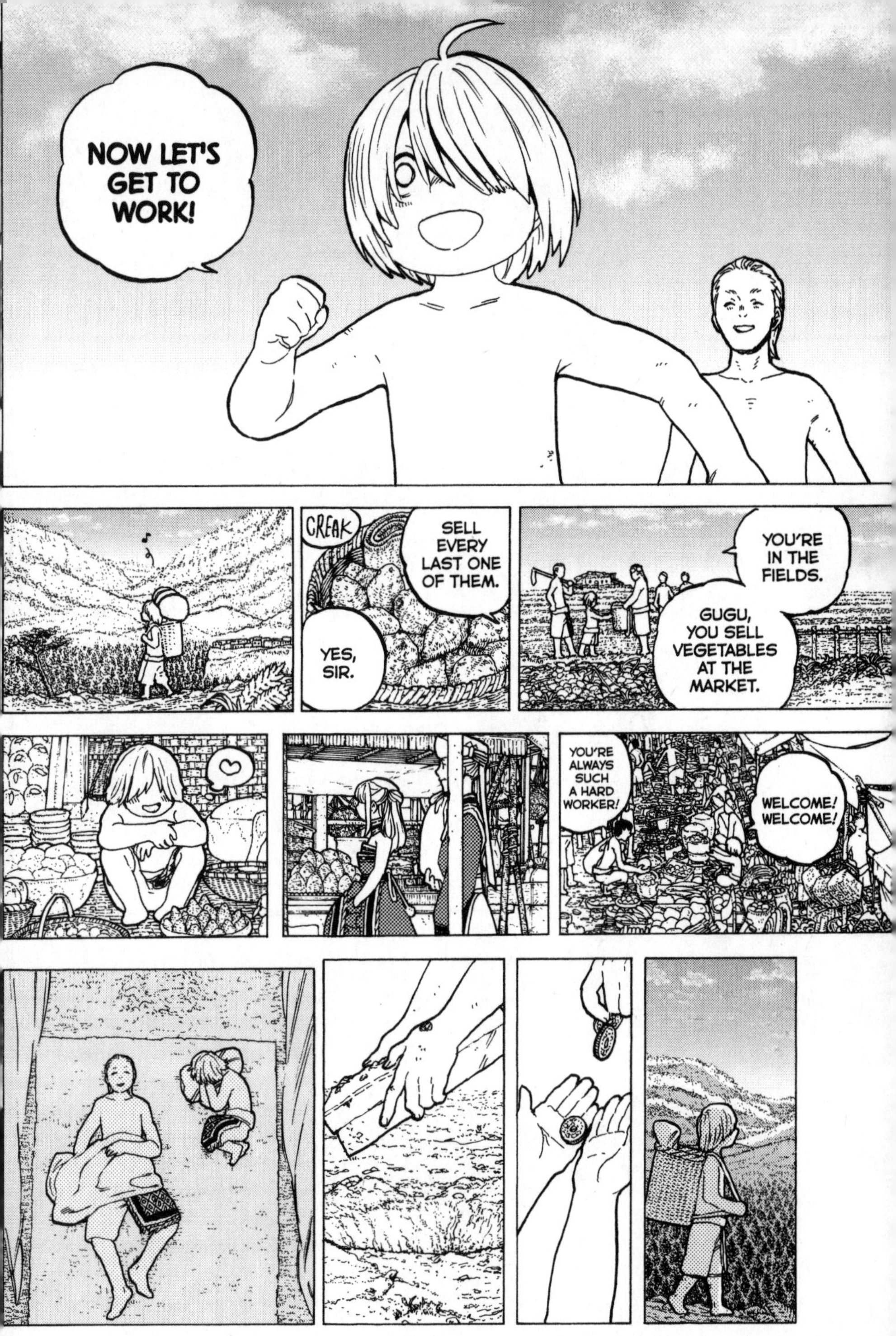
NOW LET'S GET TO WORK!
YOU'RE IN THE FIELDS.
GUGU, YOU SELL VEGETABLES AT THE MARKET.
SELL EVERY LAST ONE OF THEM.
CREAK
YES, SIR.
WELCOME! WELCOME!
YOU'RE ALWAYS SUCH A HARD WORKER!

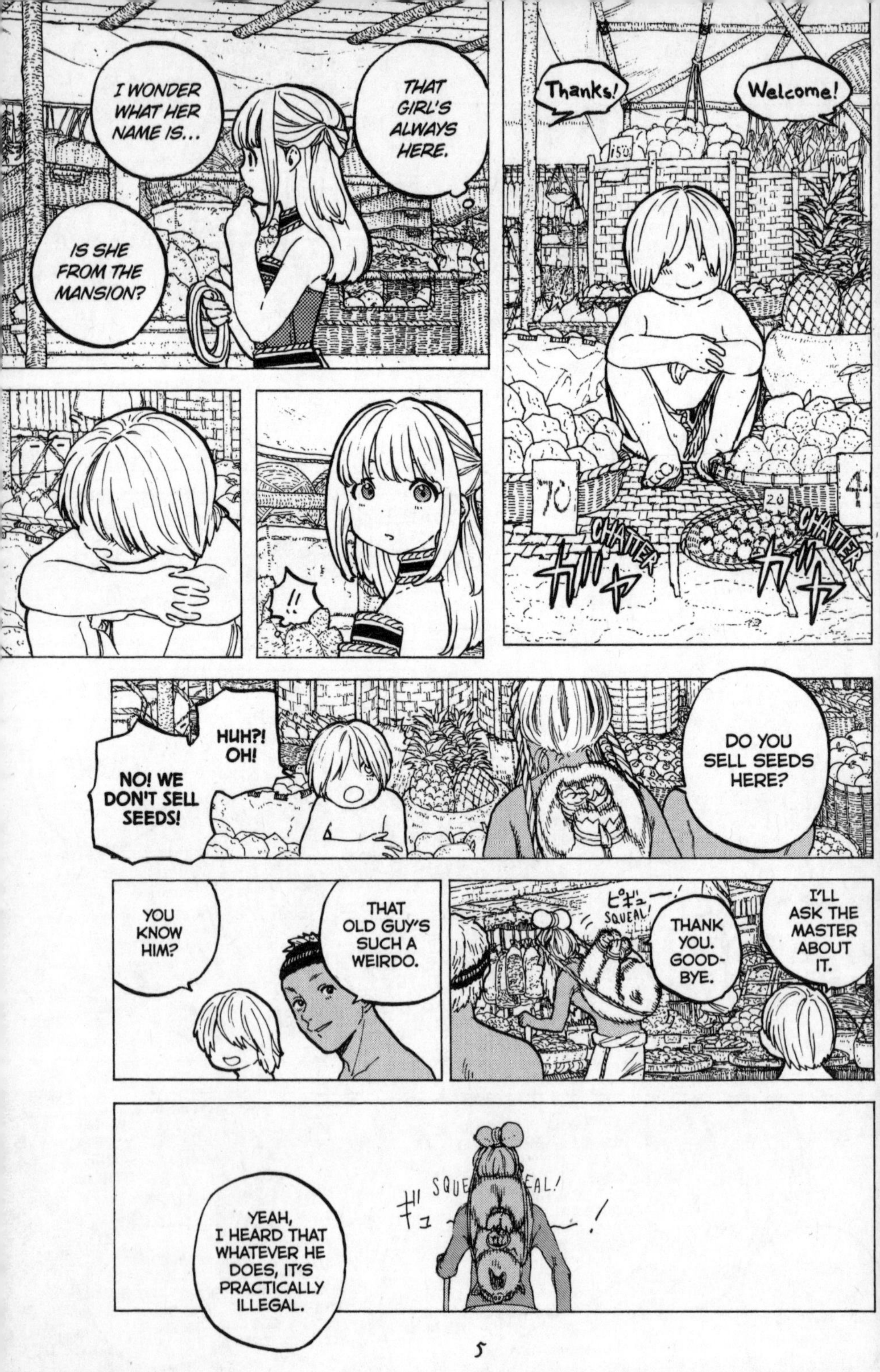
Welcome!
Thanks!
150
100
70
20
CHATTER
CHATTER
THAT GIRL'S ALWAYS HERE.
I WONDER WHAT HER NAME IS...
IS SHE FROM THE MANSION?
!!
DO YOU SELL SEEDS HERE?
HUH?! OH!
NO! WE DON'T SELL SEEDS!
I'LL ASK THE MASTER ABOUT IT.
THANK YOU. GOOD-BYE.
SQUEAL!
THAT OLD GUY'S SUCH A WEIRDO.
YOU KNOW HIM?
YEAH, I HEARD THAT WHATEVER HE DOES, IT'S PRACTICALLY ILLEGAL.

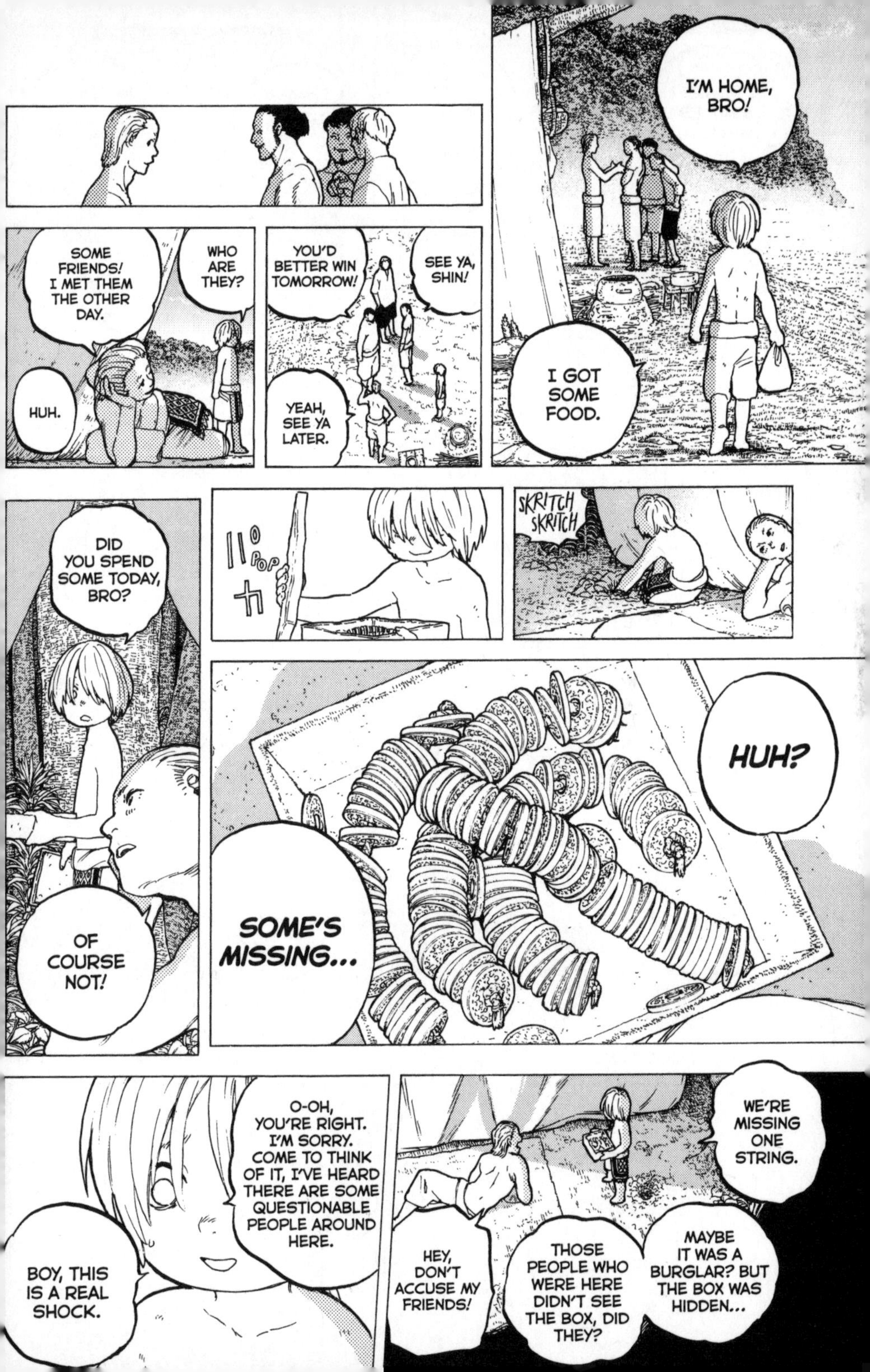
I'M HOME, BRO!
I GOT SOME FOOD.
SEE YA, SHIN!
YOU'D BETTER WIN TOMORROW!
YEAH, SEE YA LATER.
WHO ARE THEY?
SOME FRIENDS! I MET THEM THE OTHER DAY.
HUH.
SKRITCH SKRITCH
POP
HUH?
SOME'S MISSING...
DID YOU SPEND SOME TODAY, BRO?
OF COURSE NOT!
WE'RE MISSING ONE STRING.
MAYBE IT WAS A BURGLAR? BUT THE BOX WAS HIDDEN...
THOSE PEOPLE WHO WERE HERE DIDN'T SEE THE BOX, DID THEY?
HEY, DON'T ACCUSE MY FRIENDS!
O-OH, YOU'RE RIGHT. I'M SORRY. COME TO THINK OF IT, I'VE HEARD THERE ARE SOME QUESTIONABLE PEOPLE AROUND HERE.
BOY, THIS IS A REAL SHOCK.

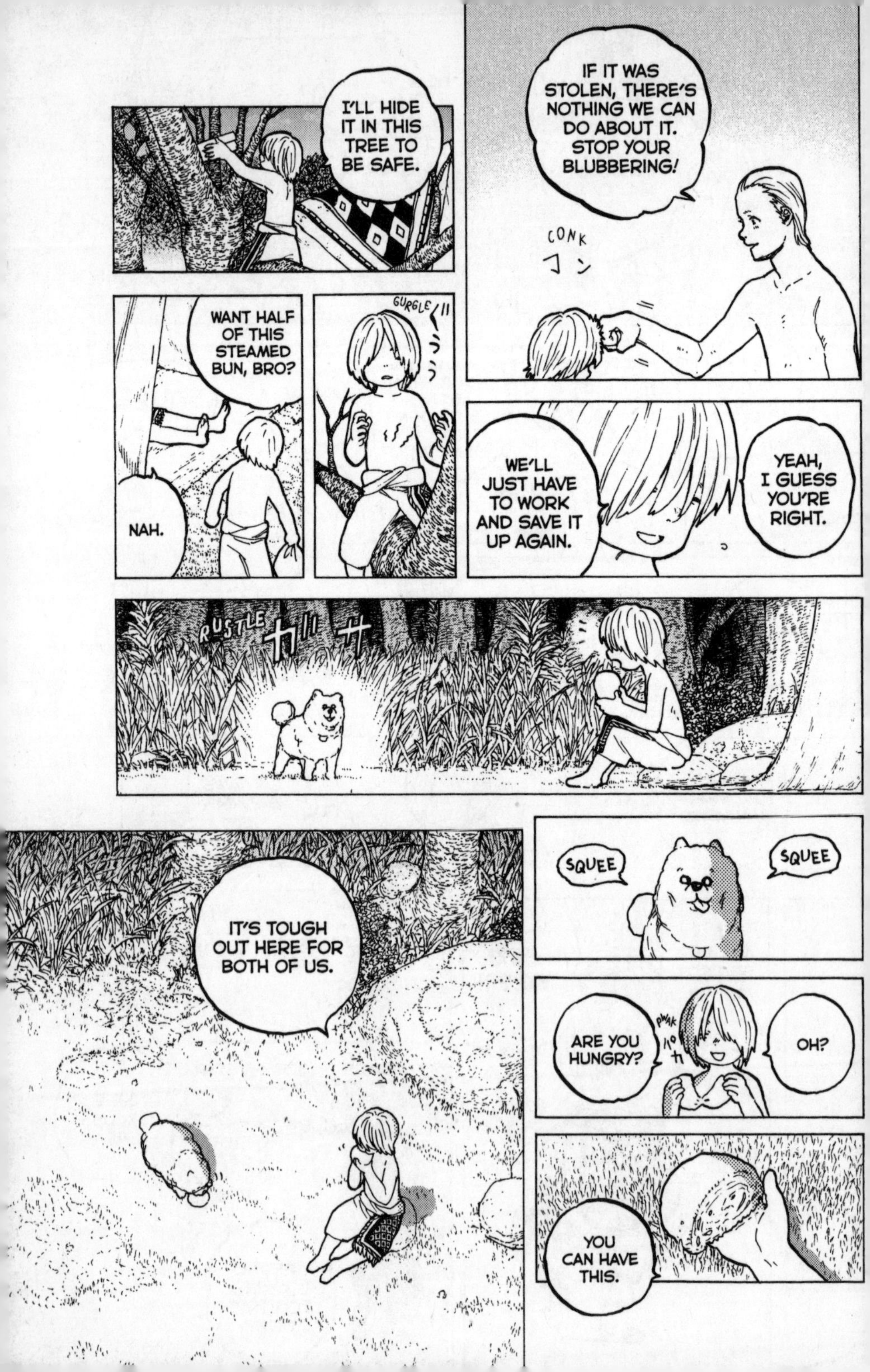
IF IT WAS STOLEN, THERE'S NOTHING WE CAN DO ABOUT IT. STOP YOUR BLUBBERING!
CONK
YEAH, I GUESS YOU'RE RIGHT.
WE'LL JUST HAVE TO WORK AND SAVE IT UP AGAIN.
I'LL HIDE IT IN THIS TREE TO BE SAFE.
GURGLE
WANT HALF OF THIS STEAMED BUN, BRO?
NAH.
RUSTLE
SQUEE
SQUEE
OH?
PWAK
ARE YOU HUNGRY?
YOU CAN HAVE THIS.
IT'S TOUGH OUT HERE FOR BOTH OF US.

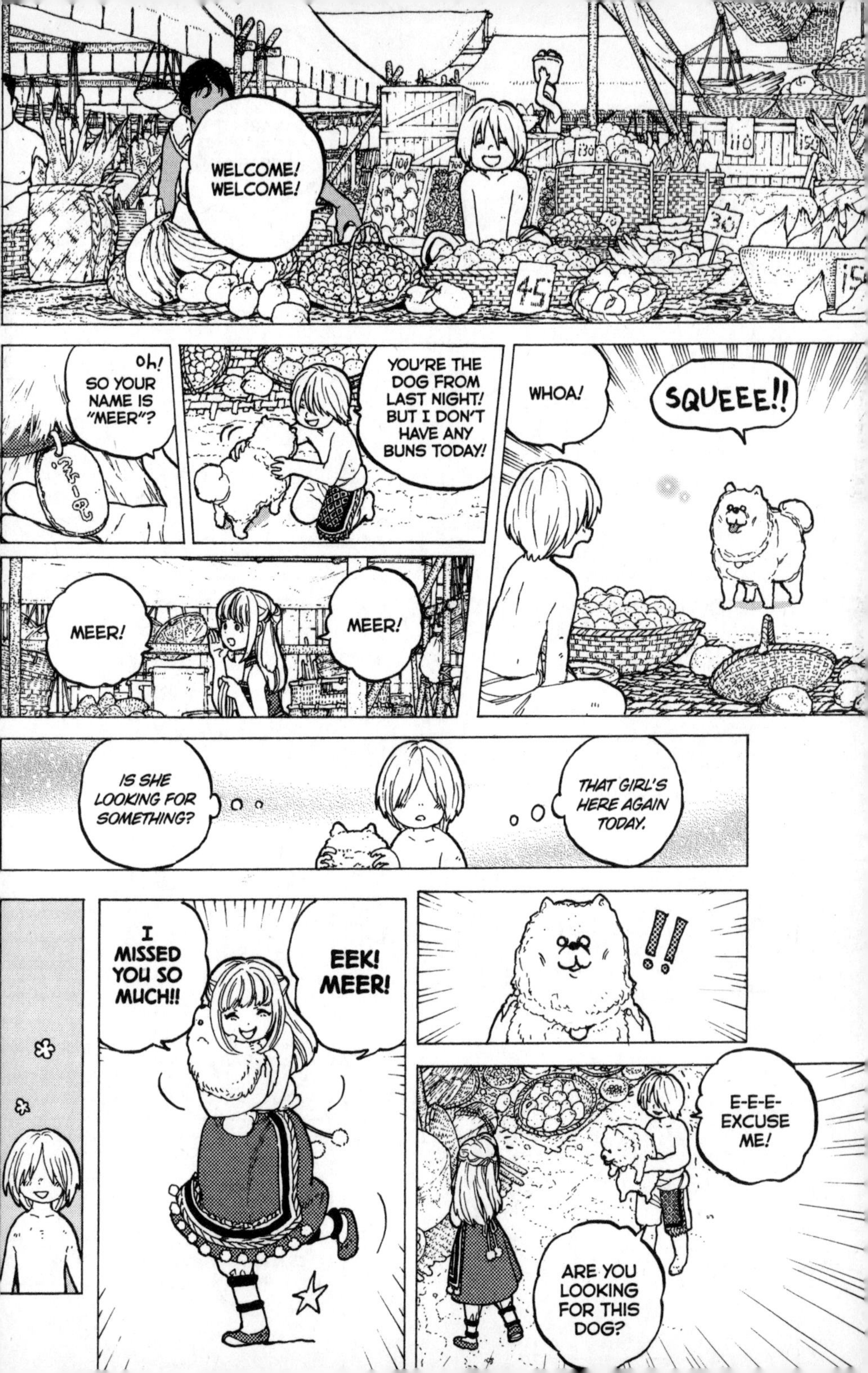
WELCOME! WELCOME!
SQUEEE!!
WHOA!
YOU'RE THE DOG FROM LAST NIGHT! BUT I DON'T HAVE ANY BUNS TODAY!
Oh! SO YOUR NAME IS "MEER"?
MEER!
MEER!
THAT GIRL'S HERE AGAIN TODAY.
IS SHE LOOKING FOR SOMETHING?
!!
E-E-E-EXCUSE ME!
ARE YOU LOOKING FOR THIS DOG?
EEK! MEER!
I MISSED YOU SO MUCH!!

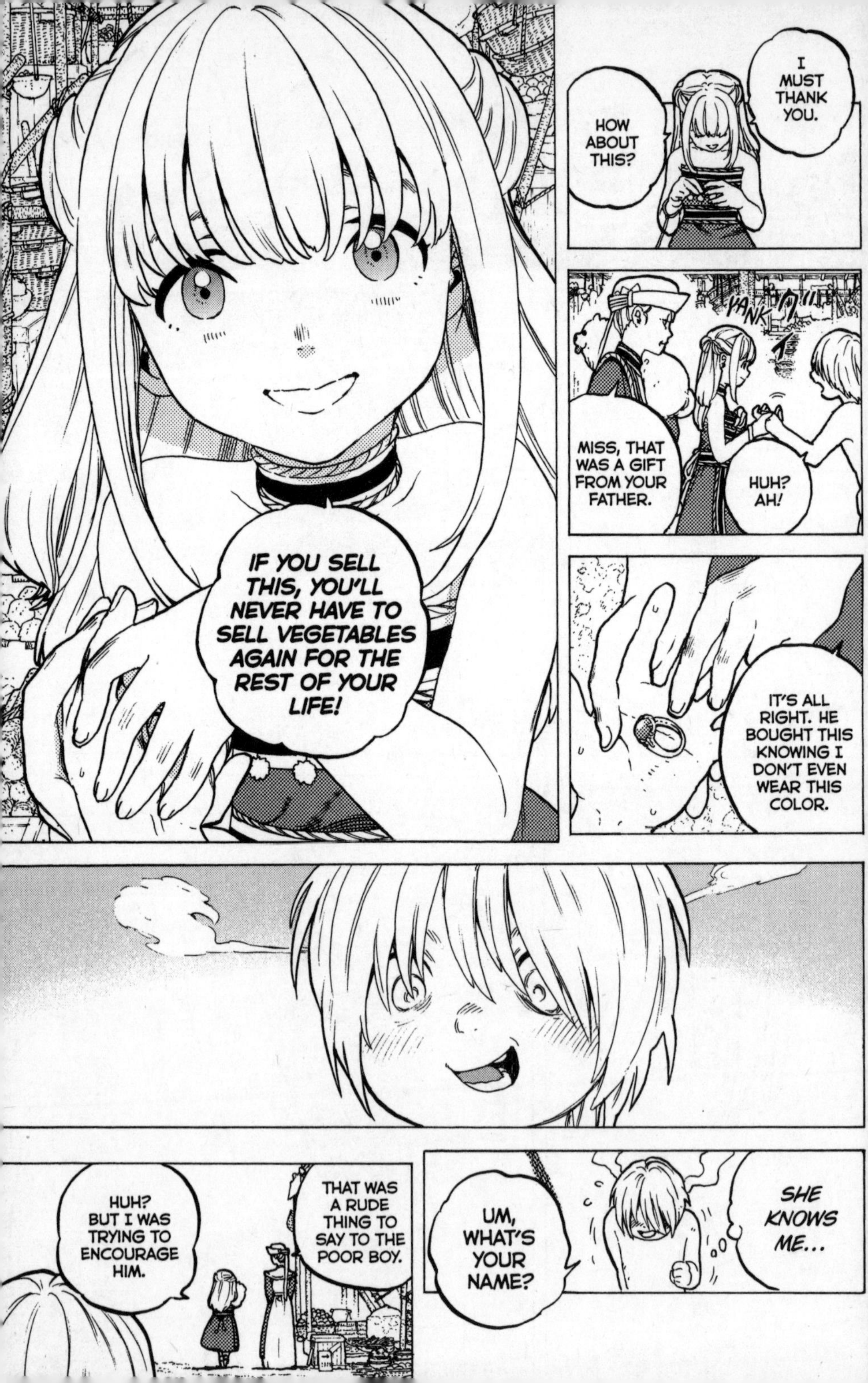
I MUST THANK YOU.
HOW ABOUT THIS?
YANK
MISS, THAT WAS A GIFT FROM YOUR FATHER.
HUH? AH!
IT'S ALL RIGHT. HE BOUGHT THIS KNOWING I DON'T EVEN WEAR THIS COLOR.
IF YOU SELL THIS, YOU'LL NEVER HAVE TO SELL VEGETABLES AGAIN FOR THE REST OF YOUR LIFE!
SHE KNOWS ME...
UM, WHAT'S YOUR NAME?
THAT WAS A RUDE THING TO SAY TO THE POOR BOY.
HUH? BUT I WAS TRYING TO ENCOURAGE HIM.

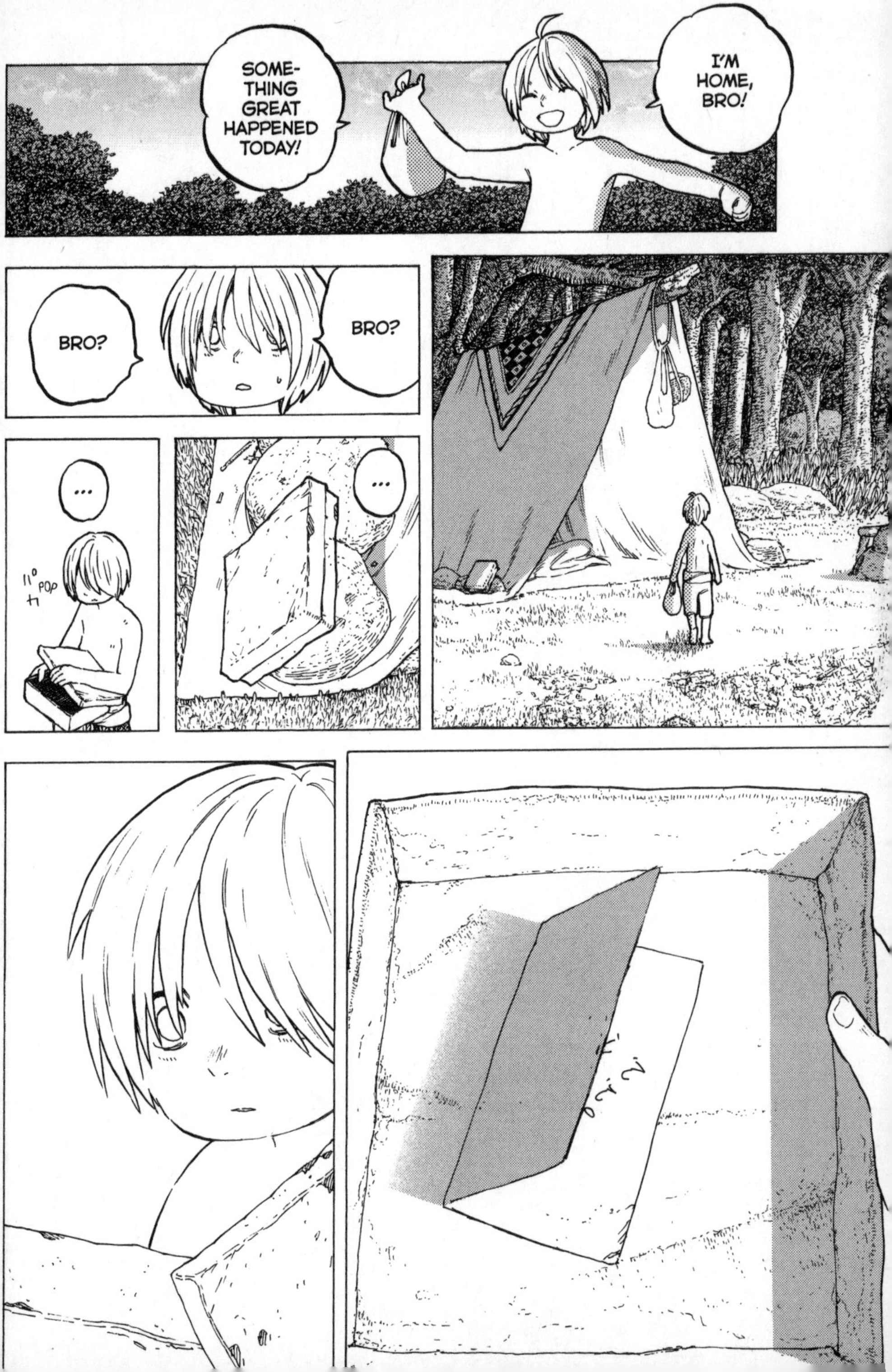
I'M HOME, BRO!
SOME-THING GREAT HAPPENED TODAY!
BRO?
BRO?
...
...
POP

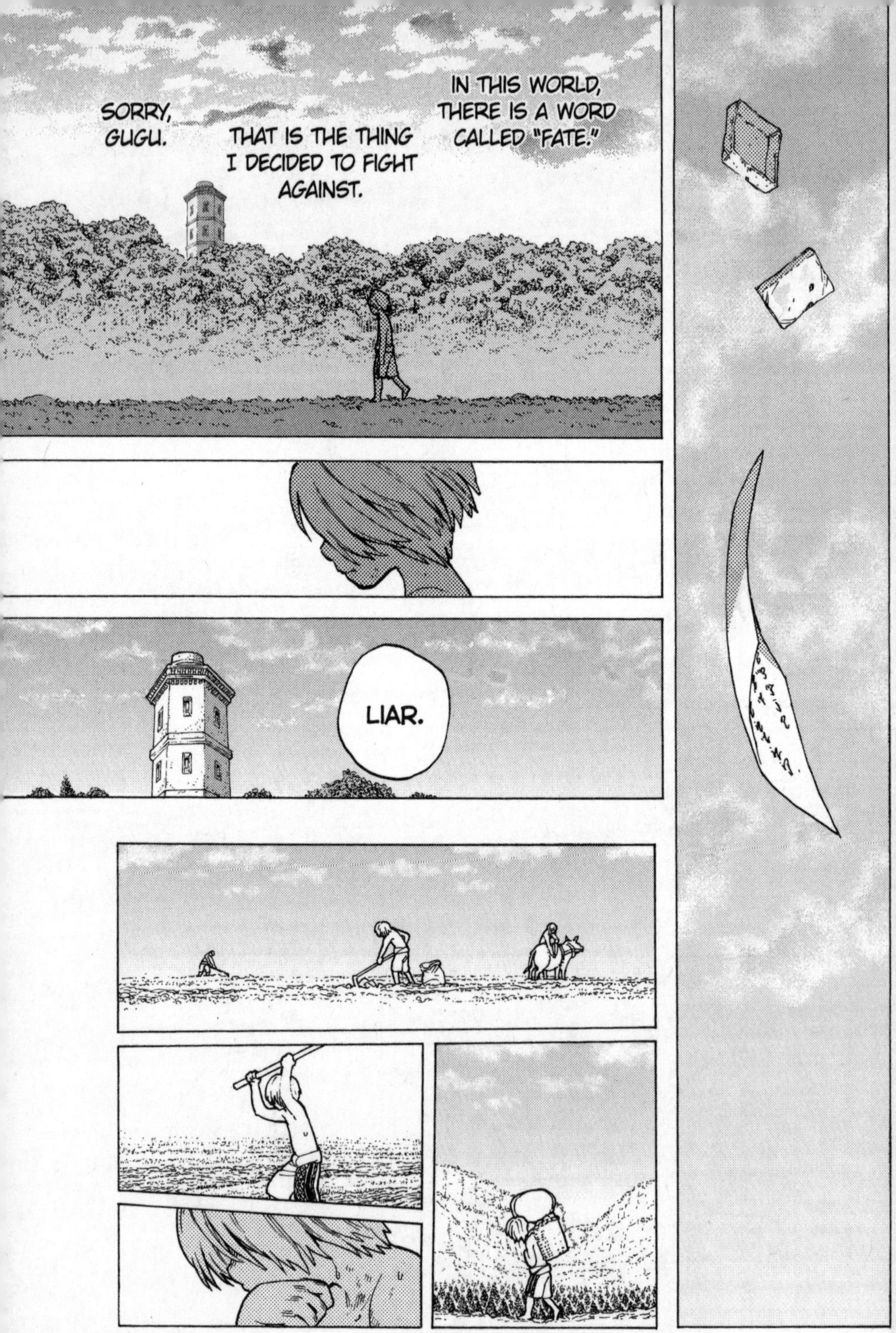
IN THIS WORLD, THERE IS A WORD CALLED "FATE."
THAT IS THE THING I DECIDED TO FIGHT AGAINST.
SORRY, GUGU.
LIAR.

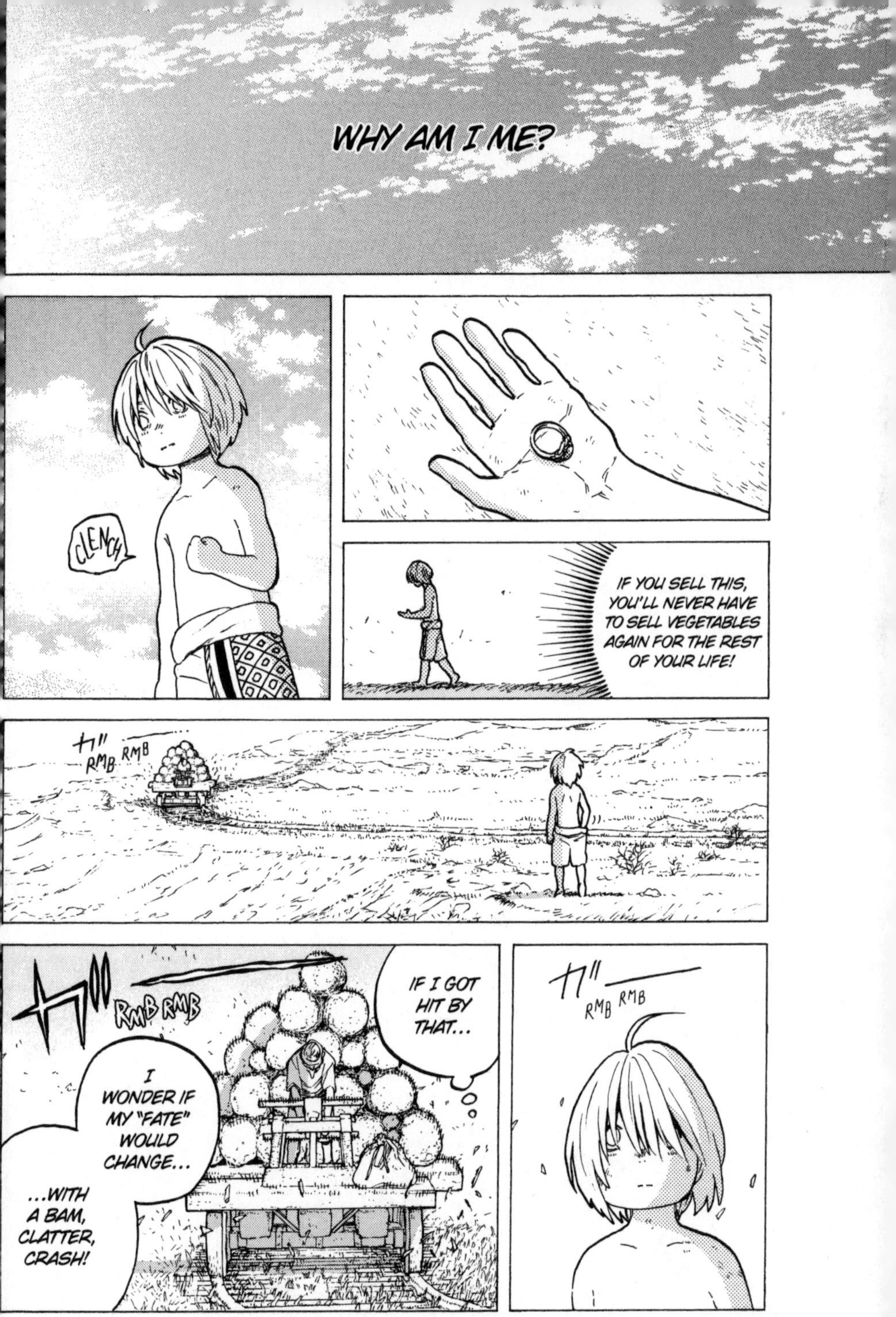
WHY AM I ME?
IF YOU SELL THIS, YOU'LL NEVER HAVE TO SELL VEGETABLES AGAIN FOR THE REST OF YOUR LIFE!
CLENCH
RMB RMB
RMB RMB
IF I GOT HIT BY THAT...
I WONDER IF MY "FATE" WOULD CHANGE...
...WITH A BAM, CLATTER, CRASH!
RMB RMB

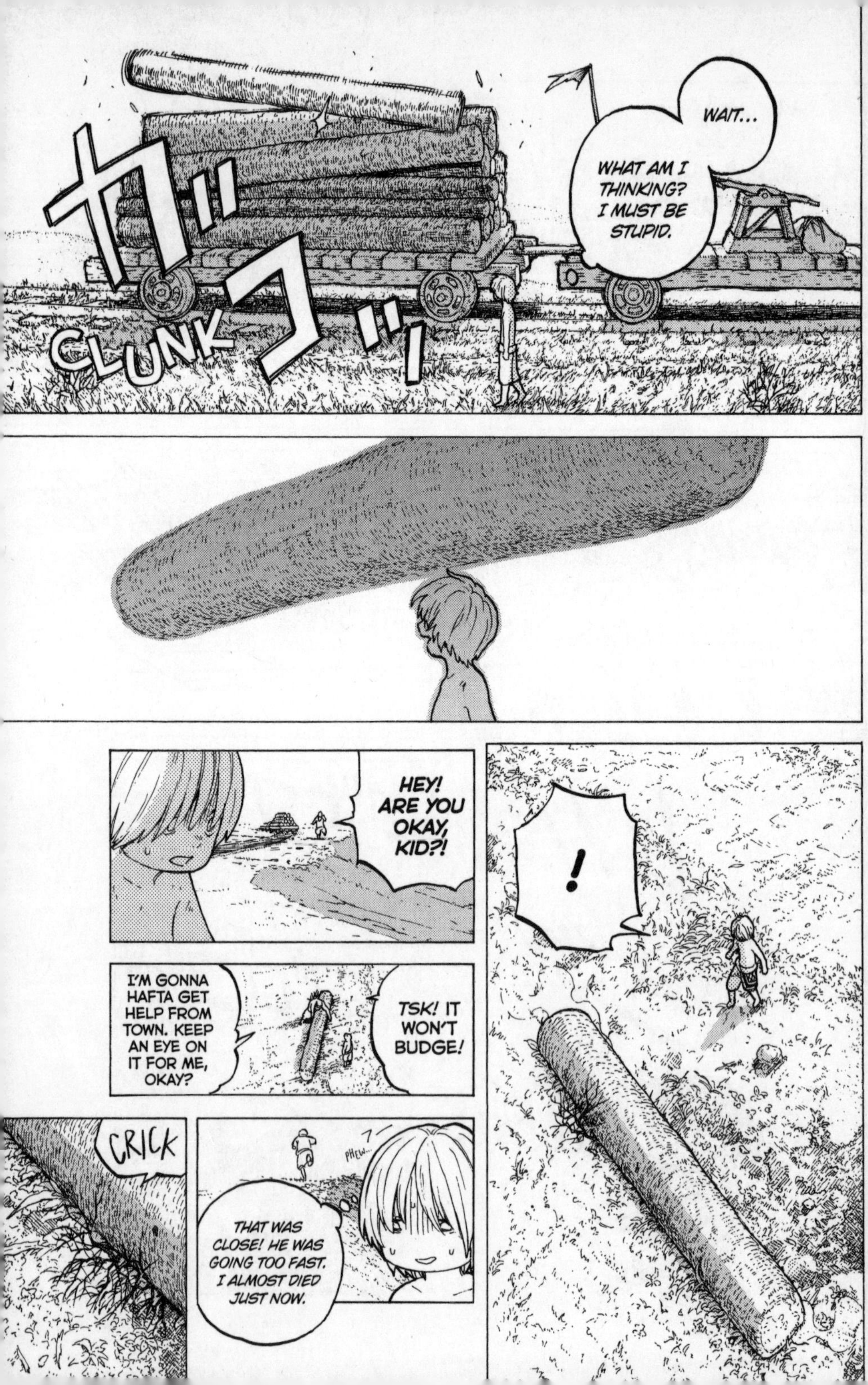
WAIT...
WHAT AM I THINKING? I MUST BE STUPID.
ガッ
ゴッ
CLUNK
!
HEY! ARE YOU OKAY, KID?!
TSK! IT WON'T BUDGE!
I'M GONNA HAFTA GET HELP FROM TOWN. KEEP AN EYE ON IT FOR ME, OKAY?
PHEW...
THAT WAS CLOSE! HE WAS GOING TOO FAST. I ALMOST DIED JUST NOW.
CRICK

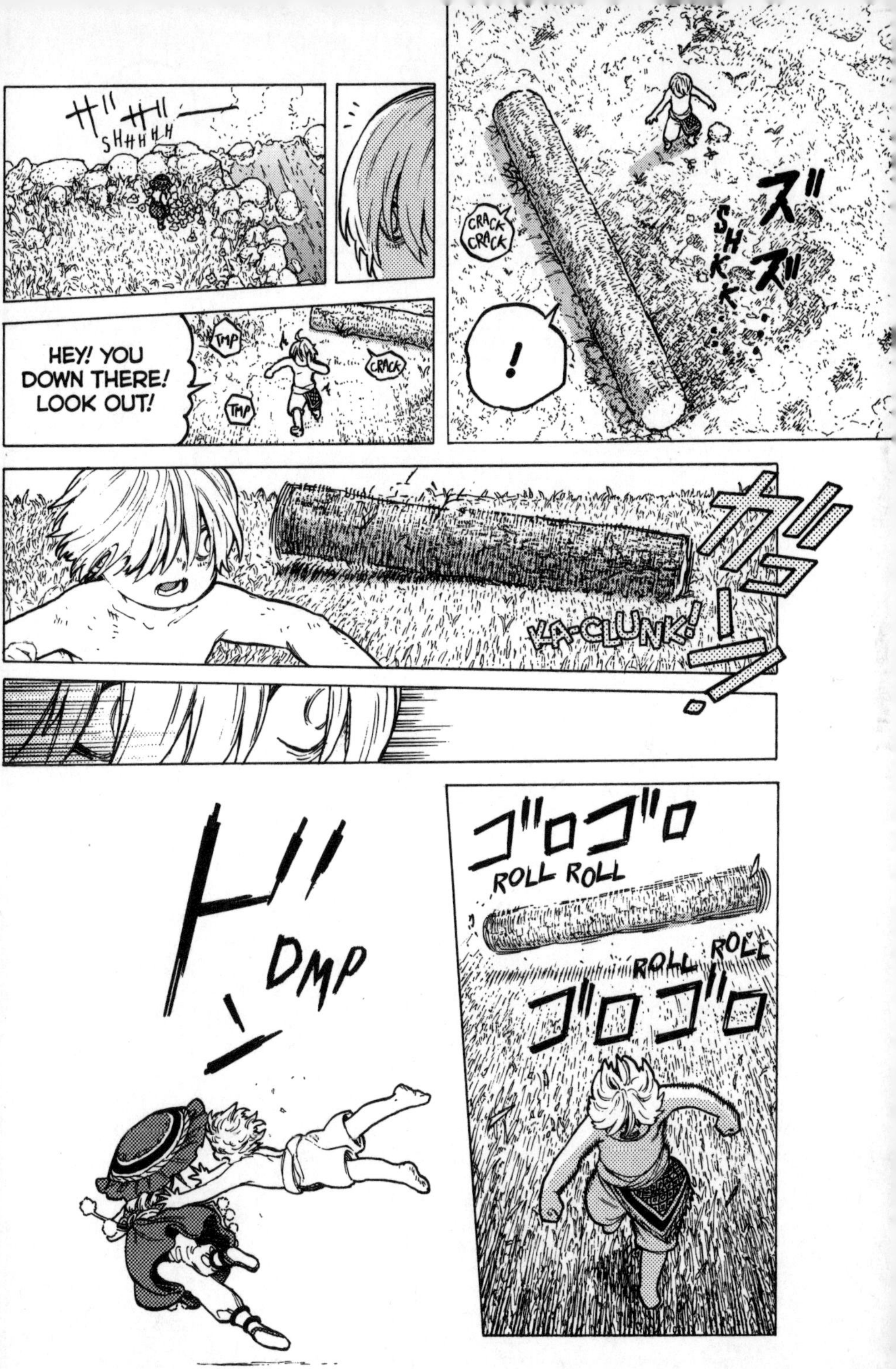
CRACK CRACK
ズズ
SHKK...
!
SHHHHH
HEY! YOU DOWN THERE! LOOK OUT!
TMP
CRACK
TMP
KA-CLUNK!
ゴロゴロ
ROLL ROLL
ROLL ROLL
ゴロゴロ
DMP

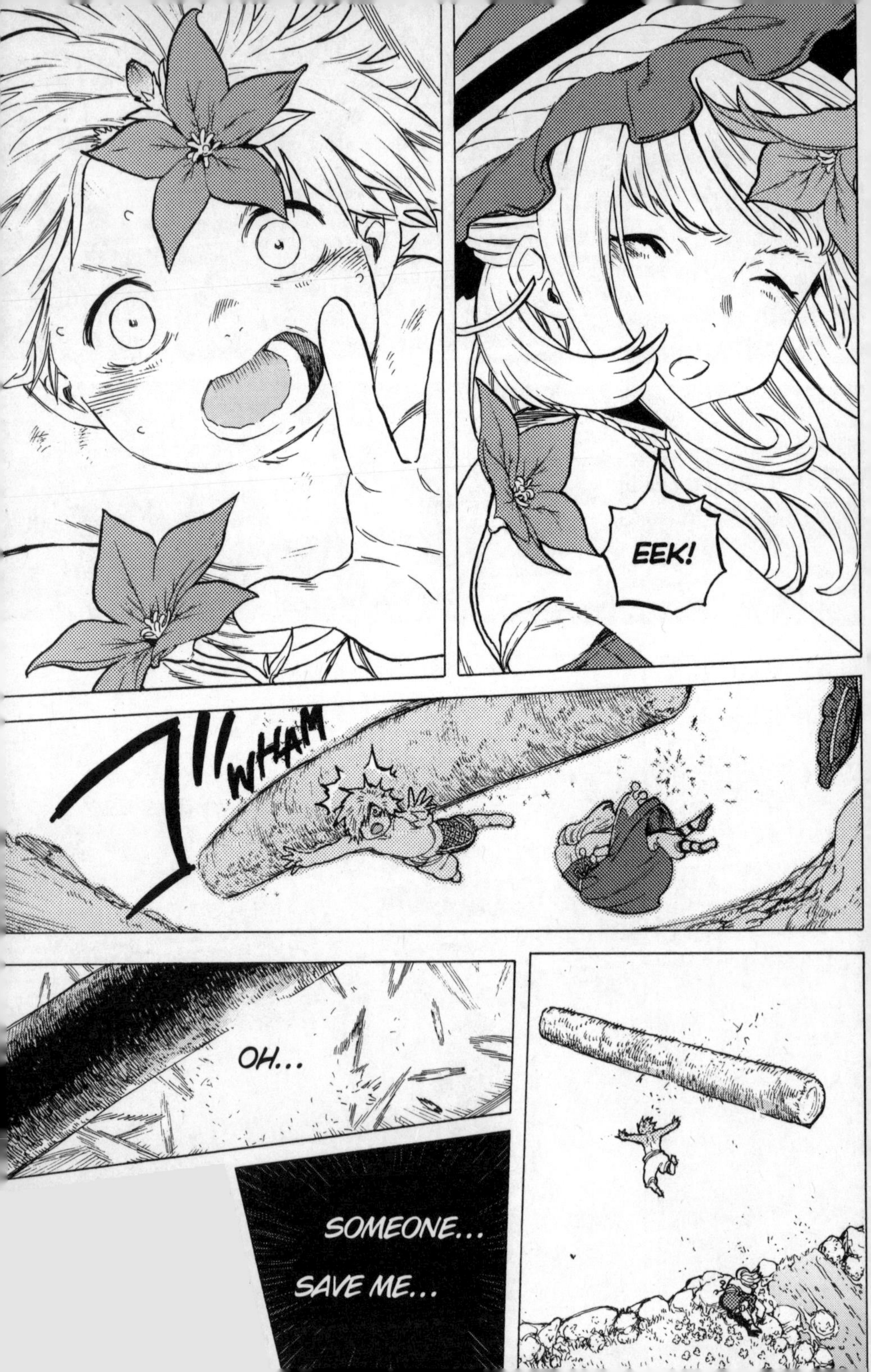
EEK!
WHAM
OH...
SOMEONE...
SAVE ME...

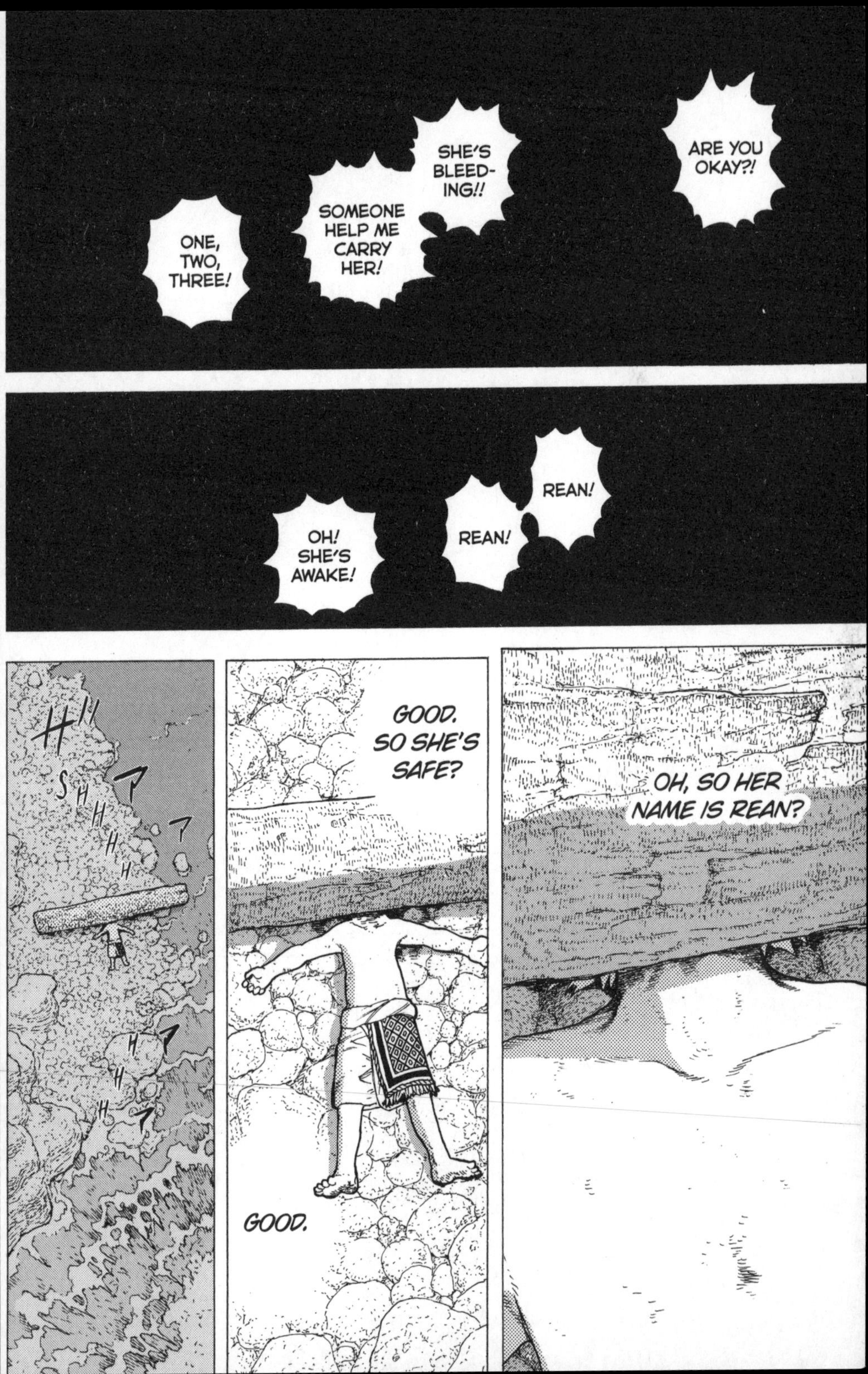
ARE YOU OKAY?!
SHE'S BLEEDING!!
SOMEONE HELP ME CARRY HER!
ONE, TWO, THREE!
REAN!
REAN!
OH! SHE'S AWAKE!
OH, SO HER NAME IS REAN?
GOOD. SO SHE'S SAFE?
GOOD.
SHHHHH

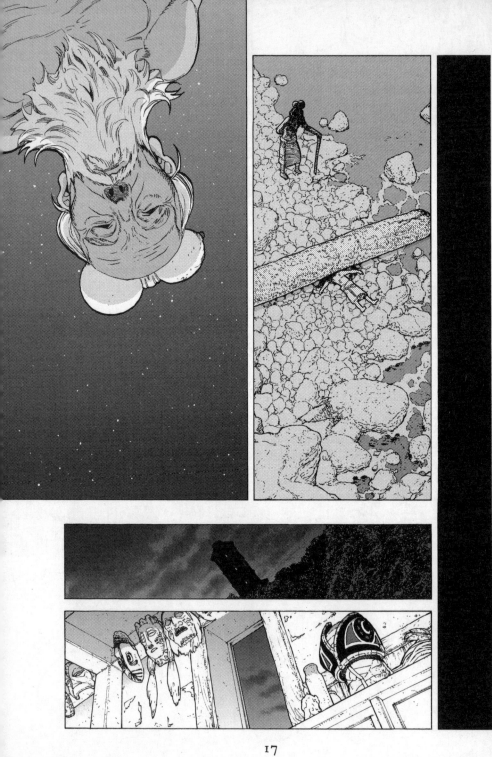

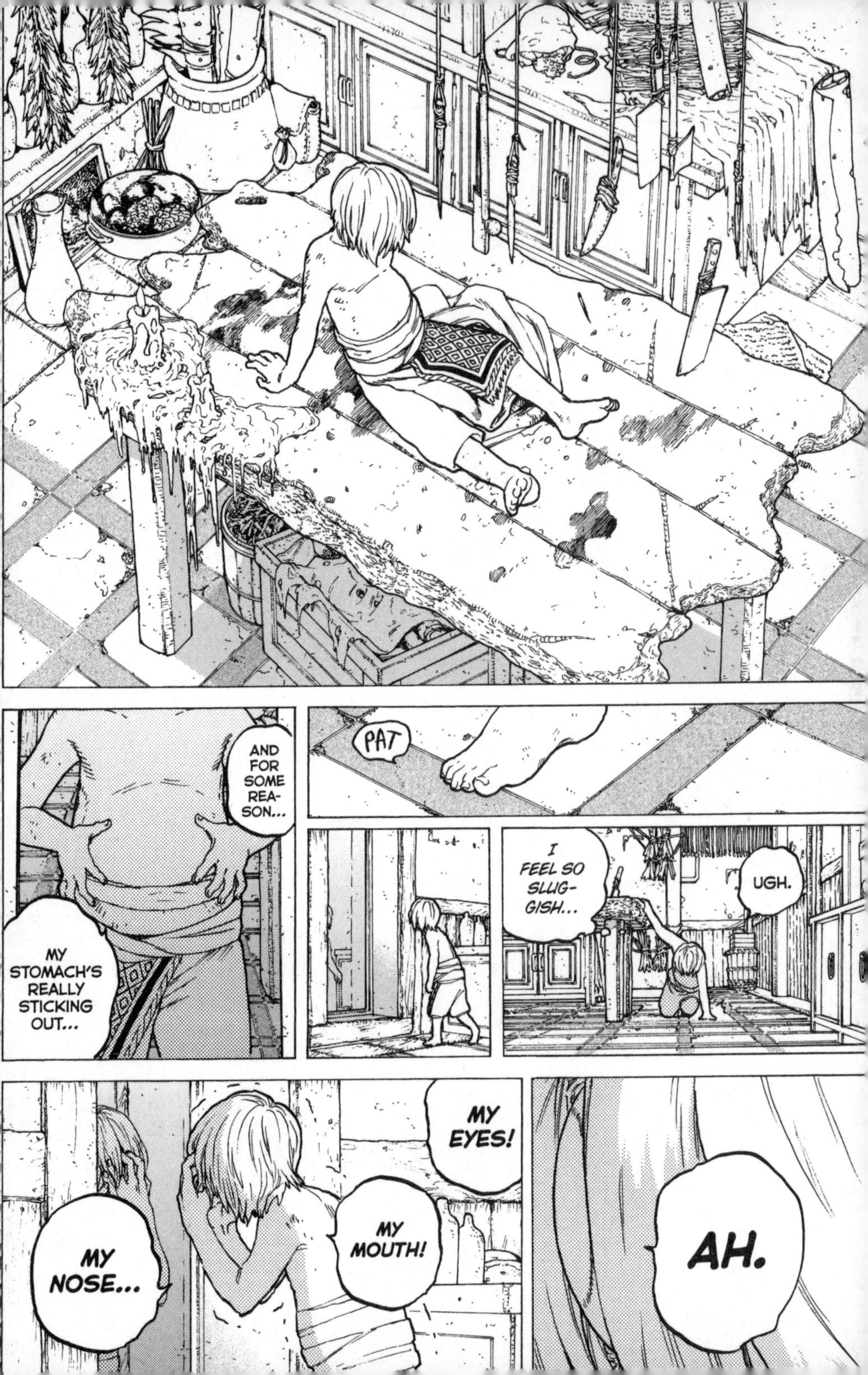
PAT
UGH.
I FEEL SO SLUG-GISH...
AND FOR SOME REA-SON...
MY STOMACH'S REALLY STICKING OUT...
AH.
MY EYES!
MY MOUTH!
MY NOSE...

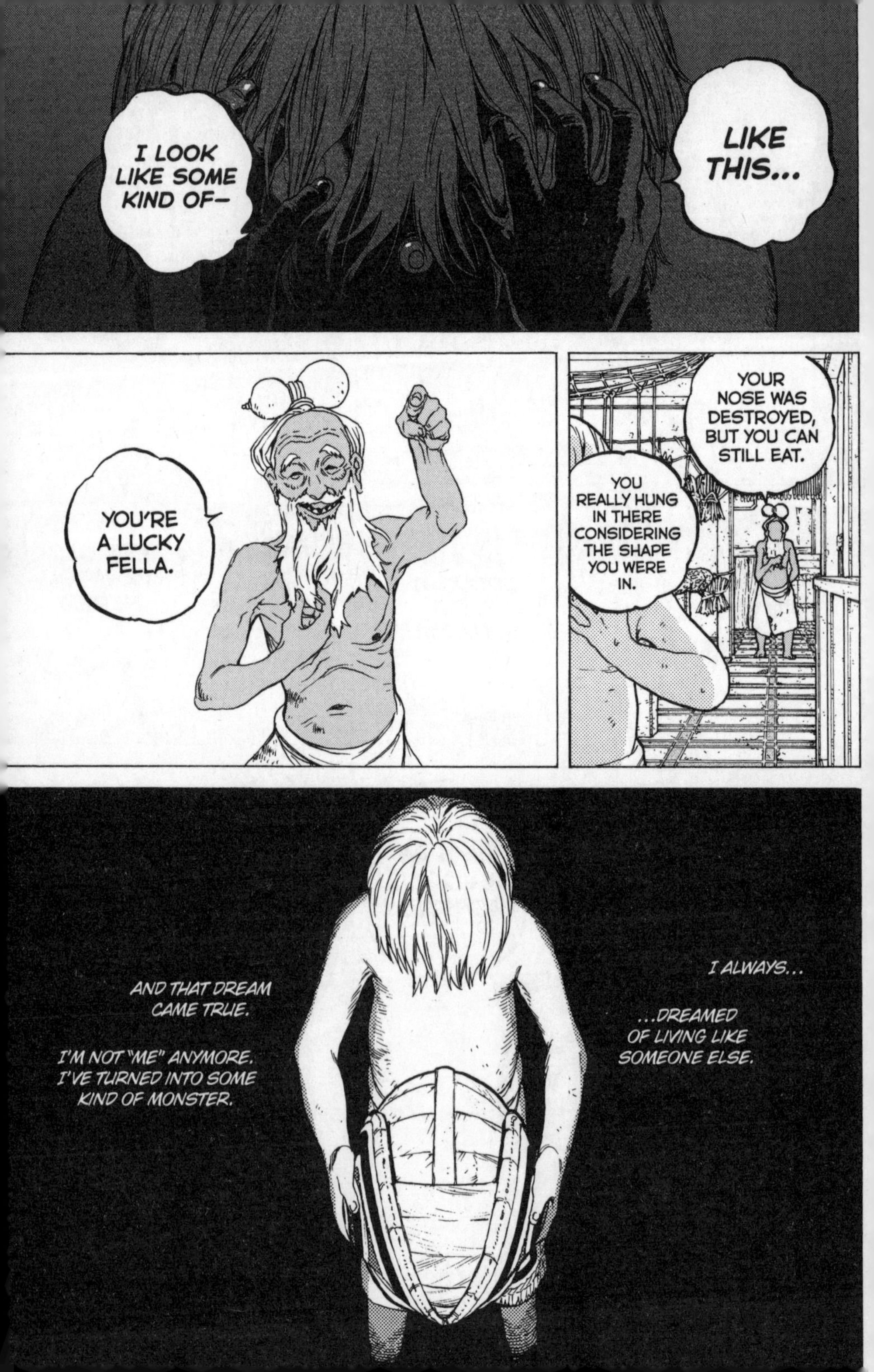
I LOOK LIKE SOME KIND OF—
LIKE THIS...
YOUR NOSE WAS DESTROYED, BUT YOU CAN STILL EAT.
YOU REALLY HUNG IN THERE CONSIDERING THE SHAPE YOU WERE IN.
YOU'RE A LUCKY FELLA.
I ALWAYS...
...DREAMED OF LIVING LIKE SOMEONE ELSE.
AND THAT DREAM CAME TRUE.
I'M NOT "ME" ANYMORE. I'VE TURNED INTO SOME KIND OF MONSTER.

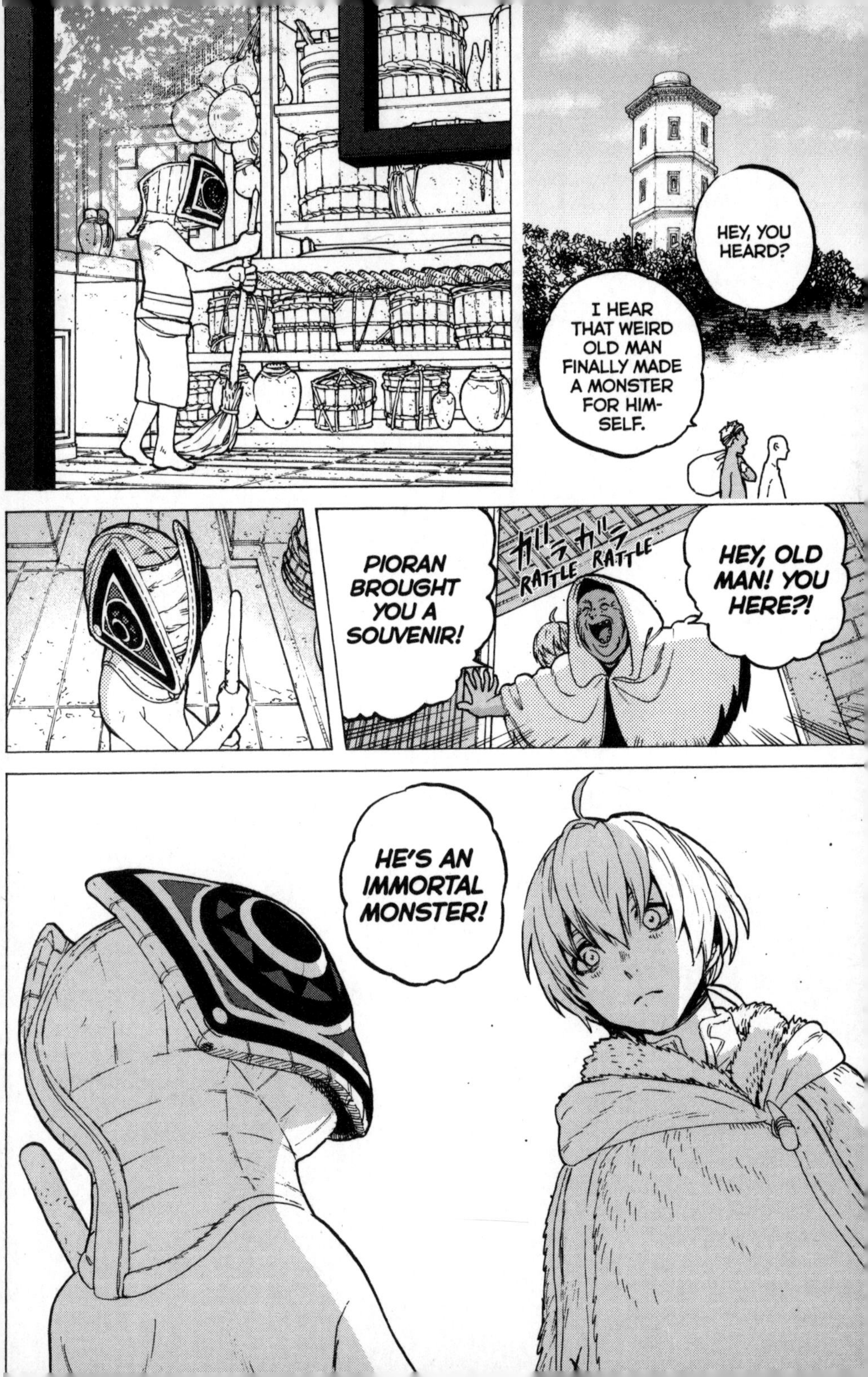
HEY, YOU HEARD?
I HEAR THAT WEIRD OLD MAN FINALLY MADE A MONSTER FOR HIM-SELF.
カラカラ
RATTLE RATTLE
HEY, OLD MAN! YOU HERE?!
PIORAN BROUGHT YOU A SOUVENIR!
HE'S AN IMMORTAL MONSTER!

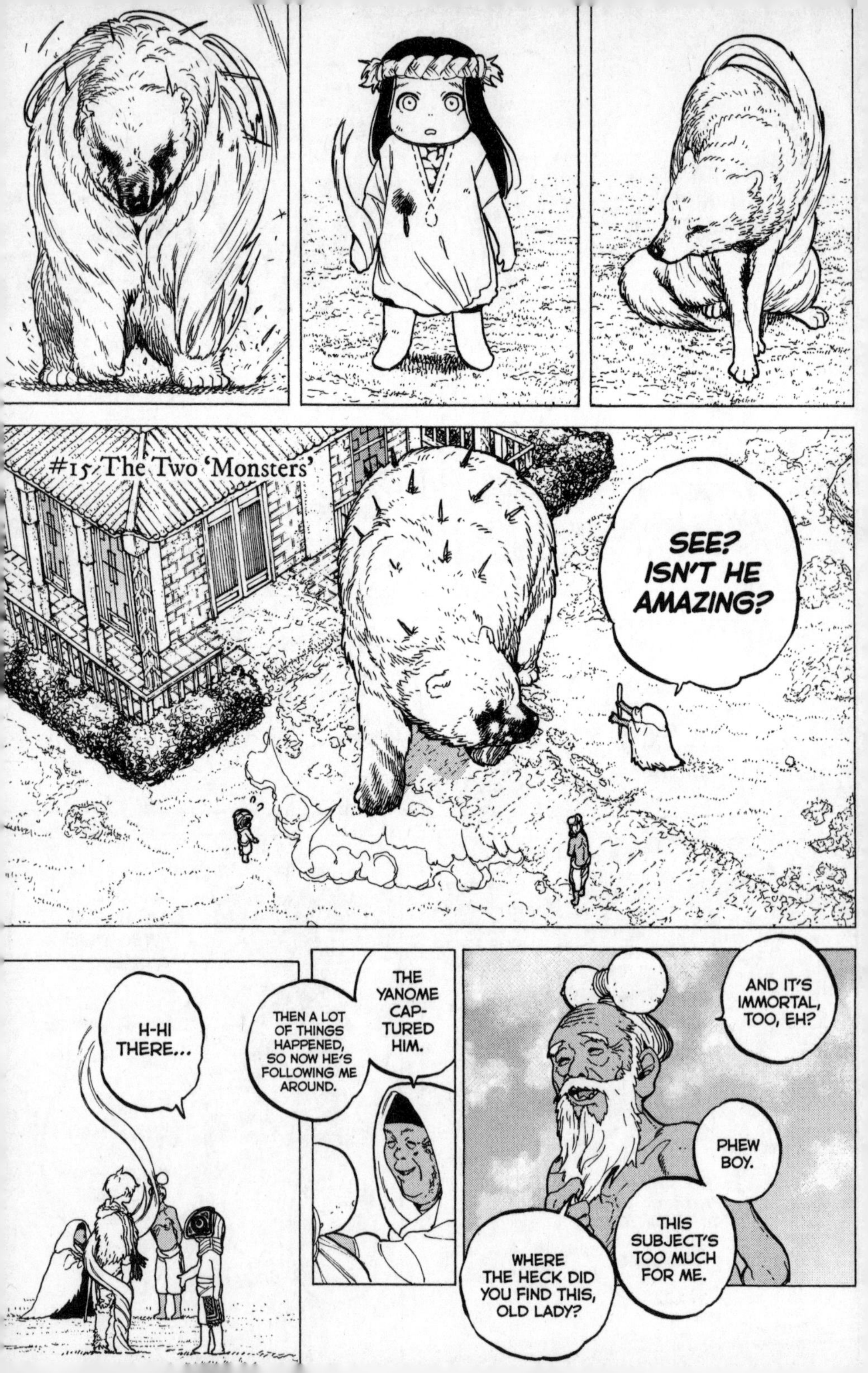
#15 The Two 'Monsters'
SEE? ISN'T HE AMAZING?
AND IT'S IMMORTAL, TOO, EH?
PHEW BOY.
THIS SUBJECT'S TOO MUCH FOR ME.
WHERE THE HECK DID YOU FIND THIS, OLD LADY?
THE YANOME CAPTURED HIM.
THEN A LOT OF THINGS HAPPENED, SO NOW HE'S FOLLOWING ME AROUND.
H-HI THERE...

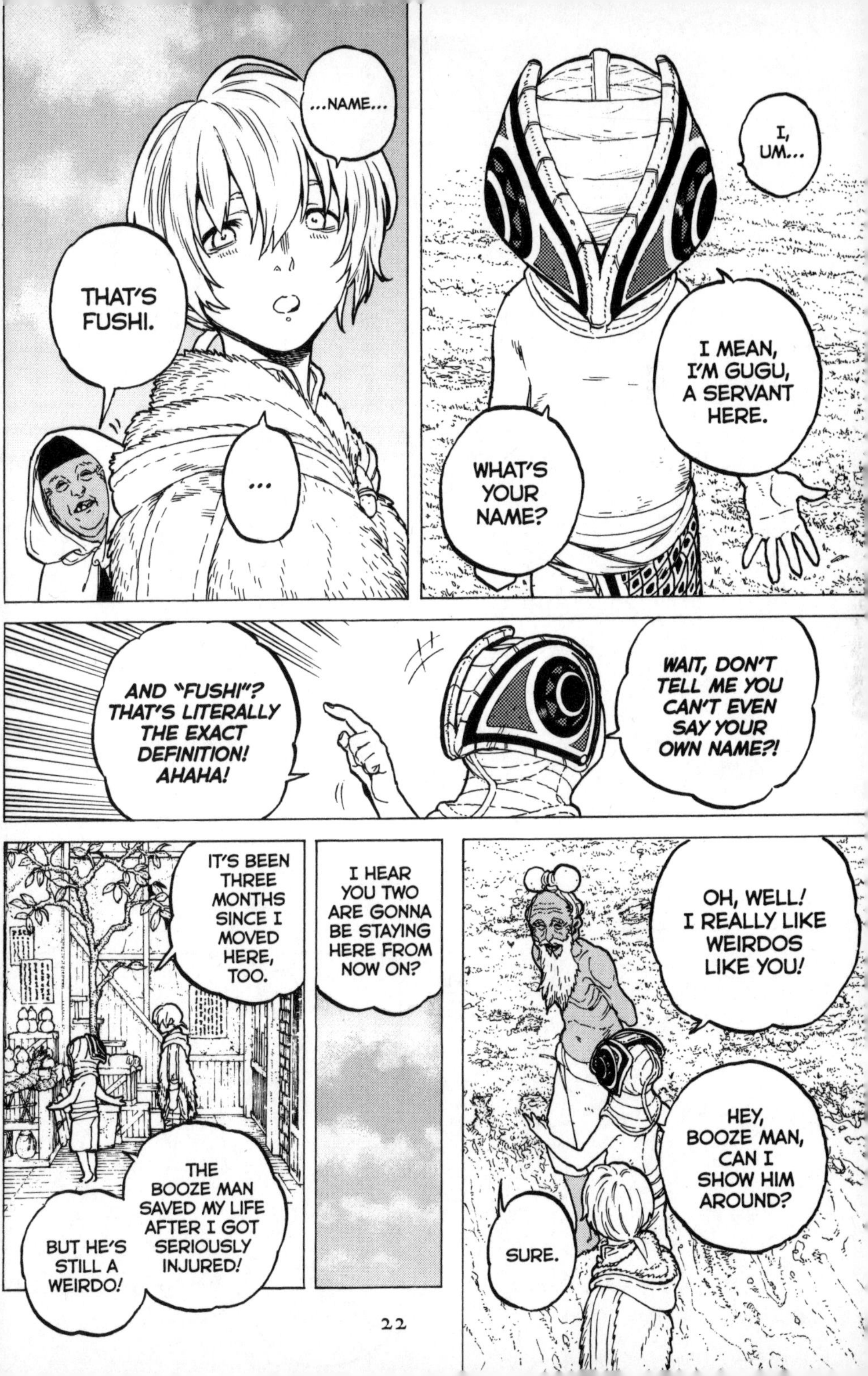
I, UM...
I MEAN, I'M GUGU, A SERVANT HERE.
WHAT'S YOUR NAME?
...NAME...
...
THAT'S FUSHI.
WAIT, DON'T TELL ME YOU CAN'T EVEN SAY YOUR OWN NAME?!
AND "FUSHI"? THAT'S LITERALLY THE EXACT DEFINITION! AHAHA!
OH, WELL! I REALLY LIKE WEIRDOS LIKE YOU!
HEY, BOOZE MAN, CAN I SHOW HIM AROUND?
SURE.
I HEAR YOU TWO ARE GONNA BE STAYING HERE FROM NOW ON?
IT'S BEEN THREE MONTHS SINCE I MOVED HERE, TOO.
THE BOOZE MAN SAVED MY LIFE AFTER I GOT SERIOUSLY INJURED!
BUT HE'S STILL A WEIRDO!

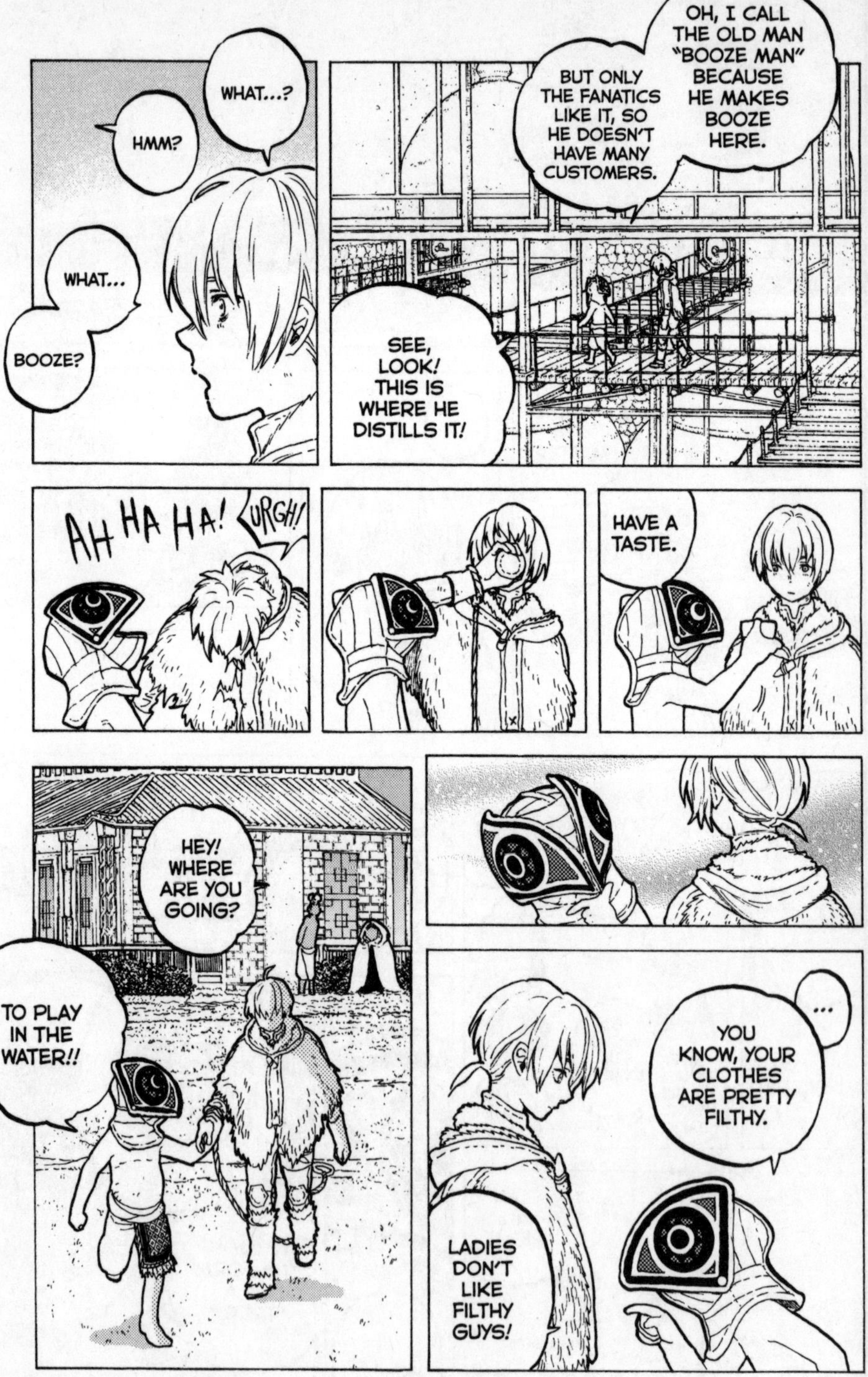

OH, I CALL THE OLD MAN "BOOZE MAN" BECAUSE HE MAKES BOOZE HERE.
BUT ONLY THE FANATICS LIKE IT, SO HE DOESN'T HAVE MANY CUSTOMERS.
SEE, LOOK! THIS IS WHERE HE DISTILLS IT!
WHAT...?
HMM?
WHAT...
BOOZE?
HAVE A TASTE.
URGH!
AH HA HA!
...
YOU KNOW, YOUR CLOTHES ARE PRETTY FILTHY.
LADIES DON'T LIKE FILTHY GUYS!
HEY! WHERE ARE YOU GOING?
TO PLAY IN THE WATER!!

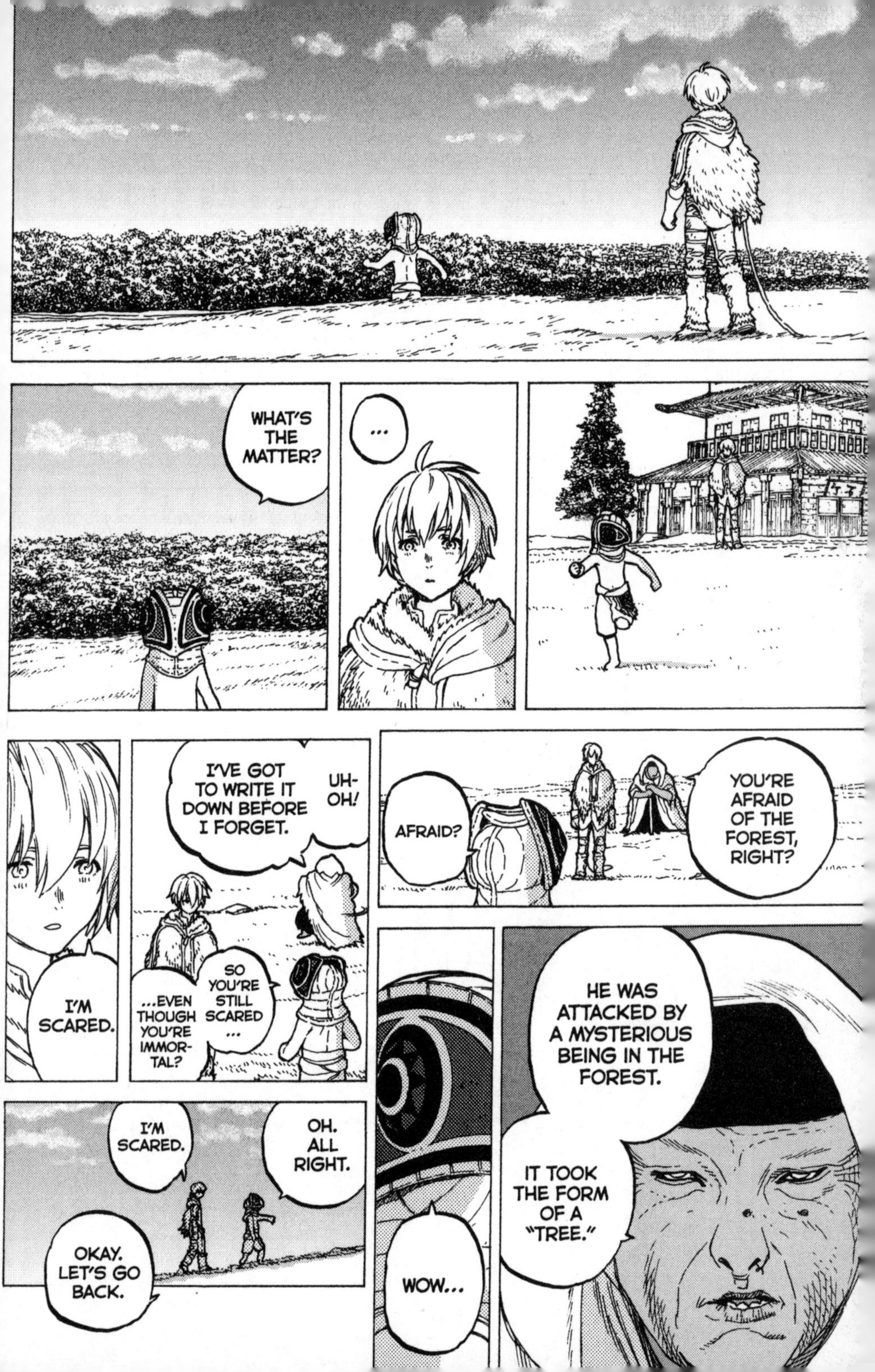
...
WHAT'S THE MATTER?
YOU'RE AFRAID OF THE FOREST, RIGHT?
AFRAID?
UH-OH!
I'VE GOT TO WRITE IT DOWN BEFORE I FORGET.
SO YOU'RE STILL SCARED ...
...EVEN THOUGH YOU'RE IMMORTAL?
I'M SCARED.
HE WAS ATTACKED BY A MYSTERIOUS BEING IN THE FOREST.
IT TOOK THE FORM OF A "TREE."
WOW...
OH. ALL RIGHT.
I'M SCARED.
OKAY. LET'S GO BACK.

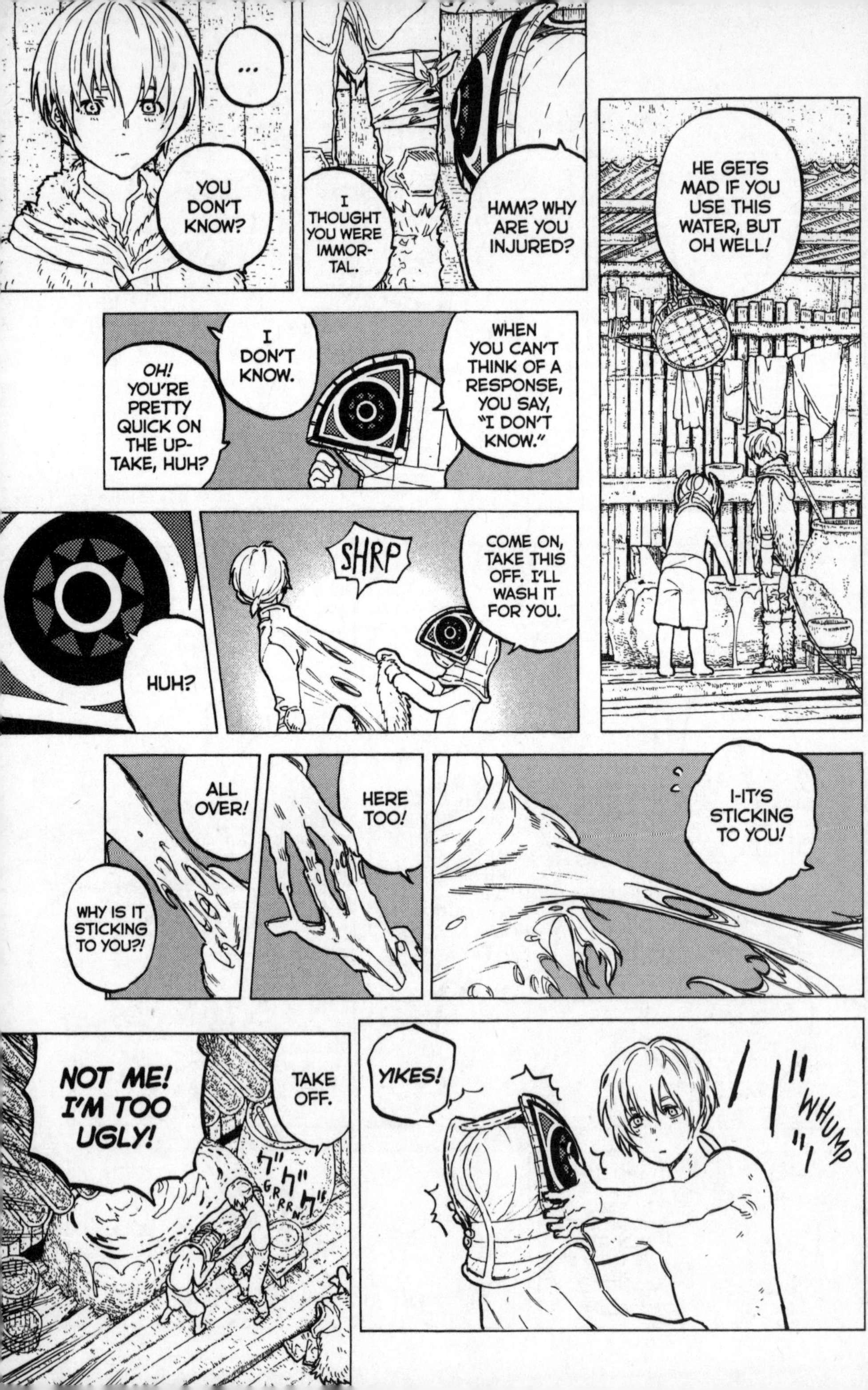
HMM? WHY ARE YOU INJURED?
I THOUGHT YOU WERE IMMORTAL.
...
YOU DON'T KNOW?
HE GETS MAD IF YOU USE THIS WATER, BUT OH WELL!
WHEN YOU CAN'T THINK OF A RESPONSE, YOU SAY, "I DON'T KNOW."
I DON'T KNOW.
OH! YOU'RE PRETTY QUICK ON THE UPTAKE, HUH?
COME ON, TAKE THIS OFF. I'LL WASH IT FOR YOU.
SHRP
HUH?
I-IT'S STICKING TO YOU!
HERE TOO!
ALL OVER!
WHY IS IT STICKING TO YOU?!
WHUMP
YIKES!
TAKE OFF.
NOT ME! I'M TOO UGLY!
GRRRN

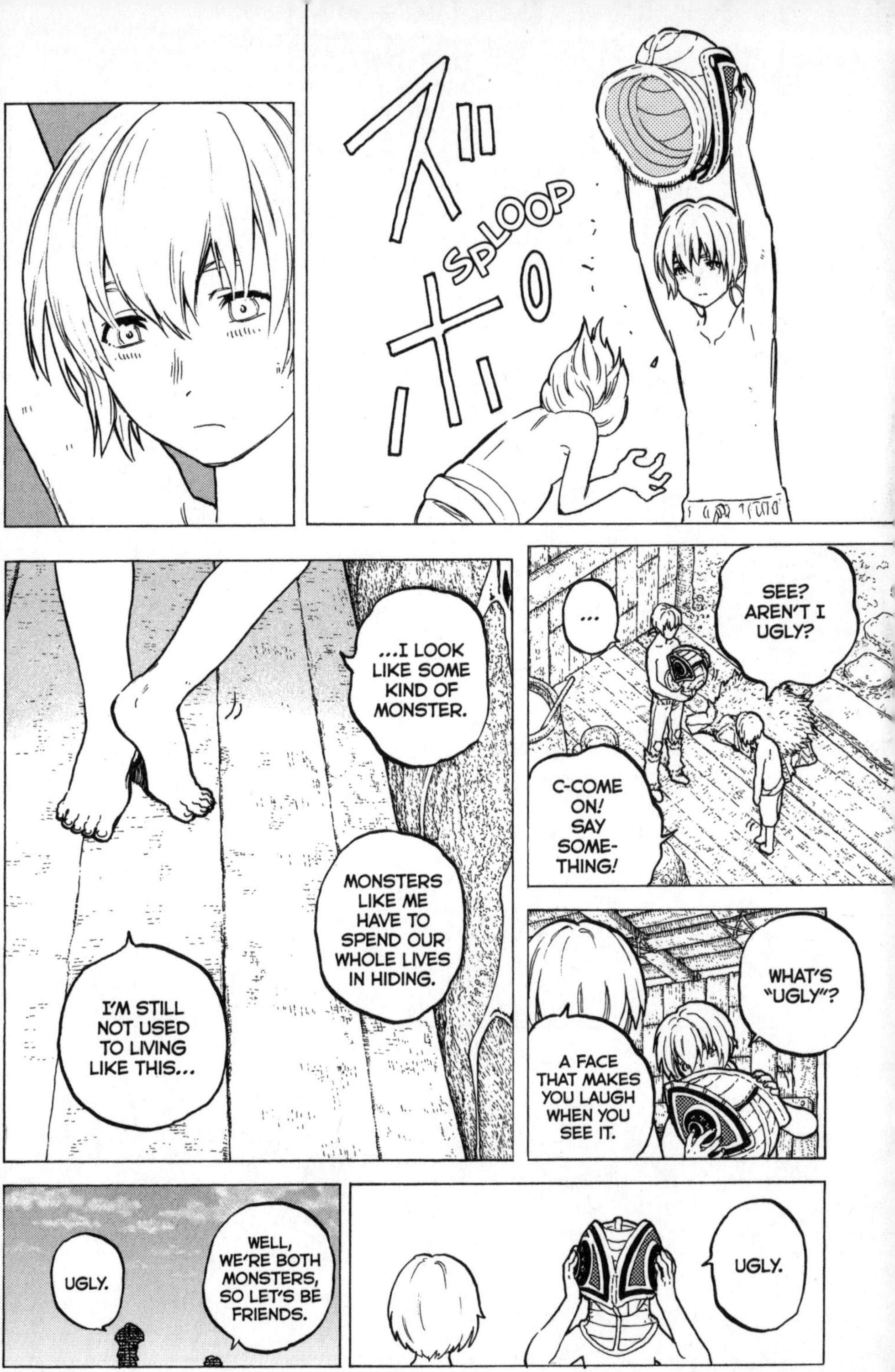
SPLOOP
SEE? AREN'T I UGLY?
...
C-COME ON! SAY SOME-THING!
WHAT'S "UGLY"?
A FACE THAT MAKES YOU LAUGH WHEN YOU SEE IT.
...I LOOK LIKE SOME KIND OF MONSTER.
MONSTERS LIKE ME HAVE TO SPEND OUR WHOLE LIVES IN HIDING.
I'M STILL NOT USED TO LIVING LIKE THIS...
UGLY.
WELL, WE'RE BOTH MONSTERS, SO LET'S BE FRIENDS.
UGLY.

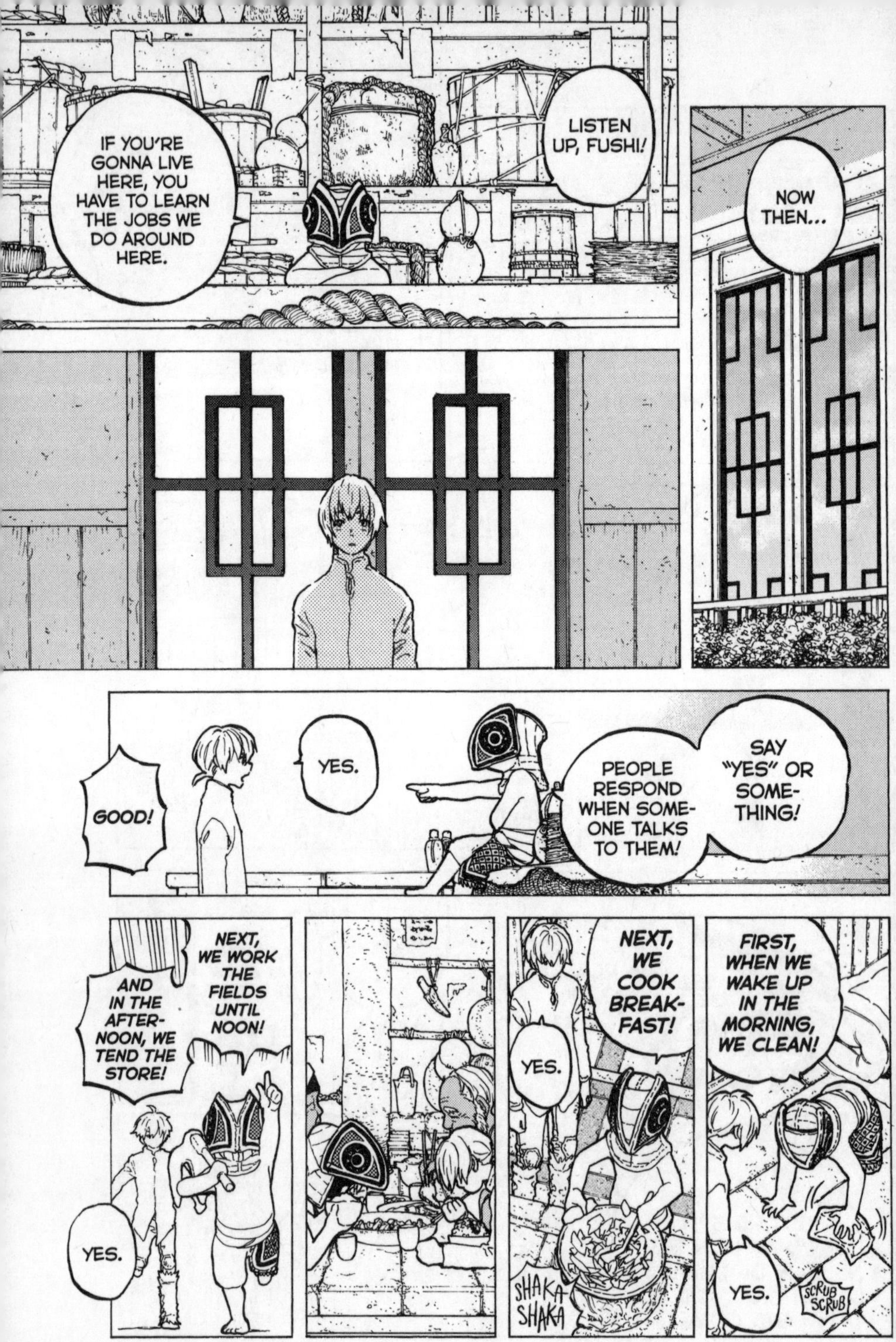
NOW THEN...
LISTEN UP, FUSHI!
IF YOU'RE GONNA LIVE HERE, YOU HAVE TO LEARN THE JOBS WE DO AROUND HERE.
SAY "YES" OR SOME-THING!
PEOPLE RESPOND WHEN SOME-ONE TALKS TO THEM!
YES.
GOOD!
FIRST, WHEN WE WAKE UP IN THE MORNING, WE CLEAN!
YES.
SCRUB SCRUB
NEXT, WE COOK BREAK-FAST!
YES.
SHAKA-SHAKA
NEXT, WE WORK THE FIELDS UNTIL NOON!
AND IN THE AFTER-NOON, WE TEND THE STORE!
YES.

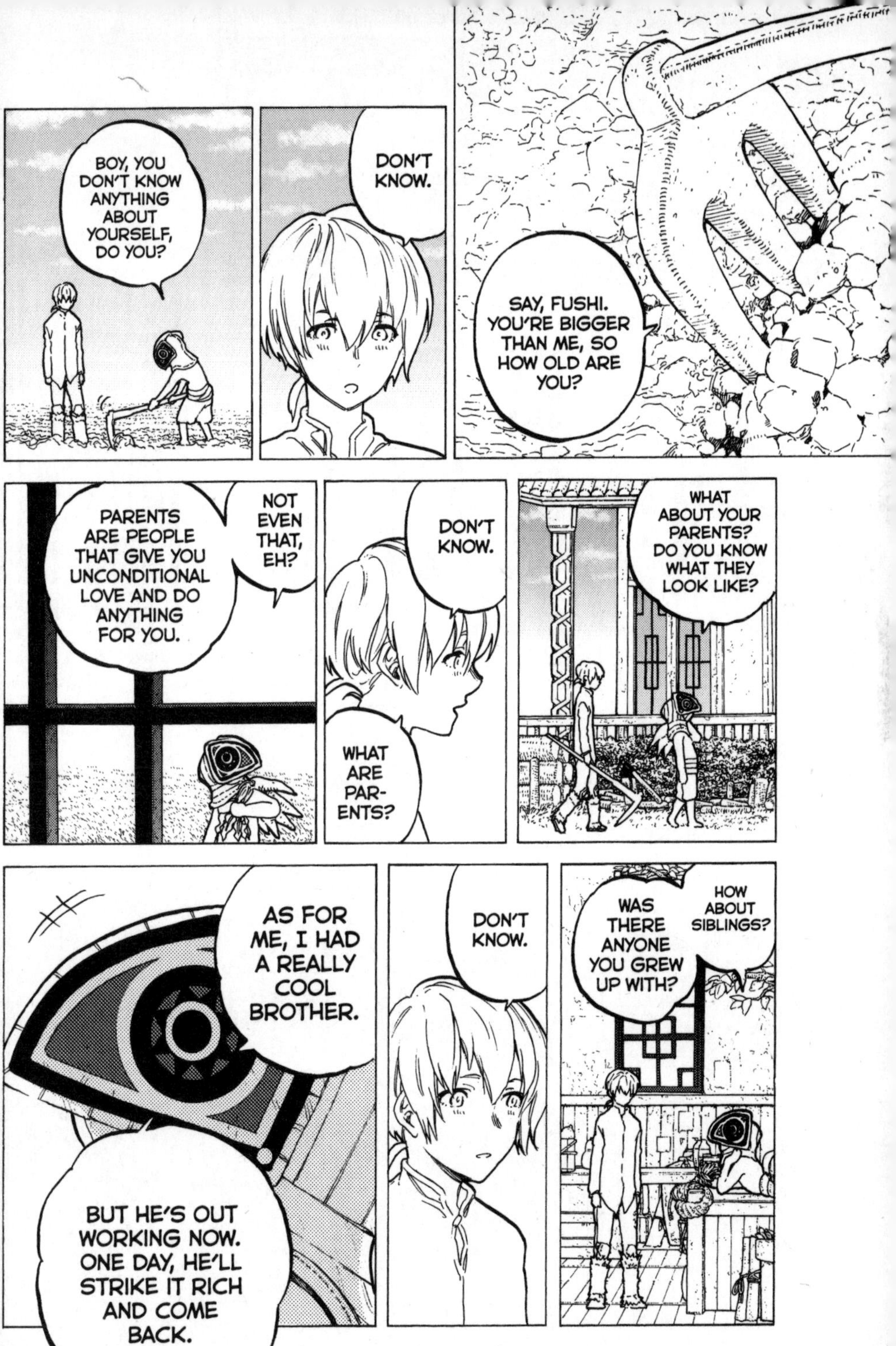
SAY, FUSHI. YOU'RE BIGGER THAN ME, SO HOW OLD ARE YOU?
DON'T KNOW.
BOY, YOU DON'T KNOW ANYTHING ABOUT YOURSELF, DO YOU?
WHAT ABOUT YOUR PARENTS? DO YOU KNOW WHAT THEY LOOK LIKE?
DON'T KNOW.
WHAT ARE PAR-ENTS?
NOT EVEN THAT, EH?
PARENTS ARE PEOPLE THAT GIVE YOU UNCONDITIONAL LOVE AND DO ANYTHING FOR YOU.
HOW ABOUT SIBLINGS?
WAS THERE ANYONE YOU GREW UP WITH?
DON'T KNOW.
AS FOR ME, I HAD A REALLY COOL BROTHER.
BUT HE'S OUT WORKING NOW. ONE DAY, HE'LL STRIKE IT RICH AND COME BACK.

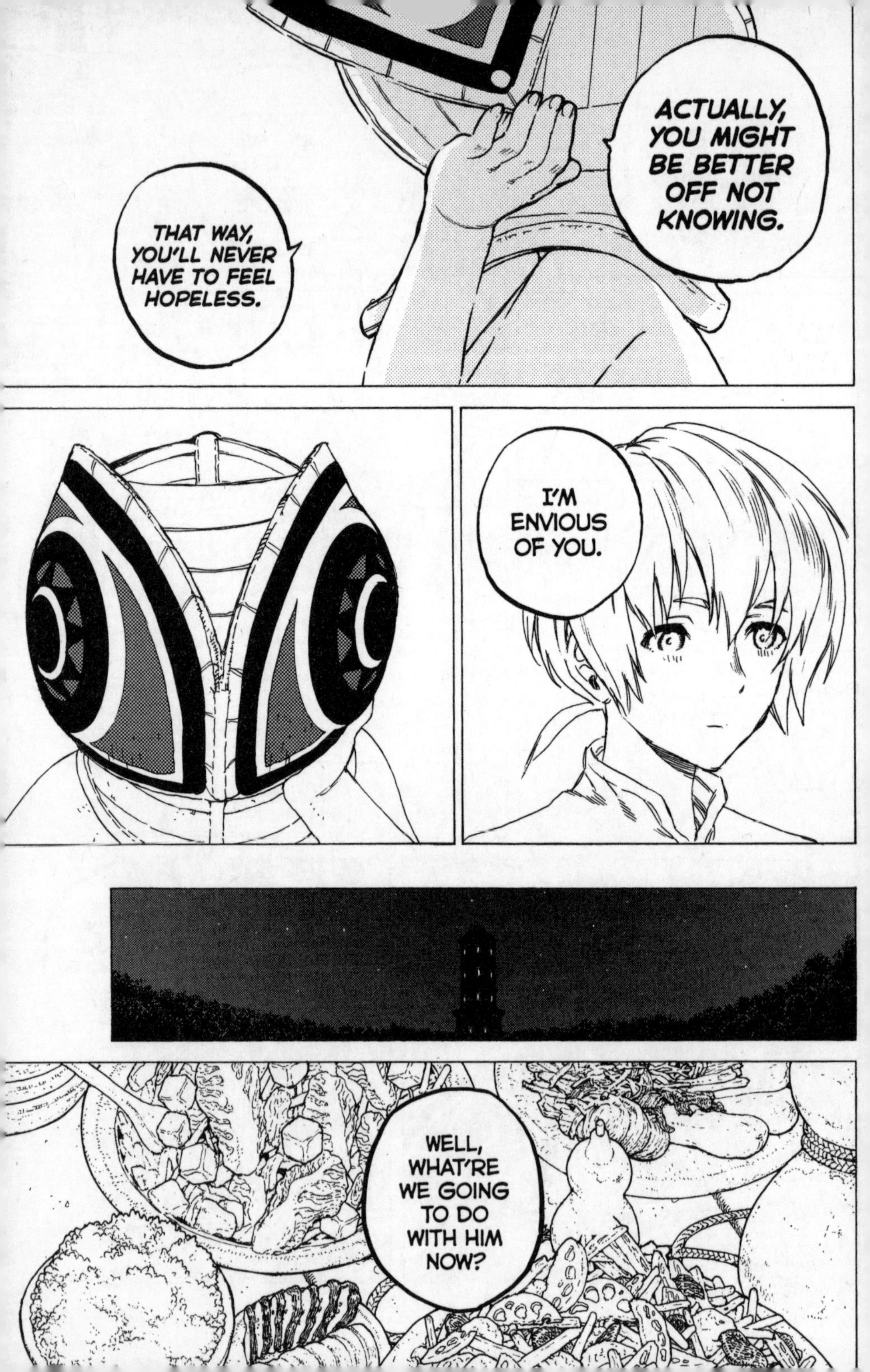
ACTUALLY, YOU MIGHT BE BETTER OFF NOT KNOWING.
THAT WAY, YOU'LL NEVER HAVE TO FEEL HOPELESS.
I'M ENVIOUS OF YOU.
WELL, WHAT'RE WE GOING TO DO WITH HIM NOW?

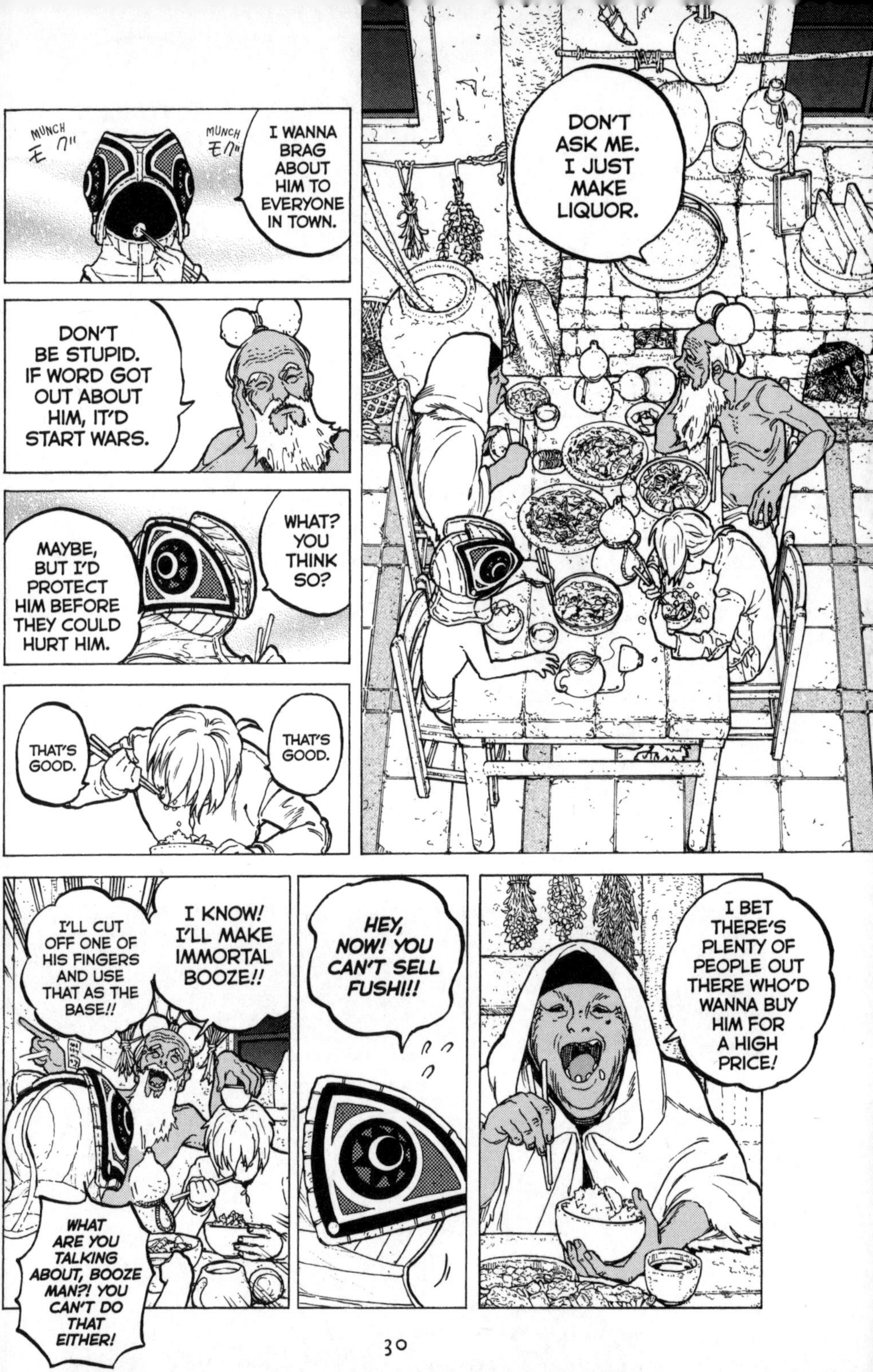

DON'T ASK ME. I JUST MAKE LIQUOR.
I WANNA BRAG ABOUT HIM TO EVERYONE IN TOWN.
MUNCH
MUNCH
DON'T BE STUPID. IF WORD GOT OUT ABOUT HIM, IT'D START WARS.
WHAT? YOU THINK SO?
MAYBE, BUT I'D PROTECT HIM BEFORE THEY COULD HURT HIM.
THAT'S GOOD.
THAT'S GOOD.
I BET THERE'S PLENTY OF PEOPLE OUT THERE WHO'D WANNA BUY HIM FOR A HIGH PRICE!
HEY, NOW! YOU CAN'T SELL FUSHI!!
I KNOW! I'LL MAKE IMMORTAL BOOZE!!
I'LL CUT OFF ONE OF HIS FINGERS AND USE THAT AS THE BASE!!
WHAT ARE YOU TALKING ABOUT, BOOZE MAN?! YOU CAN'T DO THAT EITHER!

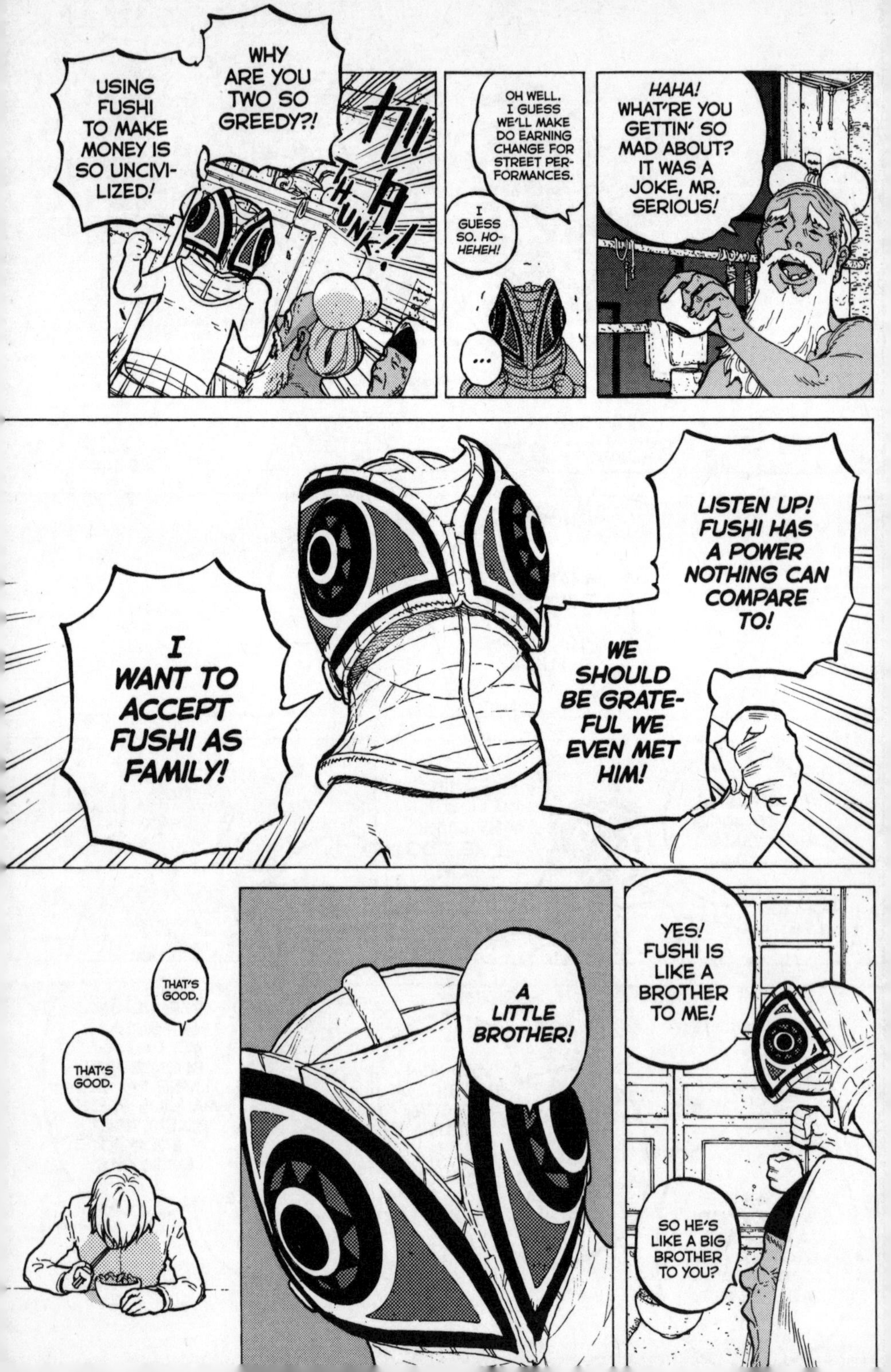
HAHA! WHAT'RE YOU GETTIN' SO MAD ABOUT? IT WAS A JOKE, MR. SERIOUS!
OH WELL. I GUESS WE'LL MAKE DO EARNING CHANGE FOR STREET PERFORMANCES.
I GUESS SO. HOHEHEH!
...
WHY ARE YOU TWO SO GREEDY?!
USING FUSHI TO MAKE MONEY IS SO UNCIVILIZED!
THUNK!!
LISTEN UP! FUSHI HAS A POWER NOTHING CAN COMPARE TO!
WE SHOULD BE GRATEFUL WE EVEN MET HIM!
I WANT TO ACCEPT FUSHI AS FAMILY!
YES! FUSHI IS LIKE A BROTHER TO ME!
SO HE'S LIKE A BIG BROTHER TO YOU?
A LITTLE BROTHER!
THAT'S GOOD.
THAT'S GOOD.

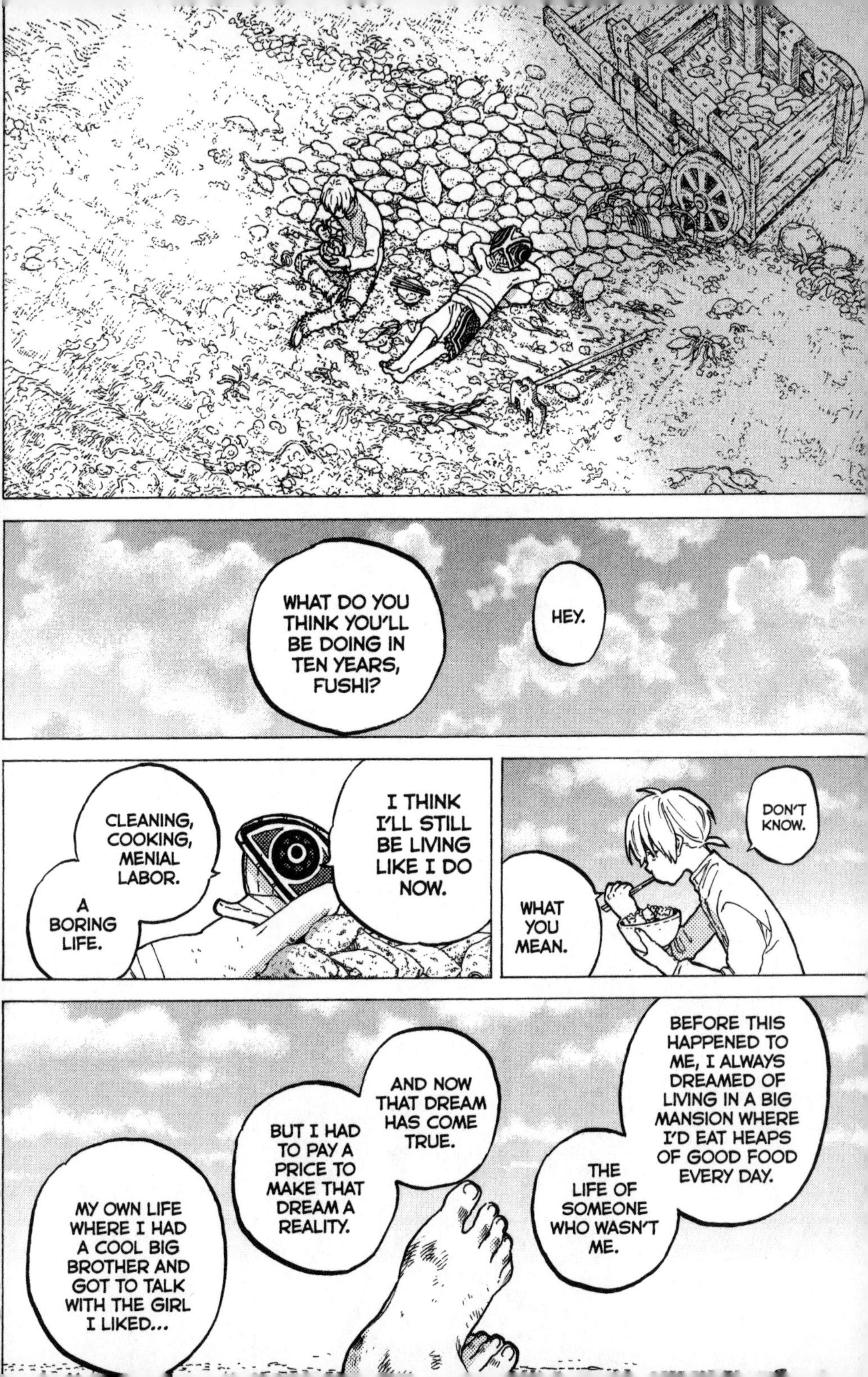
HEY.
WHAT DO YOU THINK YOU'LL BE DOING IN TEN YEARS, FUSHI?
DON'T KNOW.
WHAT YOU MEAN.
I THINK I'LL STILL BE LIVING LIKE I DO NOW.
CLEANING, COOKING, MENIAL LABOR.
A BORING LIFE.
BEFORE THIS HAPPENED TO ME, I ALWAYS DREAMED OF LIVING IN A BIG MANSION WHERE I'D EAT HEAPS OF GOOD FOOD EVERY DAY.
THE LIFE OF SOMEONE WHO WASN'T ME.
AND NOW THAT DREAM HAS COME TRUE.
BUT I HAD TO PAY A PRICE TO MAKE THAT DREAM A REALITY.
MY OWN LIFE WHERE I HAD A COOL BIG BROTHER AND GOT TO TALK WITH THE GIRL I LIKED...

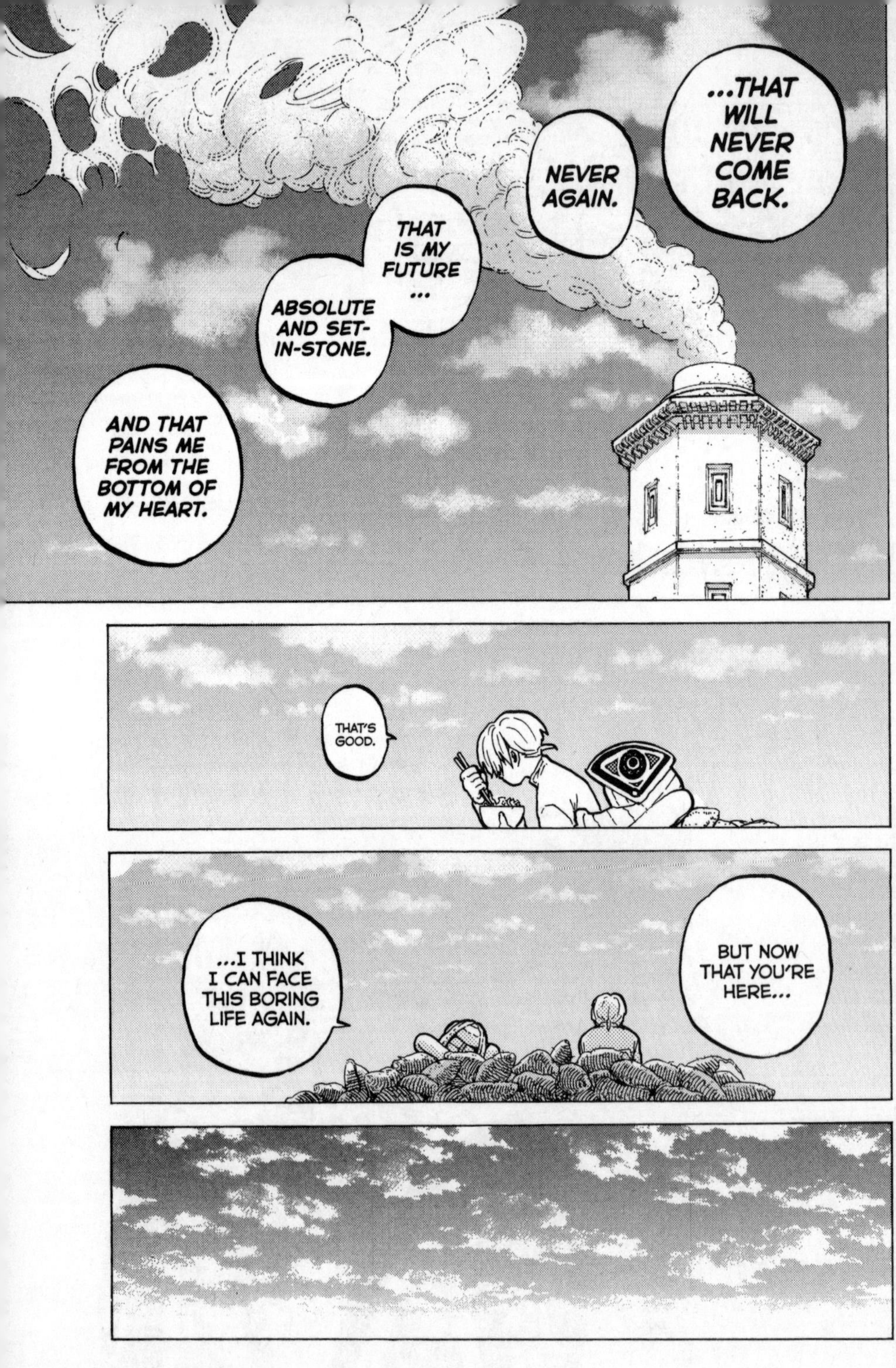
...THAT WILL NEVER COME BACK.
NEVER AGAIN.
THAT IS MY FUTURE ...
ABSOLUTE AND SET-IN-STONE.
AND THAT PAINS ME FROM THE BOTTOM OF MY HEART.
THAT'S GOOD.
BUT NOW THAT YOU'RE HERE...
...I THINK I CAN FACE THIS BORING LIFE AGAIN.

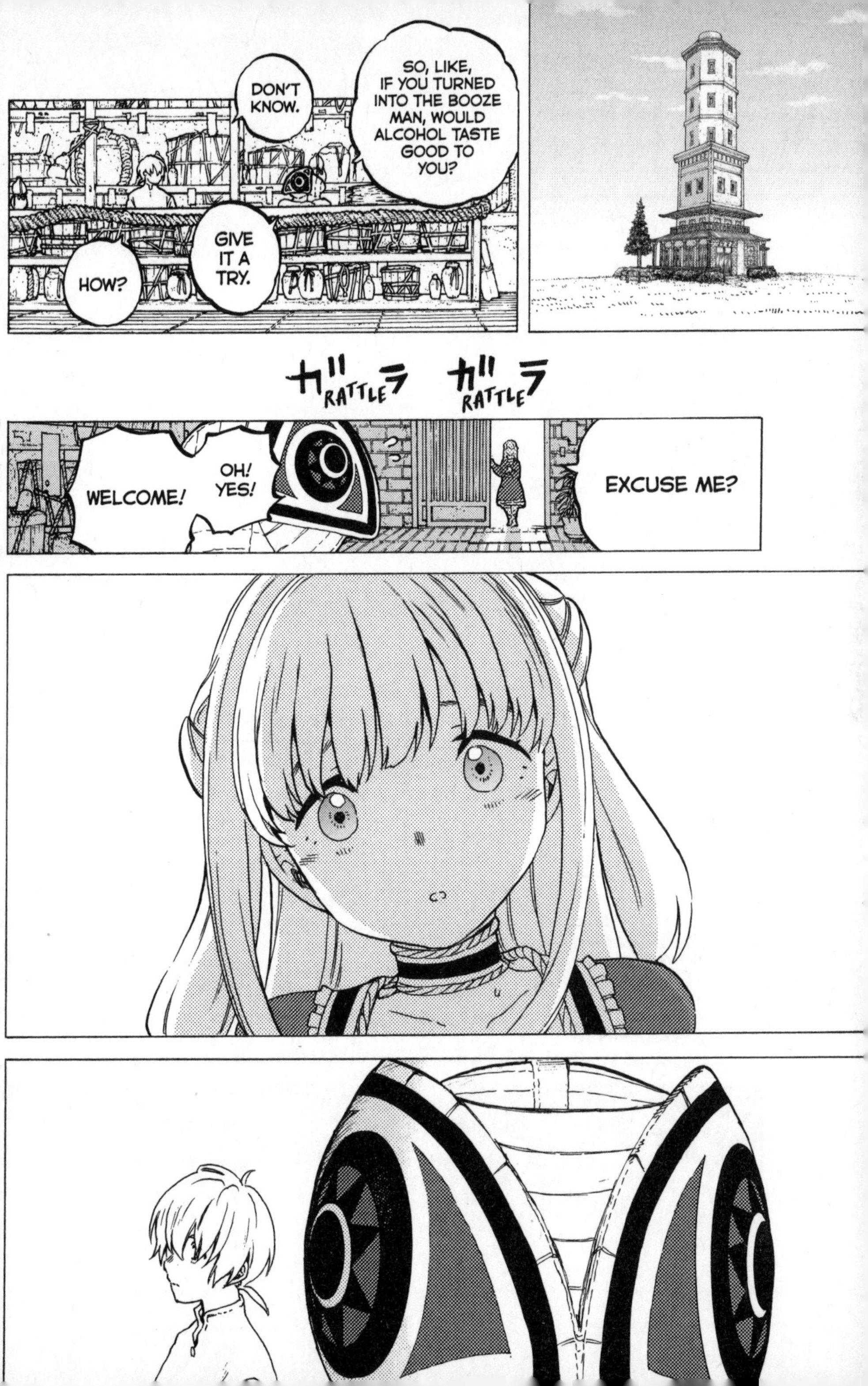
SO, LIKE, IF YOU TURNED INTO THE BOOZE MAN, WOULD ALCOHOL TASTE GOOD TO YOU?
DON'T KNOW.
GIVE IT A TRY.
HOW?
ガラ RATTLE
ガラ RATTLE
EXCUSE ME?
OH! YES!
WELCOME!

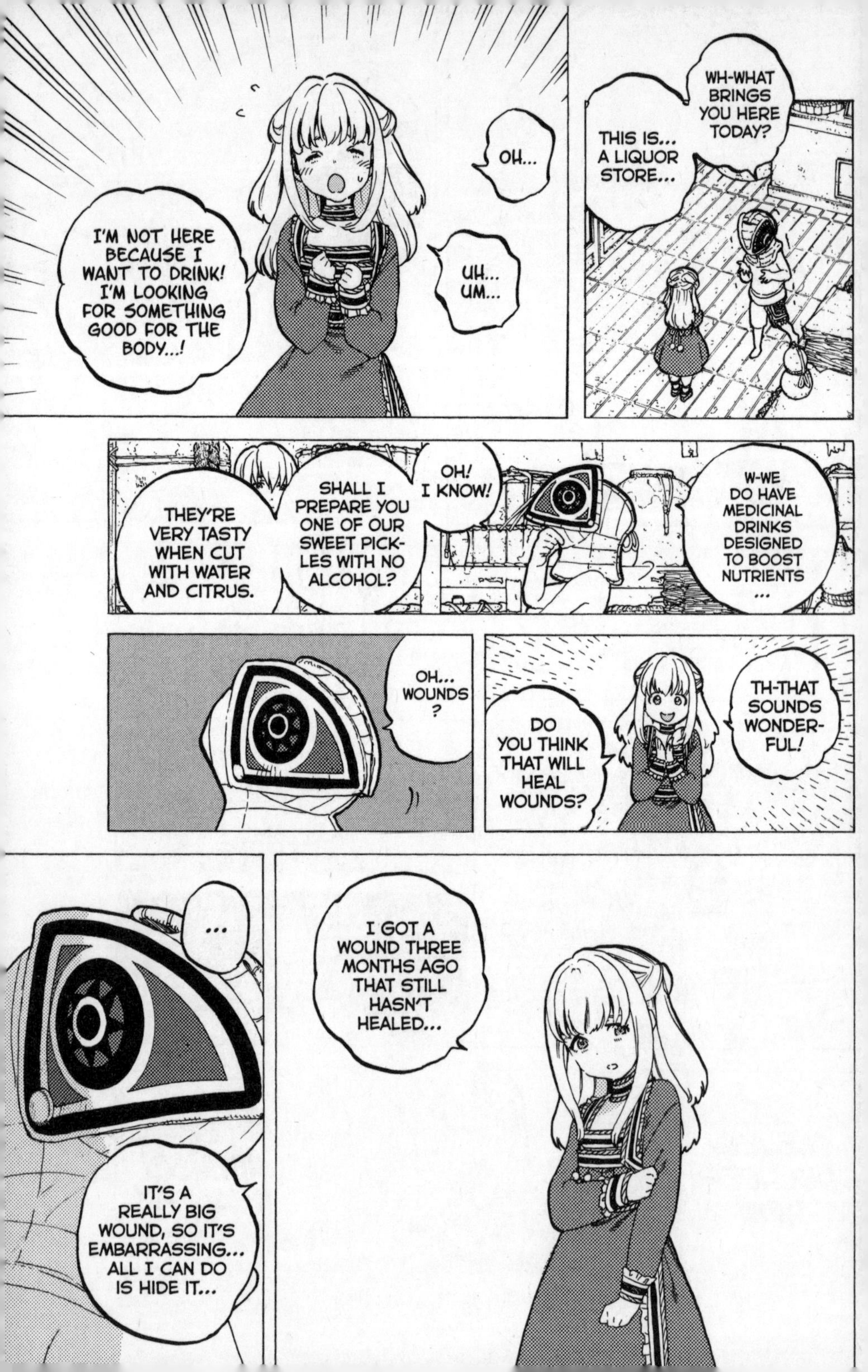
WH-WHAT BRINGS YOU HERE TODAY?
THIS IS... A LIQUOR STORE...
OH...
UH... UM...
I'M NOT HERE BECAUSE I WANT TO DRINK! I'M LOOKING FOR SOMETHING GOOD FOR THE BODY...!
W-WE DO HAVE MEDICINAL DRINKS DESIGNED TO BOOST NUTRIENTS...
OH! I KNOW!
SHALL I PREPARE YOU ONE OF OUR SWEET PICKLES WITH NO ALCOHOL?
THEY'RE VERY TASTY WHEN CUT WITH WATER AND CITRUS.
TH-THAT SOUNDS WONDERFUL!
DO YOU THINK THAT WILL HEAL WOUNDS?
OH... WOUNDS?
I GOT A WOUND THREE MONTHS AGO THAT STILL HASN'T HEALED...
...
IT'S A REALLY BIG WOUND, SO IT'S EMBARRASSING... ALL I CAN DO IS HIDE IT...

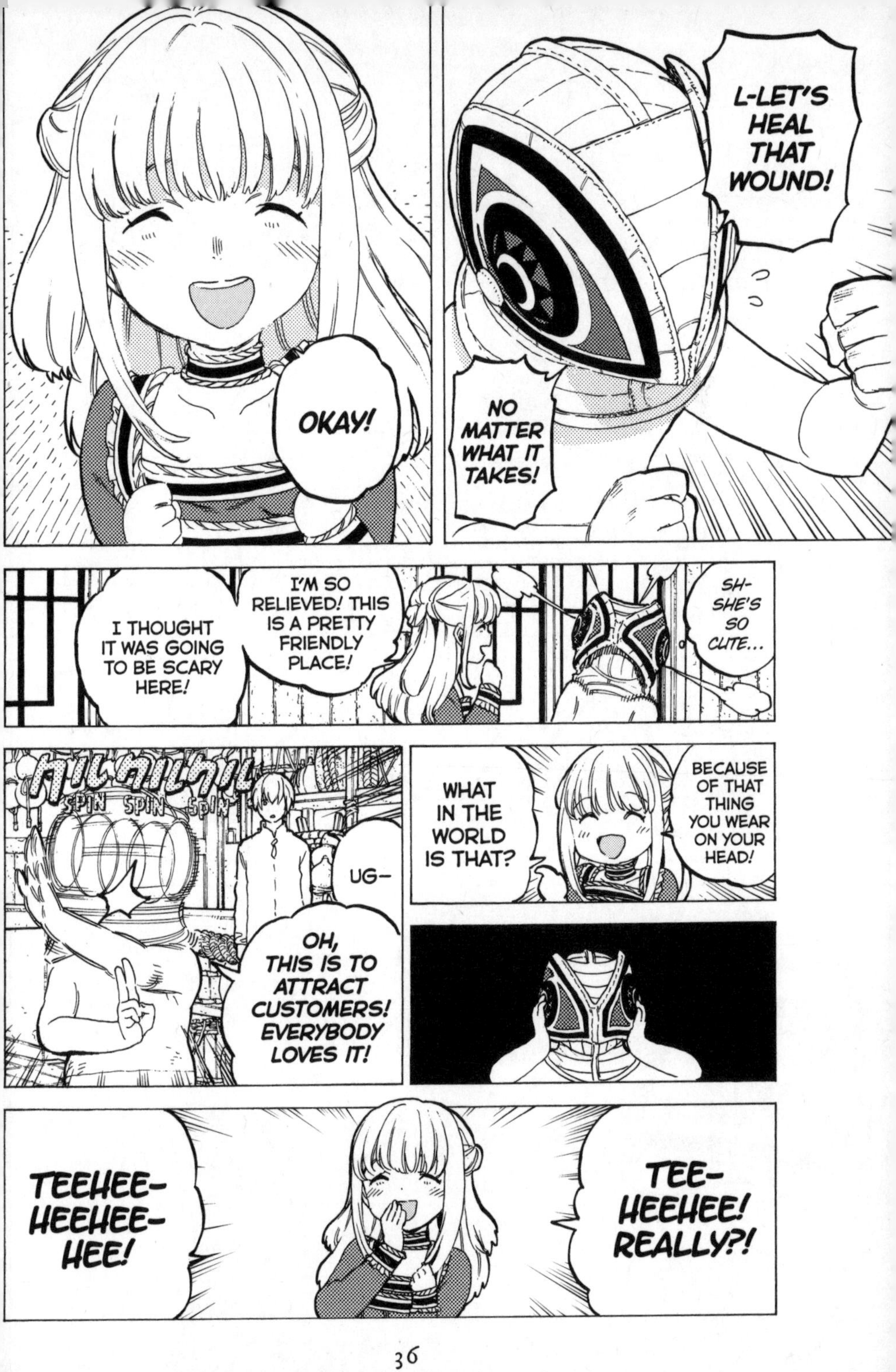
L-LET'S HEAL THAT WOUND!
NO MATTER WHAT IT TAKES!
OKAY!
SH-SHE'S SO CUTE...
I'M SO RELIEVED! THIS IS A PRETTY FRIENDLY PLACE!
I THOUGHT IT WAS GOING TO BE SCARY HERE!
BECAUSE OF THAT THING YOU WEAR ON YOUR HEAD!
WHAT IN THE WORLD IS THAT?
UG–
OH, THIS IS TO ATTRACT CUSTOMERS! EVERYBODY LOVES IT!
SPIN SPIN SPIN
TEE-HEEHEE! REALLY?!
TEEHEE-HEEHEE-HEE!

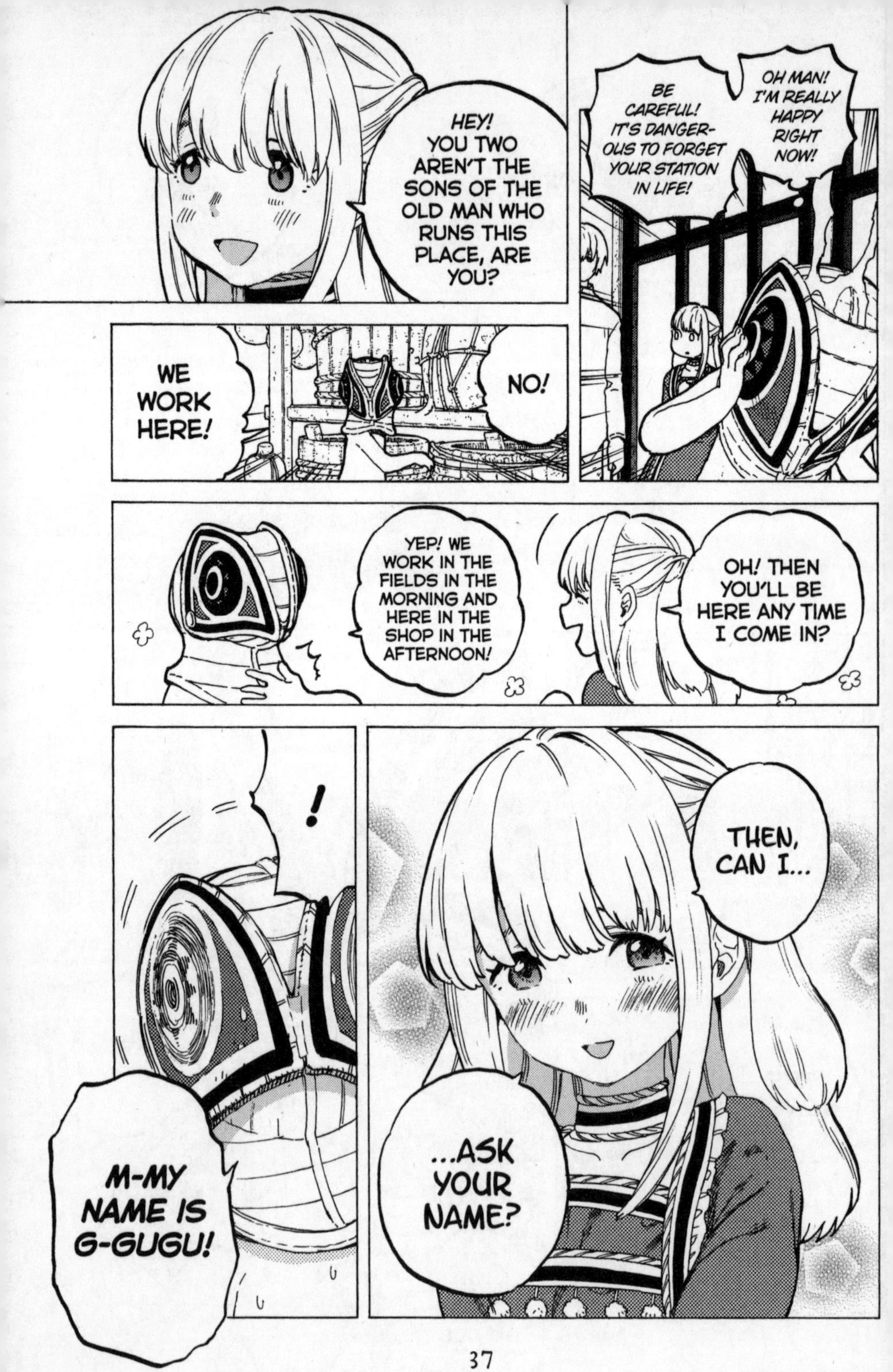
OH MAN! I'M REALLY HAPPY RIGHT NOW!
BE CAREFUL! IT'S DANGER-OUS TO FORGET YOUR STATION IN LIFE!
HEY! YOU TWO AREN'T THE SONS OF THE OLD MAN WHO RUNS THIS PLACE, ARE YOU?
NO!
WE WORK HERE!
OH! THEN YOU'LL BE HERE ANY TIME I COME IN?
YEP! WE WORK IN THE FIELDS IN THE MORNING AND HERE IN THE SHOP IN THE AFTERNOON!
THEN, CAN I...
...ASK YOUR NAME?
!
M-MY NAME IS G-GUGU!

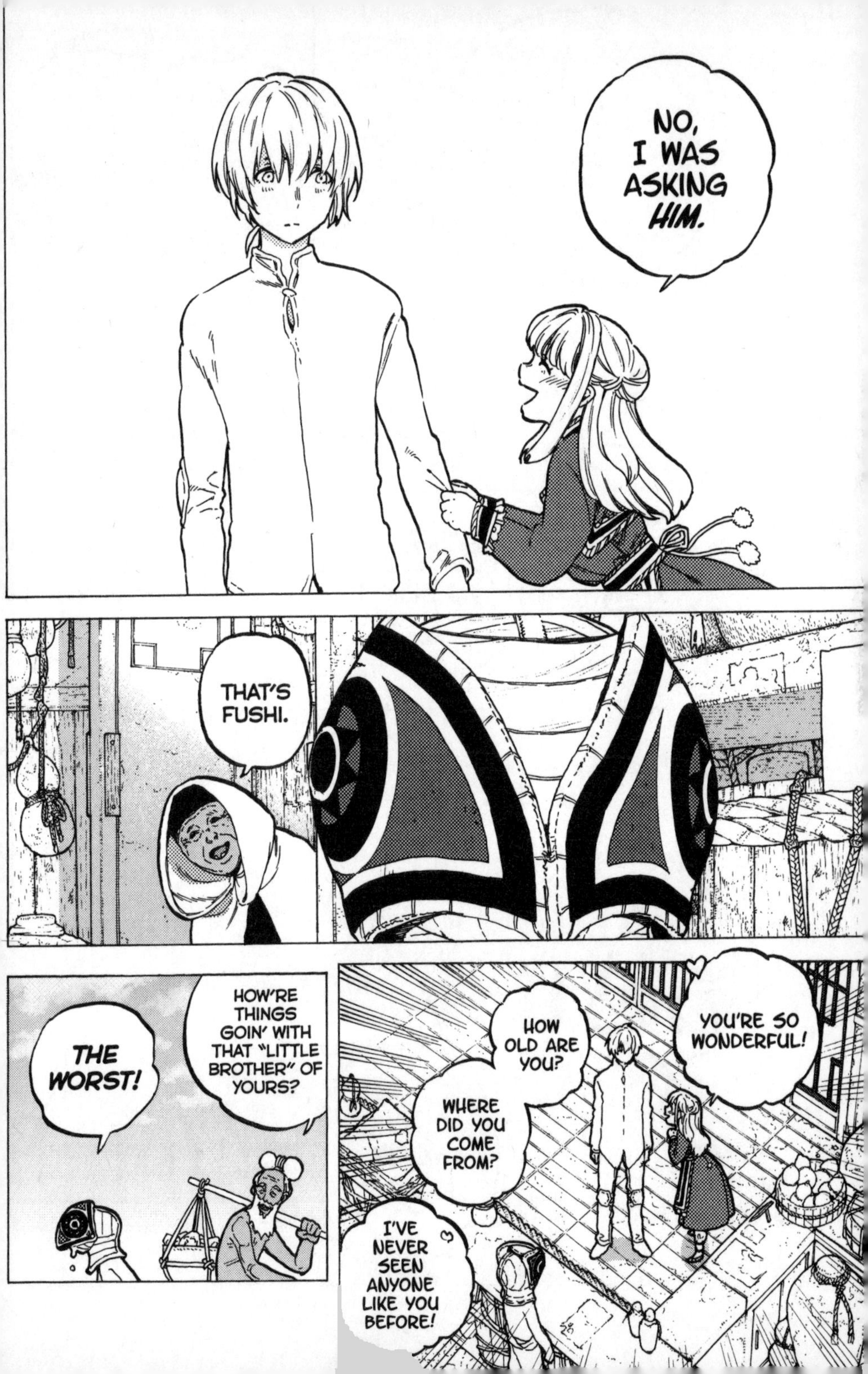
NO, I WAS ASKING HIM.
THAT'S FUSHI.
YOU'RE SO WONDERFUL!
HOW OLD ARE YOU?
WHERE DID YOU COME FROM?
I'VE NEVER SEEN ANYONE LIKE YOU BEFORE!
HOW'RE THINGS GOIN' WITH THAT "LITTLE BROTHER" OF YOURS?
THE WORST!

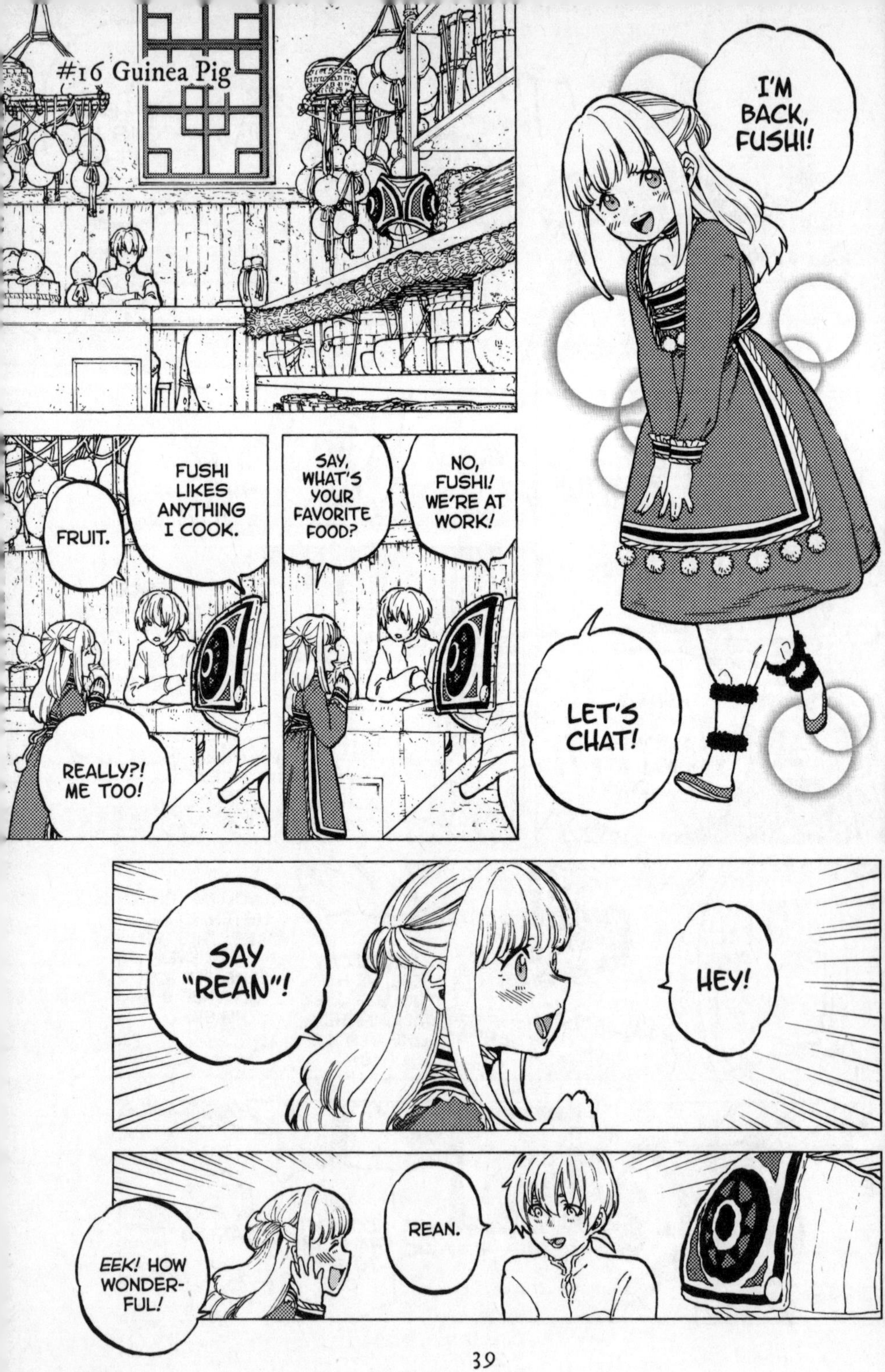
I'M BACK, FUSHI!
LET'S CHAT!
#16 Guinea Pig
NO, FUSHI! WE'RE AT WORK!
SAY, WHAT'S YOUR FAVORITE FOOD?
FUSHI LIKES ANYTHING I COOK.
FRUIT.
REALLY?! ME TOO!
HEY!
SAY "REAN"!
REAN.
EEK! HOW WONDER-FUL!

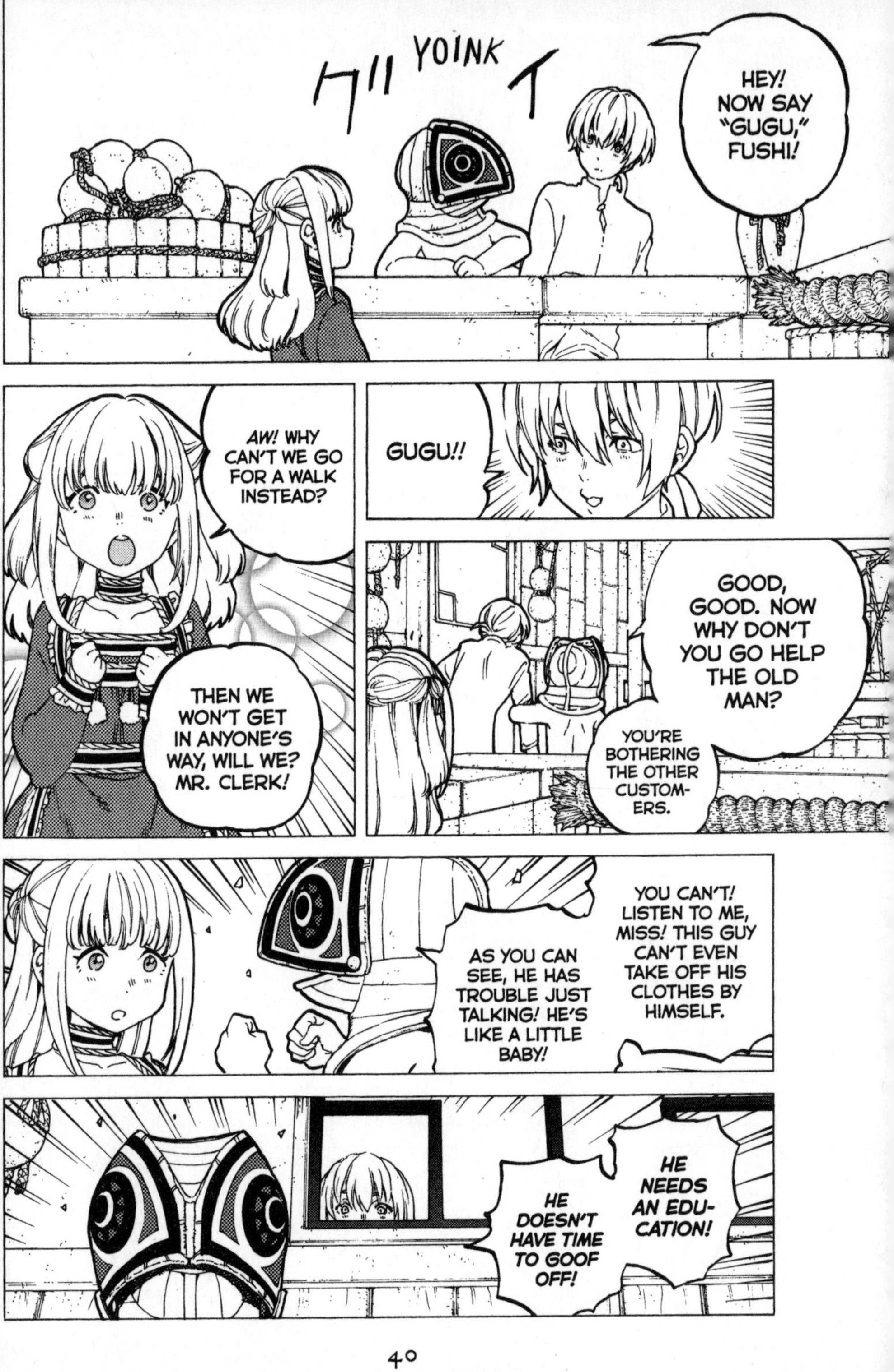
グイ YOINK
HEY! NOW SAY "GUGU," FUSHI!
GUGU!!
GOOD, GOOD. NOW WHY DON'T YOU GO HELP THE OLD MAN?
YOU'RE BOTHERING THE OTHER CUSTOM-ERS.
AW! WHY CAN'T WE GO FOR A WALK INSTEAD?
THEN WE WON'T GET IN ANYONE'S WAY, WILL WE? MR. CLERK!
YOU CAN'T! LISTEN TO ME, MISS! THIS GUY CAN'T EVEN TAKE OFF HIS CLOTHES BY HIMSELF.
AS YOU CAN SEE, HE HAS TROUBLE JUST TALKING! HE'S LIKE A LITTLE BABY!
HE NEEDS AN EDU-CATION!
HE DOESN'T HAVE TIME TO GOOF OFF!

OH, I CAN TEACH HIM HOW TO TALK.

AND HOW TO TAKE OFF HIS CLOTHES, TOO... ♡

JUST KIDDING!

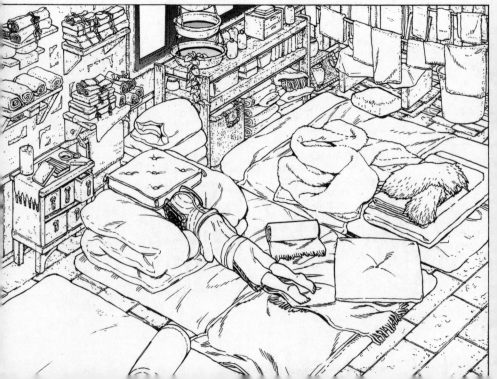

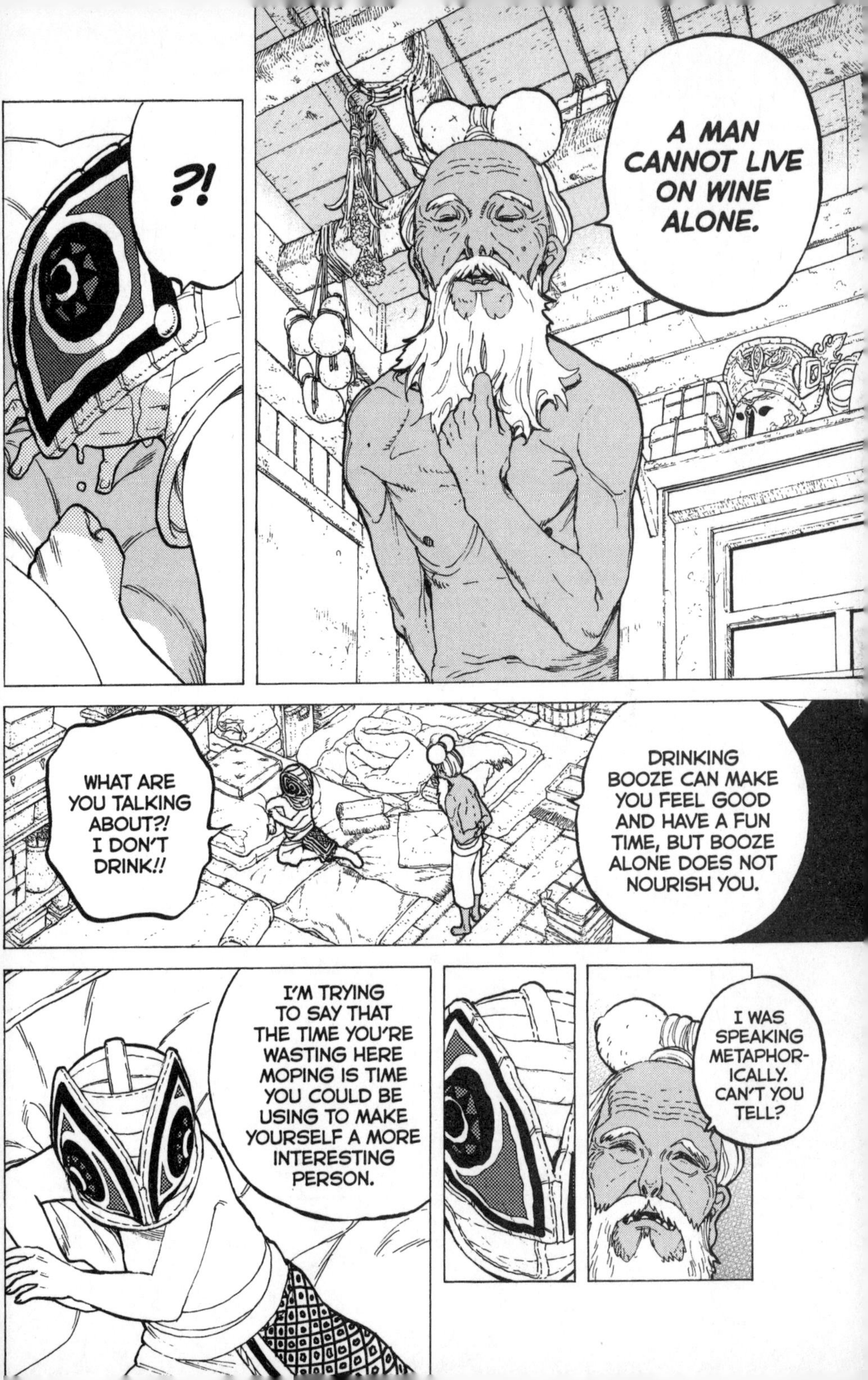
A MAN CANNOT LIVE ON WINE ALONE.
?!
DRINKING BOOZE CAN MAKE YOU FEEL GOOD AND HAVE A FUN TIME, BUT BOOZE ALONE DOES NOT NOURISH YOU.
WHAT ARE YOU TALKING ABOUT?! I DON'T DRINK!!
I WAS SPEAKING METAPHORICALLY. CAN'T YOU TELL?
I'M TRYING TO SAY THAT THE TIME YOU'RE WASTING HERE MOPING IS TIME YOU COULD BE USING TO MAKE YOURSELF A MORE INTERESTING PERSON.

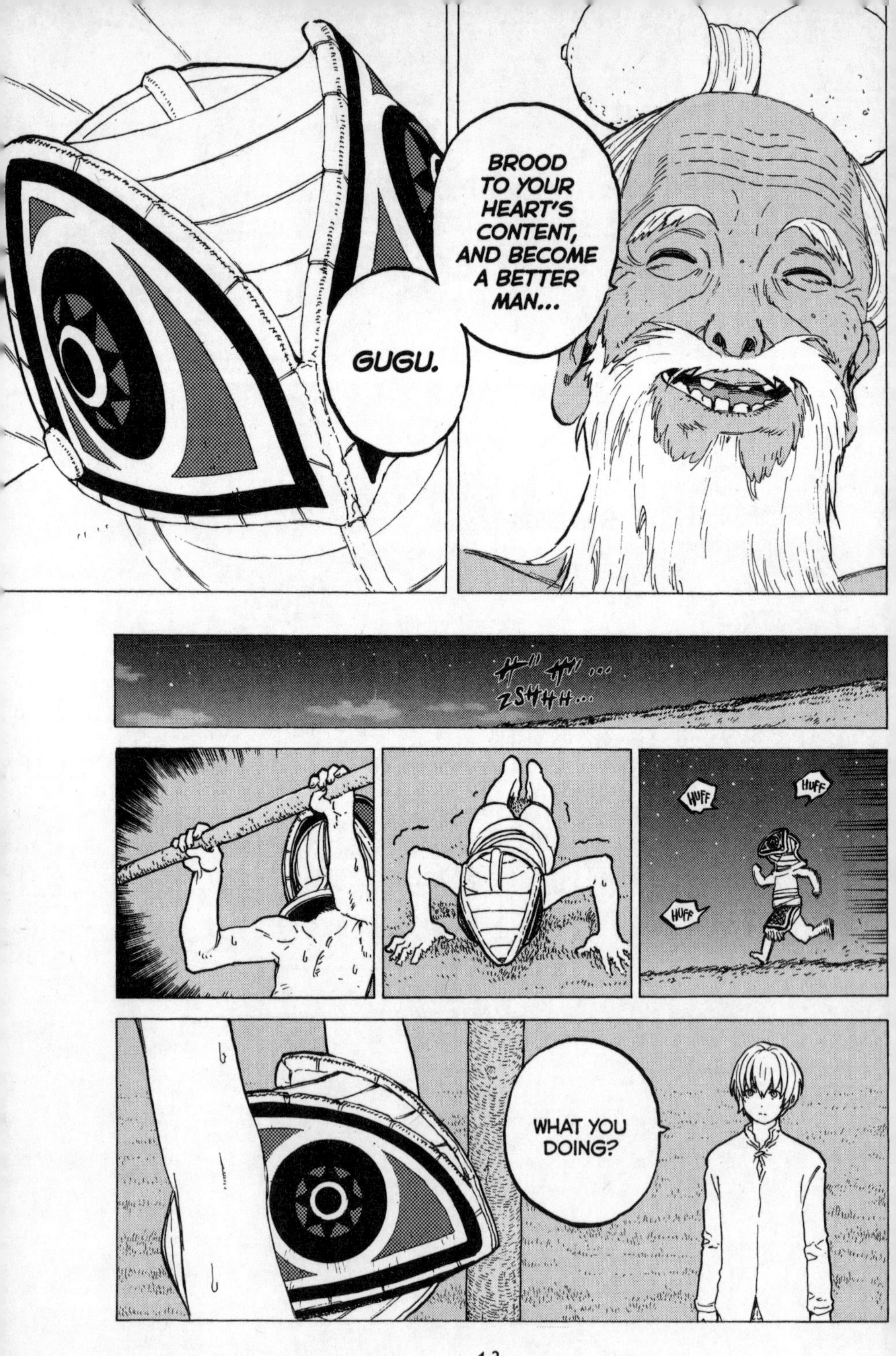
BROOD TO YOUR HEART'S CONTENT, AND BECOME A BETTER MAN...
GUGU.
ZSHHH...
HUFF
HUFF
HUFF
WHAT YOU DOING?

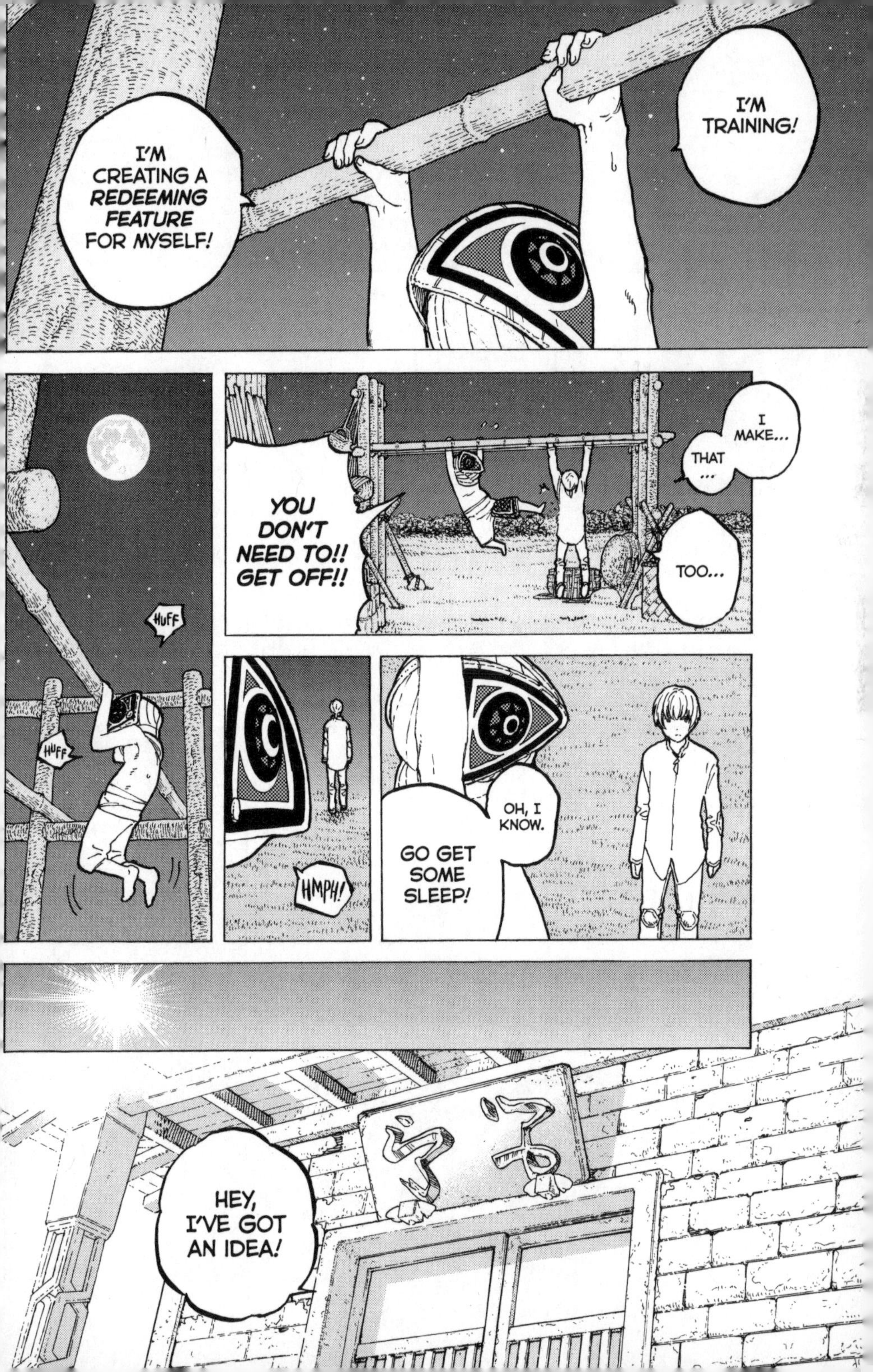
I'M TRAINING!
I'M CREATING A *REDEEMING FEATURE* FOR MYSELF!
I MAKE...
THAT ...
TOO...
YOU DON'T NEED TO!! GET OFF!!
OH, I KNOW.
GO GET SOME SLEEP!
HMPH!
HUFF
HUFF
HEY, I'VE GOT AN IDEA!

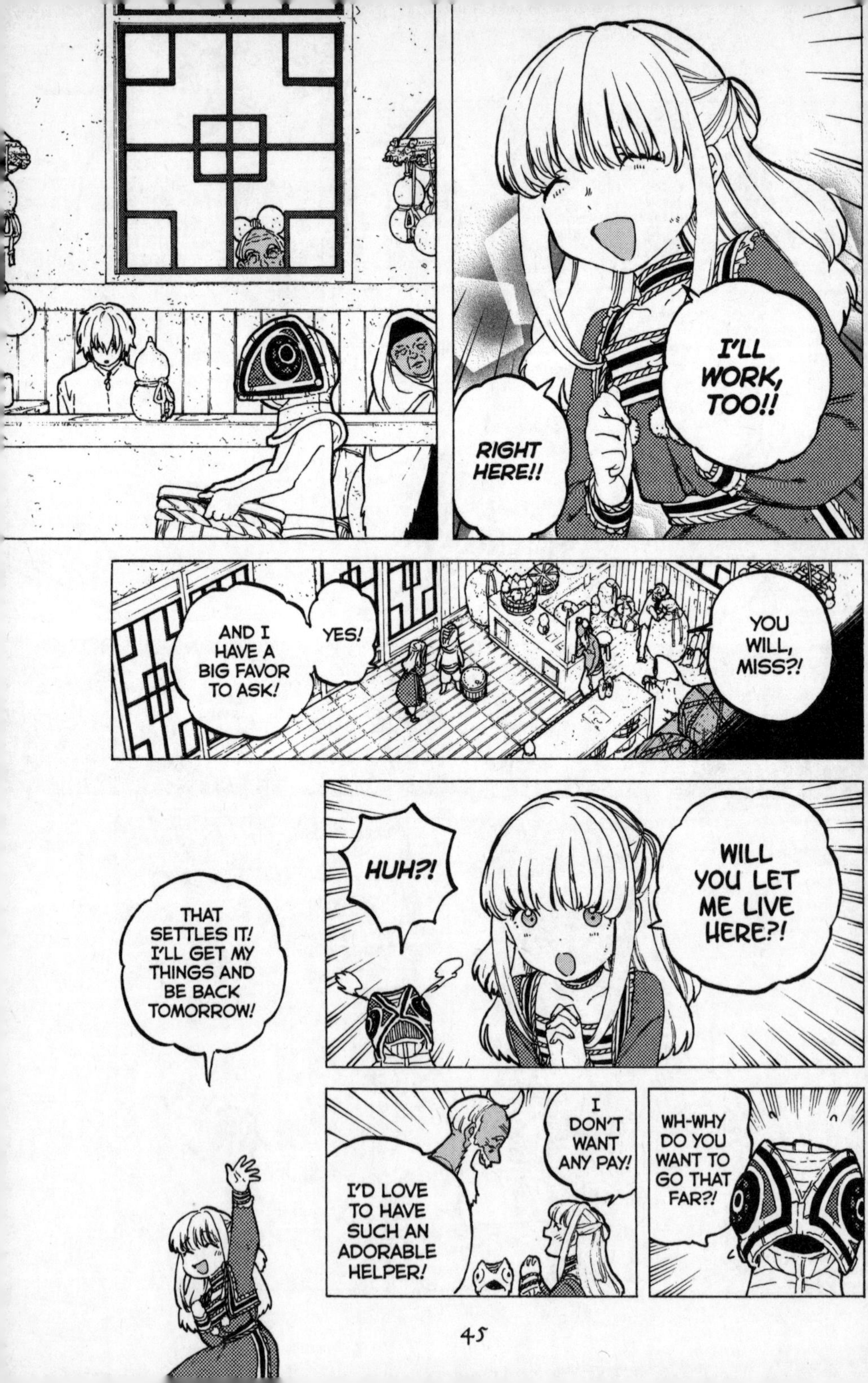
I'LL WORK, TOO!!
RIGHT HERE!!
YOU WILL, MISS?!
YES!
AND I HAVE A BIG FAVOR TO ASK!
WILL YOU LET ME LIVE HERE?!
HUH?!
WH-WHY DO YOU WANT TO GO THAT FAR?!
I DON'T WANT ANY PAY!
I'D LOVE TO HAVE SUCH AN ADORABLE HELPER!
THAT SETTLES IT! I'LL GET MY THINGS AND BE BACK TOMORROW!

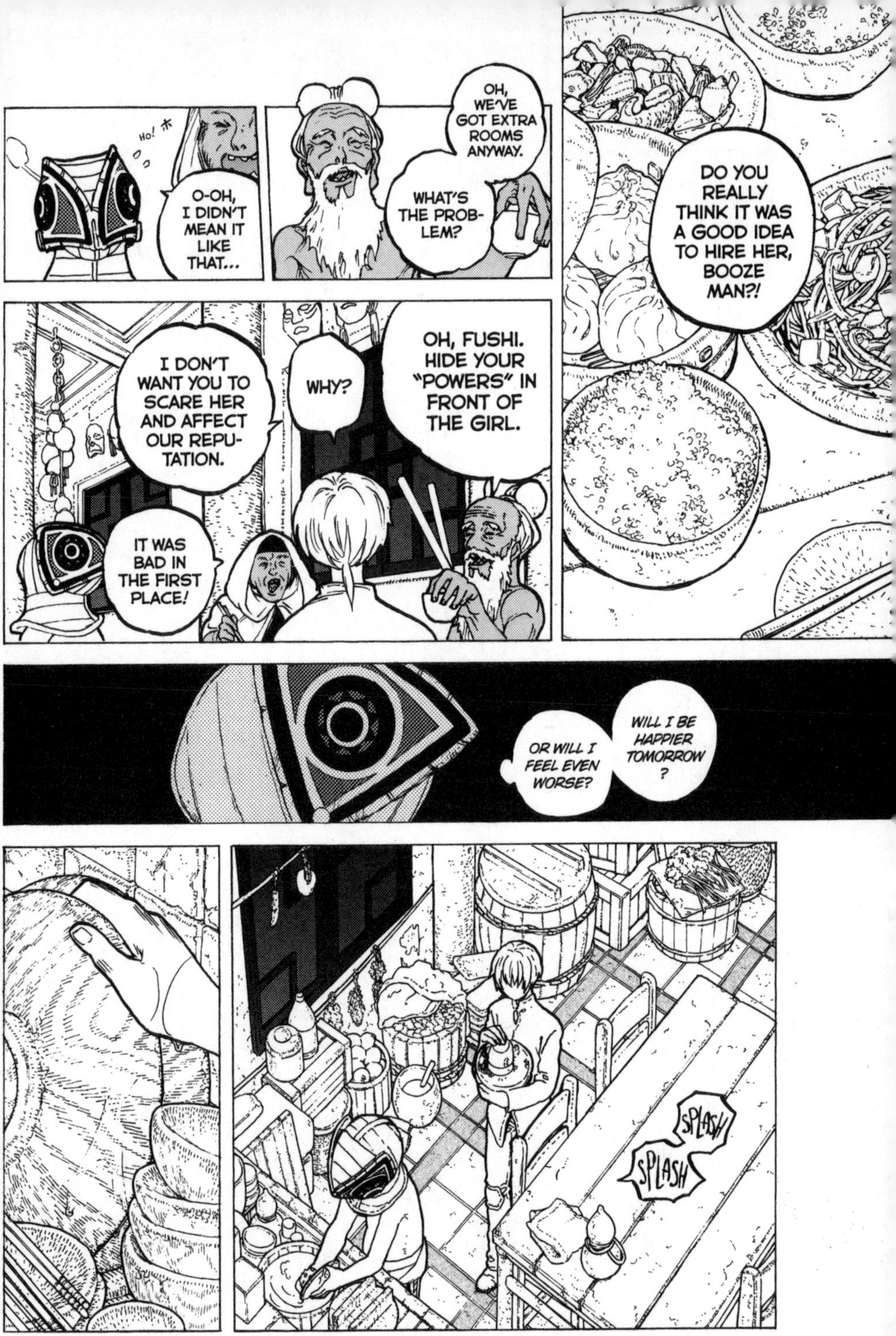
DO YOU REALLY THINK IT WAS A GOOD IDEA TO HIRE HER, BOOZE MAN?!
OH, WE'VE GOT EXTRA ROOMS ANYWAY.
WHAT'S THE PROB-LEM?
HO! ホ
O-OH, I DIDN'T MEAN IT LIKE THAT...
OH, FUSHI. HIDE YOUR "POWERS" IN FRONT OF THE GIRL.
WHY?
I DON'T WANT YOU TO SCARE HER AND AFFECT OUR REPU-TATION.
IT WAS BAD IN THE FIRST PLACE!
WILL I BE HAPPIER TOMORROW?
OR WILL I FEEL EVEN WORSE?
SPLASH
SPLASH

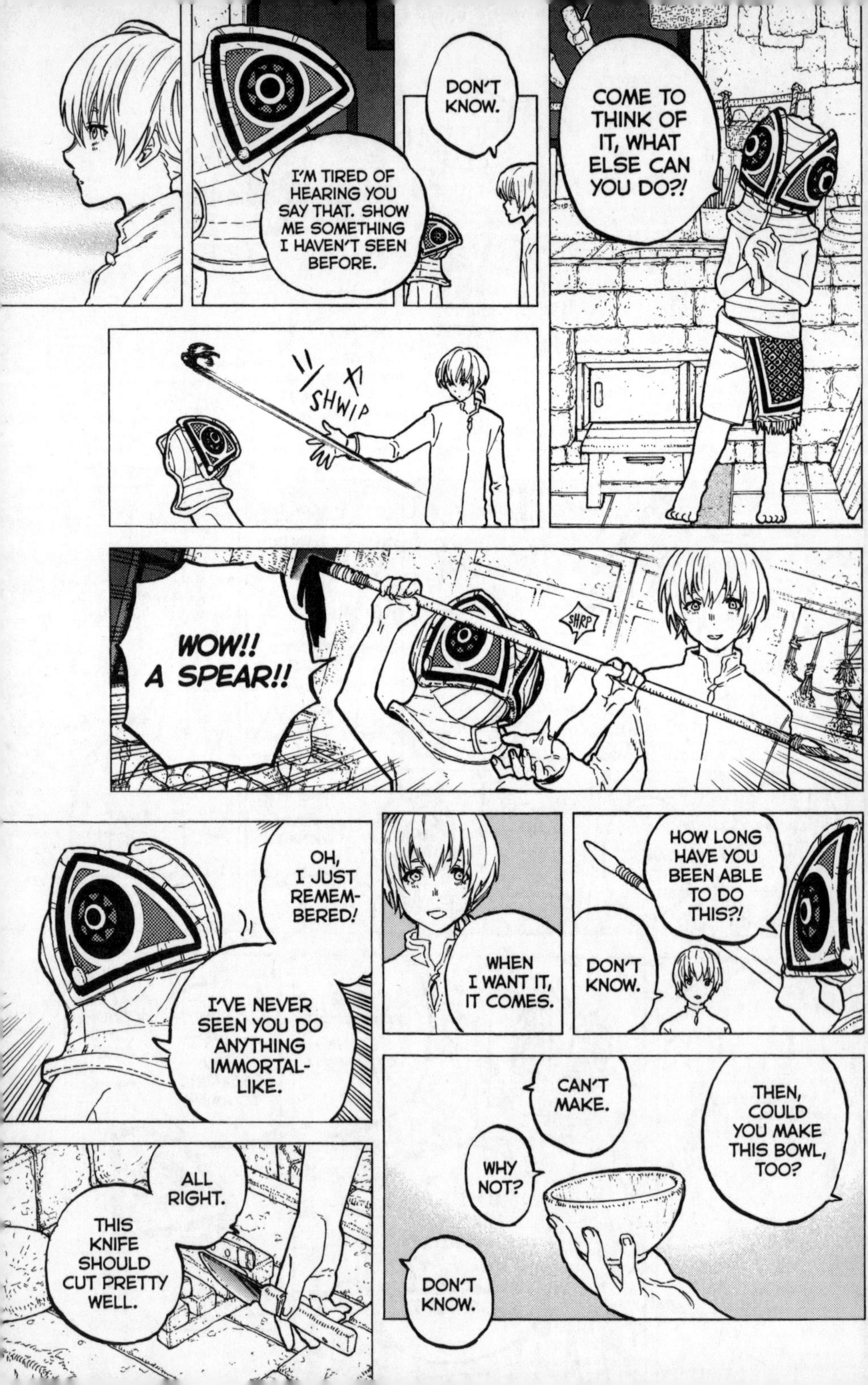
COME TO THINK OF IT, WHAT ELSE CAN YOU DO?!
DON'T KNOW.
I'M TIRED OF HEARING YOU SAY THAT. SHOW ME SOMETHING I HAVEN'T SEEN BEFORE.
SHWIP
SHRP
WOW!! A SPEAR!!
HOW LONG HAVE YOU BEEN ABLE TO DO THIS?!
DON'T KNOW.
WHEN I WANT IT, IT COMES.
OH, I JUST REMEMBERED!
I'VE NEVER SEEN YOU DO ANYTHING IMMORTAL-LIKE.
ALL RIGHT.
THIS KNIFE SHOULD CUT PRETTY WELL.
THEN, COULD YOU MAKE THIS BOWL, TOO?
CAN'T MAKE.
WHY NOT?
DON'T KNOW.

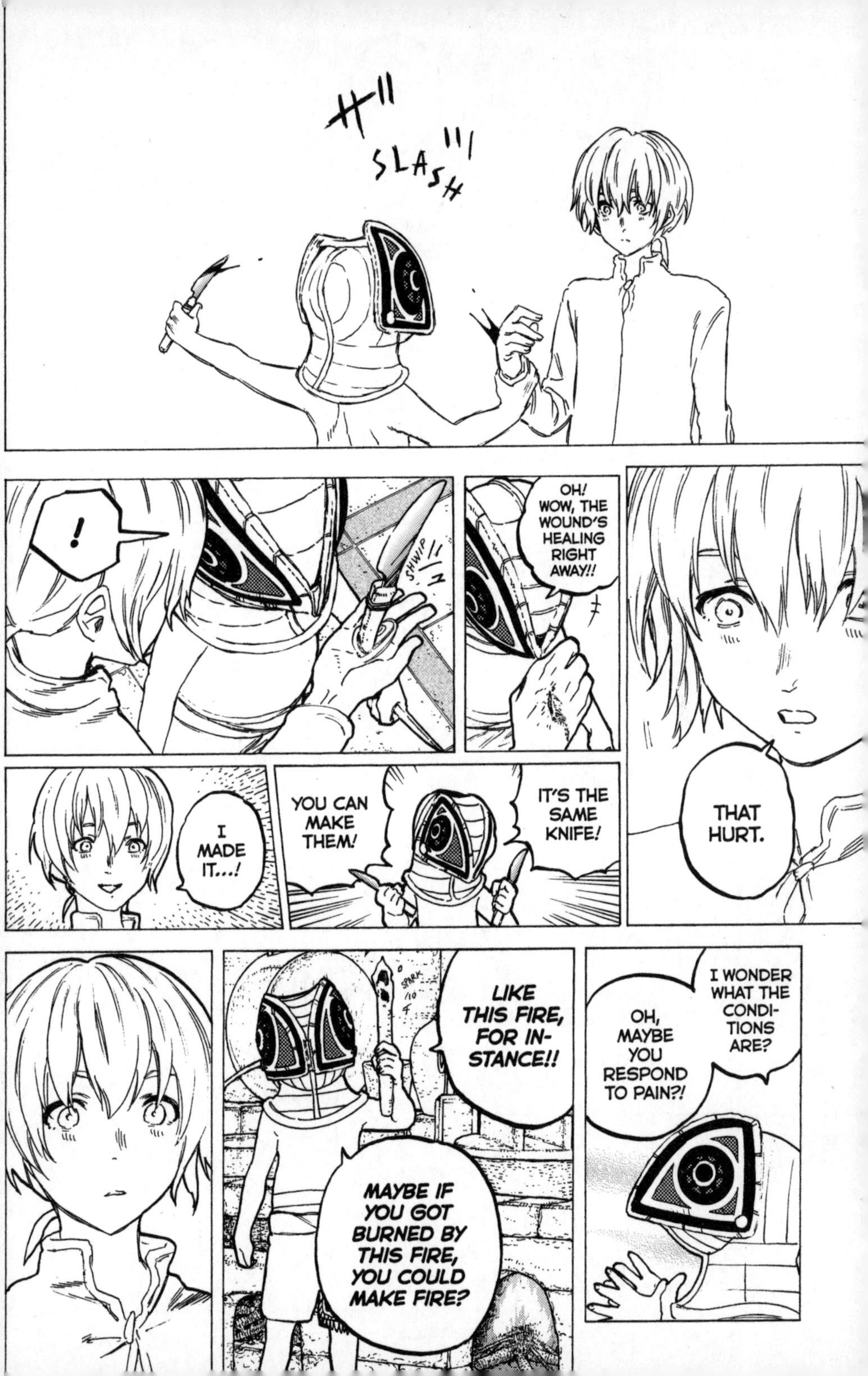
SLASH
THAT HURT.
OH! WOW, THE WOUND'S HEALING RIGHT AWAY!!
SHWIP
!
IT'S THE SAME KNIFE!
YOU CAN MAKE THEM!
I MADE IT...!
I WONDER WHAT THE CONDITIONS ARE?
OH, MAYBE YOU RESPOND TO PAIN?!
SPARK
LIKE THIS FIRE, FOR INSTANCE!!
MAYBE IF YOU GOT BURNED BY THIS FIRE, YOU COULD MAKE FIRE?

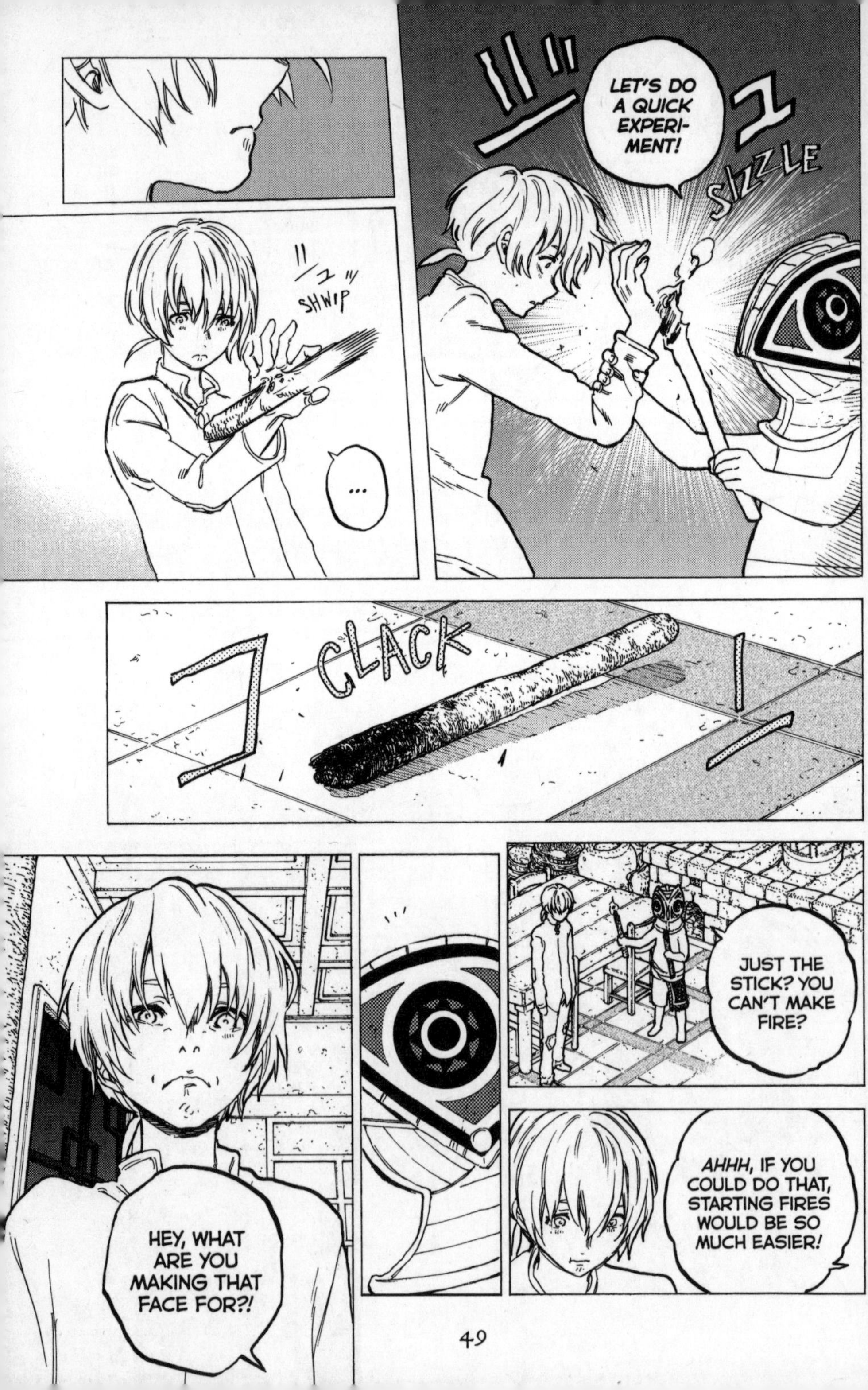
LET'S DO A QUICK EXPERI-MENT!
SIZZLE
SHWIP
...
CLACK
JUST THE STICK? YOU CAN'T MAKE FIRE?
AHHH, IF YOU COULD DO THAT, STARTING FIRES WOULD BE SO MUCH EASIER!
HEY, WHAT ARE YOU MAKING THAT FACE FOR?!

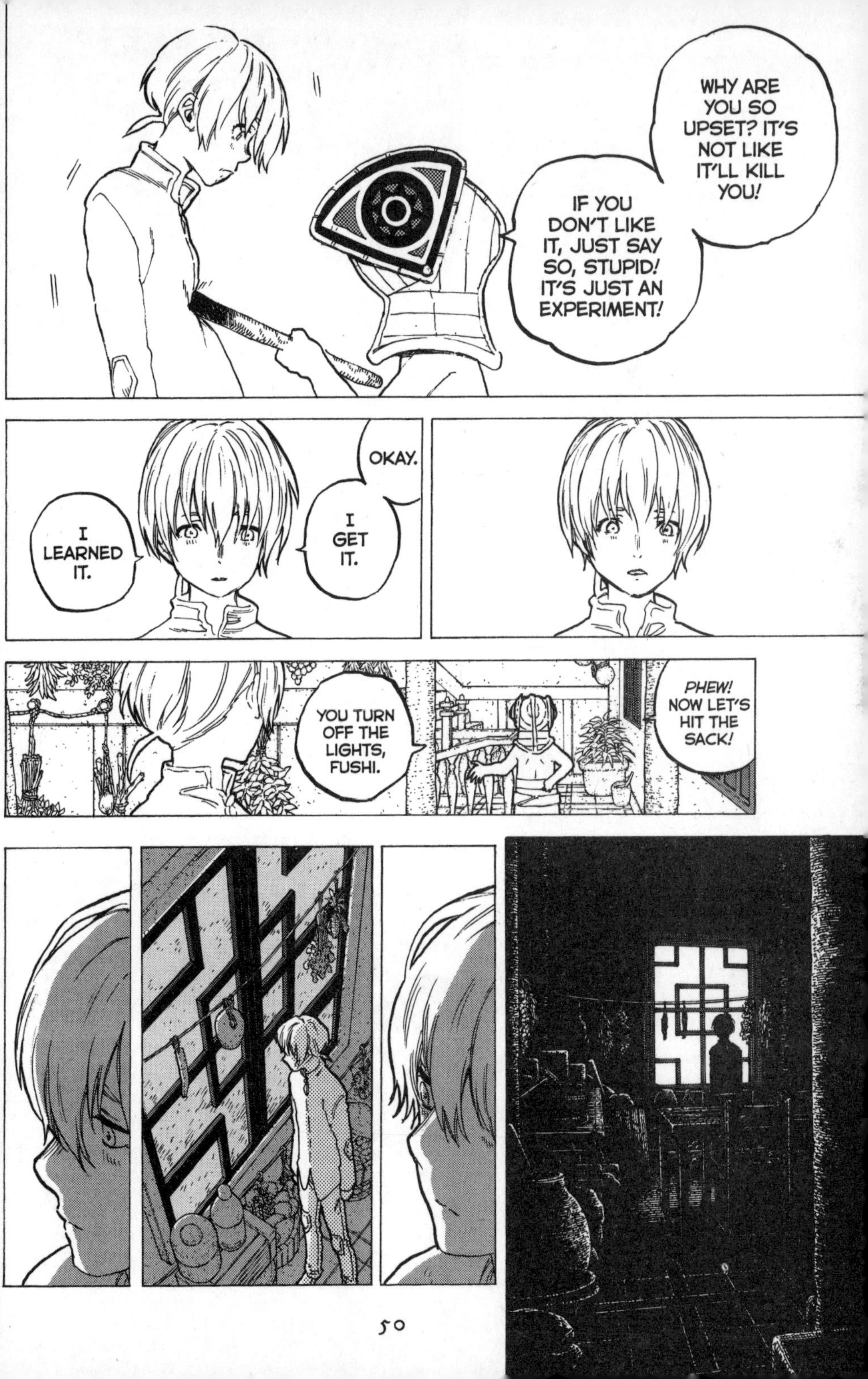
WHY ARE YOU SO UPSET? IT'S NOT LIKE IT'LL KILL YOU!
IF YOU DON'T LIKE IT, JUST SAY SO, STUPID! IT'S JUST AN EXPERIMENT!
OKAY.
I GET IT.
I LEARNED IT.
PHEW! NOW LET'S HIT THE SACK!
YOU TURN OFF THE LIGHTS, FUSHI.

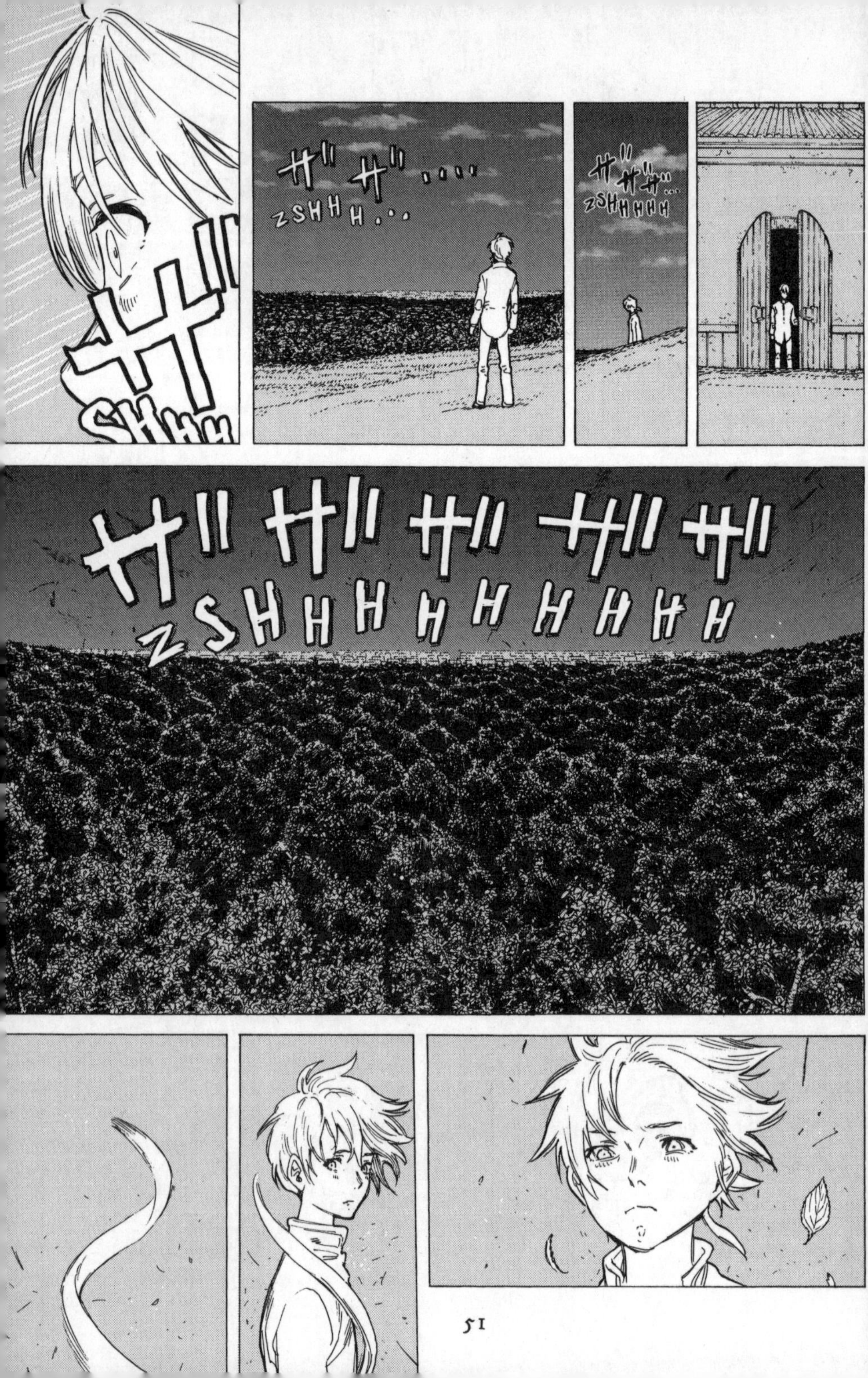
ザザザ…
ZSHHHHH
ザザ……
ZSHHH…
ザ
SHHH
ザザザザザ
ZSHHHHHHHHHH

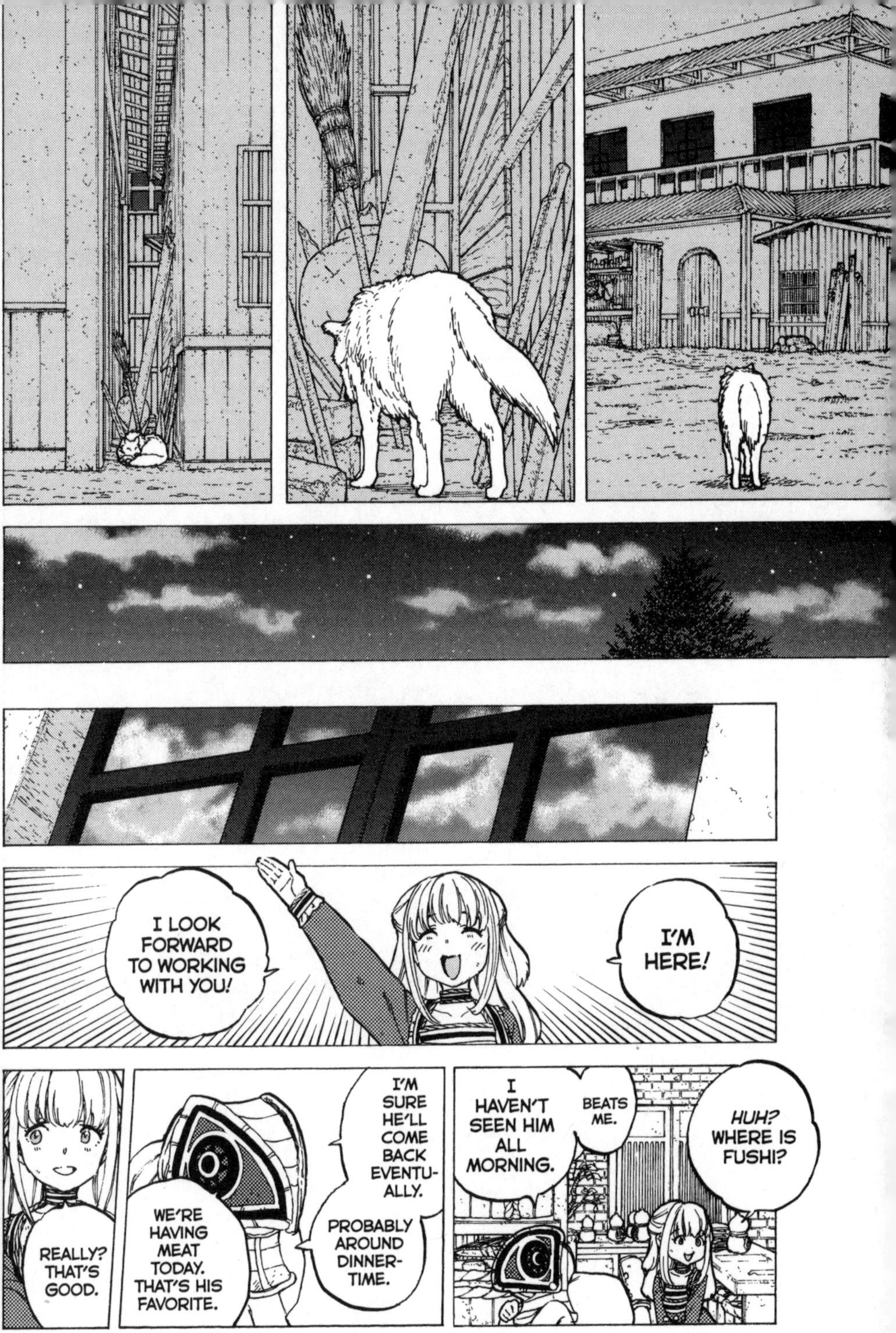
I'M HERE!
I LOOK FORWARD TO WORKING WITH YOU!
HUH? WHERE IS FUSHI?
BEATS ME.
I HAVEN'T SEEN HIM ALL MORNING.
I'M SURE HE'LL COME BACK EVENTU-ALLY.
PROBABLY AROUND DINNER-TIME.
WE'RE HAVING MEAT TODAY. THAT'S HIS FAVORITE.
REALLY? THAT'S GOOD.

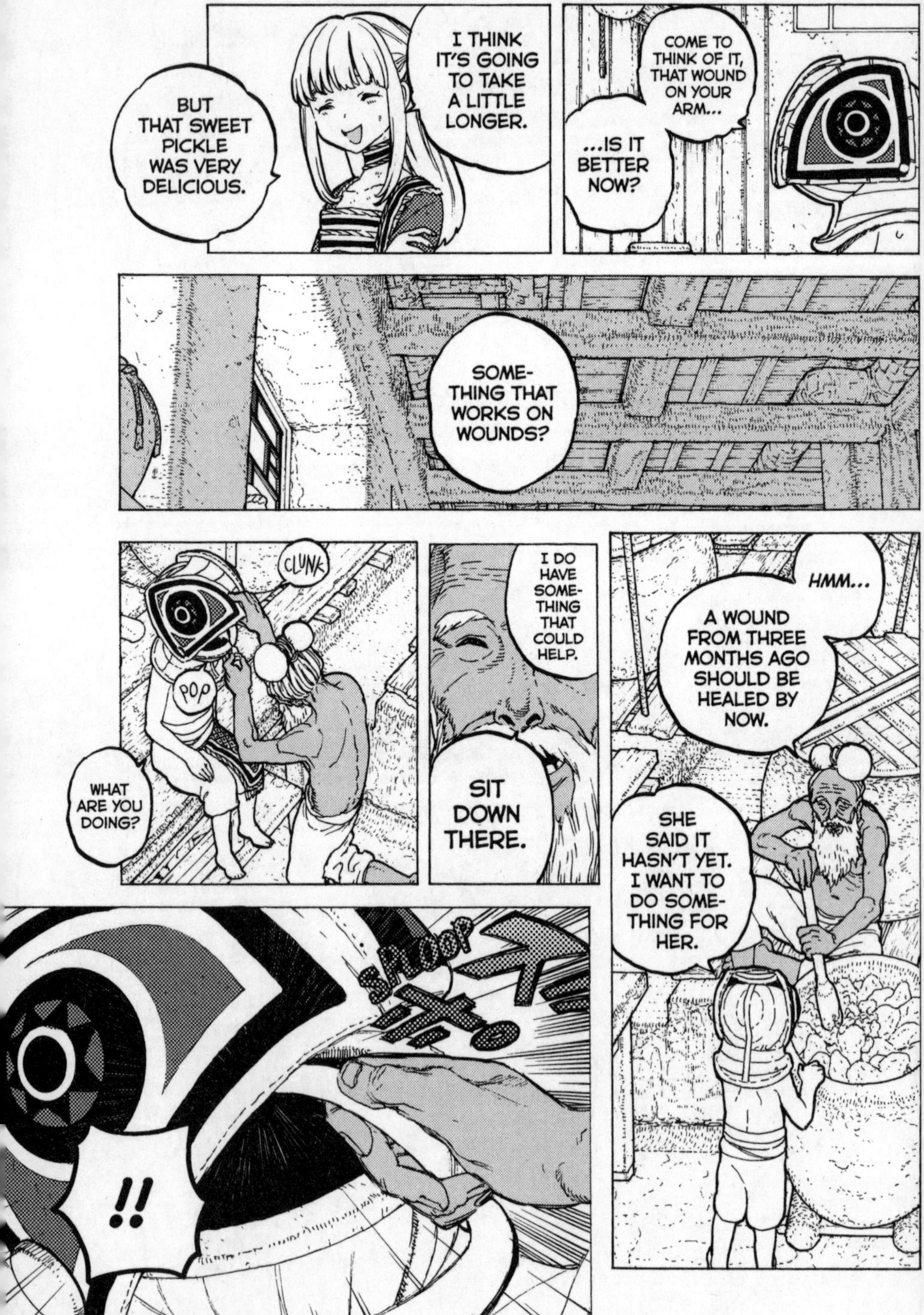

COME TO THINK OF IT, THAT WOUND ON YOUR ARM...
...IS IT BETTER NOW?
I THINK IT'S GOING TO TAKE A LITTLE LONGER.
BUT THAT SWEET PICKLE WAS VERY DELICIOUS.
SOME-THING THAT WORKS ON WOUNDS?
HMM...
A WOUND FROM THREE MONTHS AGO SHOULD BE HEALED BY NOW.
SHE SAID IT HASN'T YET. I WANT TO DO SOME-THING FOR HER.
I DO HAVE SOME-THING THAT COULD HELP.
SIT DOWN THERE.
CLUNK
POP
WHAT ARE YOU DOING?
!!

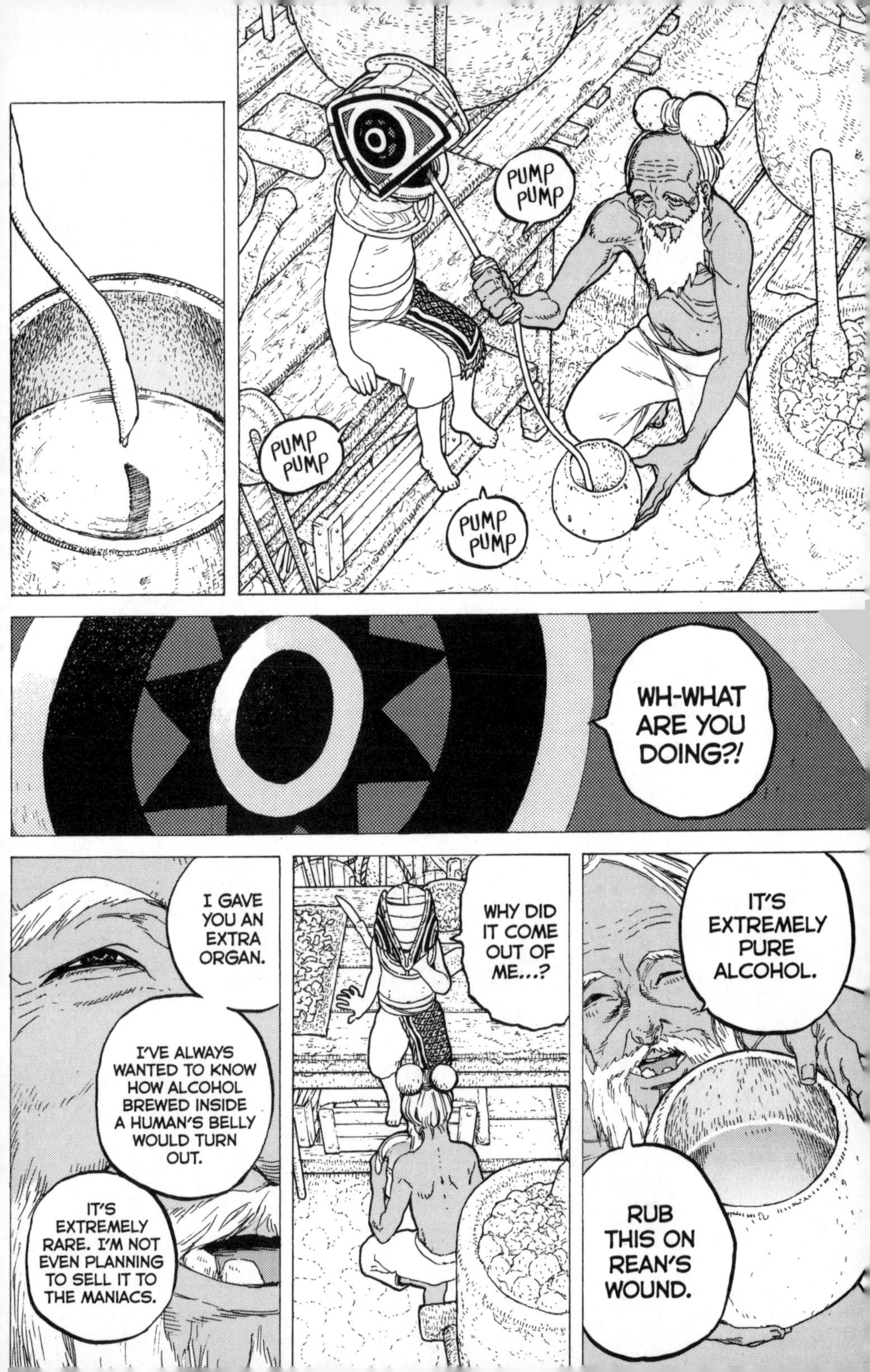
PUMP PUMP
PUMP PUMP
PUMP PUMP
WH-WHAT ARE YOU DOING?!
IT'S EXTREMELY PURE ALCOHOL.
RUB THIS ON REAN'S WOUND.
WHY DID IT COME OUT OF ME...?
I GAVE YOU AN EXTRA ORGAN.
I'VE ALWAYS WANTED TO KNOW HOW ALCOHOL BREWED INSIDE A HUMAN'S BELLY WOULD TURN OUT.
IT'S EXTREMELY RARE. I'M NOT EVEN PLANNING TO SELL IT TO THE MANIACS.

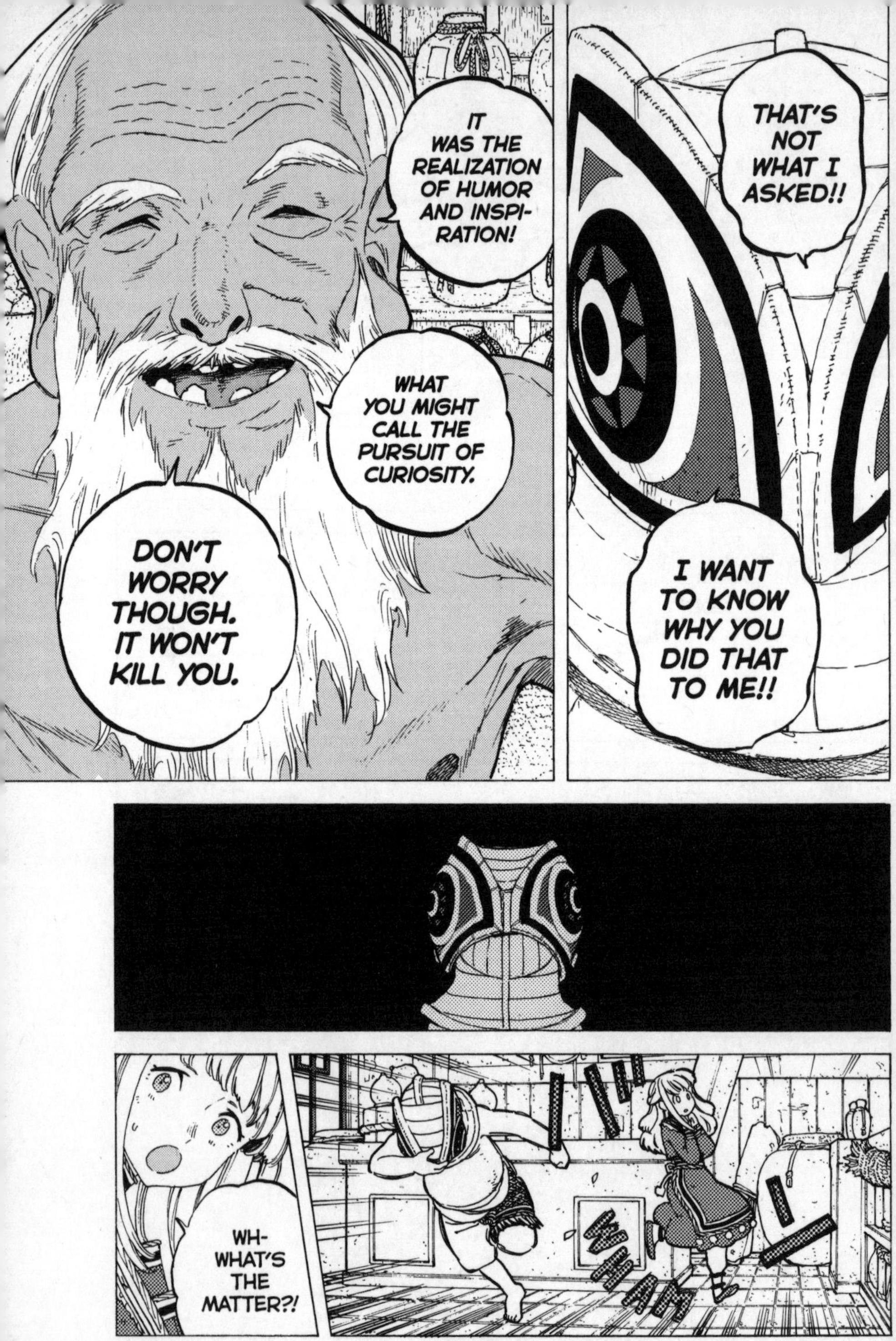
THAT'S NOT WHAT I ASKED!!
I WANT TO KNOW WHY YOU DID THAT TO ME!!
IT WAS THE REALIZATION OF HUMOR AND INSPIRATION!
WHAT YOU MIGHT CALL THE PURSUIT OF CURIOSITY.
DON'T WORRY THOUGH. IT WON'T KILL YOU.
WHAM
WH-WHAT'S THE MATTER?!

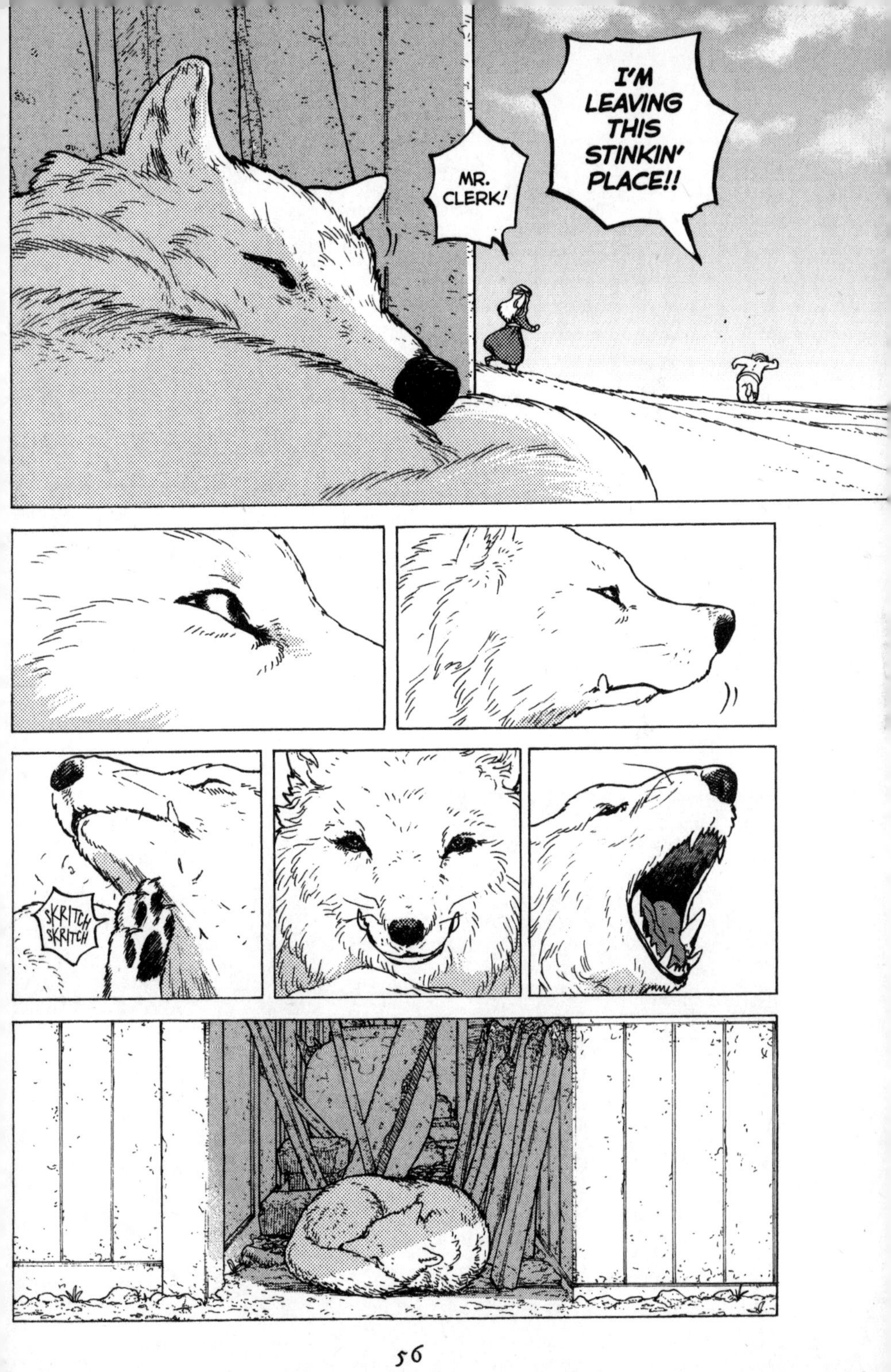
I'M LEAVING THIS STINKIN' PLACE!!
MR. CLERK!
SKRITCH SKRITCH

#17 Things Let Go

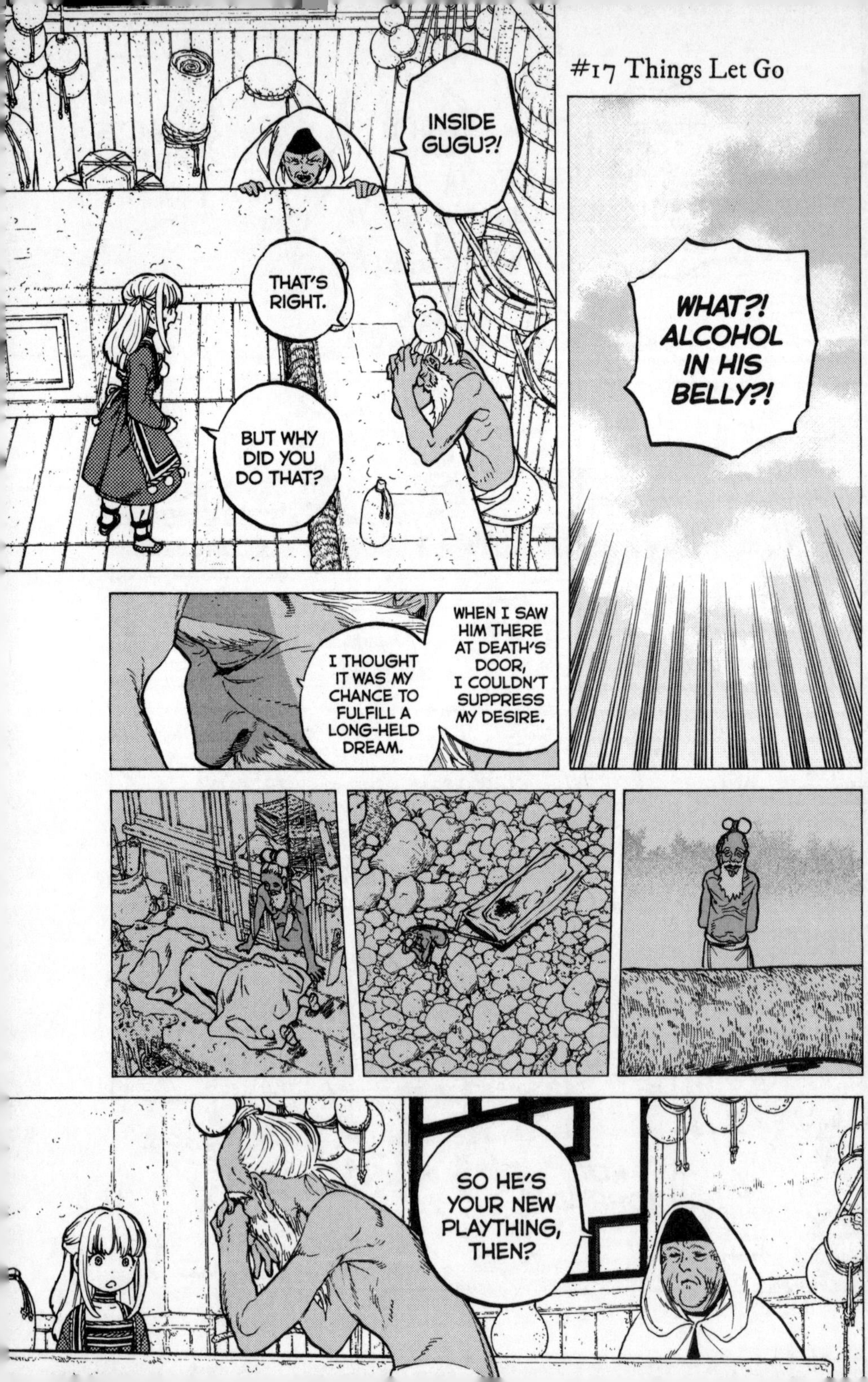
WHAT?! ALCOHOL IN HIS BELLY?!
INSIDE GUGU?!
THAT'S RIGHT.
BUT WHY DID YOU DO THAT?
WHEN I SAW HIM THERE AT DEATH'S DOOR, I COULDN'T SUPPRESS MY DESIRE.
I THOUGHT IT WAS MY CHANCE TO FULFILL A LONG-HELD DREAM.
SO HE'S YOUR NEW PLAYTHING, THEN?

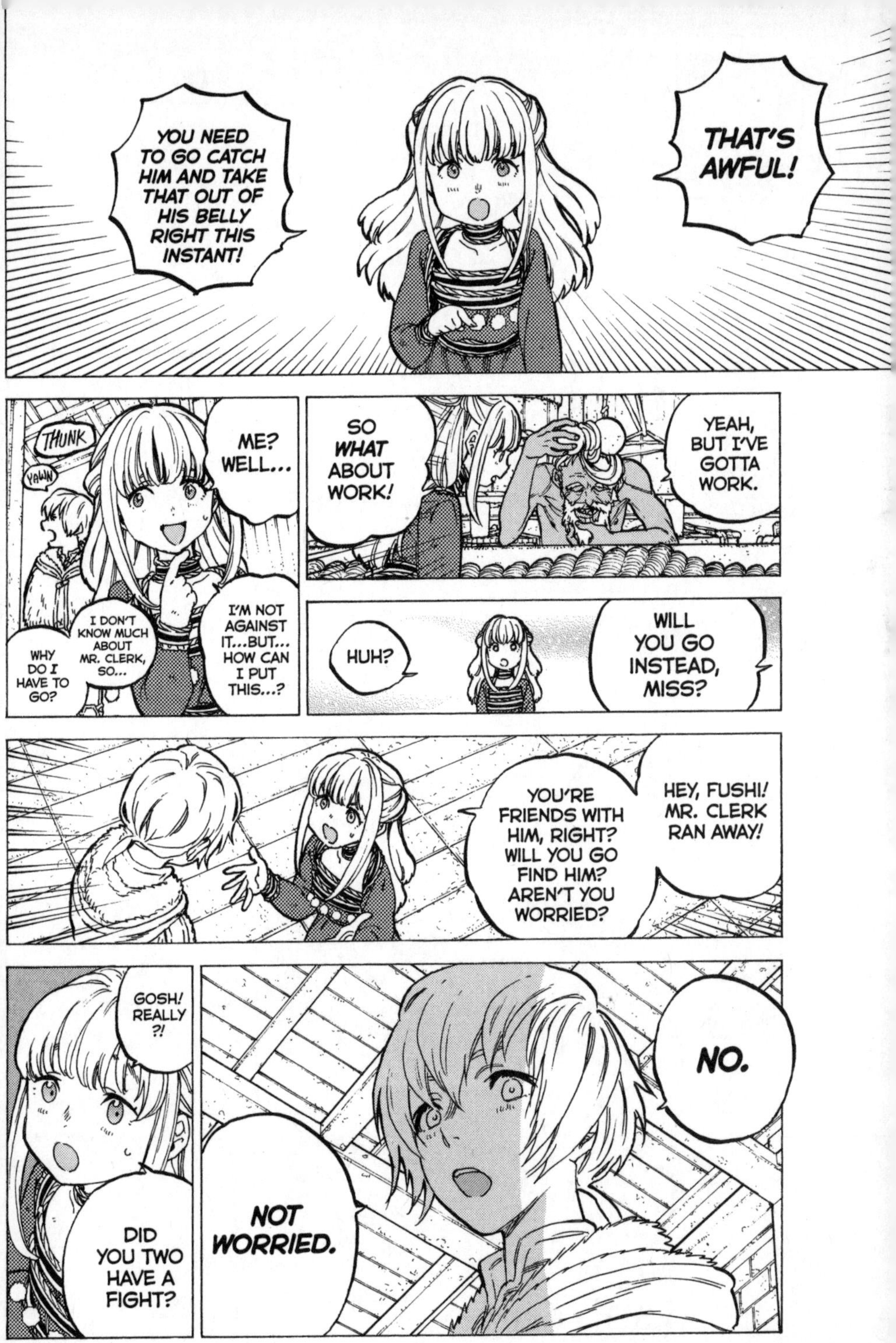
THAT'S AWFUL!
YOU NEED TO GO CATCH HIM AND TAKE THAT OUT OF HIS BELLY RIGHT THIS INSTANT!
YEAH, BUT I'VE GOTTA WORK.
SO WHAT ABOUT WORK!
WILL YOU GO INSTEAD, MISS?
HUH?
ME? WELL...
THUNK
YAWN
I'M NOT AGAINST IT...BUT... HOW CAN I PUT THIS...?
I DON'T KNOW MUCH ABOUT MR. CLERK, SO...
WHY DO I HAVE TO GO?
HEY, FUSHI! MR. CLERK RAN AWAY!
YOU'RE FRIENDS WITH HIM, RIGHT? WILL YOU GO FIND HIM? AREN'T YOU WORRIED?
NO.
NOT WORRIED.
GOSH! REALLY?!
DID YOU TWO HAVE A FIGHT?

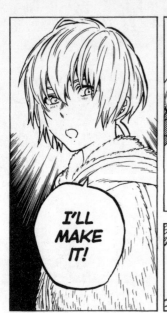

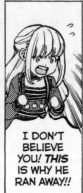

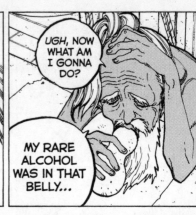

UGH, NOW WHAT AM I GONNA DO?
MY RARE ALCOHOL WAS IN THAT BELLY...
I DON'T BELIEVE YOU! THIS IS WHY HE RAN AWAY!!
WHO'S GOING TO MAKE THE FOOD WITH GUGU GONE?
ME?
I'LL MAKE IT!

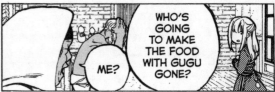

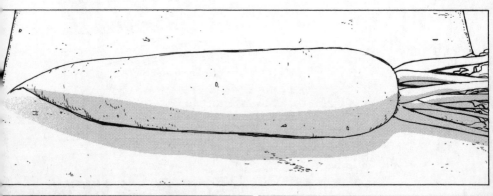

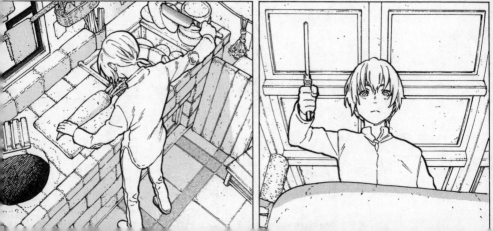

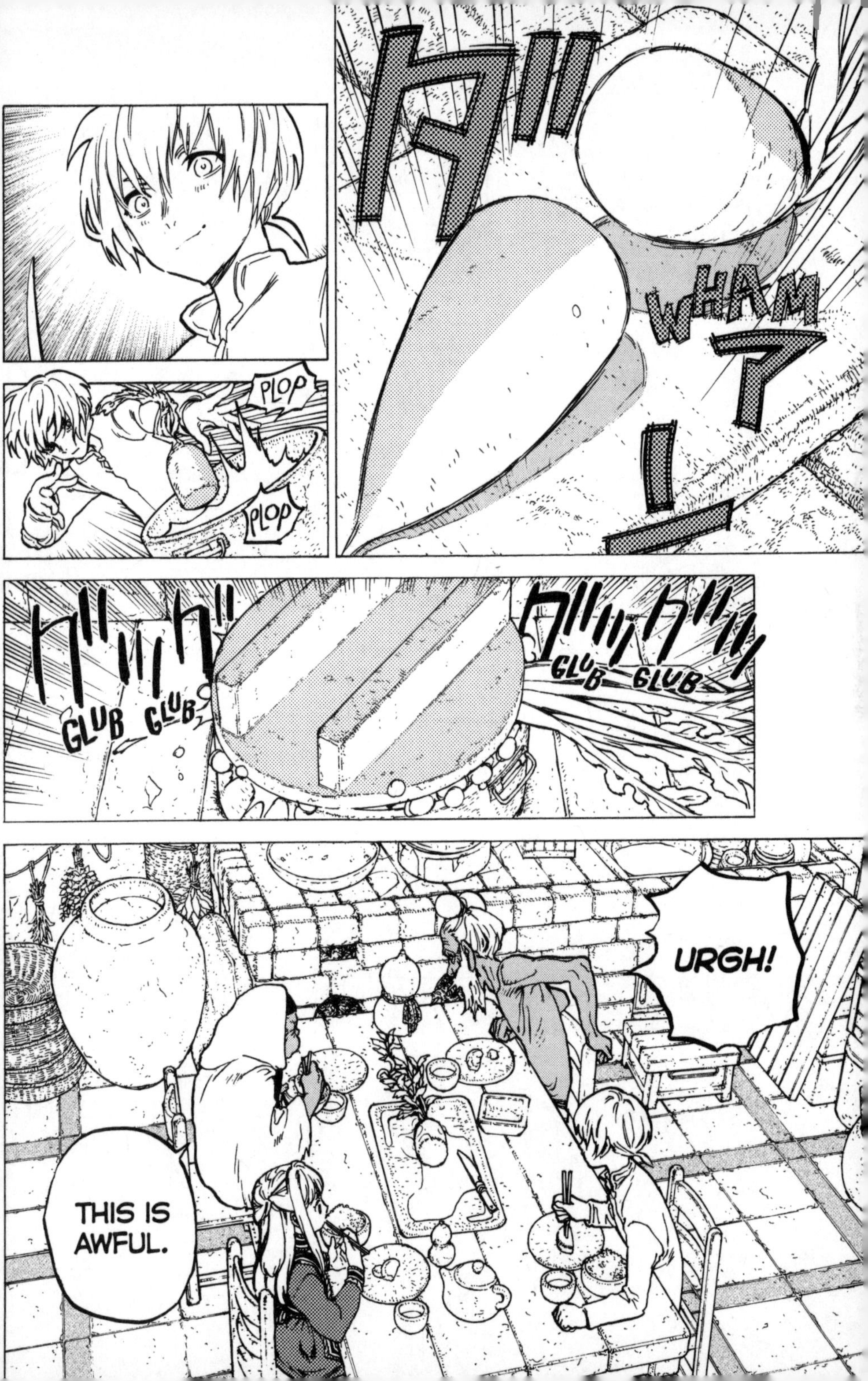
WHAM
PLOP
PLOP
GLUB GLUB
GLUB GLUB
URGH!
THIS IS AWFUL.

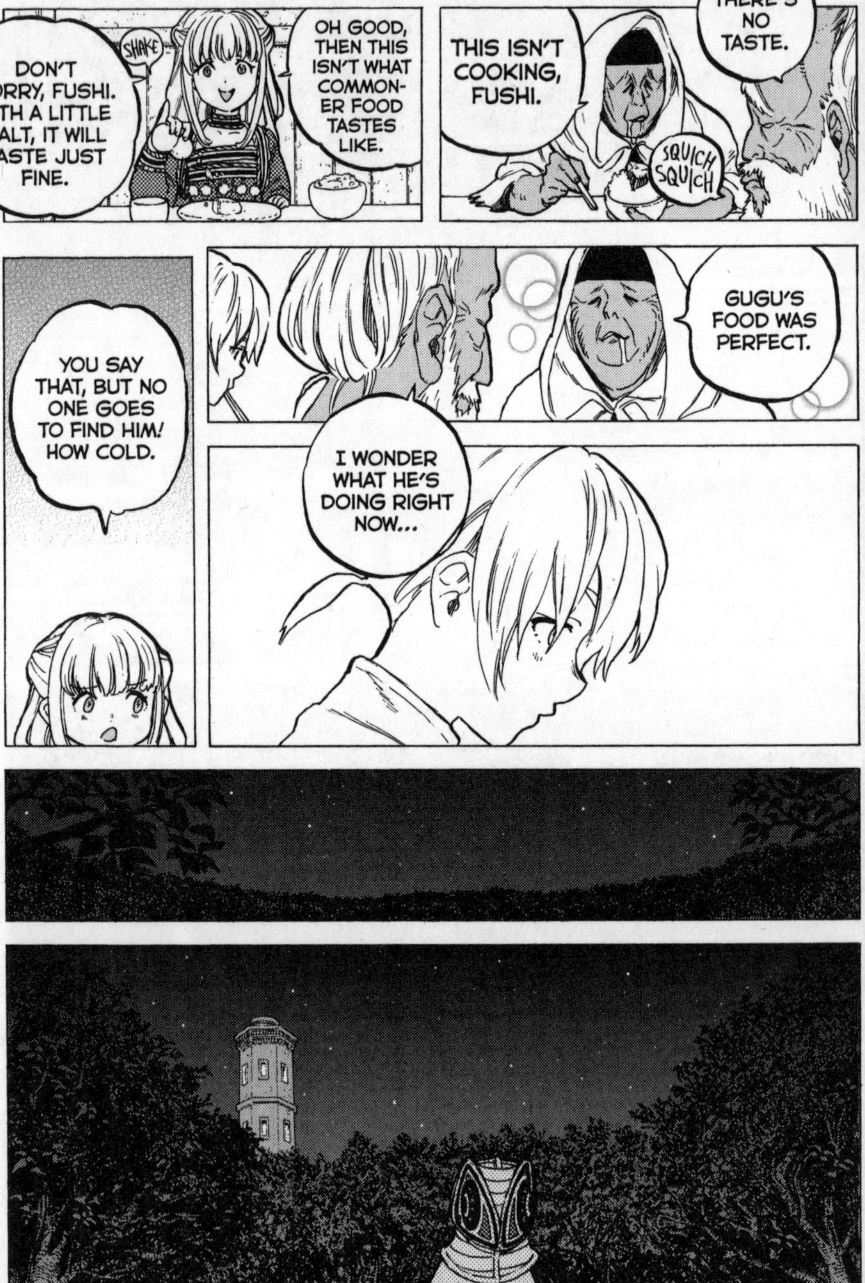
THERE'S NO TASTE.
THIS ISN'T COOKING, FUSHI.
SQUICH SQUICH
OH GOOD, THEN THIS ISN'T WHAT COMMONER FOOD TASTES LIKE.
SHAKE
DON'T WORRY, FUSHI. WITH A LITTLE SALT, IT WILL TASTE JUST FINE.
GUGU'S FOOD WAS PERFECT.
I WONDER WHAT HE'S DOING RIGHT NOW...
YOU SAY THAT, BUT NO ONE GOES TO FIND HIM! HOW COLD.

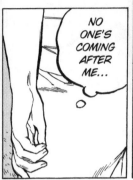

TURN
NO ONE'S COMING AFTER ME...
HMPH! THAT'S FINE WITH ME! I'LL LIVE ON MY OWN!
MORE IMPOR-TANTLY!
I'VE GOTTA GET THIS ALCOHOL OUT OF ME!
POP
HUH? IT WON'T COME OUT!
SHAKE
COME OUT! COME OUT!
HMPH! HMPH!
GAHH!
WHAP
WHAP
?!
WHERE IS THIS ATTACHED?
IF I COULD TAKE THIS OFF...
ハア
HUFF
ハア
HUFF
ハア
HUFF

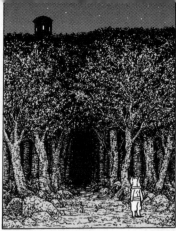

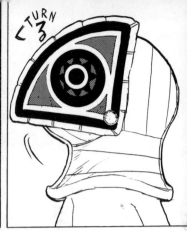

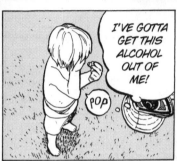

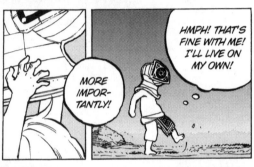

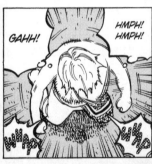

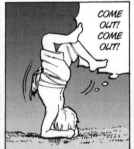

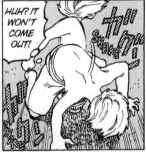

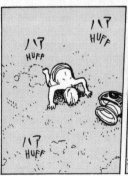

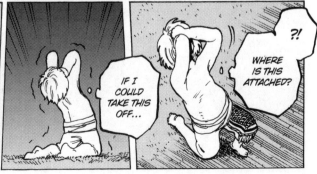

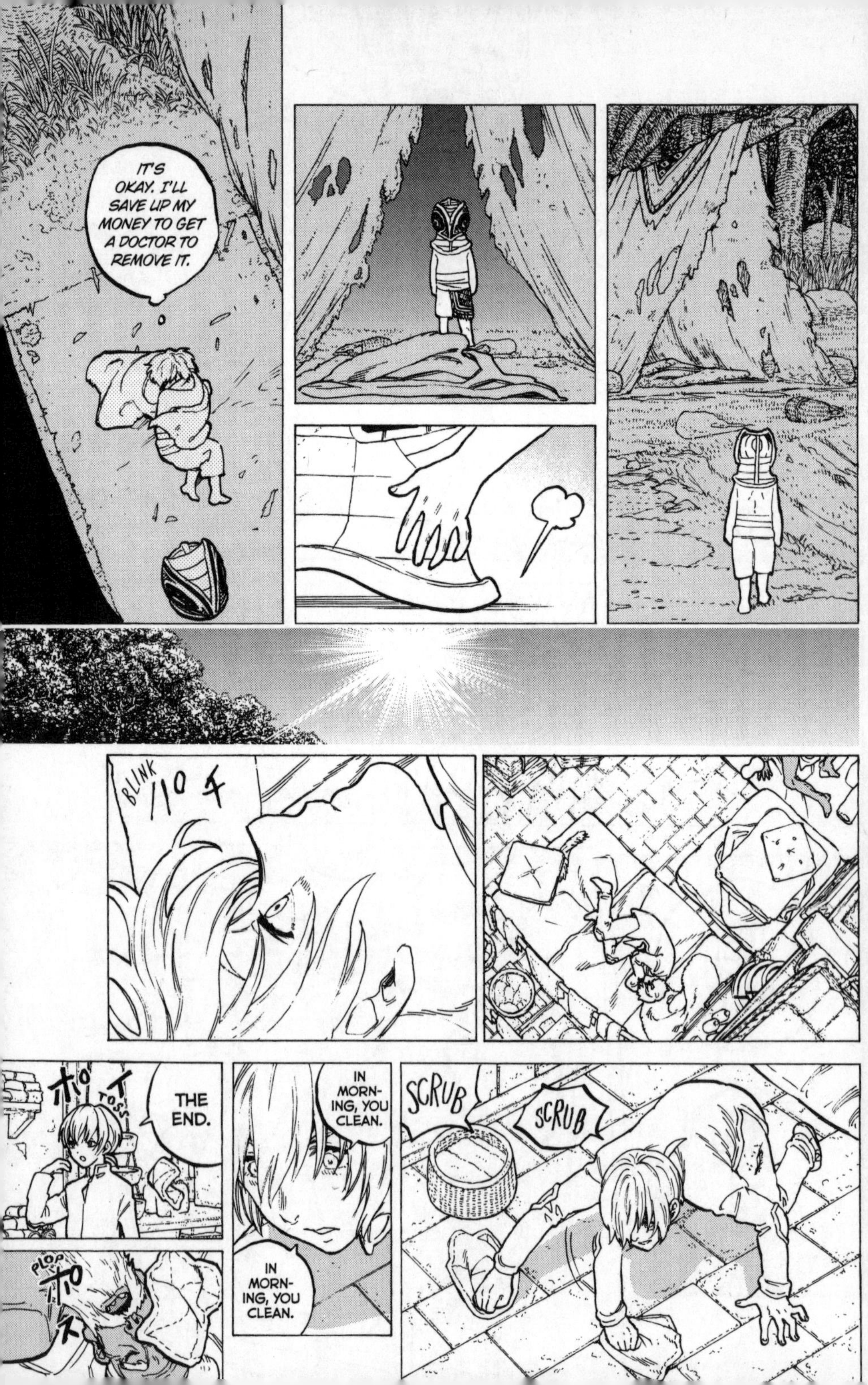
IT'S OKAY. I'LL SAVE UP MY MONEY TO GET A DOCTOR TO REMOVE IT.
BLINK
SCRUB
SCRUB
IN MORNING, YOU CLEAN.
IN MORNING, YOU CLEAN.
THE END.
TOSS
PLOP

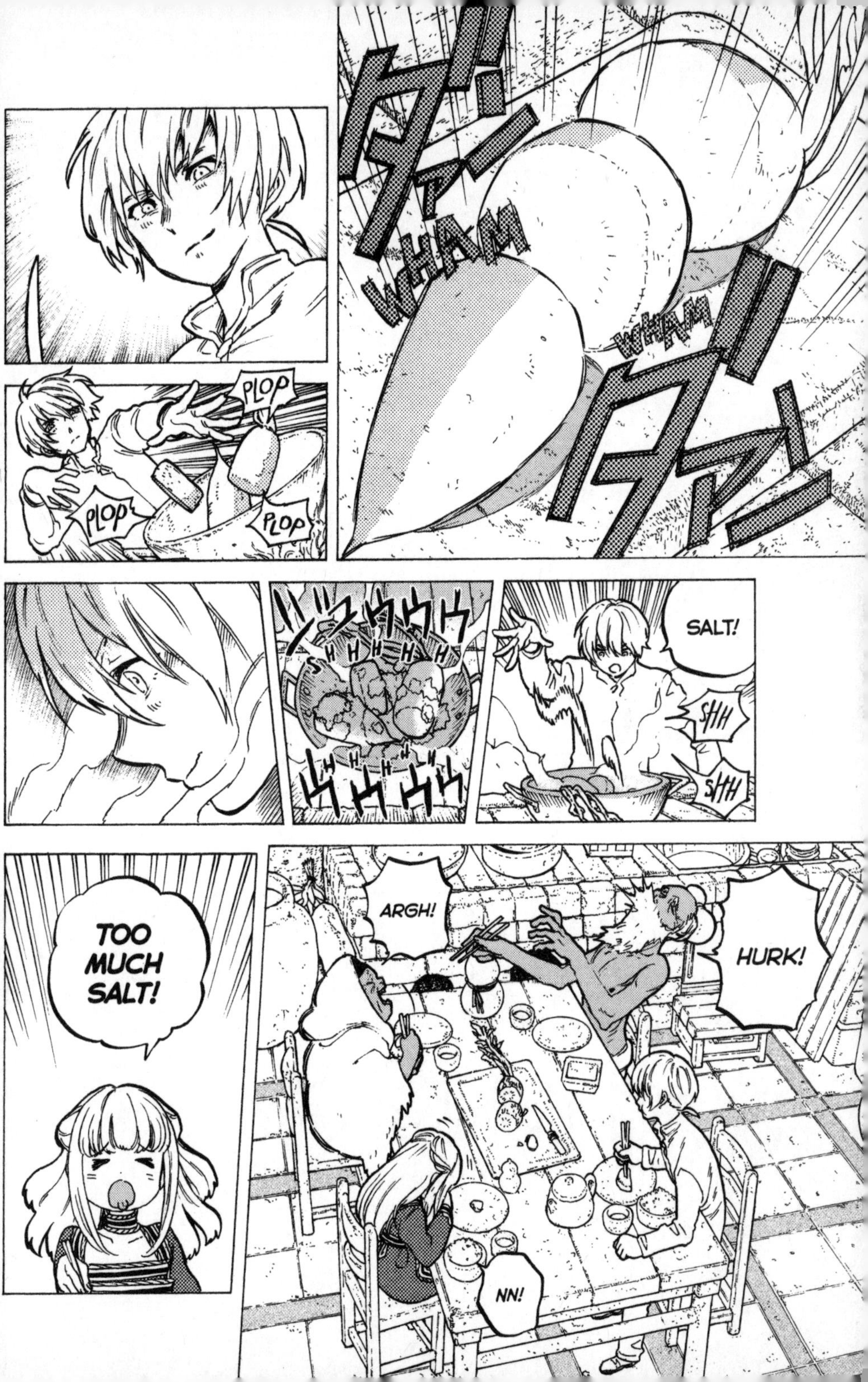
WHAM
WHAM
PLOP
PLOP
PLOP
SALT!
SHH
SHH
HURK!
ARGH!
NN!
TOO MUCH SALT!

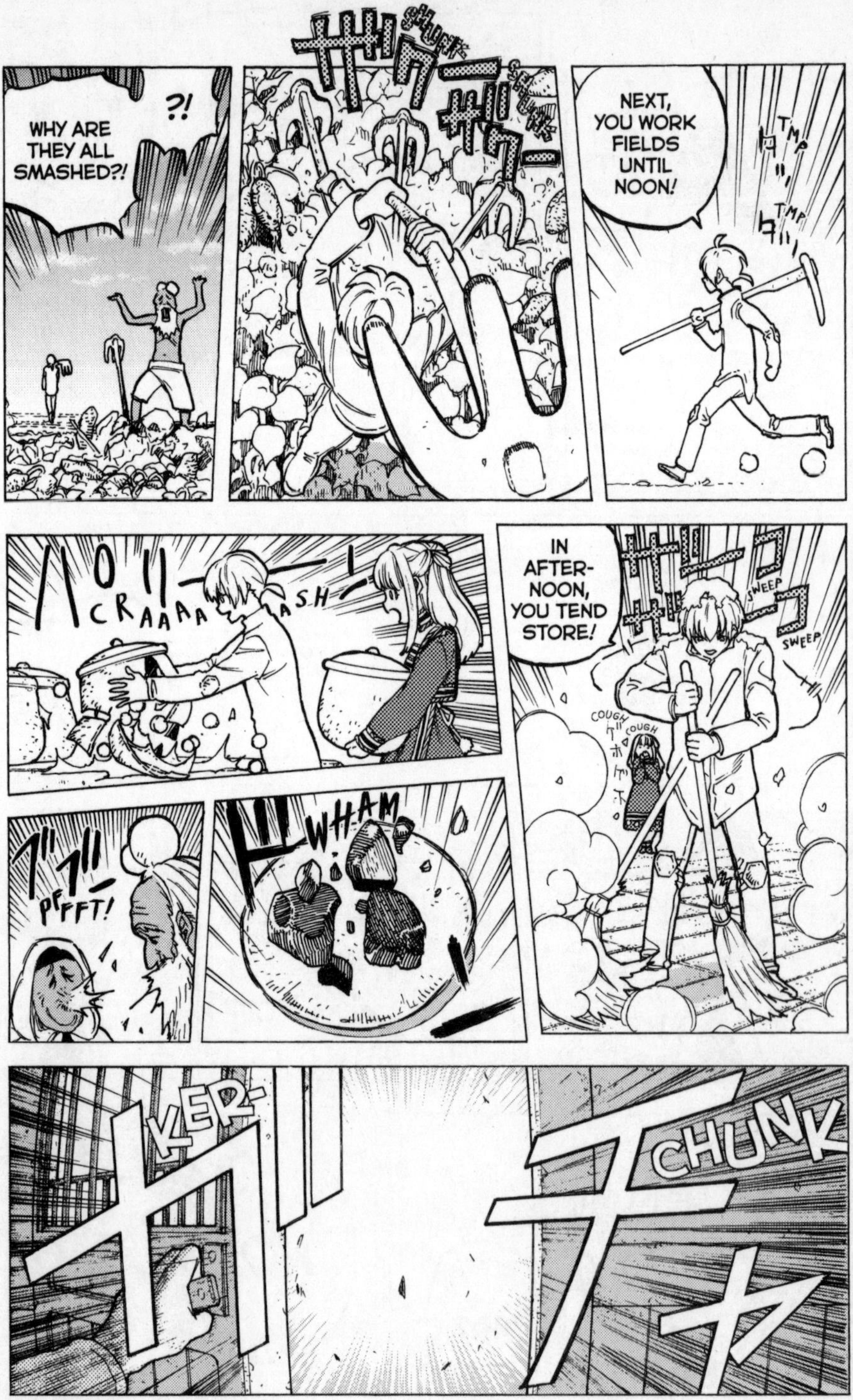
NEXT, YOU WORK FIELDS UNTIL NOON!
TMP
TMP
SHUNK
SHUNK
?!
WHY ARE THEY ALL SMASHED?!
IN AFTER-NOON, YOU TEND STORE!
SWEEP
SWEEP
COUGH
COUGH
CRAAAAASH
WHAM
PFFFT!
KER-CHUNK

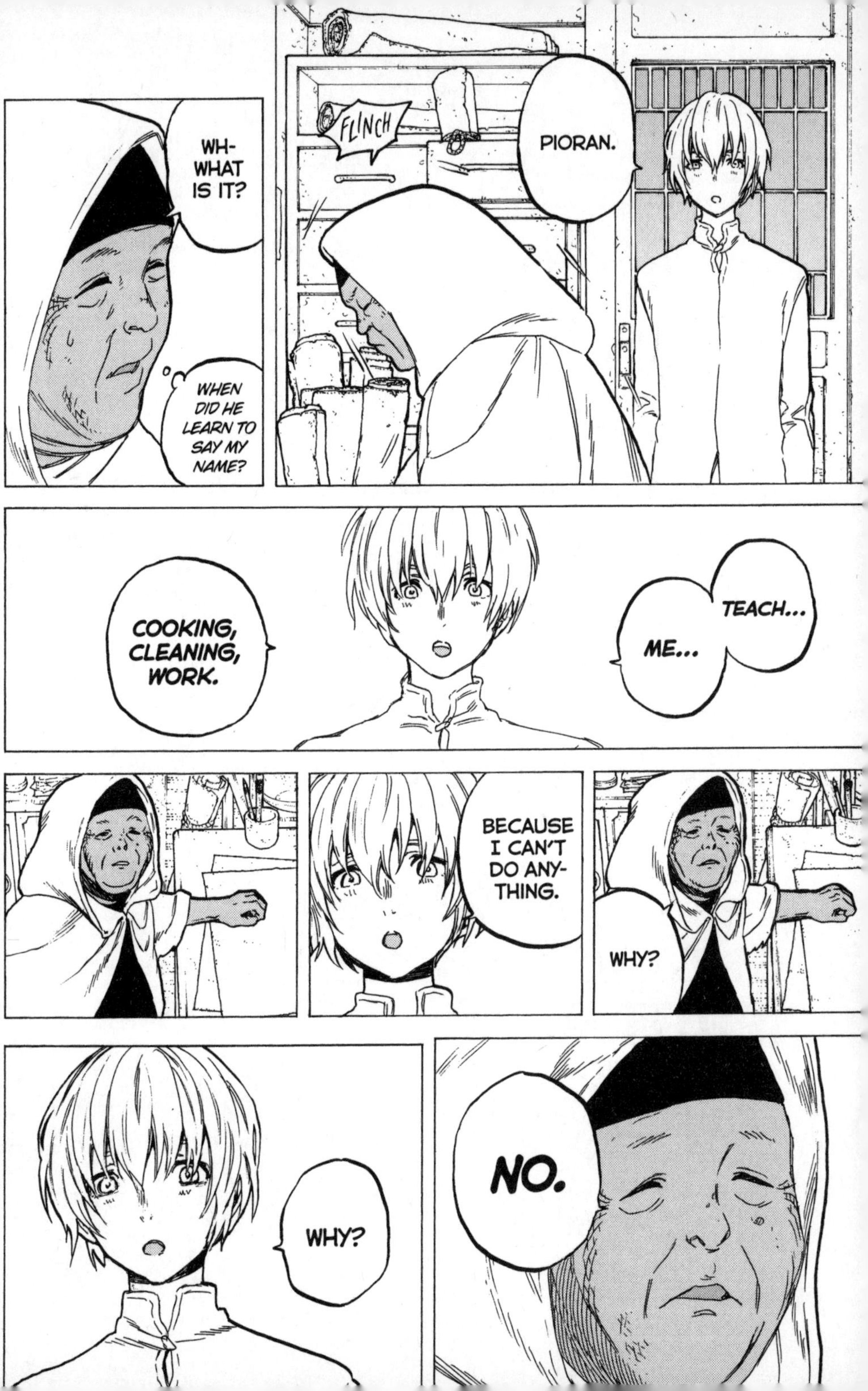
PIORAN.
FLINCH
WH- WHAT IS IT?
WHEN DID HE LEARN TO SAY MY NAME?
TEACH...
ME...
COOKING, CLEANING, WORK.
WHY?
BECAUSE I CAN'T DO ANY-THING.
NO.
WHY?

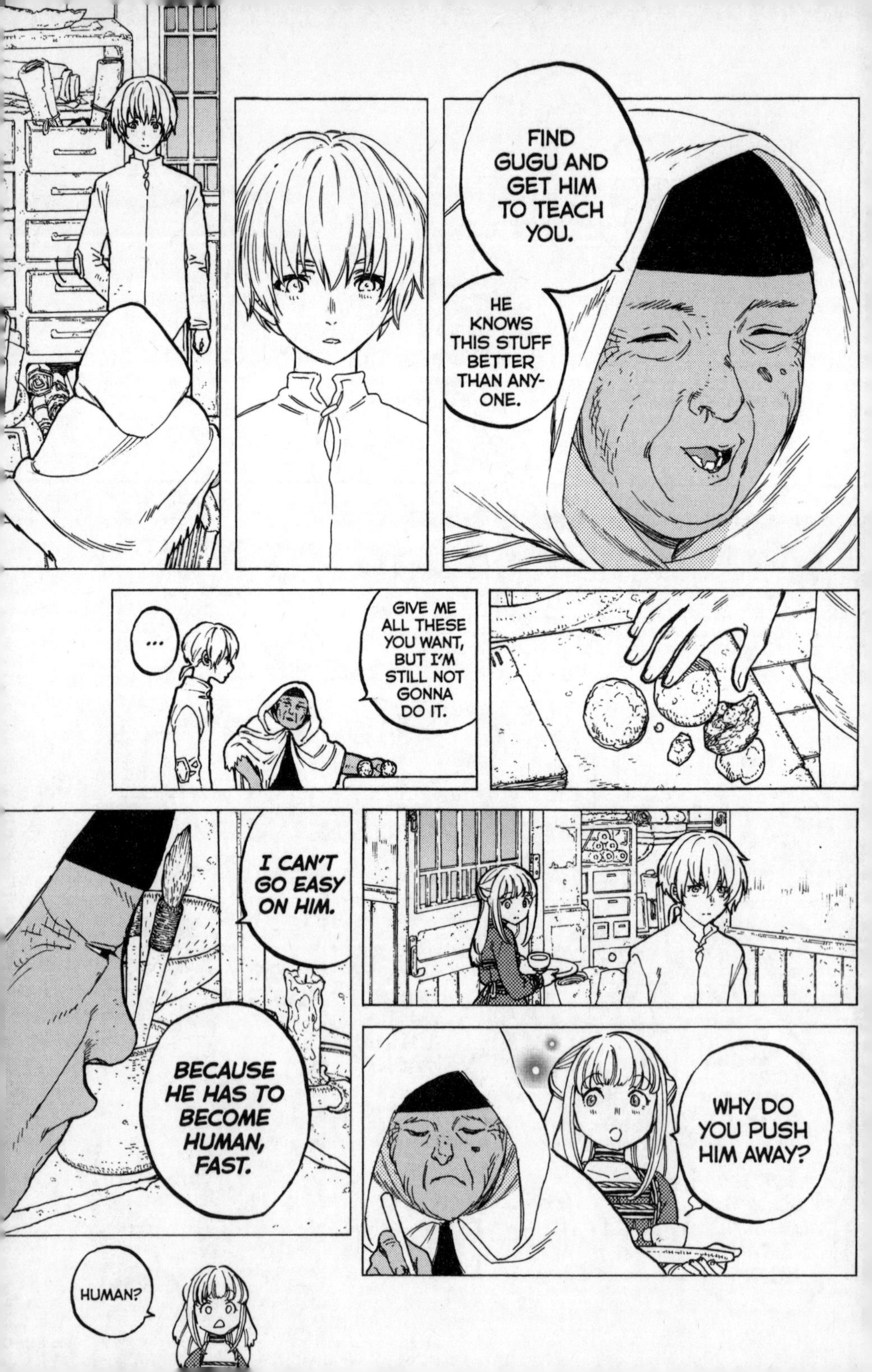
FIND GUGU AND GET HIM TO TEACH YOU.
HE KNOWS THIS STUFF BETTER THAN ANY-ONE.
GIVE ME ALL THESE YOU WANT, BUT I'M STILL NOT GONNA DO IT.
...
WHY DO YOU PUSH HIM AWAY?
I CAN'T GO EASY ON HIM.
BECAUSE HE HAS TO BECOME HUMAN, FAST.
HUMAN?

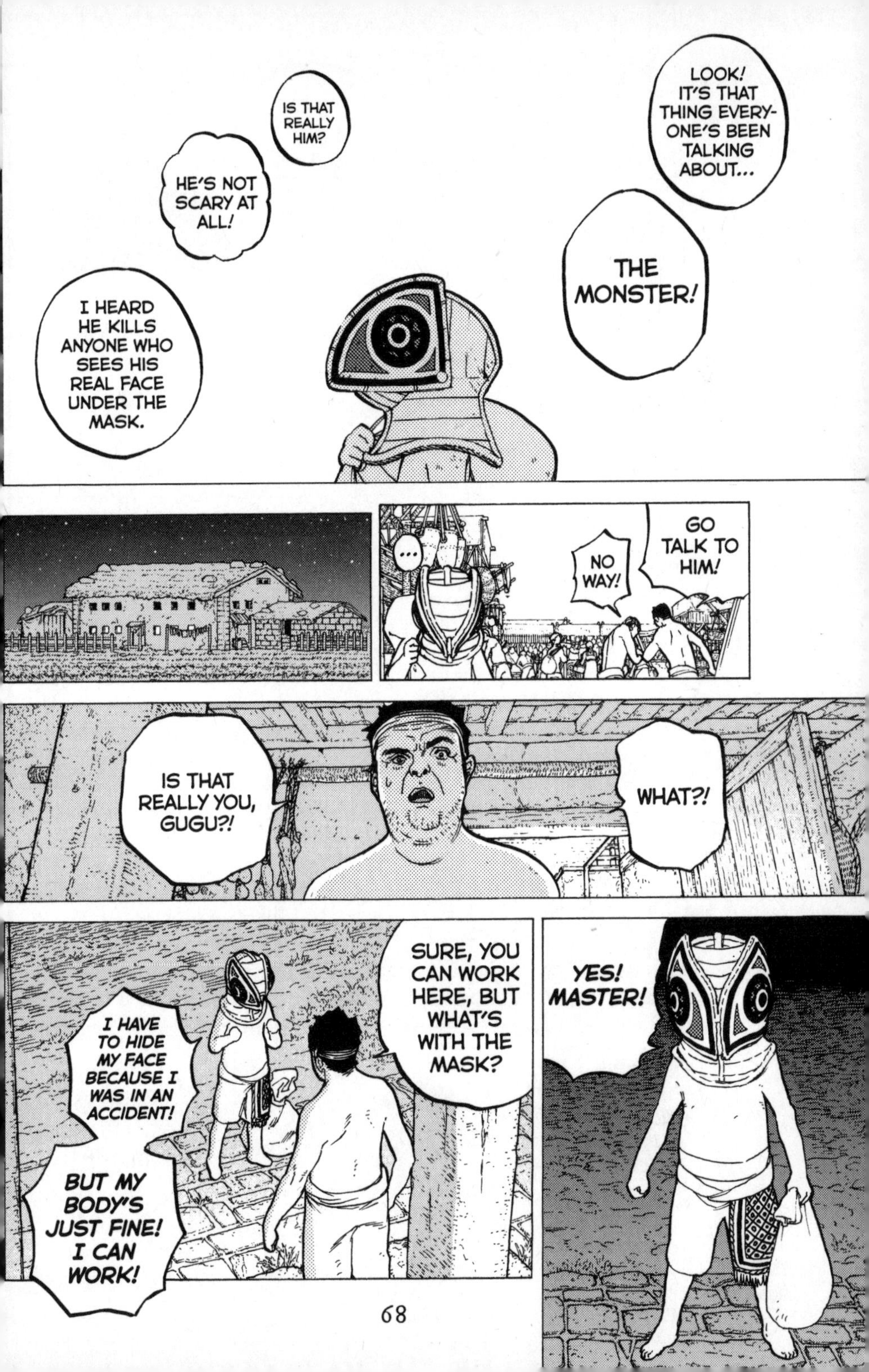
LOOK! IT'S THAT THING EVERY-ONE'S BEEN TALKING ABOUT...
THE MONSTER!
IS THAT REALLY HIM?
HE'S NOT SCARY AT ALL!
I HEARD HE KILLS ANYONE WHO SEES HIS REAL FACE UNDER THE MASK.
GO TALK TO HIM!
NO WAY!
...
WHAT?!
IS THAT REALLY YOU, GUGU?!
YES! MASTER!
SURE, YOU CAN WORK HERE, BUT WHAT'S WITH THE MASK?
I HAVE TO HIDE MY FACE BECAUSE I WAS IN AN ACCIDENT!
BUT MY BODY'S JUST FINE! I CAN WORK!

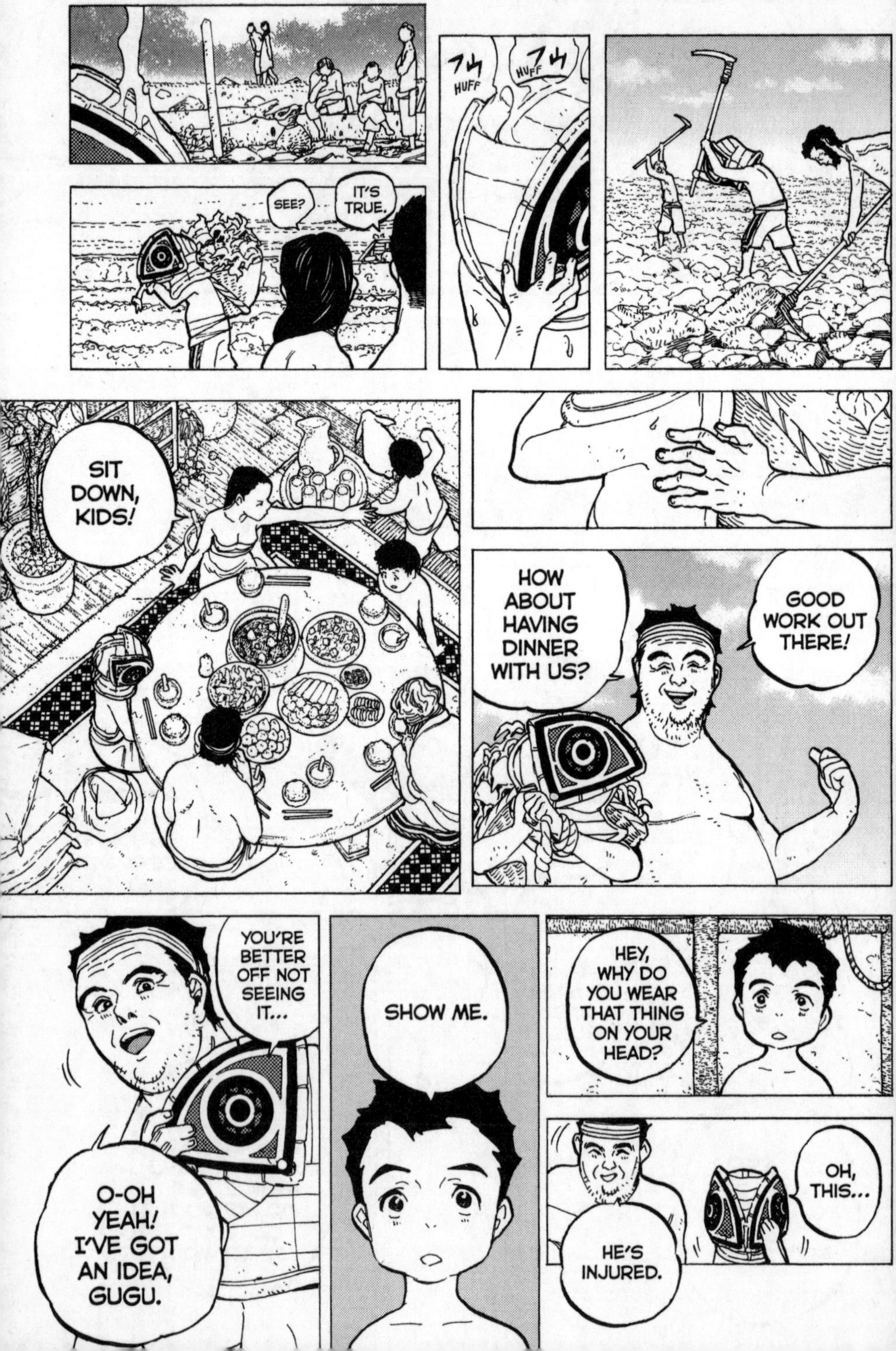
HUFF
HUFF
IT'S TRUE.
SEE?
GOOD WORK OUT THERE!
HOW ABOUT HAVING DINNER WITH US?
SIT DOWN, KIDS!
HEY, WHY DO YOU WEAR THAT THING ON YOUR HEAD?
OH, THIS...
HE'S INJURED.
SHOW ME.
YOU'RE BETTER OFF NOT SEEING IT...
O-OH YEAH! I'VE GOT AN IDEA, GUGU.

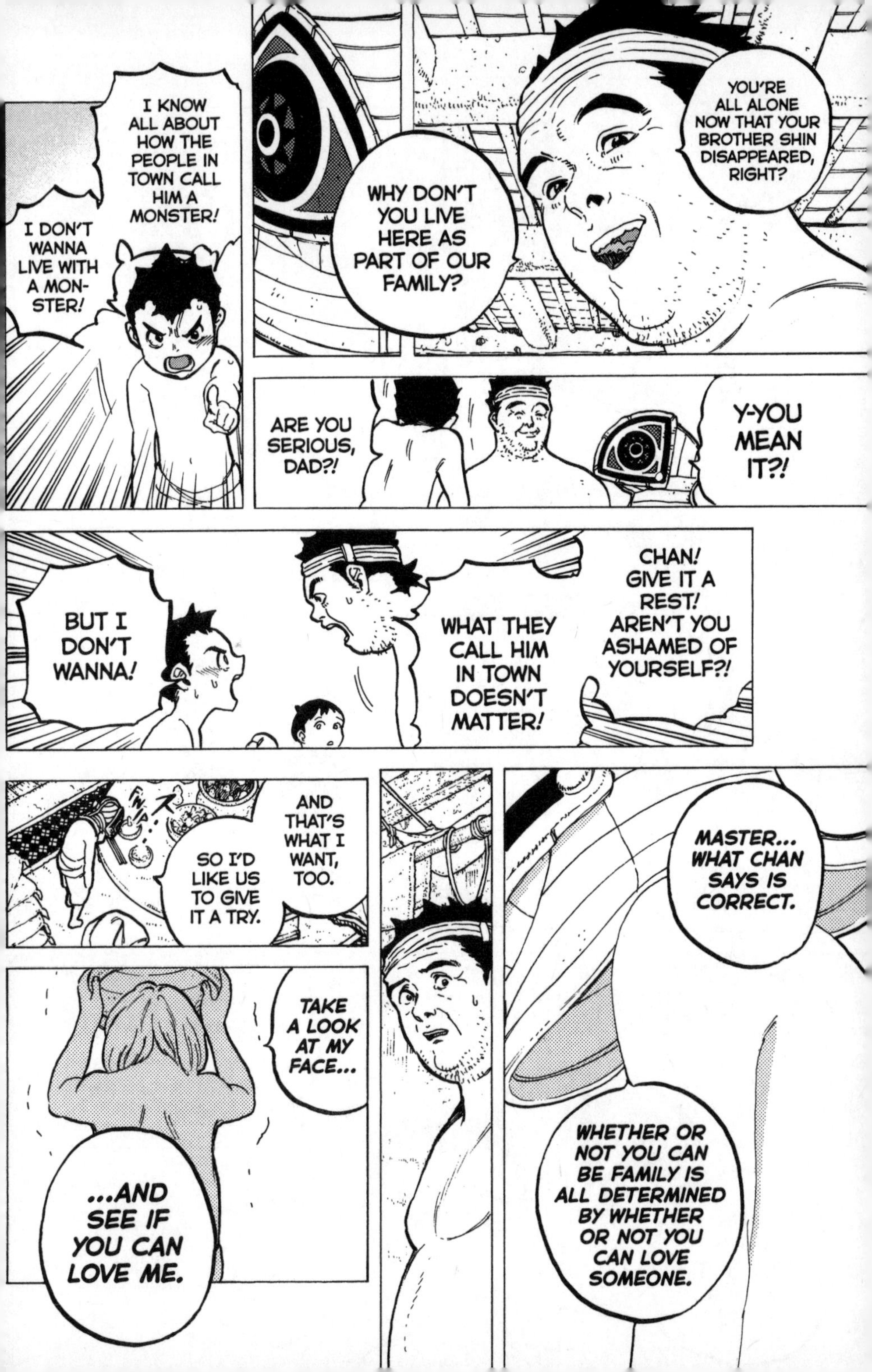
YOU'RE ALL ALONE NOW THAT YOUR BROTHER SHIN DISAPPEARED, RIGHT?
WHY DON'T YOU LIVE HERE AS PART OF OUR FAMILY?
Y-YOU MEAN IT?!
ARE YOU SERIOUS, DAD?!
I KNOW ALL ABOUT HOW THE PEOPLE IN TOWN CALL HIM A MONSTER!
I DON'T WANNA LIVE WITH A MON-STER!
CHAN! GIVE IT A REST! AREN'T YOU ASHAMED OF YOURSELF?!
WHAT THEY CALL HIM IN TOWN DOESN'T MATTER!
BUT I DON'T WANNA!
MASTER... WHAT CHAN SAYS IS CORRECT.
WHETHER OR NOT YOU CAN BE FAMILY IS ALL DETERMINED BY WHETHER OR NOT YOU CAN LOVE SOMEONE.
AND THAT'S WHAT I WANT, TOO.
SO I'D LIKE US TO GIVE IT A TRY.
TAKE A LOOK AT MY FACE...
...AND SEE IF YOU CAN LOVE ME.

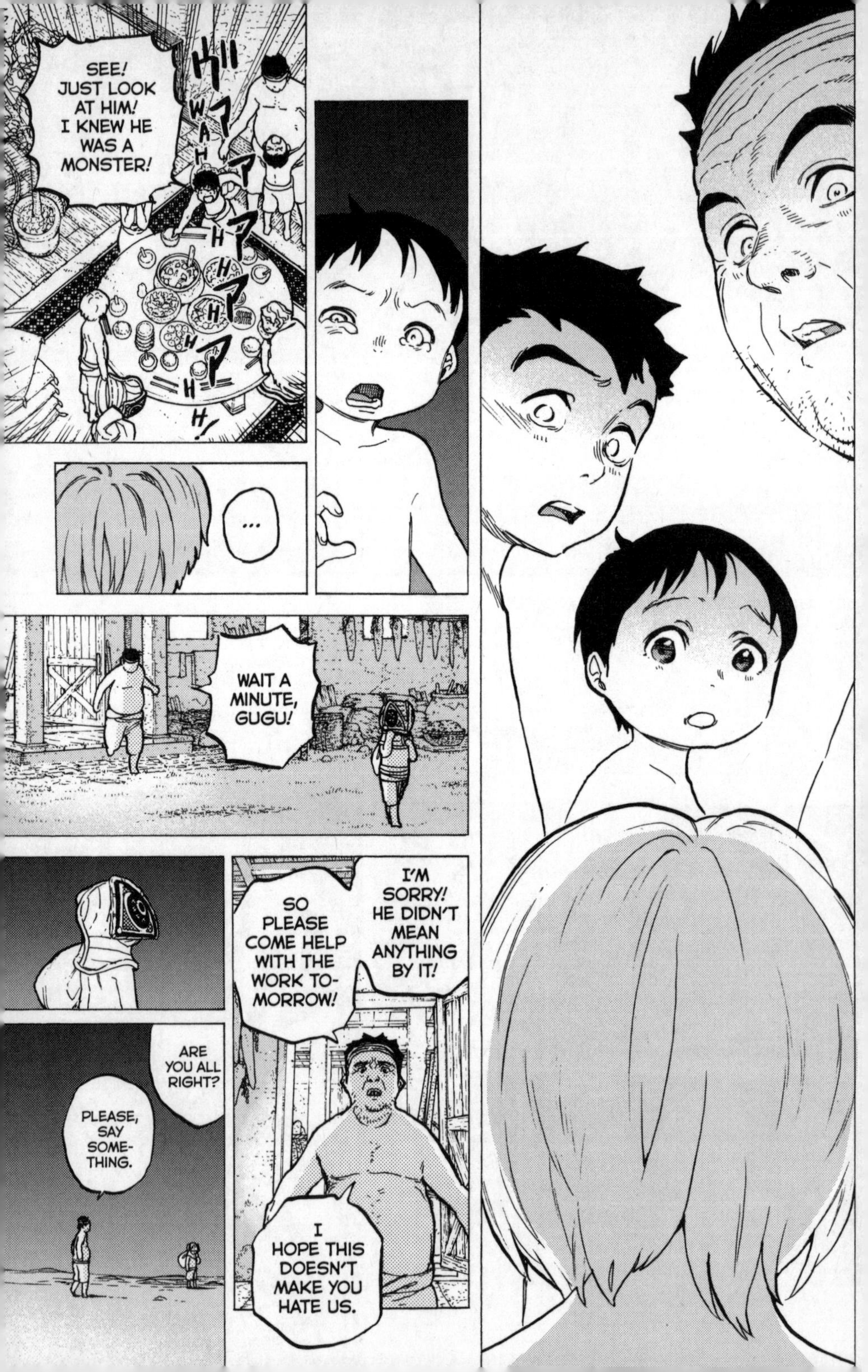
SEE! JUST LOOK AT HIM! I KNEW HE WAS A MONSTER!
WAHHHHHHH!
...
WAIT A MINUTE, GUGU!
I'M SORRY! HE DIDN'T MEAN ANYTHING BY IT!
SO PLEASE COME HELP WITH THE WORK TO-MORROW!
I HOPE THIS DOESN'T MAKE YOU HATE US.
ARE YOU ALL RIGHT?
PLEASE, SAY SOME-THING.

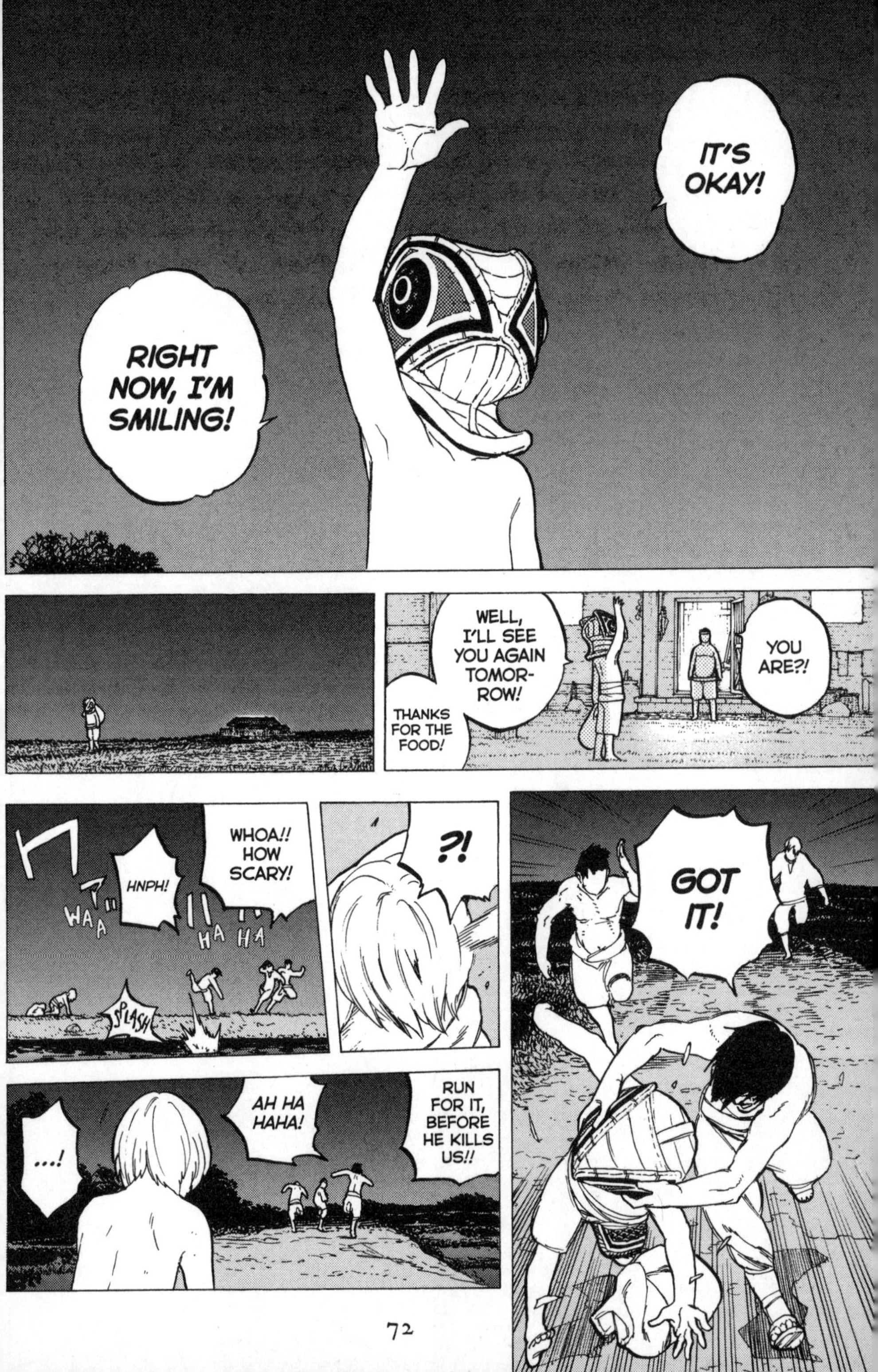
IT'S OKAY!
RIGHT NOW, I'M SMILING!
YOU ARE?!
WELL, I'LL SEE YOU AGAIN TOMOR-ROW!
THANKS FOR THE FOOD!
GOT IT!
?!
WHOA!! HOW SCARY!
HNPH!
WAA
HA HA
SPLASH
RUN FOR IT, BEFORE HE KILLS US!!
AH HA HAHA!
...!

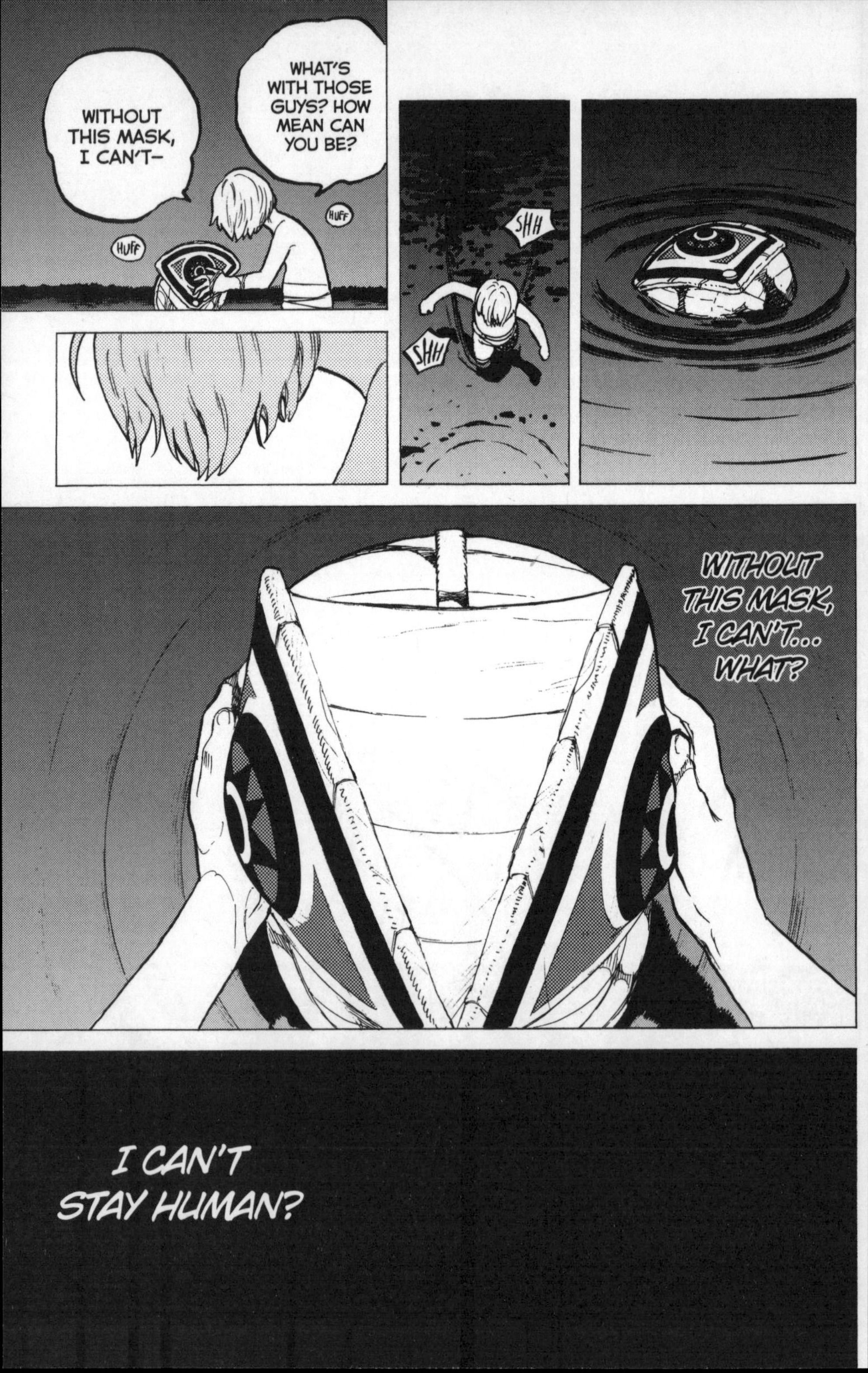
SHH
SHH
WHAT'S WITH THOSE GUYS? HOW MEAN CAN YOU BE?
WITHOUT THIS MASK, I CAN'T–
HUFF
HUFF
WITHOUT THIS MASK, I CAN'T... WHAT?
I CAN'T STAY HUMAN?

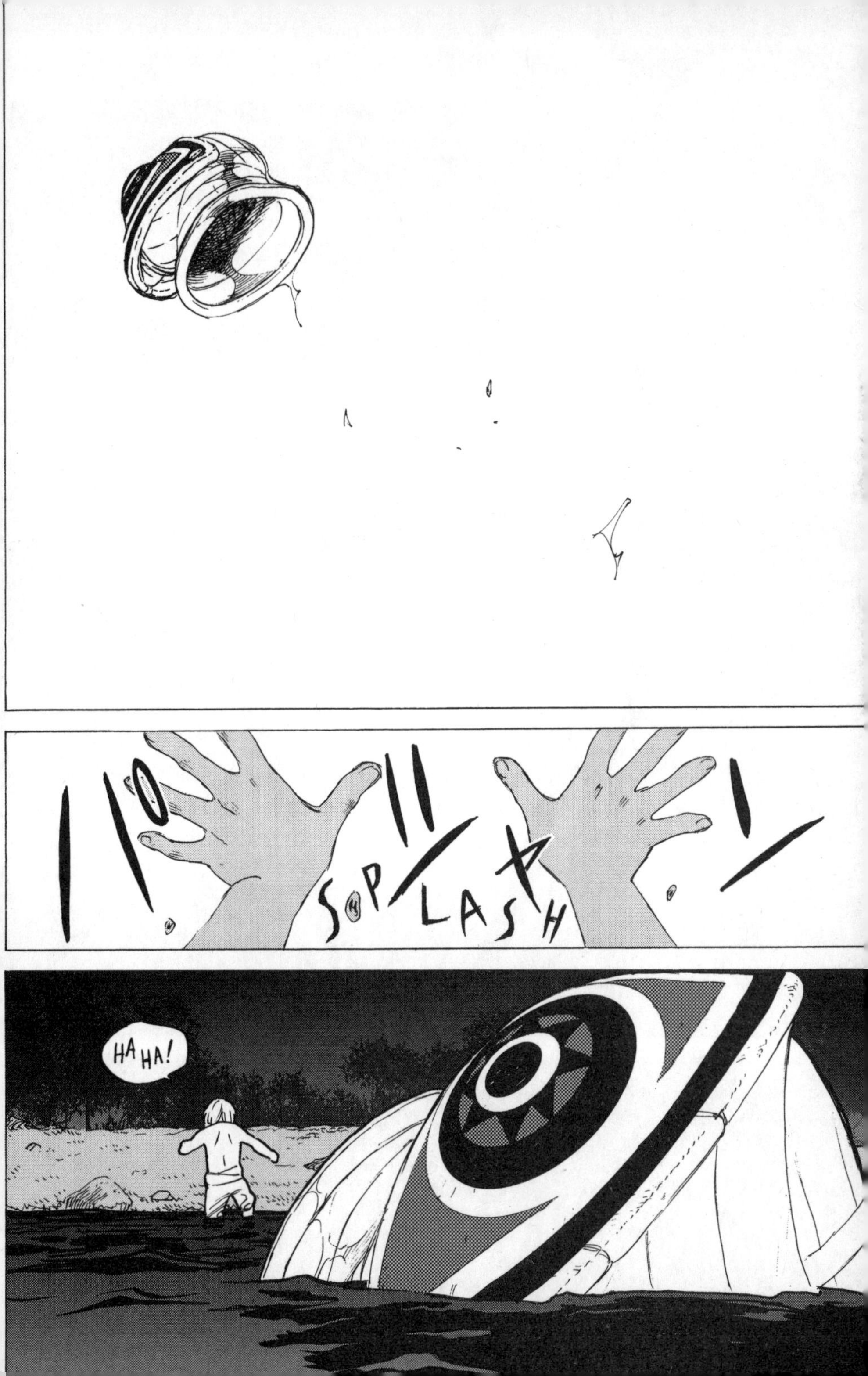
SPLASH
HAHA!

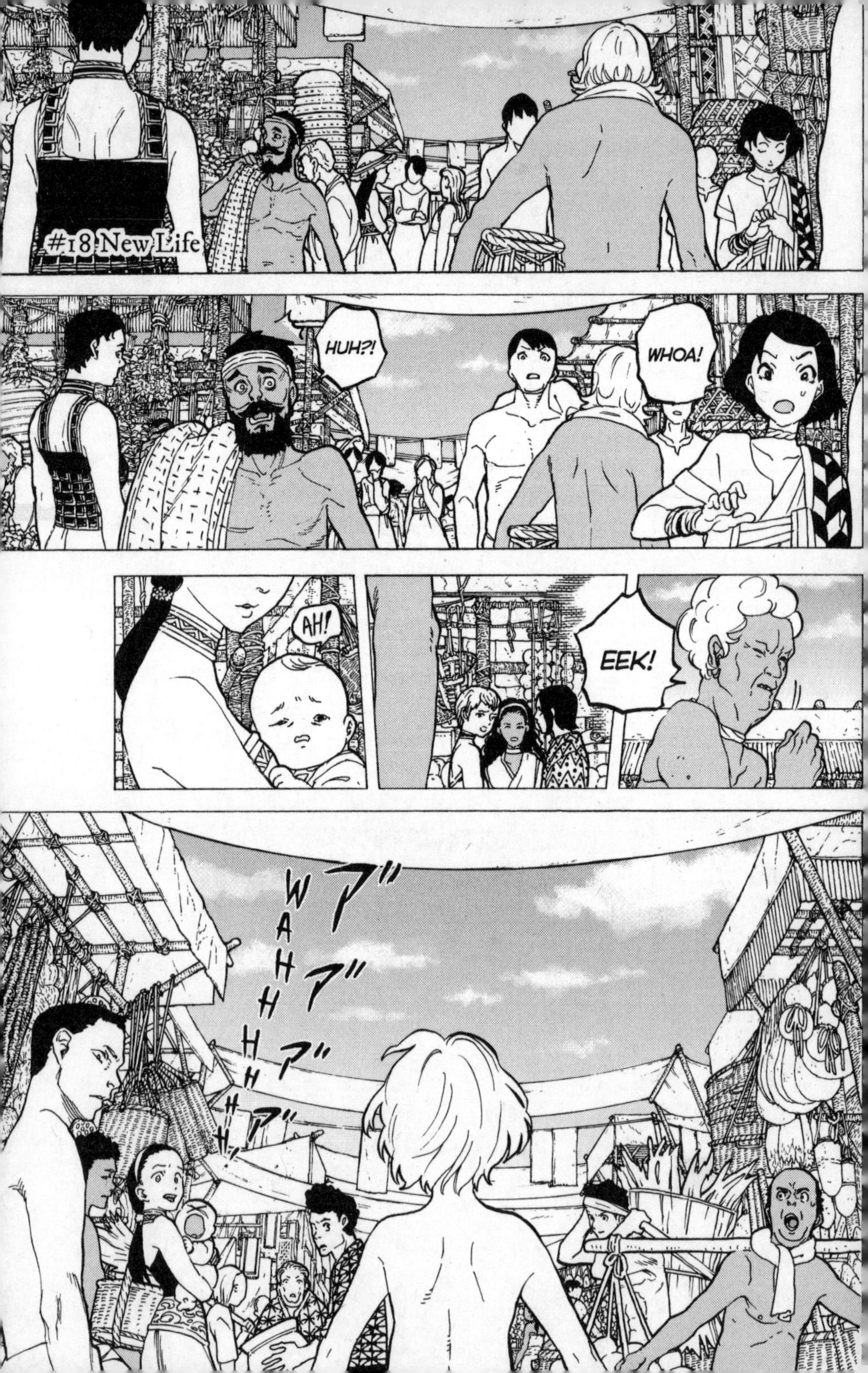
#18 New Life
WHOA!
HUH?!
EEK!
AH!
ア゛ア゛ア゛ア゛
WAHHHHHH!

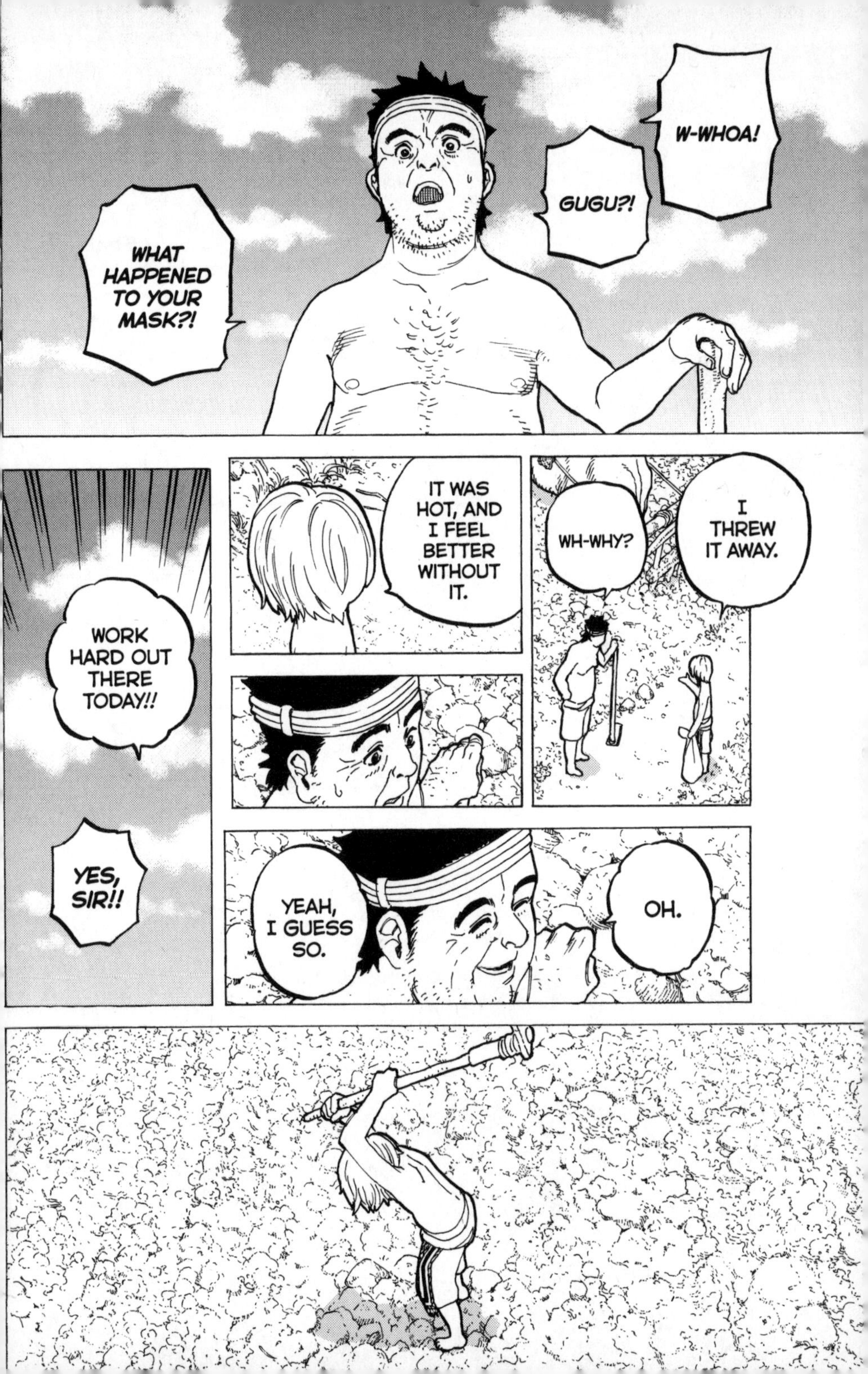
W-WHOA!
GUGU?!
WHAT HAPPENED TO YOUR MASK?!
I THREW IT AWAY.
WH-WHY?
IT WAS HOT, AND I FEEL BETTER WITHOUT IT.
OH.
YEAH, I GUESS SO.
WORK HARD OUT THERE TODAY!!
YES, SIR!!

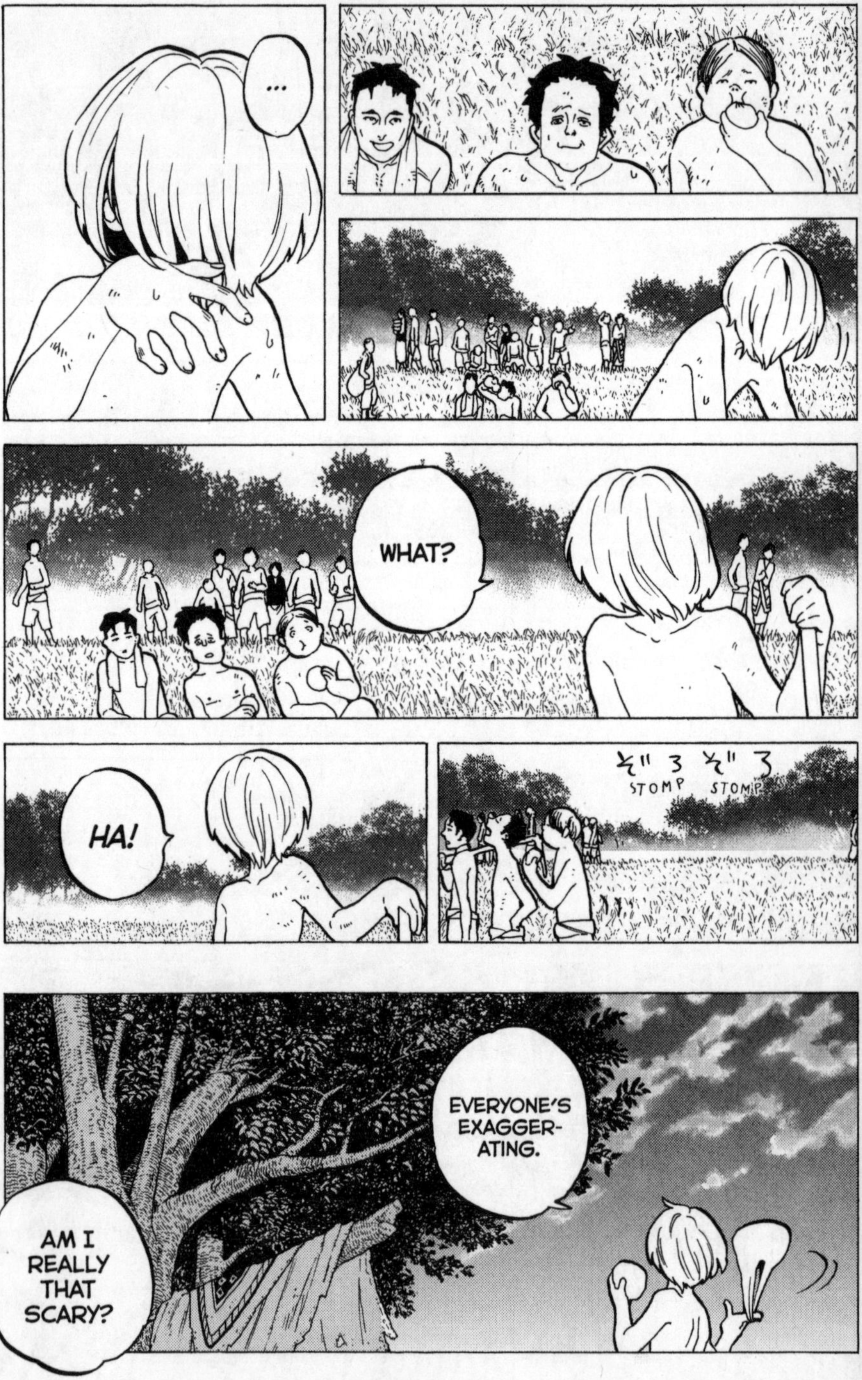
...
WHAT?
ぞろ ぞろ
STOMP STOMP
HA!
EVERYONE'S EXAGGER-ATING.
AM I REALLY THAT SCARY?

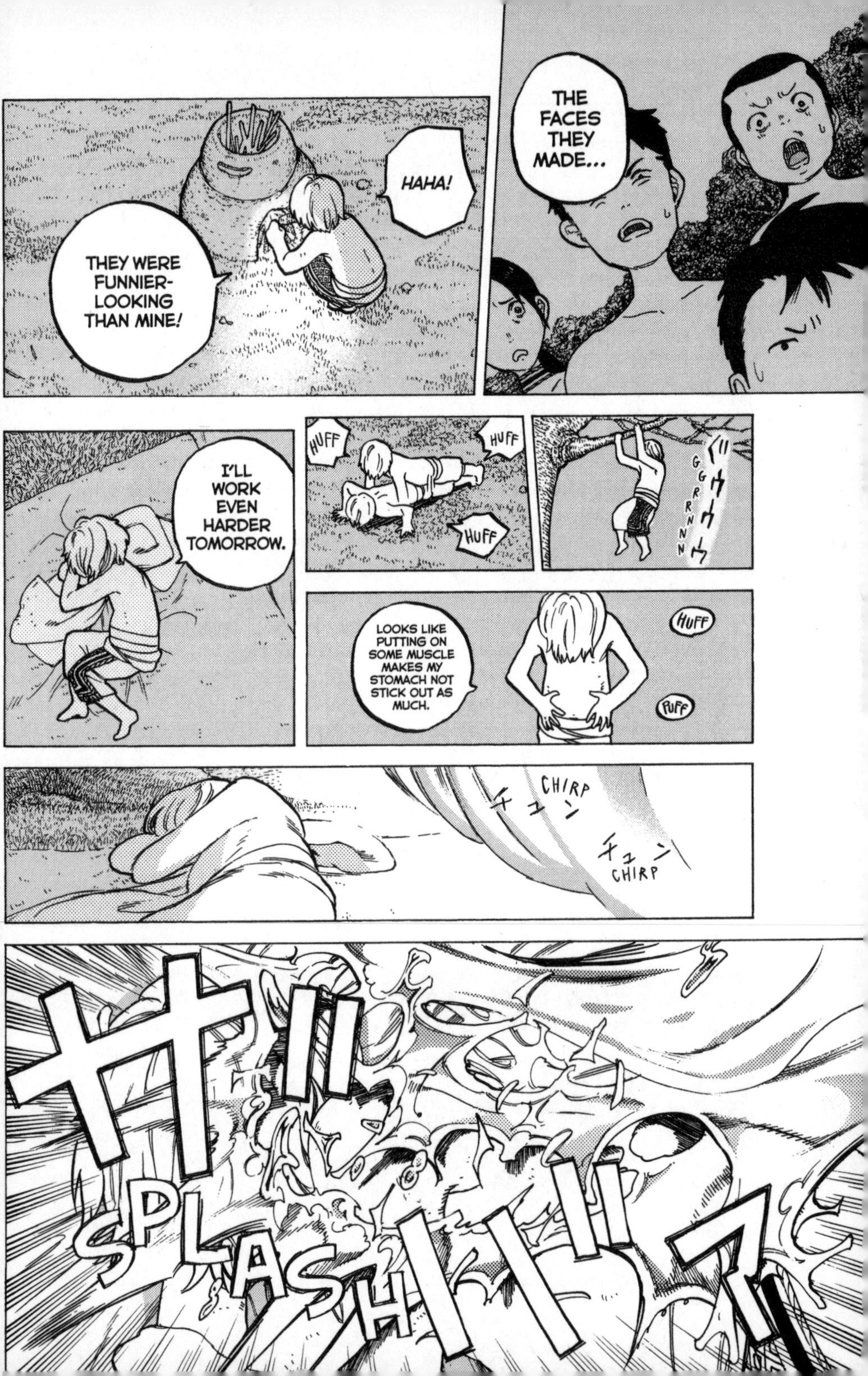
THE FACES THEY MADE...
HAHA!
THEY WERE FUNNIER-LOOKING THAN MINE!
GGRRNN
HUFF
HUFF
HUFF
HUFF
LOOKS LIKE PUTTING ON SOME MUSCLE MAKES MY STOMACH NOT STICK OUT AS MUCH.
PUFF
I'LL WORK EVEN HARDER TOMORROW.
CHIRP
CHIRP
SPLASH

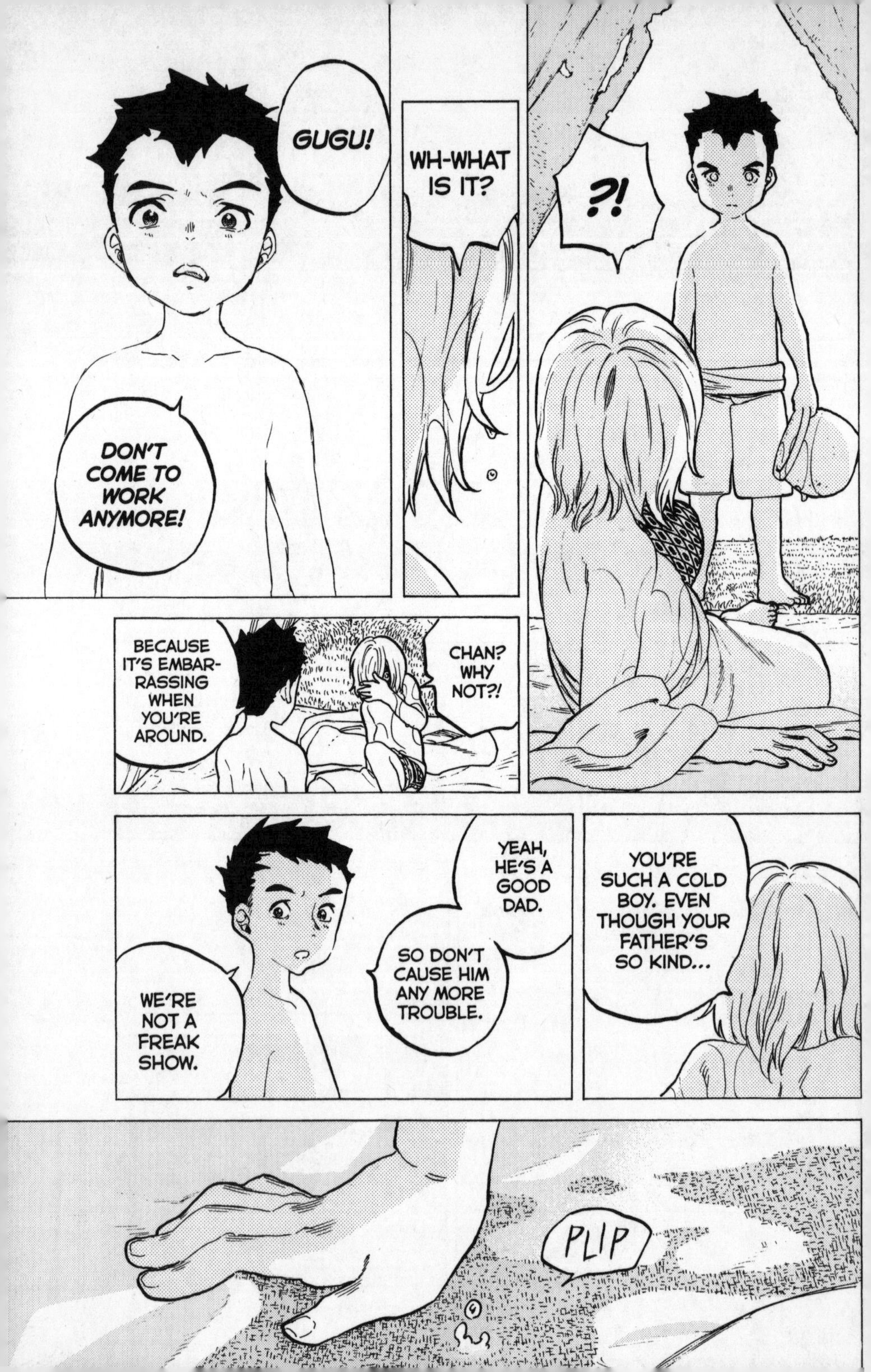
?!
WH-WHAT IS IT?
GUGU!
DON'T COME TO WORK ANYMORE!
CHAN? WHY NOT?!
BECAUSE IT'S EMBARRASSING WHEN YOU'RE AROUND.
YOU'RE SUCH A COLD BOY. EVEN THOUGH YOUR FATHER'S SO KIND...
YEAH, HE'S A GOOD DAD.
SO DON'T CAUSE HIM ANY MORE TROUBLE.
WE'RE NOT A FREAK SHOW.
PLIP

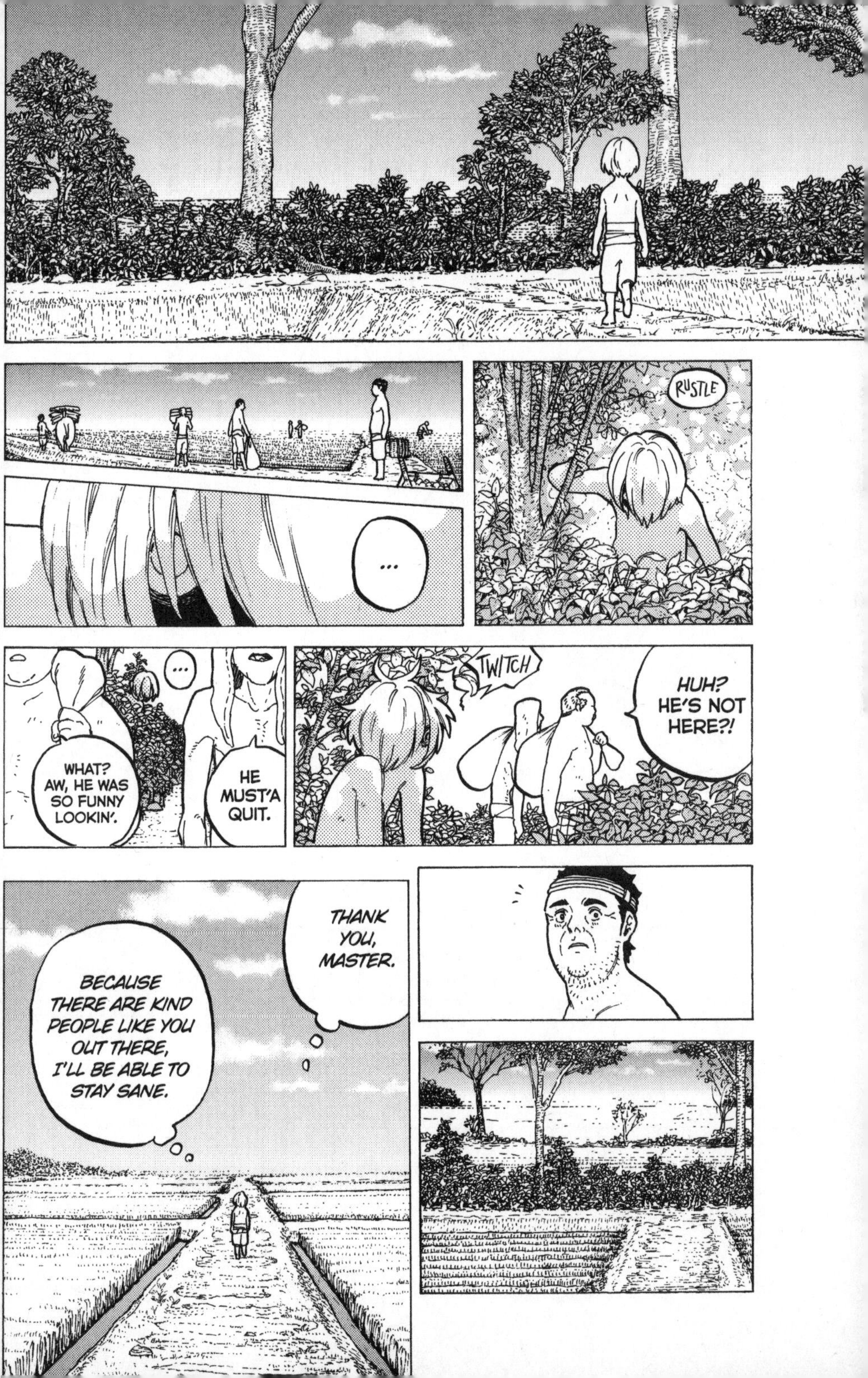
RUSTLE
...
HUH? HE'S NOT HERE?!
TWITCH
...
HE MUST'A QUIT.
WHAT? AW, HE WAS SO FUNNY LOOKIN'.
THANK YOU, MASTER.
BECAUSE THERE ARE KIND PEOPLE LIKE YOU OUT THERE, I'LL BE ABLE TO STAY SANE.

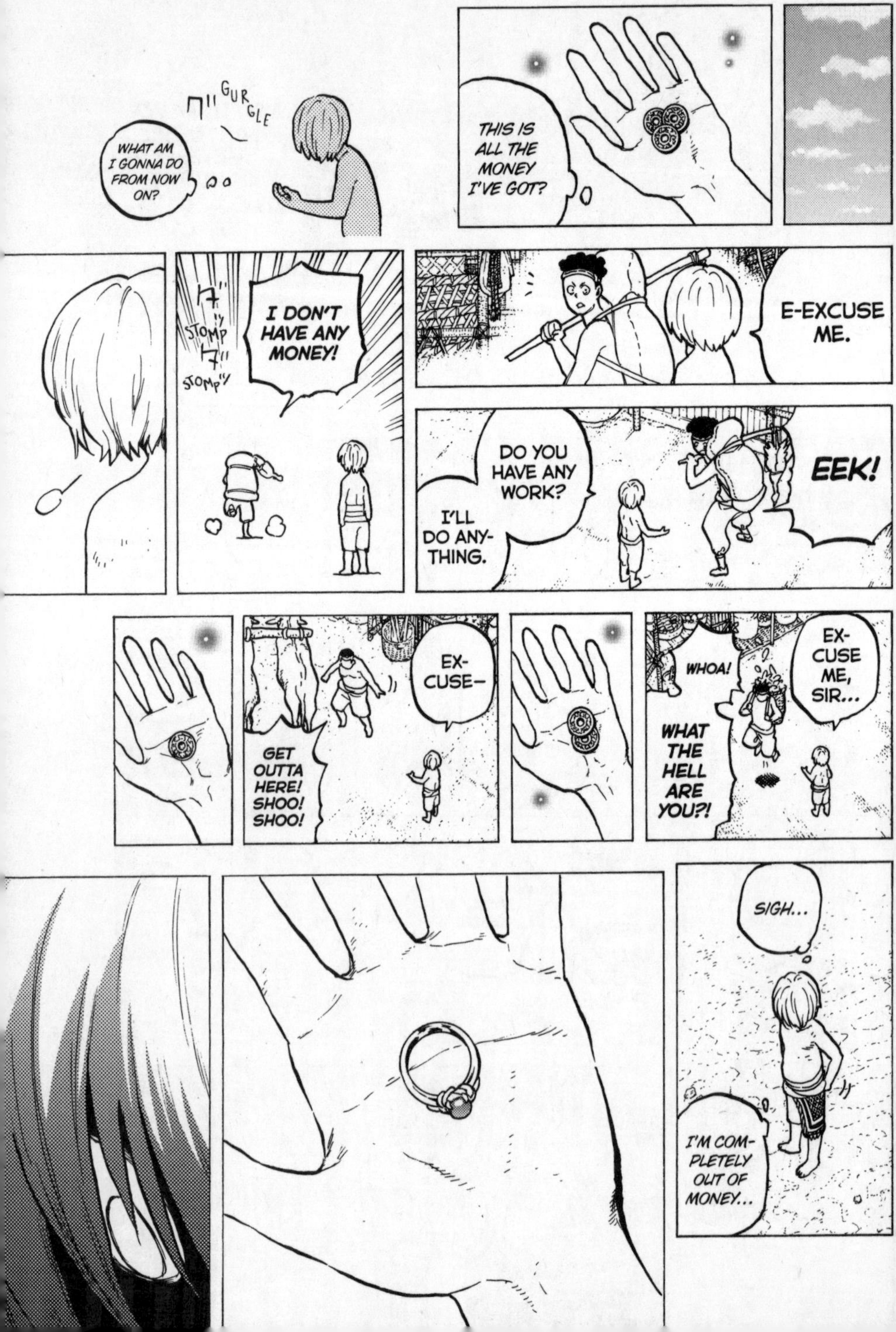
THIS IS ALL THE MONEY I'VE GOT?
GURGLE
WHAT AM I GONNA DO FROM NOW ON?
E-EXCUSE ME.
EEK!
DO YOU HAVE ANY WORK?
I'LL DO ANY-THING.
I DON'T HAVE ANY MONEY!
STOMP
STOMP
EX-CUSE ME, SIR...
WHOA!
WHAT THE HELL ARE YOU?!
EX-CUSE—
GET OUTTA HERE! SHOO! SHOO!
SIGH...
I'M COM-PLETELY OUT OF MONEY...

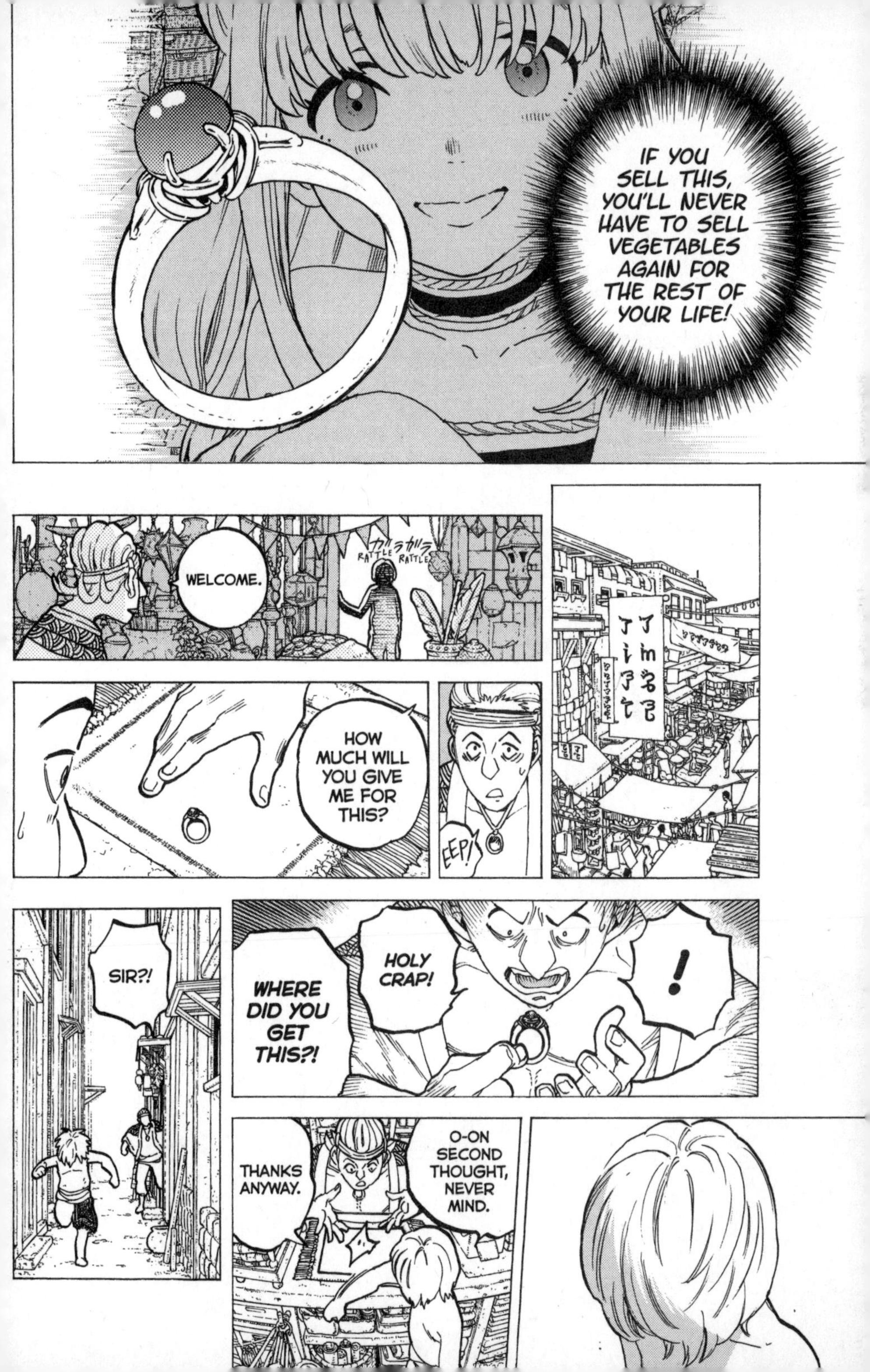
IF YOU SELL THIS, YOU'LL NEVER HAVE TO SELL VEGETABLES AGAIN FOR THE REST OF YOUR LIFE!
RATTLE RATTLE
WELCOME.
EEP!
HOW MUCH WILL YOU GIVE ME FOR THIS?
!
HOLY CRAP!
WHERE DID YOU GET THIS?!
O-ON SECOND THOUGHT, NEVER MIND.
THANKS ANYWAY.
SIR?!

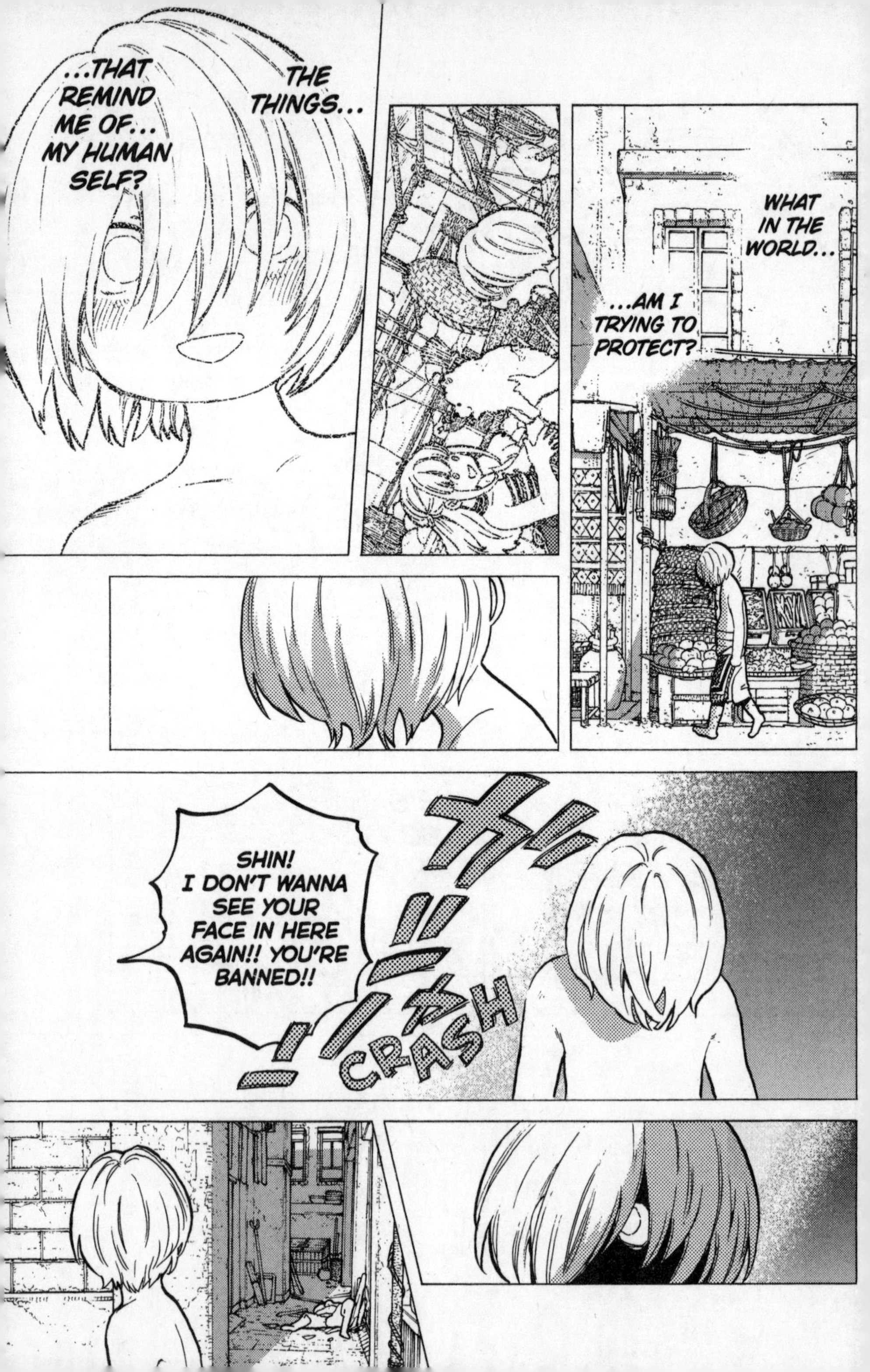
WHAT IN THE WORLD...
...AM I TRYING TO PROTECT?
THE THINGS...
...THAT REMIND ME OF... MY HUMAN SELF?
SHIN! I DON'T WANNA SEE YOUR FACE IN HERE AGAIN!! YOU'RE BANNED!!
CRASH

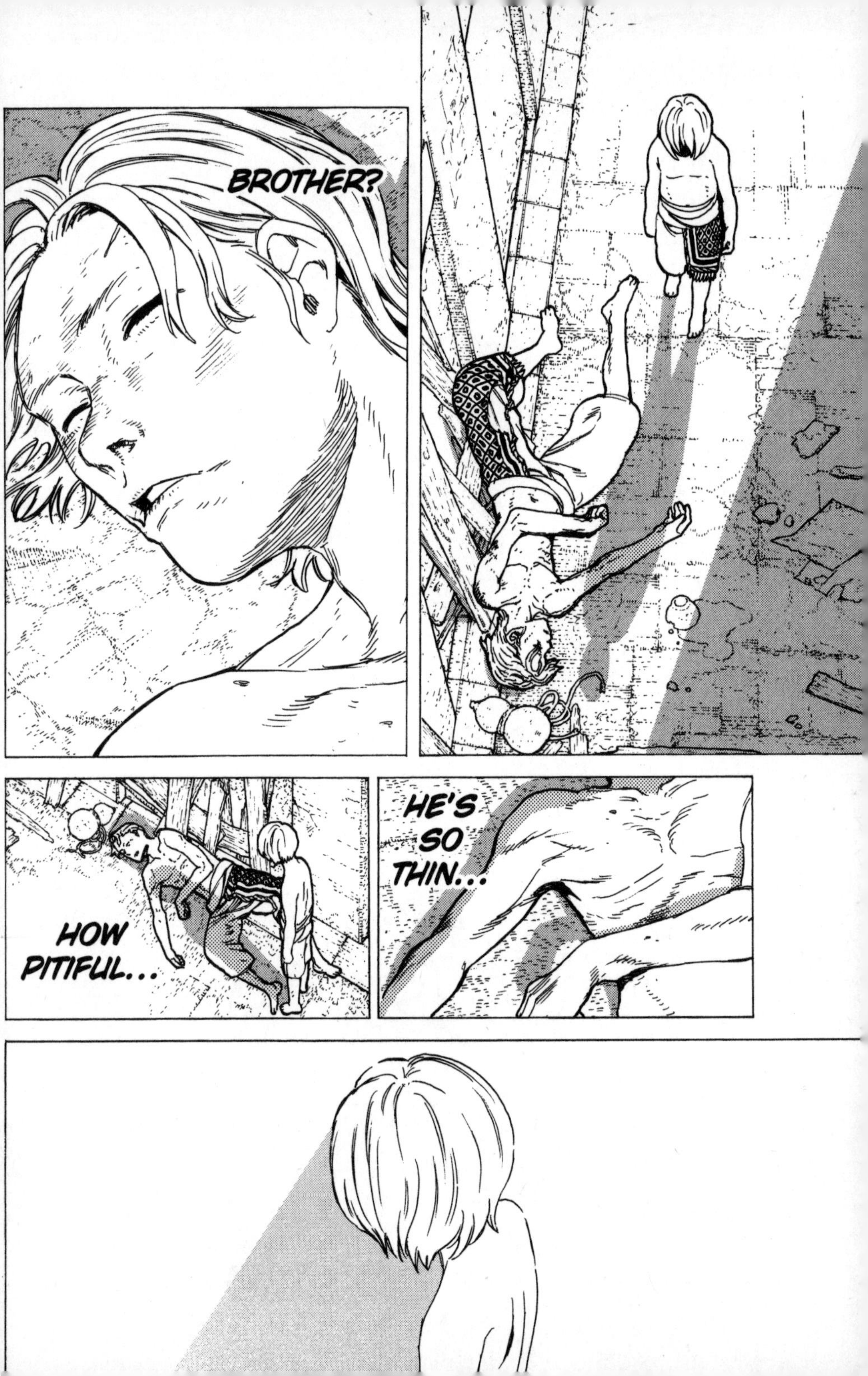
BROTHER?
HE'S SO THIN...
HOW PITIFUL...

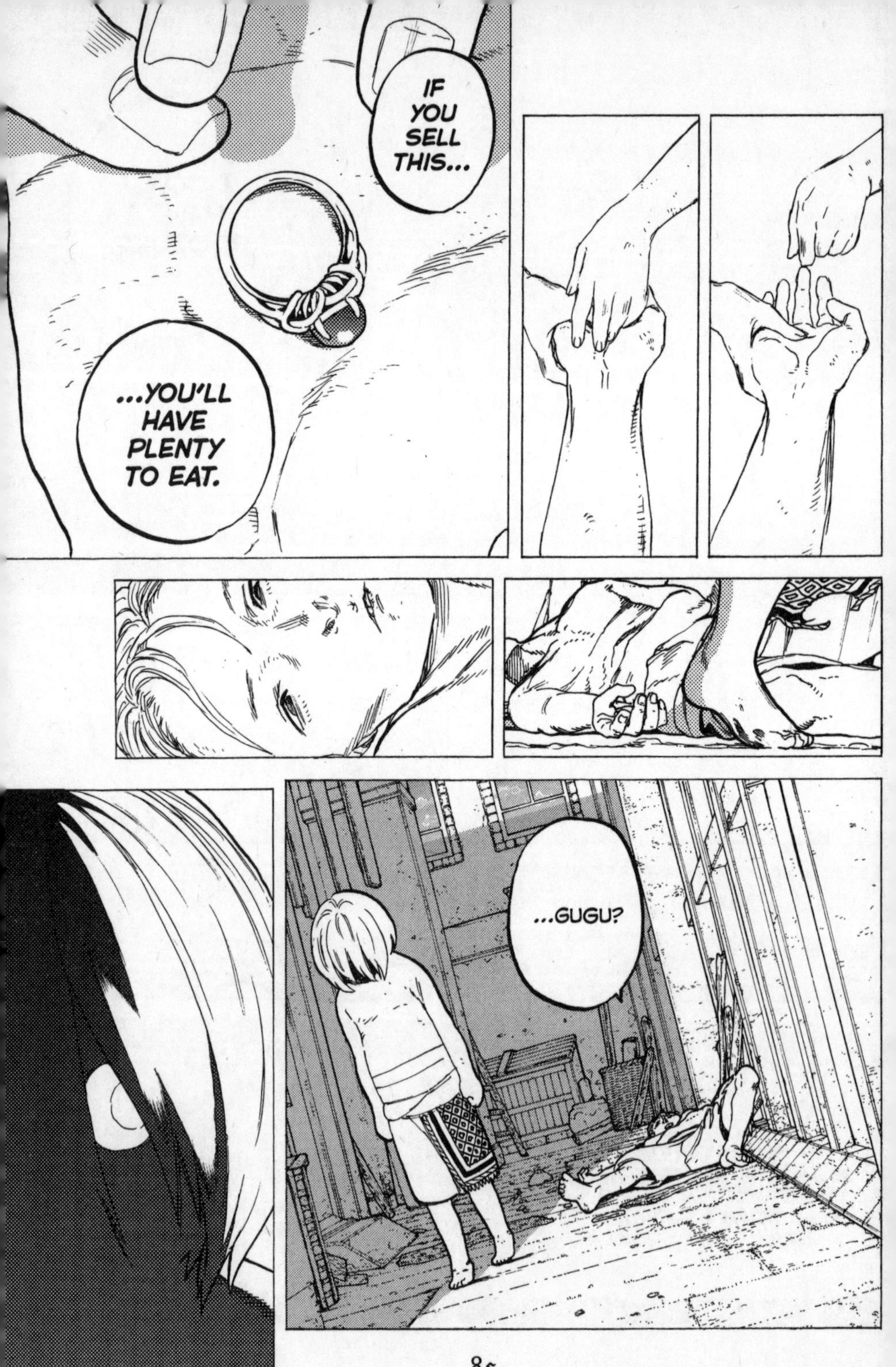
IF YOU SELL THIS...
...YOU'LL HAVE PLENTY TO EAT.
...GUGU?

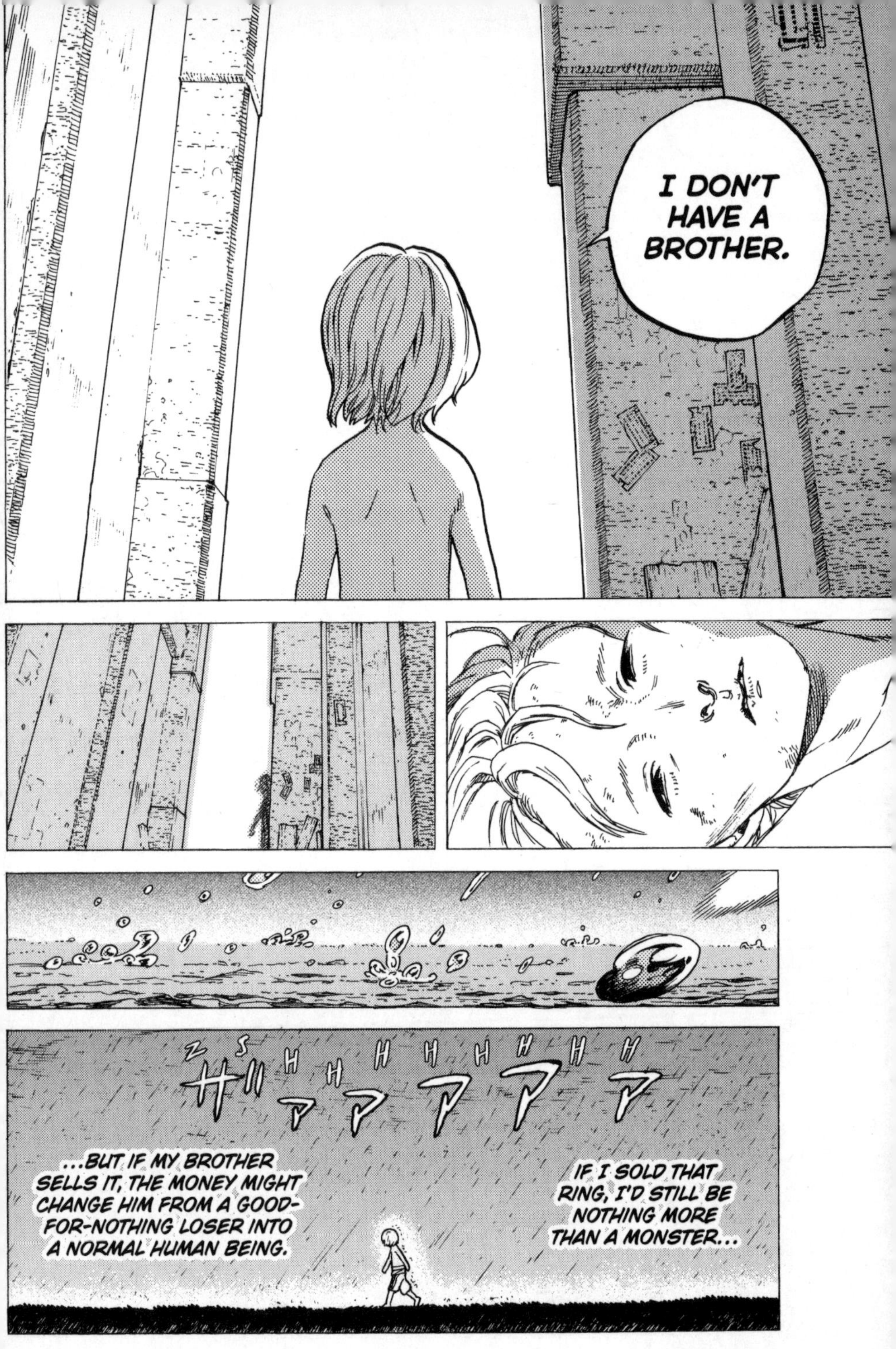
I DON'T HAVE A BROTHER.
ZSHHHHHHHH
IF I SOLD THAT RING, I'D STILL BE NOTHING MORE THAN A MONSTER...
...BUT IF MY BROTHER SELLS IT, THE MONEY MIGHT CHANGE HIM FROM A GOOD-FOR-NOTHING LOSER INTO A NORMAL HUMAN BEING.

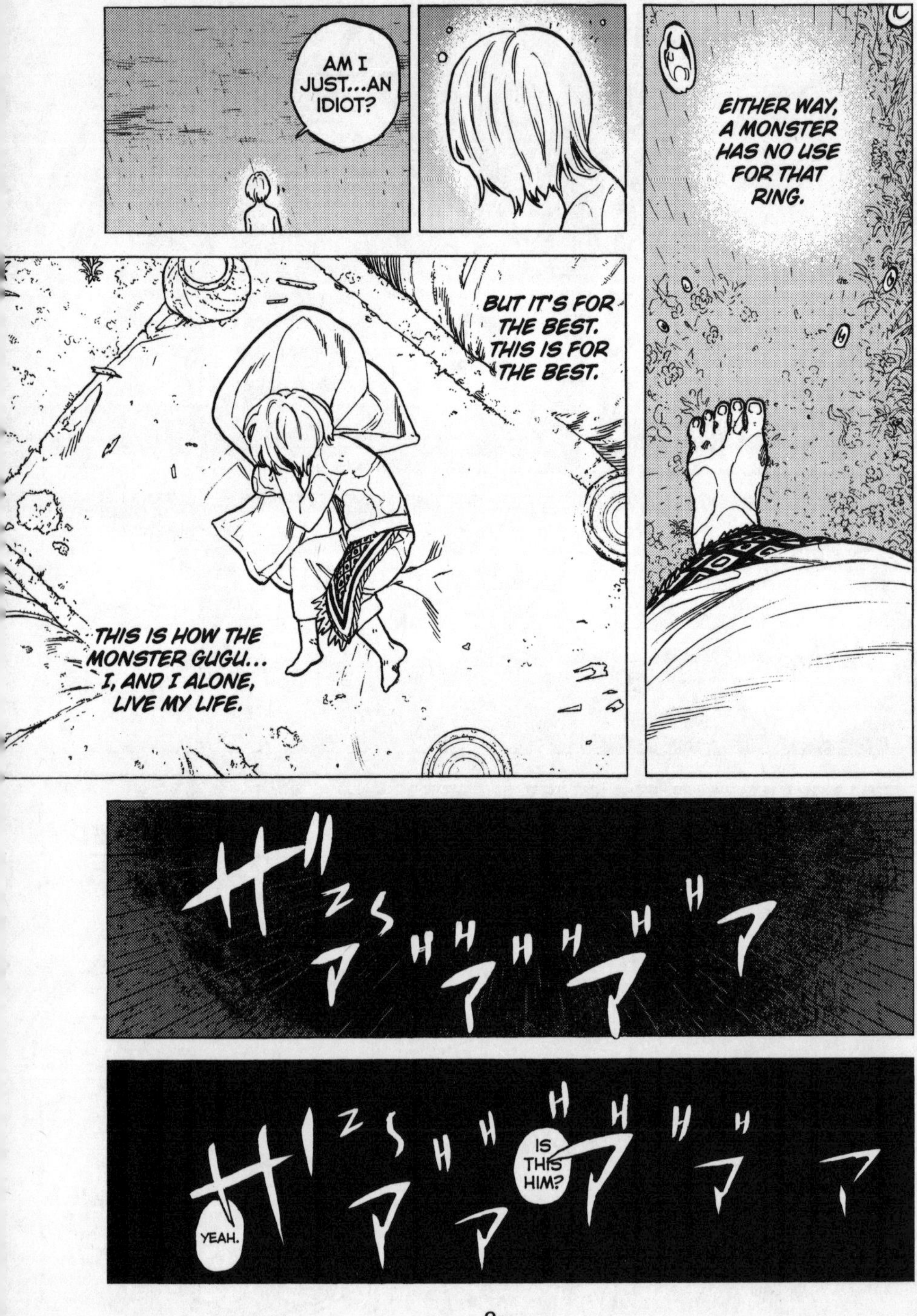
EITHER WAY, A MONSTER HAS NO USE FOR THAT RING.
AM I JUST...AN IDIOT?
BUT IT'S FOR THE BEST. THIS IS FOR THE BEST.
THIS IS HOW THE MONSTER GUGU... I, AND I ALONE, LIVE MY LIFE.
ZSHHHHHH
ZSHHHHHH
IS THIS HIM?
YEAH.

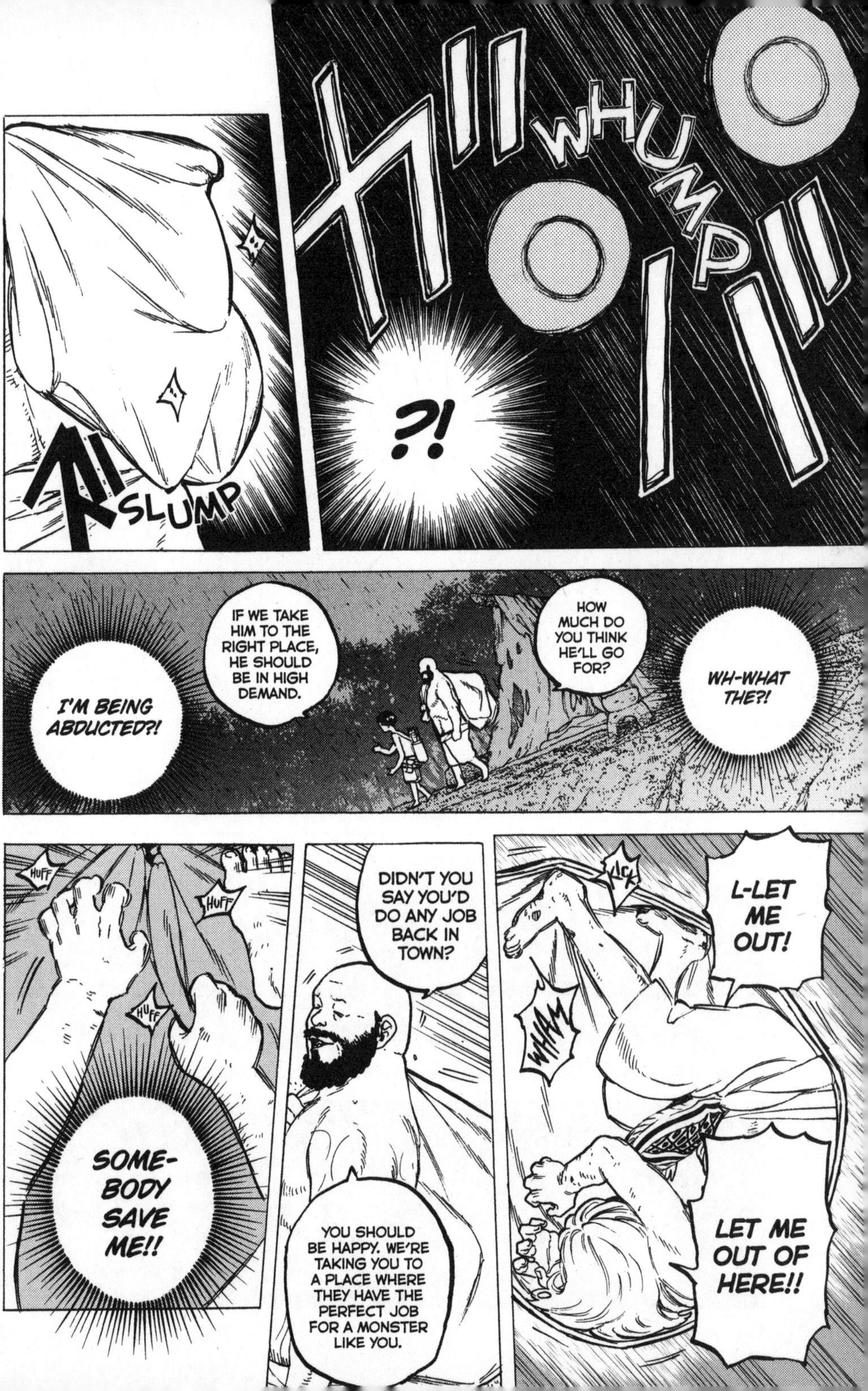
WHUMP
?!
SLUMP
WH-WHAT THE?!
HOW MUCH DO YOU THINK HE'LL GO FOR?
IF WE TAKE HIM TO THE RIGHT PLACE, HE SHOULD BE IN HIGH DEMAND.
I'M BEING ABDUCTED?!
KICK
L-LET ME OUT!
WHAM
LET ME OUT OF HERE!!
DIDN'T YOU SAY YOU'D DO ANY JOB BACK IN TOWN?
YOU SHOULD BE HAPPY. WE'RE TAKING YOU TO A PLACE WHERE THEY HAVE THE PERFECT JOB FOR A MONSTER LIKE YOU.
HUFF
HUFF
HUFF
SOME-BODY SAVE ME!!

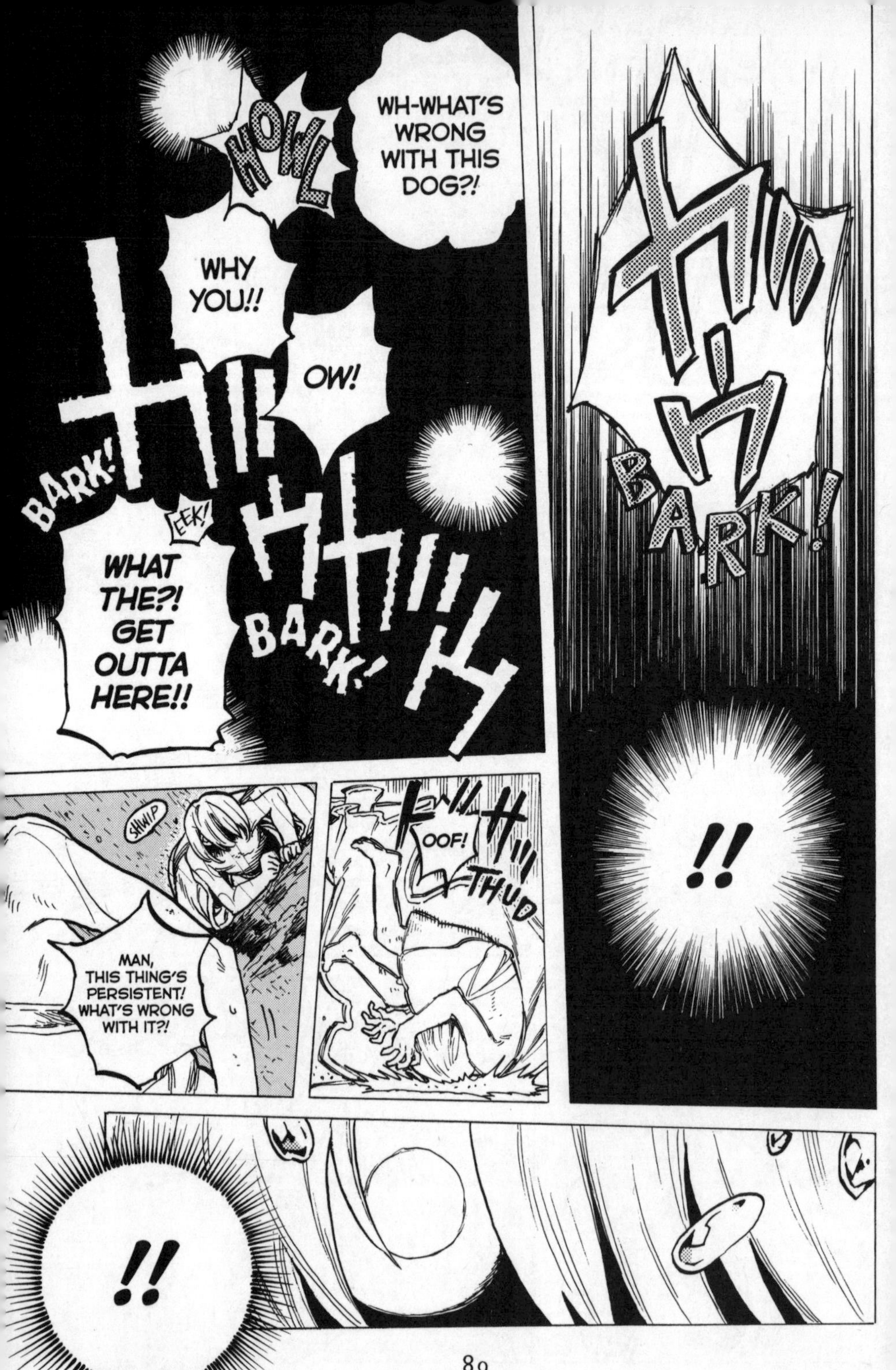
BARK!
!!
WH-WHAT'S WRONG WITH THIS DOG?!
HOWL
WHY YOU!!
OW!
BARK!
BARK!
EEK!
WHAT THE?! GET OUTTA HERE!!
OOF!
THUD
SHWIP
MAN, THIS THING'S PERSISTENT! WHAT'S WRONG WITH IT?!
!!

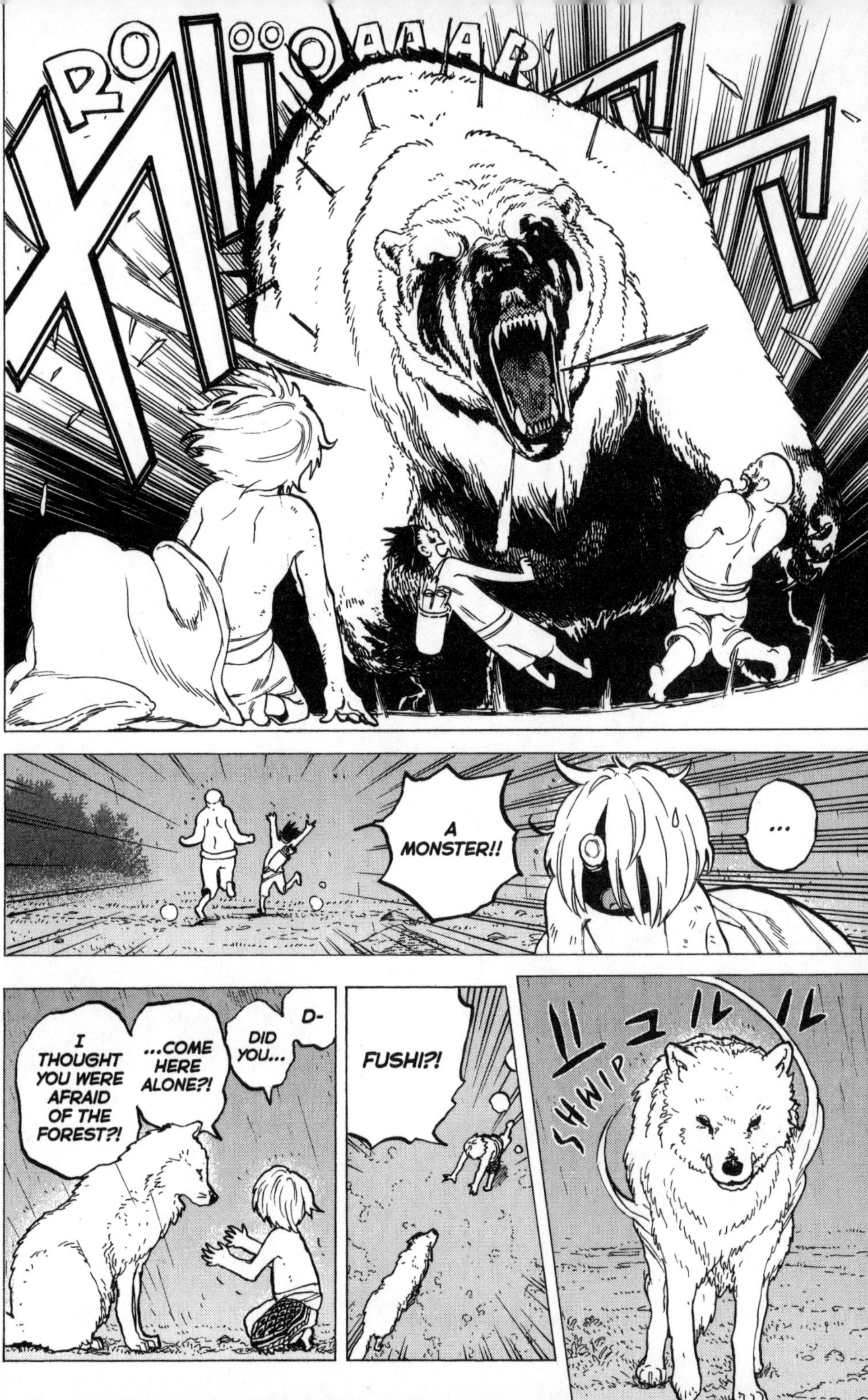
ROOOAAAR
...
A MONSTER!!
SHWIP
FUSHI?!
D-
DID YOU...
...COME HERE ALONE?!
I THOUGHT YOU WERE AFRAID OF THE FOREST?!

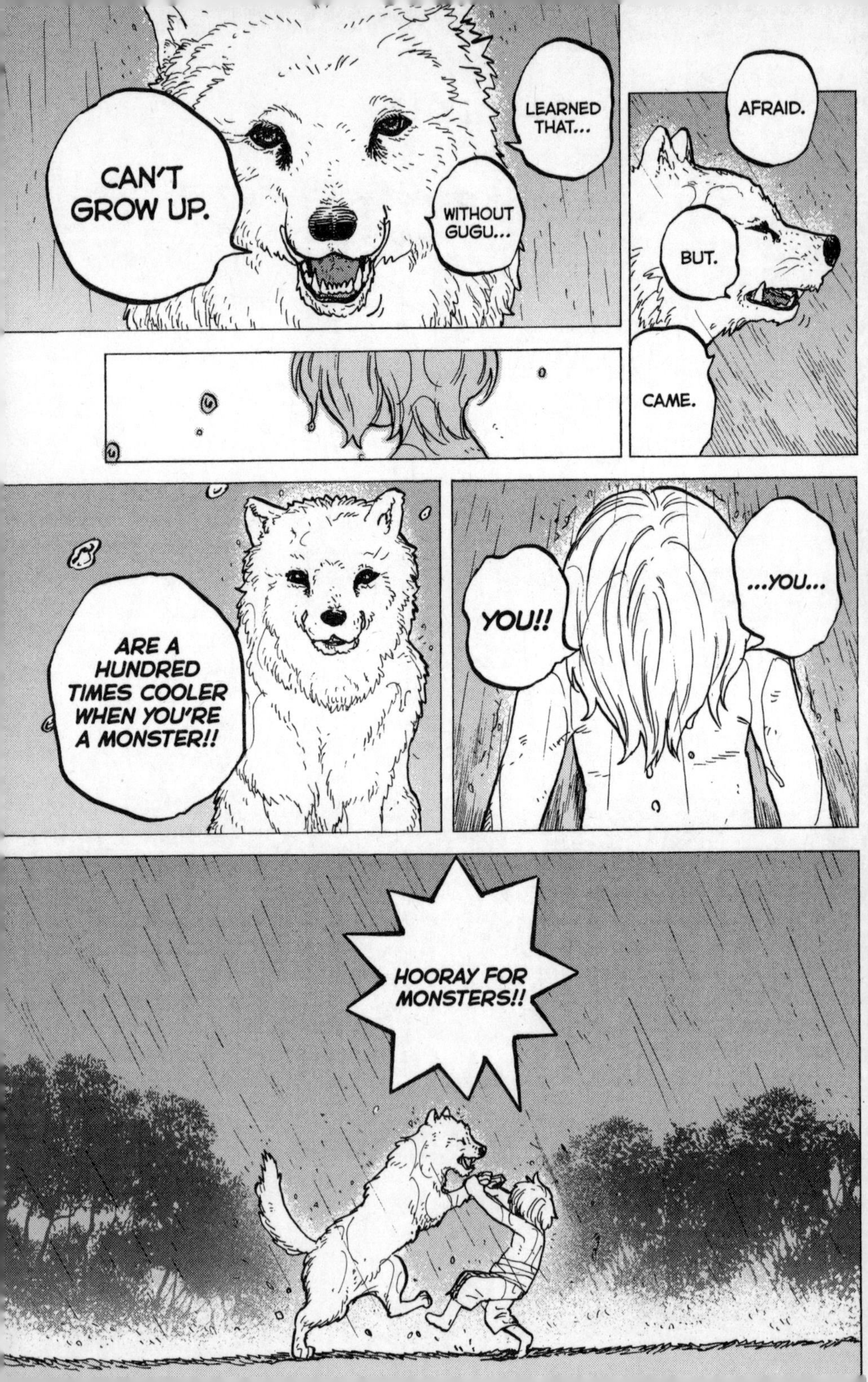
LEARNED THAT...
WITHOUT GUGU...
CAN'T GROW UP.
AFRAID.
BUT.
CAME.
...YOU...
YOU!!
ARE A HUNDRED TIMES COOLER WHEN YOU'RE A MONSTER!!
HOORAY FOR MONSTERS!!

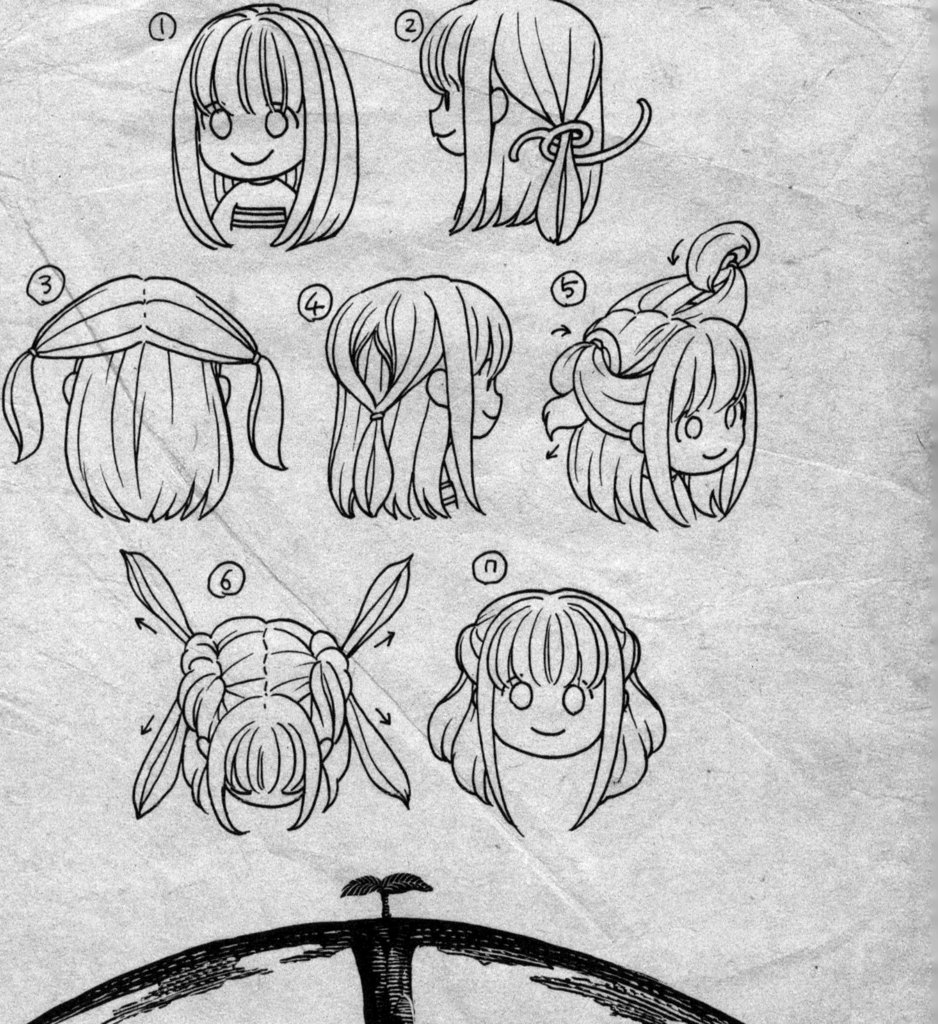

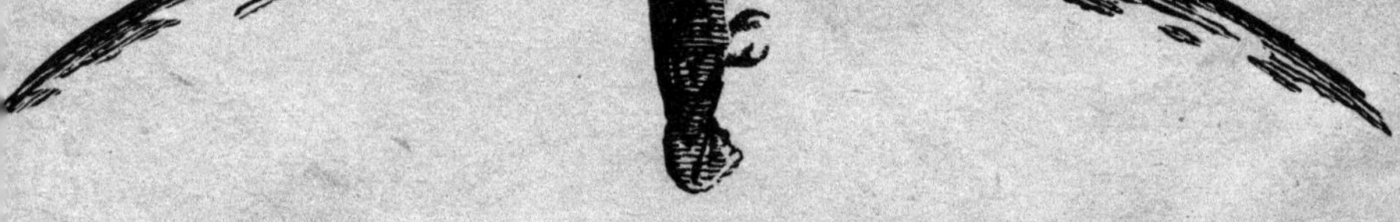

#19 Deep Memory

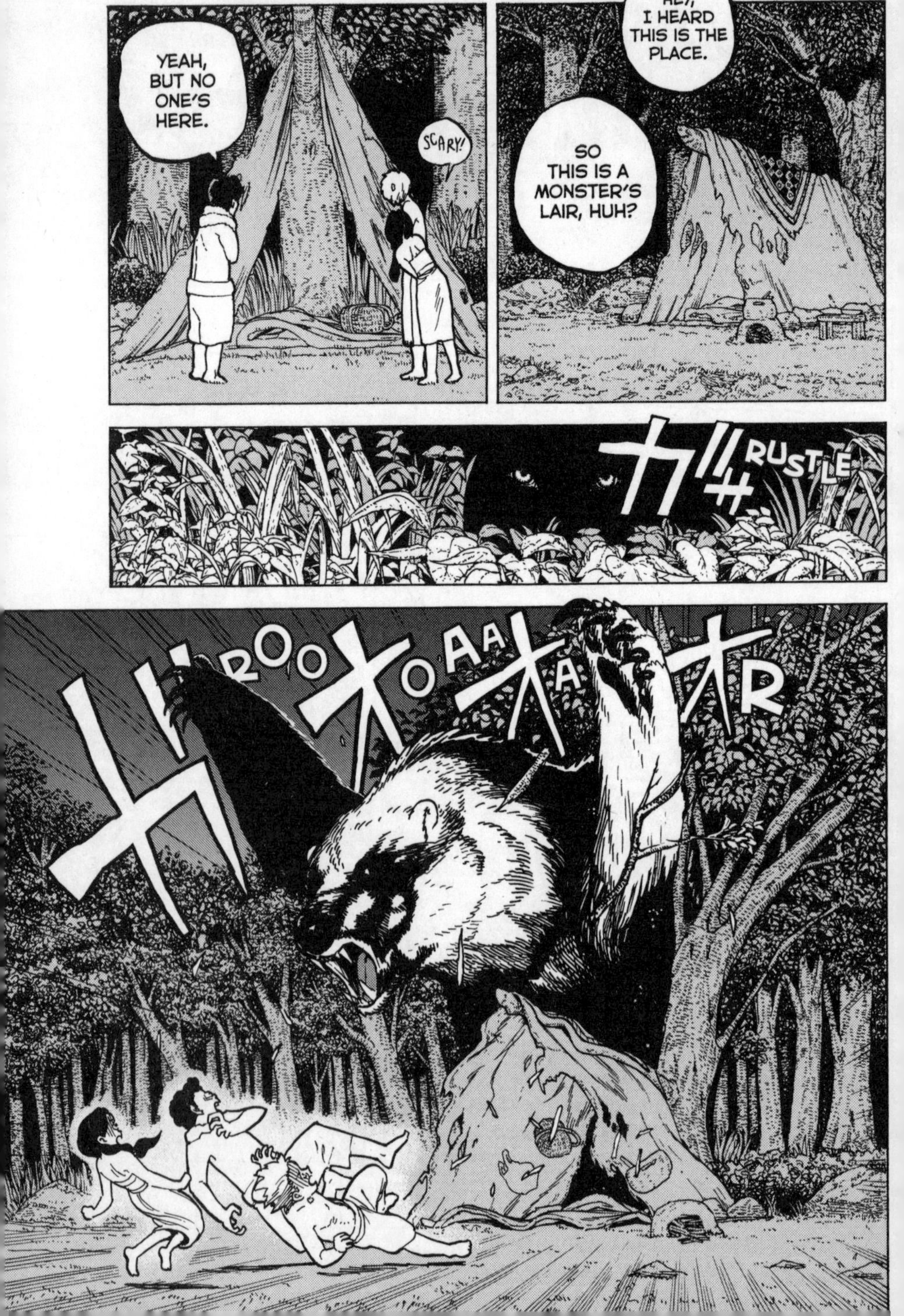

HEY, I HEARD THIS IS THE PLACE.
SO THIS IS A MONSTER'S LAIR, HUH?
YEAH, BUT NO ONE'S HERE.
SCARY!
RUSTLE
ROOOAAAR

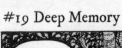

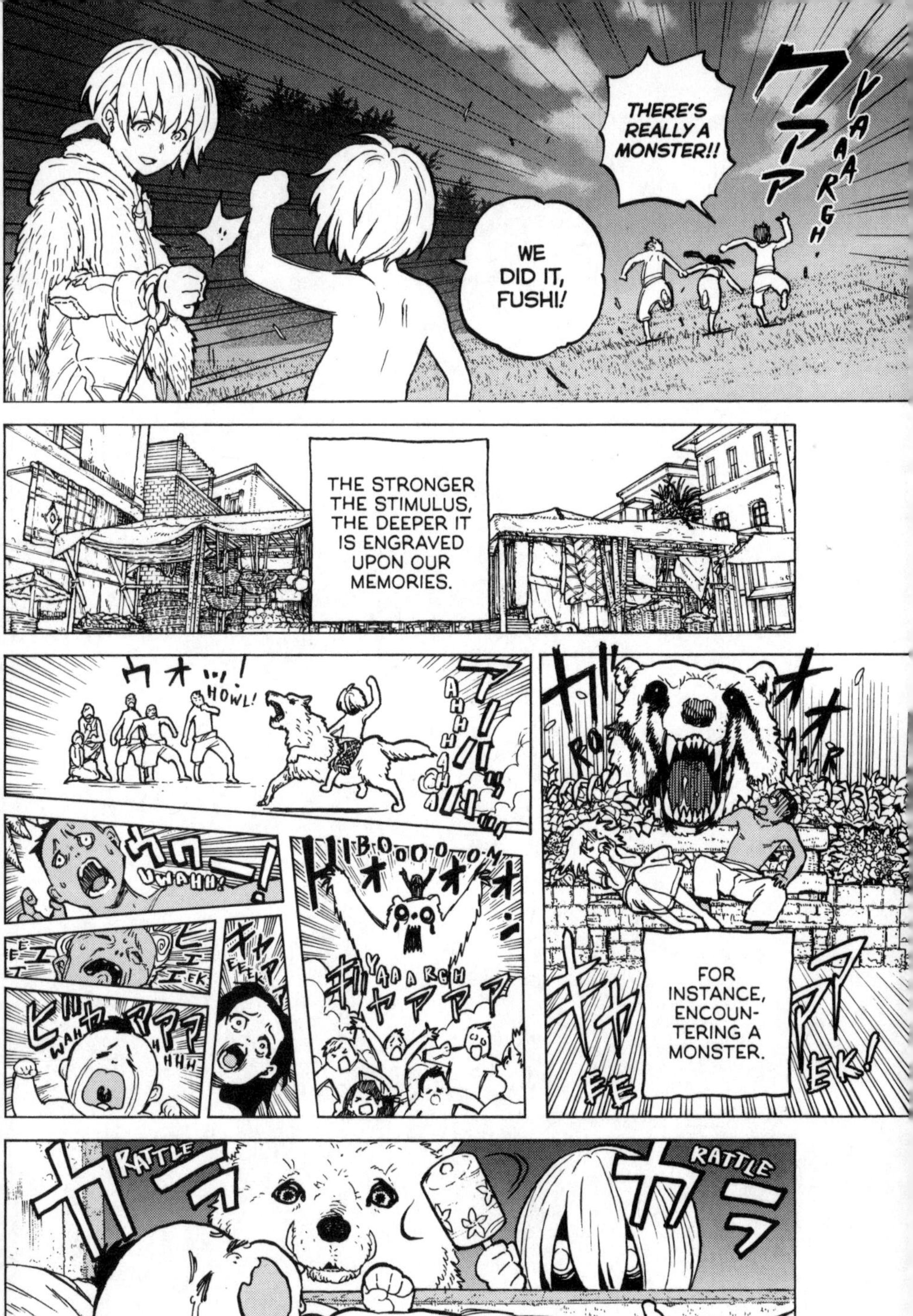
YAAARGH
THERE'S REALLY A MONSTER!!
WE DID IT, FUSHI!
THE STRONGER THE STIMULUS, THE DEEPER IT IS ENGRAVED UPON OUR MEMORIES.
ROAR
FOR INSTANCE, ENCOUNTERING A MONSTER.
EEEK!
AHHHHAHAHA
HOWL!
BOOOOOOM
YAAARGH
UWAHH!
EEEK
EEEK
WAHHHHH
RATTLE
RATTLE

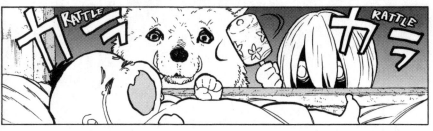

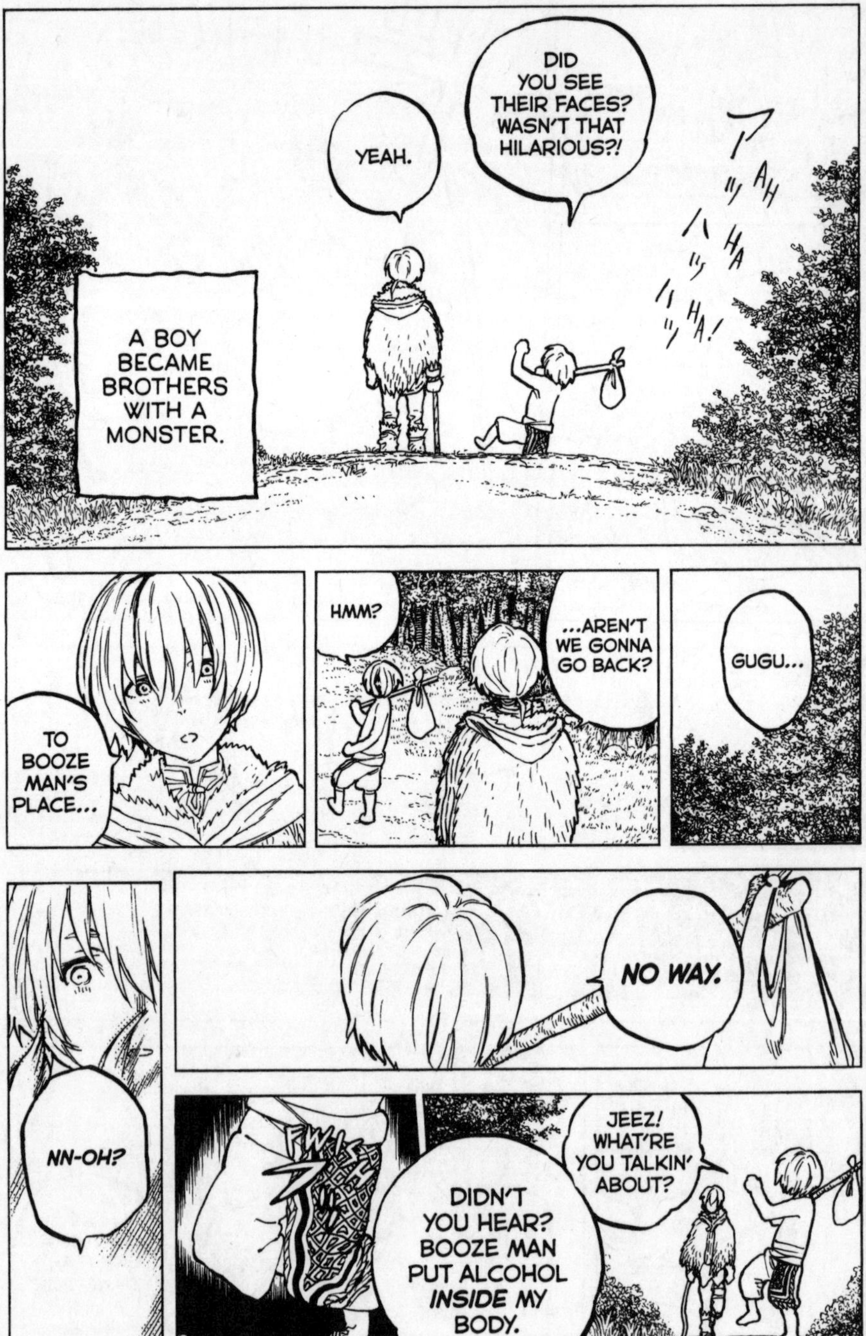
DID YOU SEE THEIR FACES? WASN'T THAT HILARIOUS?!
AH HA HA HA!
YEAH.
A BOY BECAME BROTHERS WITH A MONSTER.
GUGU...
...AREN'T WE GONNA GO BACK?
HMM?
TO BOOZE MAN'S PLACE...
NO WAY.
JEEZ! WHAT'RE YOU TALKIN' ABOUT?
DIDN'T YOU HEAR? BOOZE MAN PUT ALCOHOL INSIDE MY BODY.
FWISH
NN-OH?

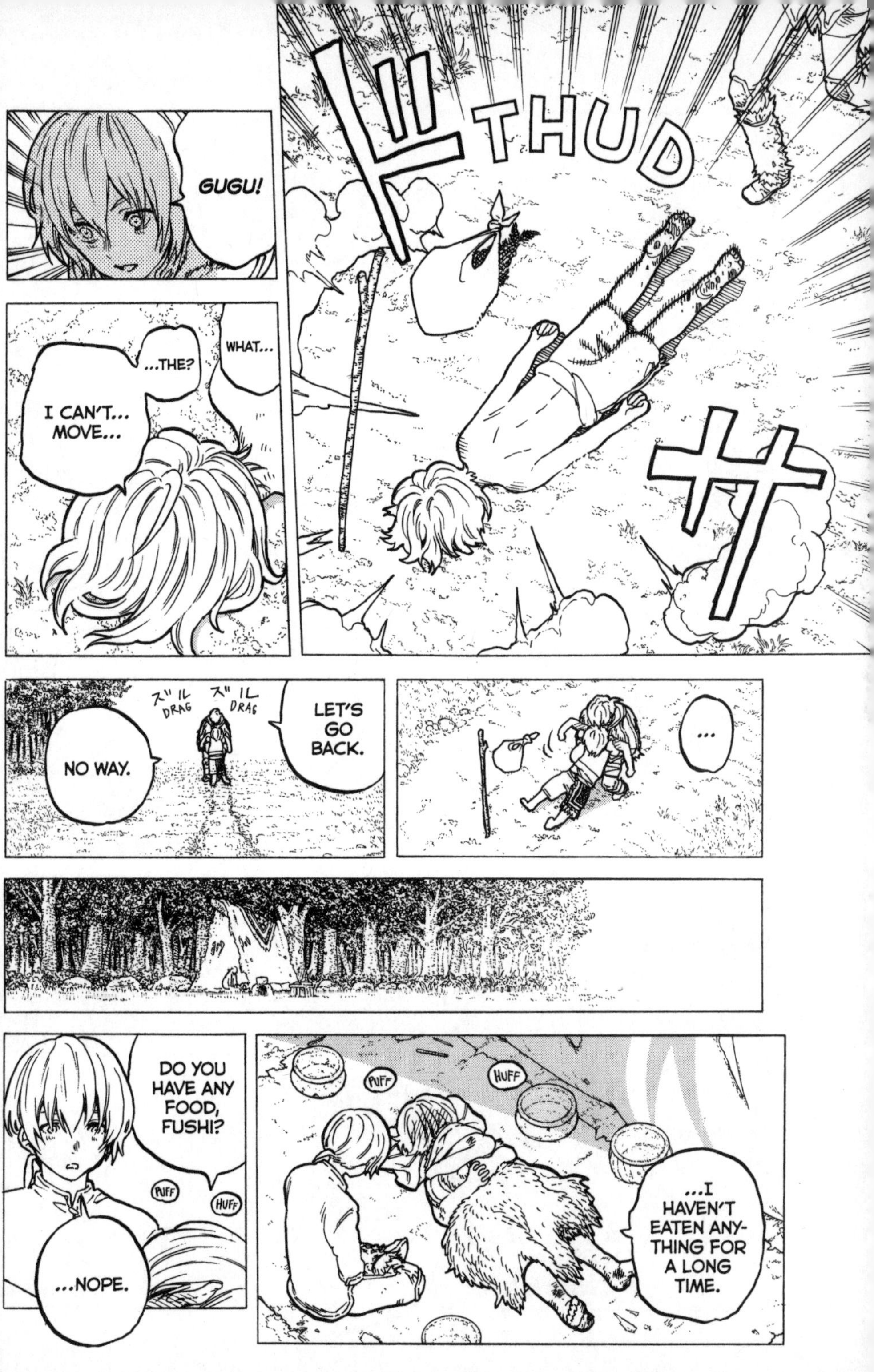
THUD
GUGU!
WHAT...
...THE?
I CAN'T... MOVE...
...
LET'S GO BACK.
ズル DRAG ズル DRAG
NO WAY.
HUFF
PUFF
...I HAVEN'T EATEN ANY-THING FOR A LONG TIME.
DO YOU HAVE ANY FOOD, FUSHI?
HUFF
PUFF
...NOPE.

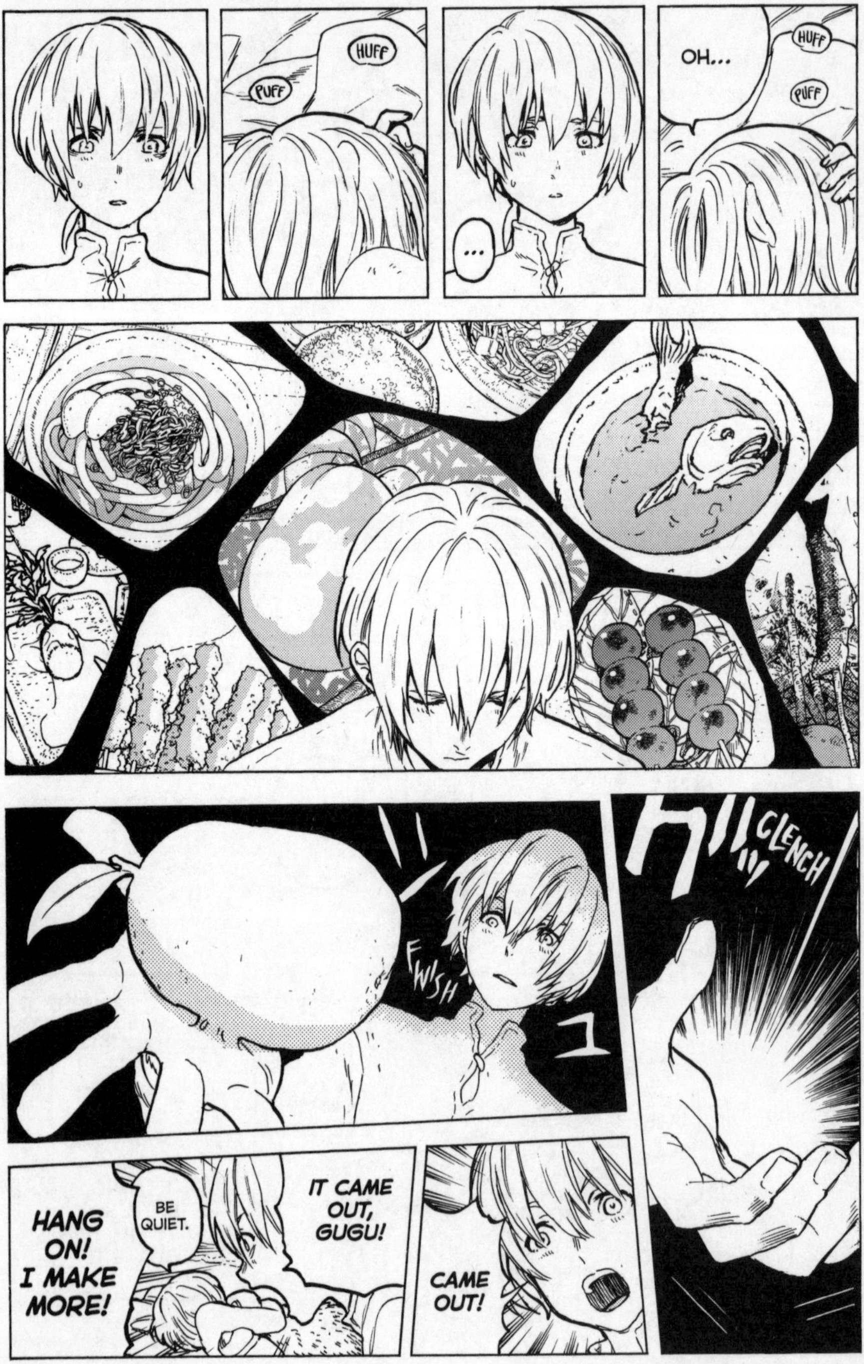
OH...
HUFF
PUFF
...
HUFF
PUFF
CLENCH
FWISH
CAME OUT!
IT CAME OUT, GUGU!
BE QUIET.
HANG ON! I MAKE MORE!

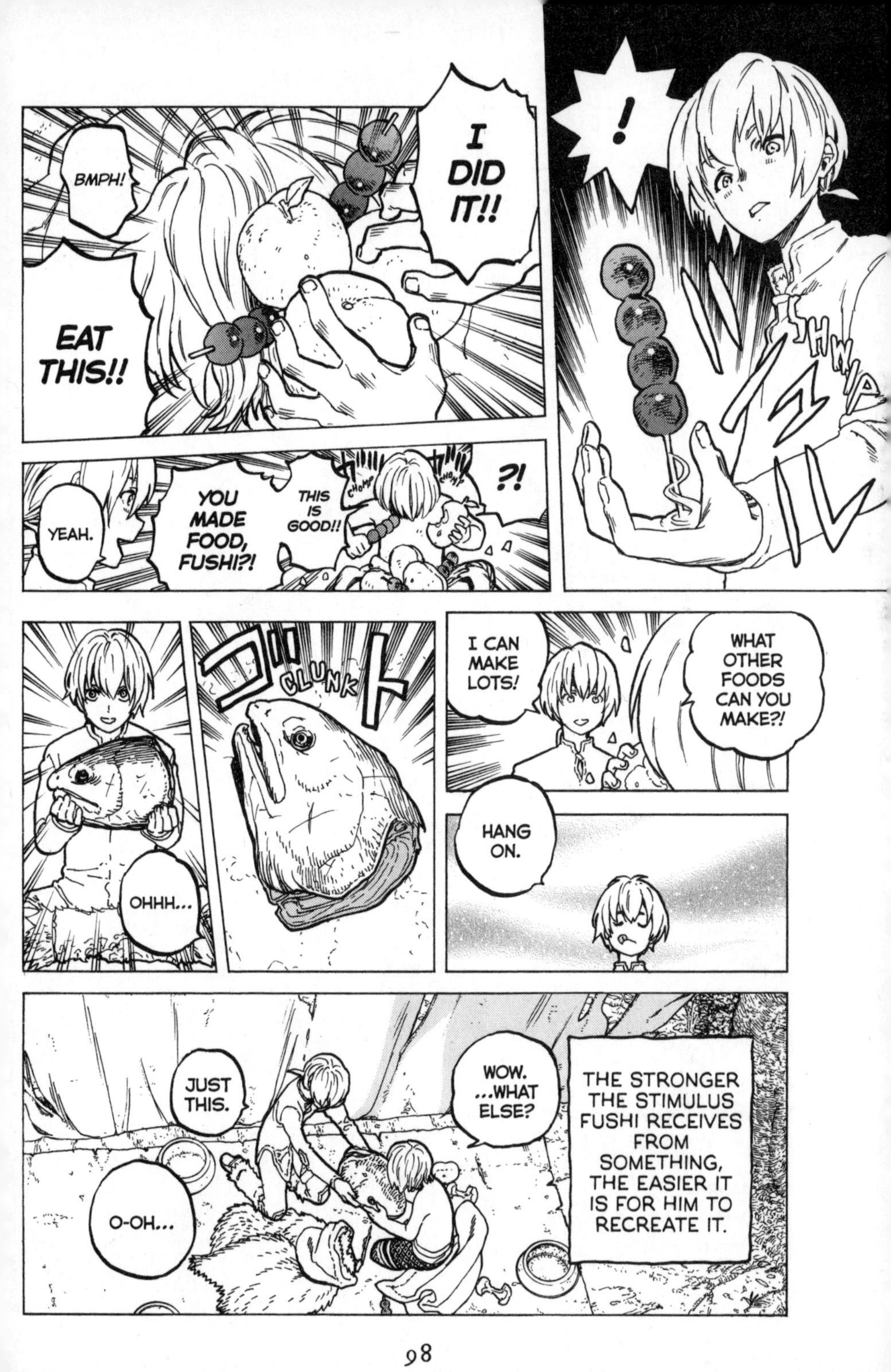
!
SHWIP
I DID IT!!
BMPH!
EAT THIS!!
?!
CHOMP
CHOMP
THIS IS GOOD!!
YOU MADE FOOD, FUSHI?!
YEAH.
WHAT OTHER FOODS CAN YOU MAKE?!
I CAN MAKE LOTS!
HANG ON.
CLUNK
OHHH...
THE STRONGER THE STIMULUS FUSHI RECEIVES FROM SOMETHING, THE EASIER IT IS FOR HIM TO RECREATE IT.
WOW. ...WHAT ELSE?
JUST THIS.
O-OH...

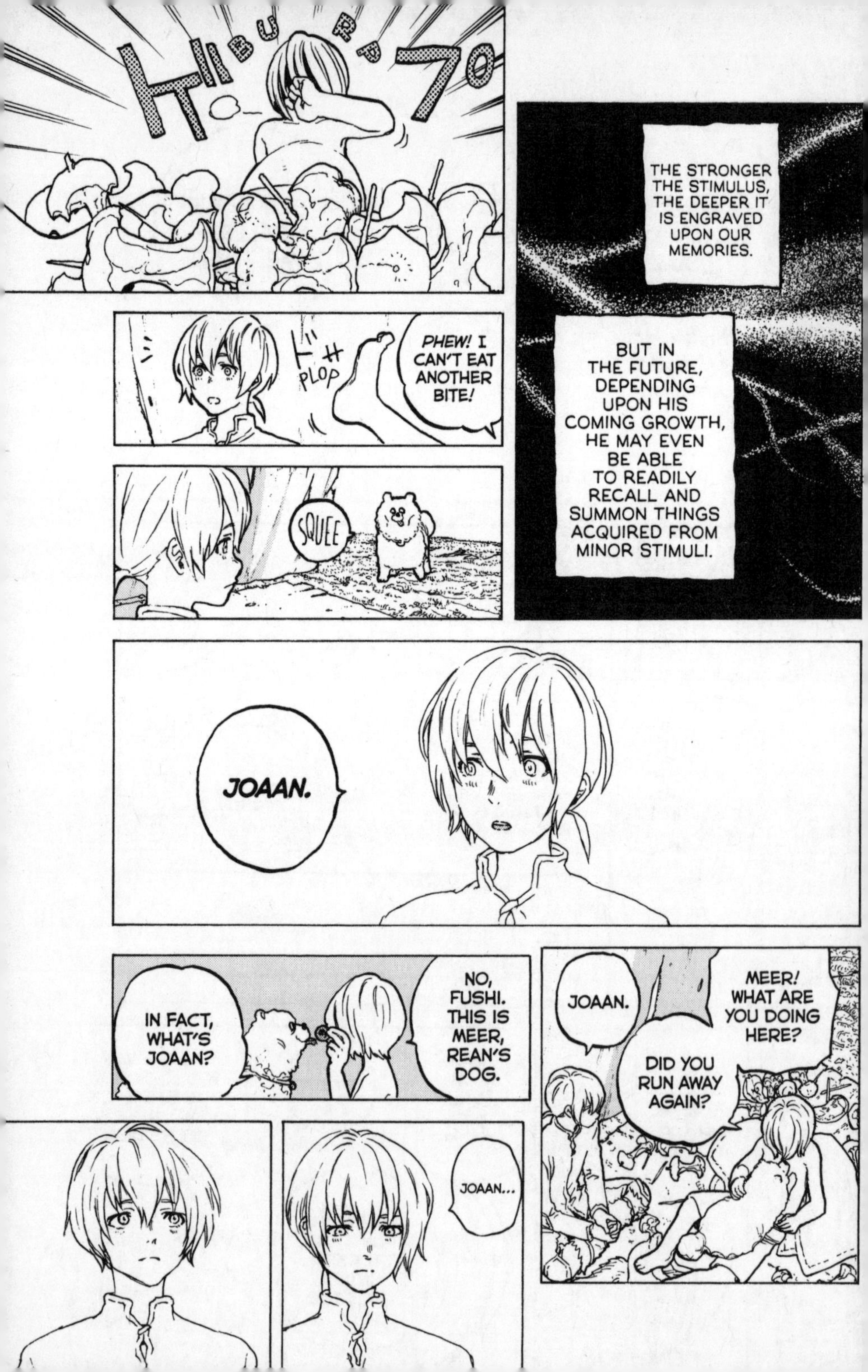

THE STRONGER THE STIMULUS, THE DEEPER IT IS ENGRAVED UPON OUR MEMORIES.
BUT IN THE FUTURE, DEPENDING UPON HIS COMING GROWTH, HE MAY EVEN BE ABLE TO READILY RECALL AND SUMMON THINGS ACQUIRED FROM MINOR STIMULI.
BURP
PHEW! I CAN'T EAT ANOTHER BITE!
PLOP
SQUEE
JOAAN.
MEER! WHAT ARE YOU DOING HERE?
JOAAN.
DID YOU RUN AWAY AGAIN?
NO, FUSHI. THIS IS MEER, REAN'S DOG.
IN FACT, WHAT'S JOAAN?
JOAAN...

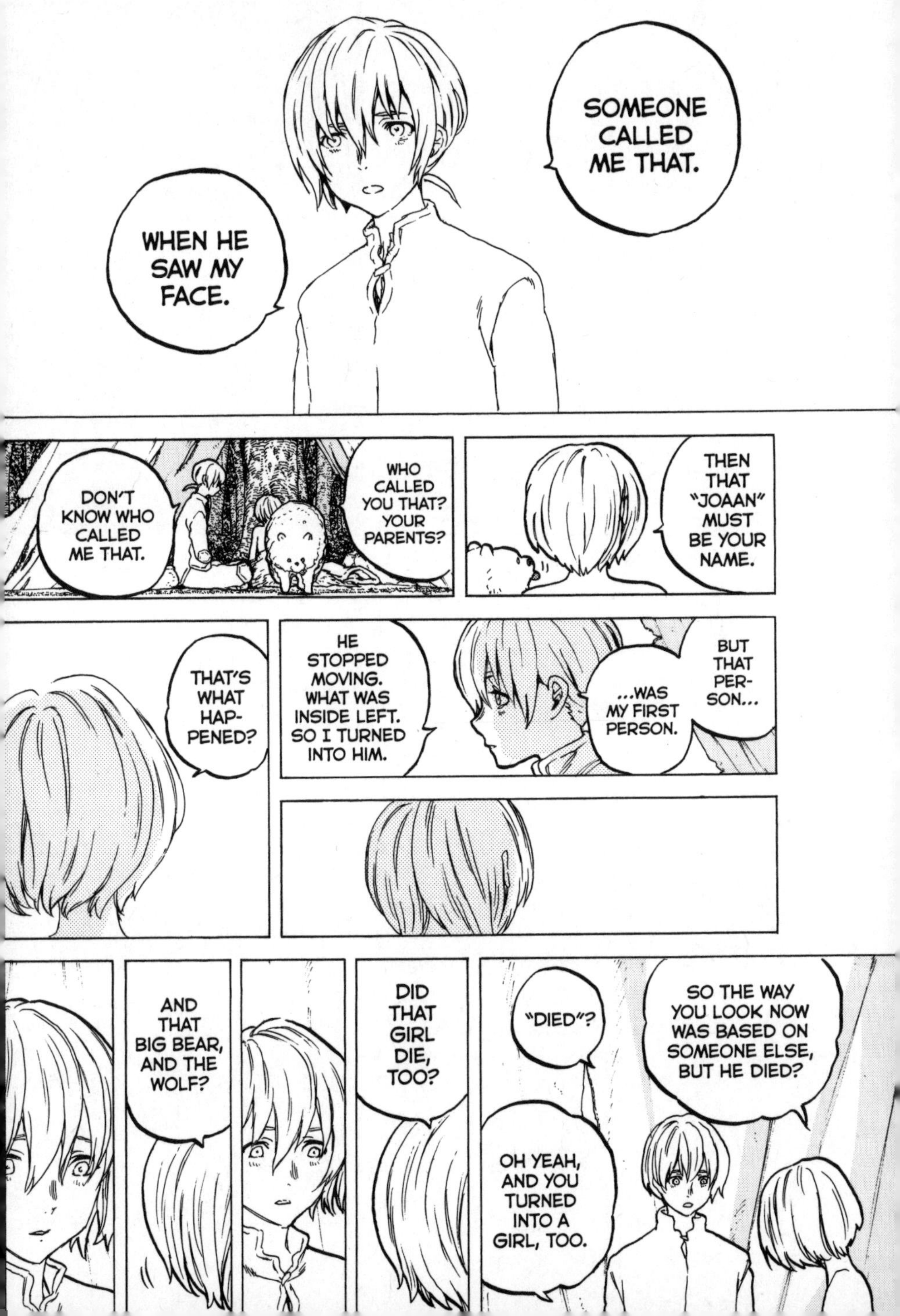
SOMEONE CALLED ME THAT.
WHEN HE SAW MY FACE.
THEN THAT "JOAAN" MUST BE YOUR NAME.
WHO CALLED YOU THAT? YOUR PARENTS?
DON'T KNOW WHO CALLED ME THAT.
BUT THAT PERSON...
...WAS MY FIRST PERSON.
HE STOPPED MOVING. WHAT WAS INSIDE LEFT. SO I TURNED INTO HIM.
THAT'S WHAT HAPPENED?
SO THE WAY YOU LOOK NOW WAS BASED ON SOMEONE ELSE, BUT HE DIED?
"DIED"?
OH YEAH, AND YOU TURNED INTO A GIRL, TOO.
DID THAT GIRL DIE, TOO?
AND THAT BIG BEAR, AND THE WOLF?

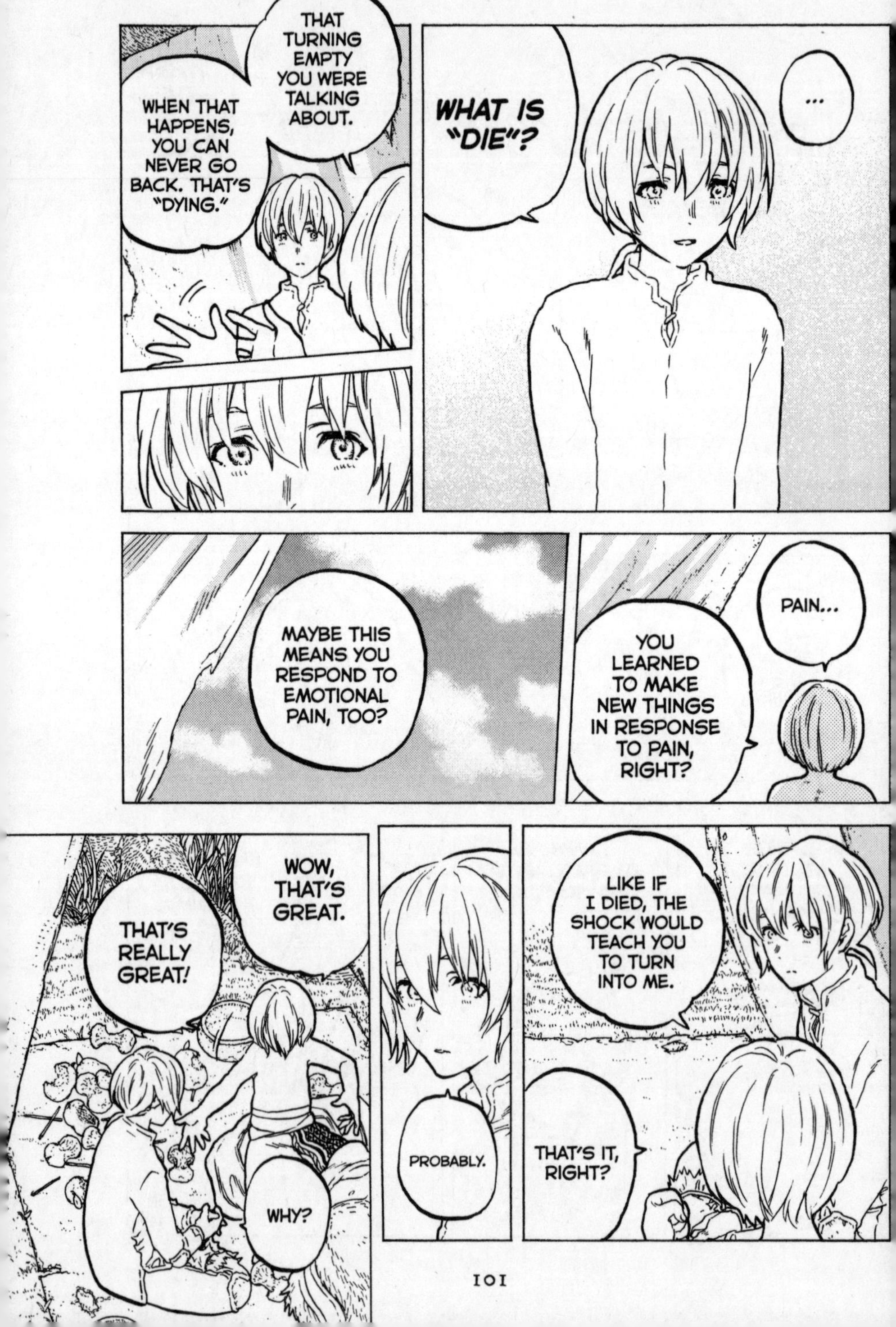
...
WHAT IS "DIE"?
THAT TURNING EMPTY YOU WERE TALKING ABOUT.
WHEN THAT HAPPENS, YOU CAN NEVER GO BACK. THAT'S "DYING."
PAIN...
YOU LEARNED TO MAKE NEW THINGS IN RESPONSE TO PAIN, RIGHT?
MAYBE THIS MEANS YOU RESPOND TO EMOTIONAL PAIN, TOO?
LIKE IF I DIED, THE SHOCK WOULD TEACH YOU TO TURN INTO ME.
THAT'S IT, RIGHT?
PROBABLY.
WOW, THAT'S GREAT.
THAT'S REALLY GREAT!
WHY?

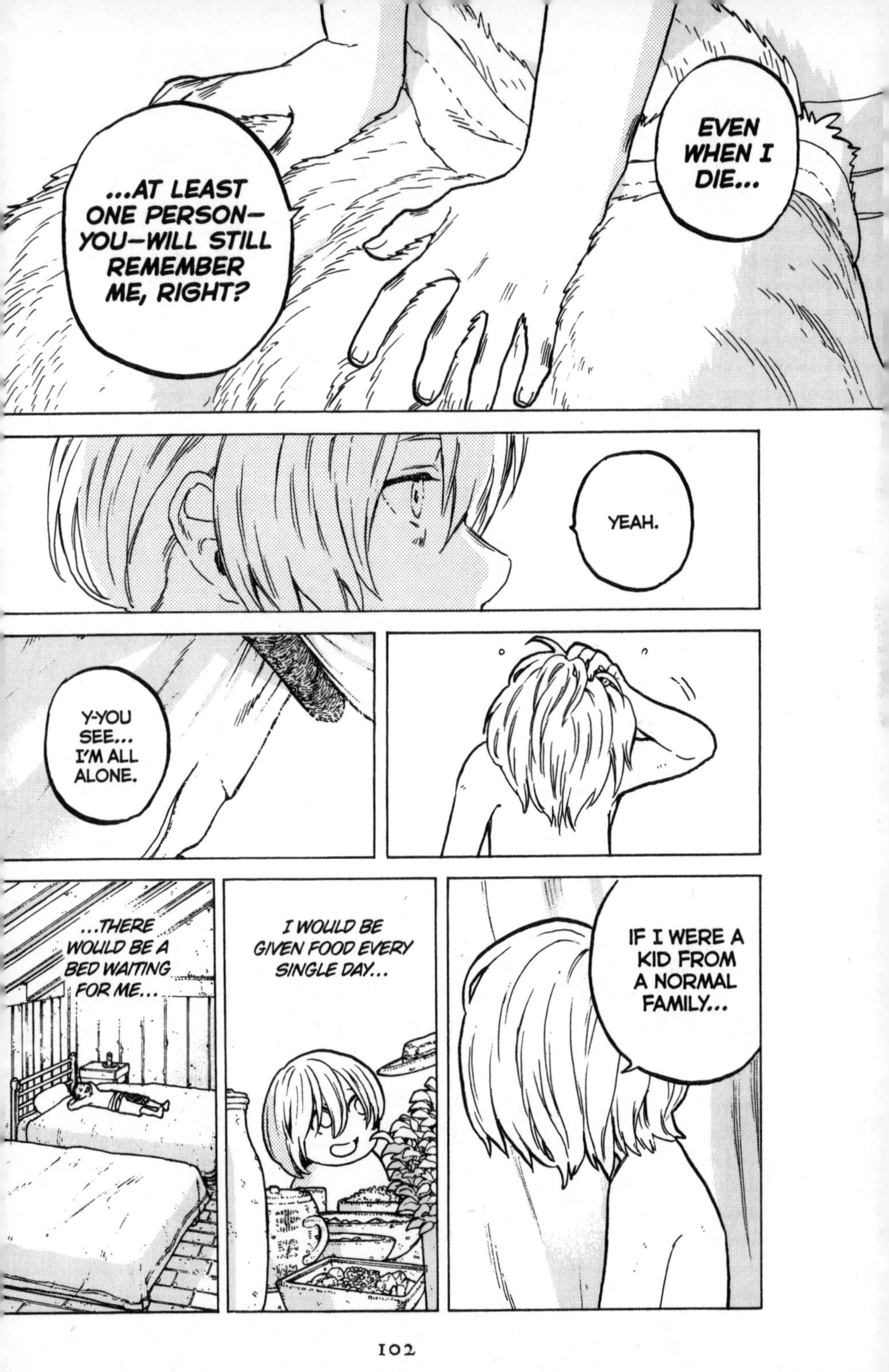
EVEN WHEN I DIE...
...AT LEAST ONE PERSON—YOU—WILL STILL REMEMBER ME, RIGHT?
YEAH.
Y-YOU SEE... I'M ALL ALONE.
IF I WERE A KID FROM A NORMAL FAMILY...
I WOULD BE GIVEN FOOD EVERY SINGLE DAY...
...THERE WOULD BE A BED WAITING FOR ME...

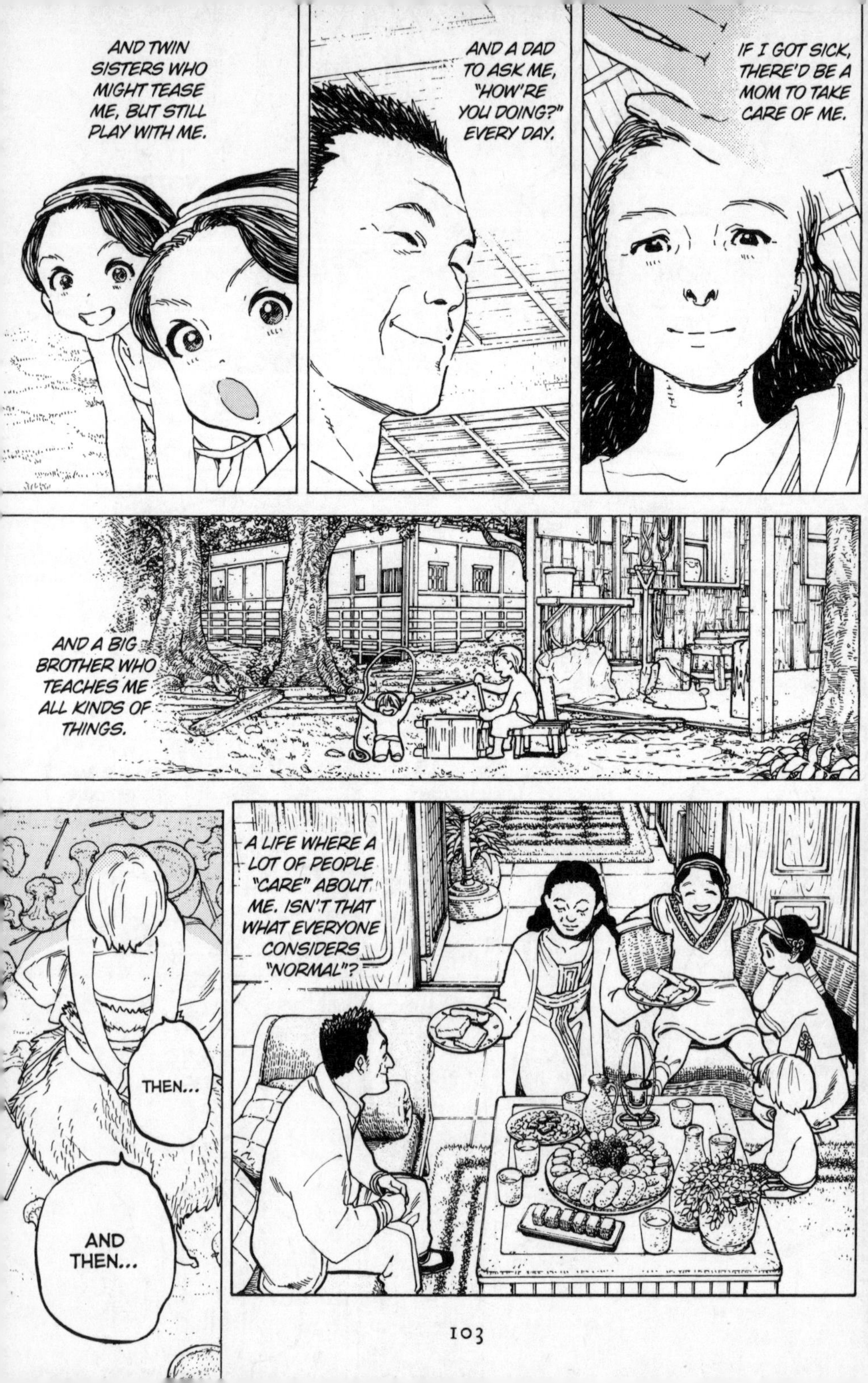
IF I GOT SICK, THERE'D BE A MOM TO TAKE CARE OF ME.
AND A DAD TO ASK ME, "HOW'RE YOU DOING?" EVERY DAY.
AND TWIN SISTERS WHO MIGHT TEASE ME, BUT STILL PLAY WITH ME.
AND A BIG BROTHER WHO TEACHES ME ALL KINDS OF THINGS.
A LIFE WHERE A LOT OF PEOPLE "CARE" ABOUT ME. ISN'T THAT WHAT EVERYONE CONSIDERS "NORMAL"?
THEN...
AND THEN...

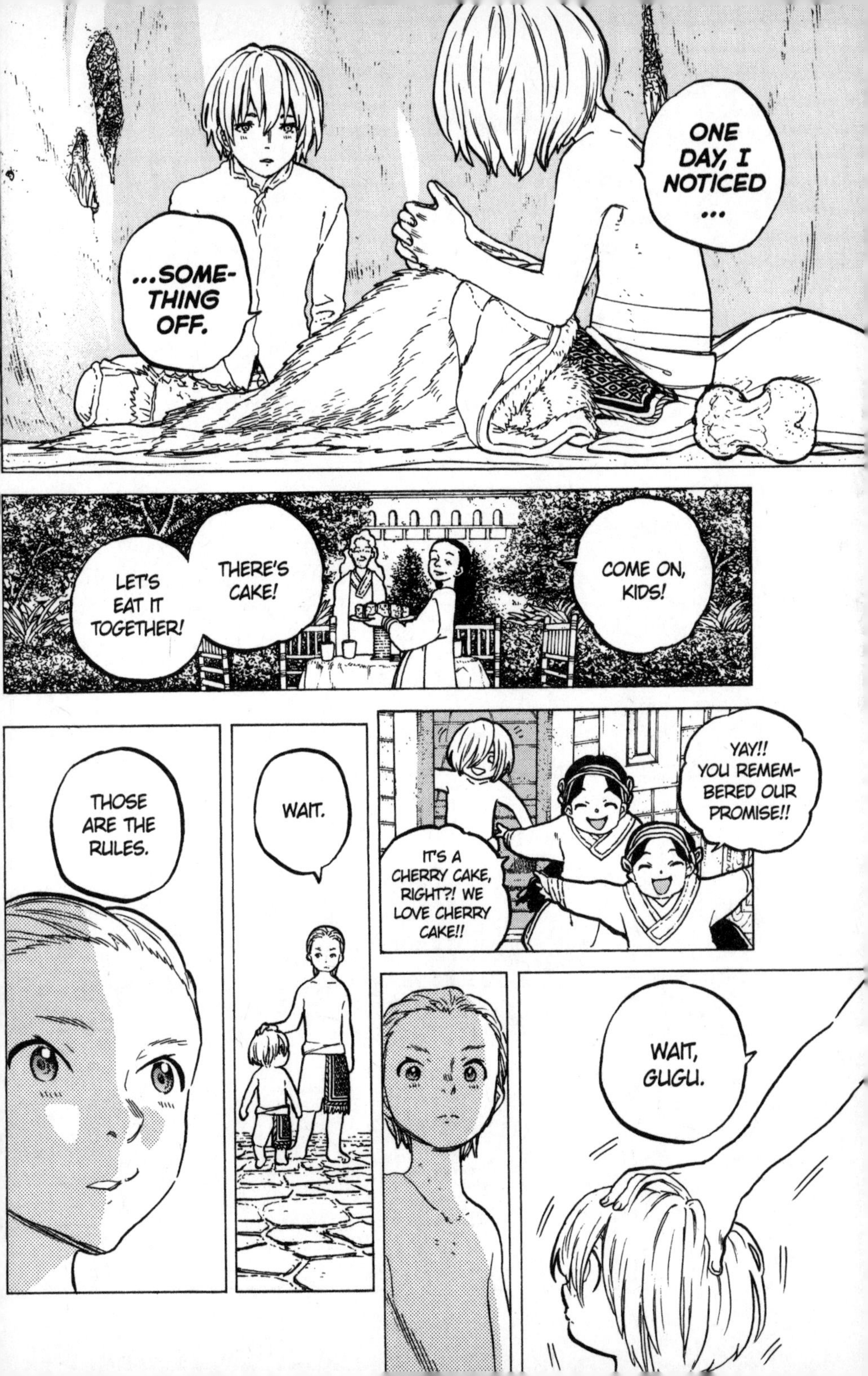
ONE DAY, I NOTICED ...
...SOME-THING OFF.
COME ON, KIDS!
THERE'S CAKE!
LET'S EAT IT TOGETHER!
YAY!! YOU REMEM-BERED OUR PROMISE!!
IT'S A CHERRY CAKE, RIGHT?! WE LOVE CHERRY CAKE!!
WAIT, GUGU.
WAIT.
THOSE ARE THE RULES.

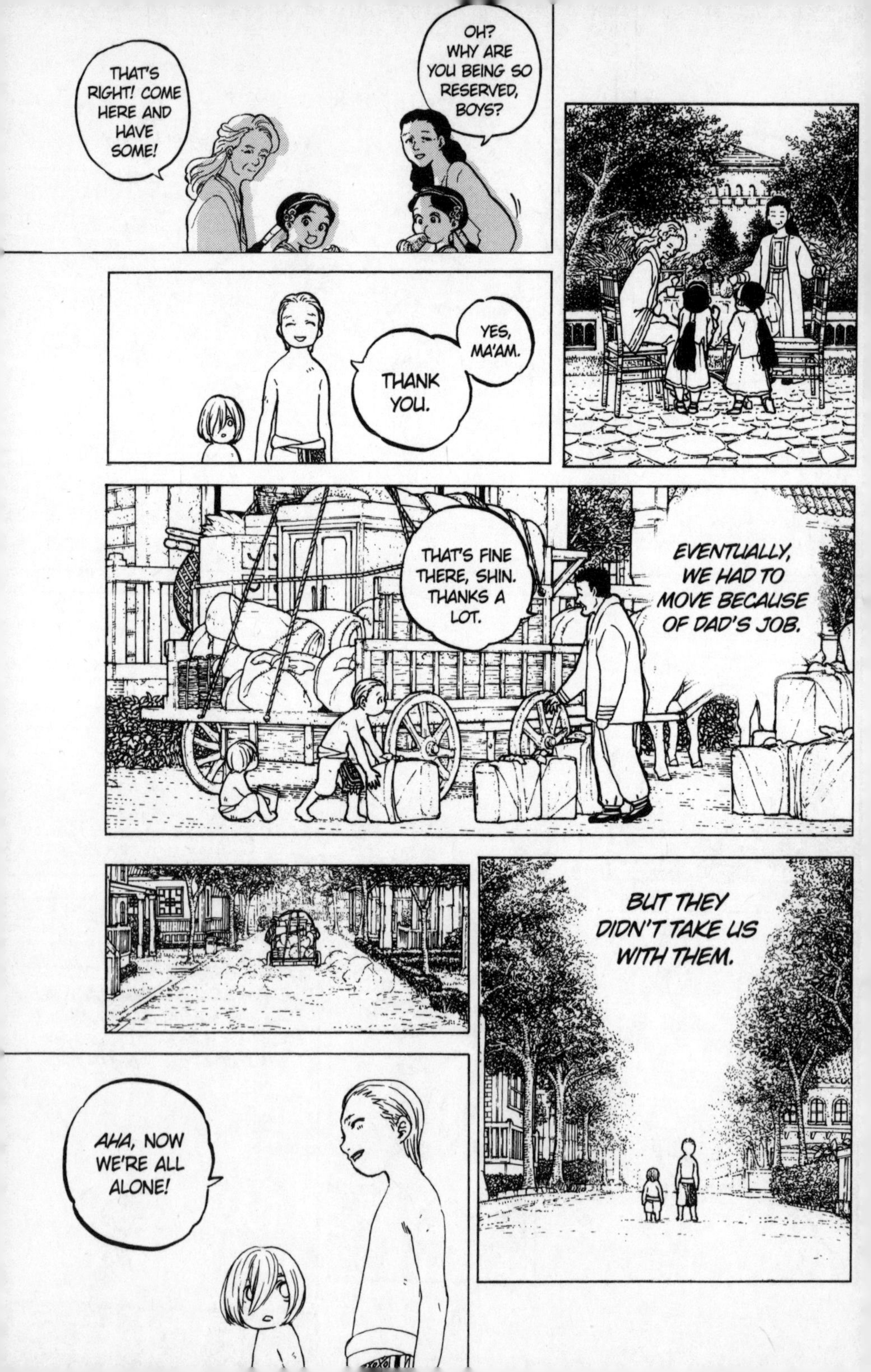
OH? WHY ARE YOU BEING SO RESERVED, BOYS?
THAT'S RIGHT! COME HERE AND HAVE SOME!
YES, MA'AM.
THANK YOU.
EVENTUALLY, WE HAD TO MOVE BECAUSE OF DAD'S JOB.
THAT'S FINE THERE, SHIN. THANKS A LOT.
BUT THEY DIDN'T TAKE US WITH THEM.
AHA, NOW WE'RE ALL ALONE!

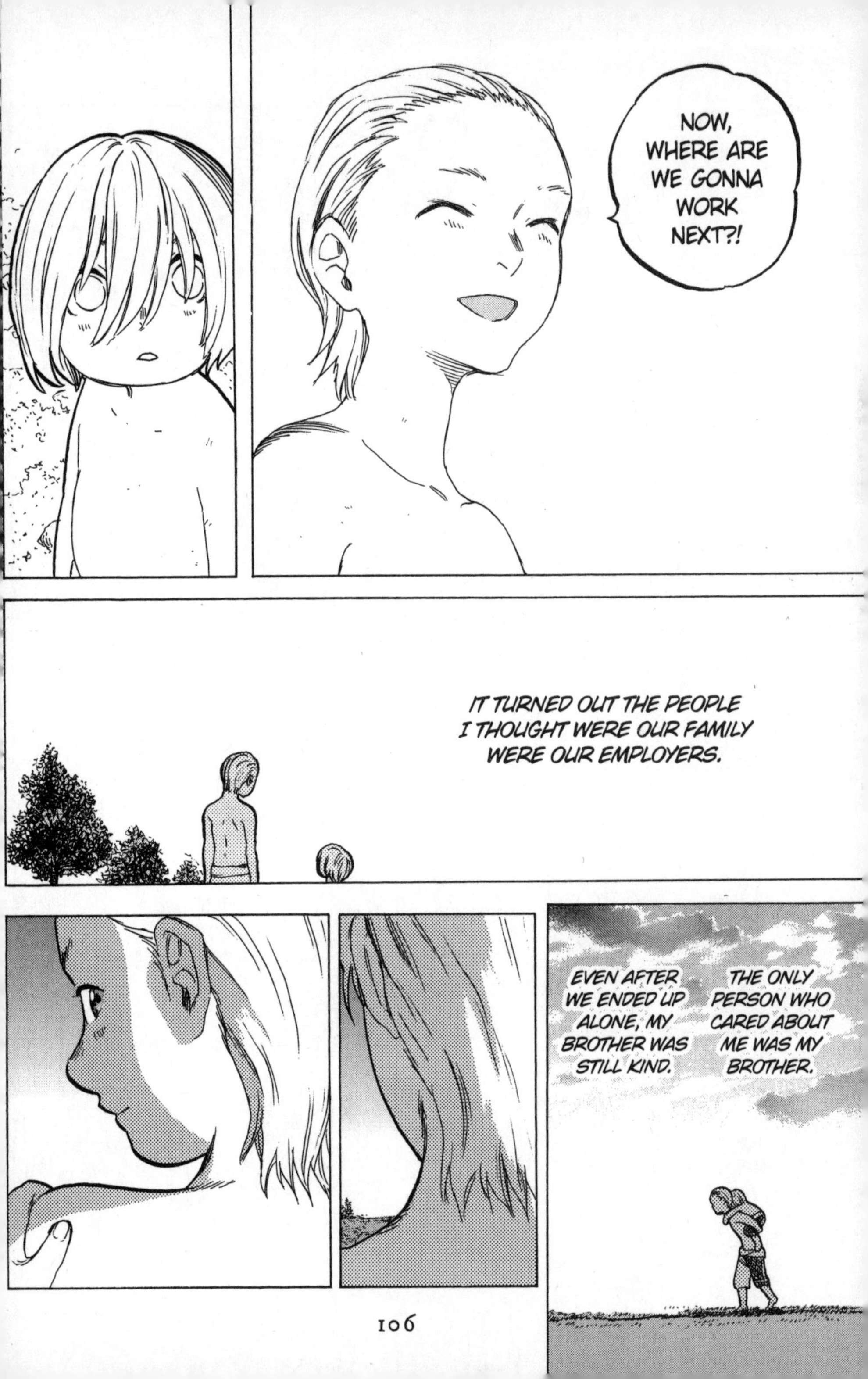
NOW, WHERE ARE WE GONNA WORK NEXT?!
IT TURNED OUT THE PEOPLE I THOUGHT WERE OUR FAMILY WERE OUR EMPLOYERS.
THE ONLY PERSON WHO CARED ABOUT ME WAS MY BROTHER.
EVEN AFTER WE ENDED UP ALONE, MY BROTHER WAS STILL KIND.

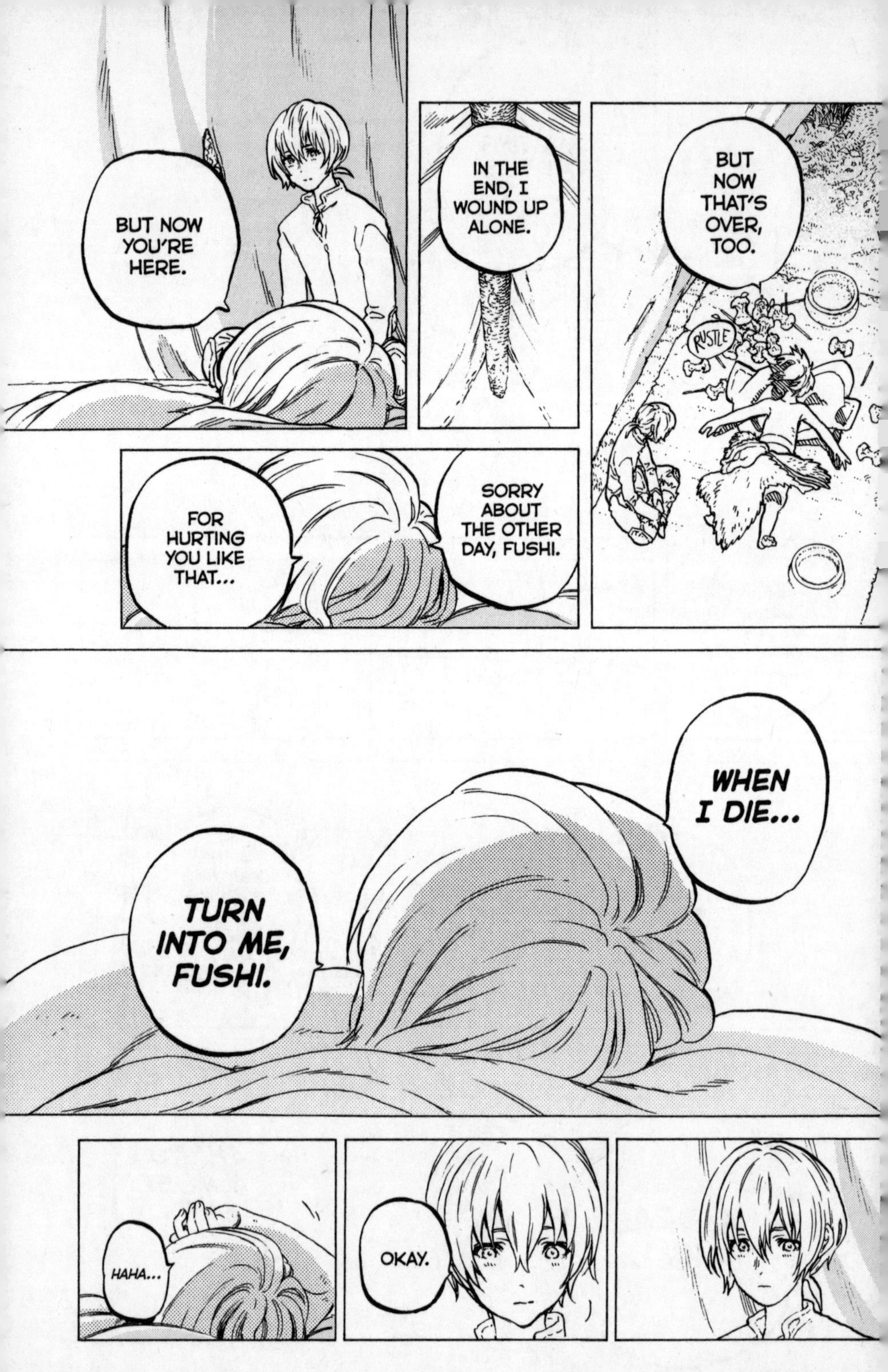
BUT NOW THAT'S OVER, TOO.
RUSTLE
IN THE END, I WOUND UP ALONE.
BUT NOW YOU'RE HERE.
SORRY ABOUT THE OTHER DAY, FUSHI.
FOR HURTING YOU LIKE THAT...
WHEN I DIE...
TURN INTO ME, FUSHI.
OKAY.
HAHA...

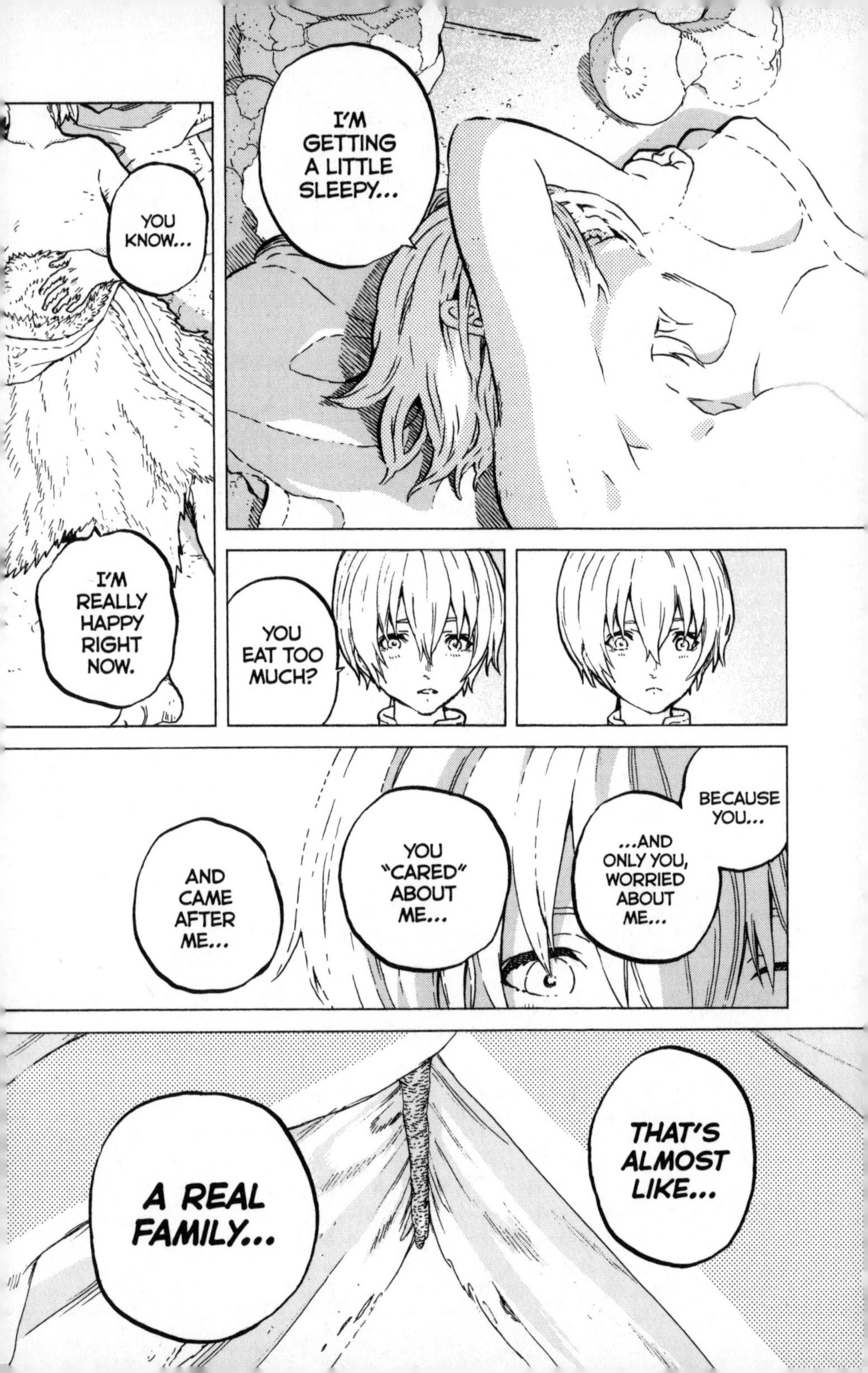
I'M GETTING A LITTLE SLEEPY...
YOU EAT TOO MUCH?
YOU KNOW...
I'M REALLY HAPPY RIGHT NOW.
BECAUSE YOU...
...AND ONLY YOU, WORRIED ABOUT ME...
YOU "CARED" ABOUT ME...
AND CAME AFTER ME...
THAT'S ALMOST LIKE...
A REAL FAMILY...

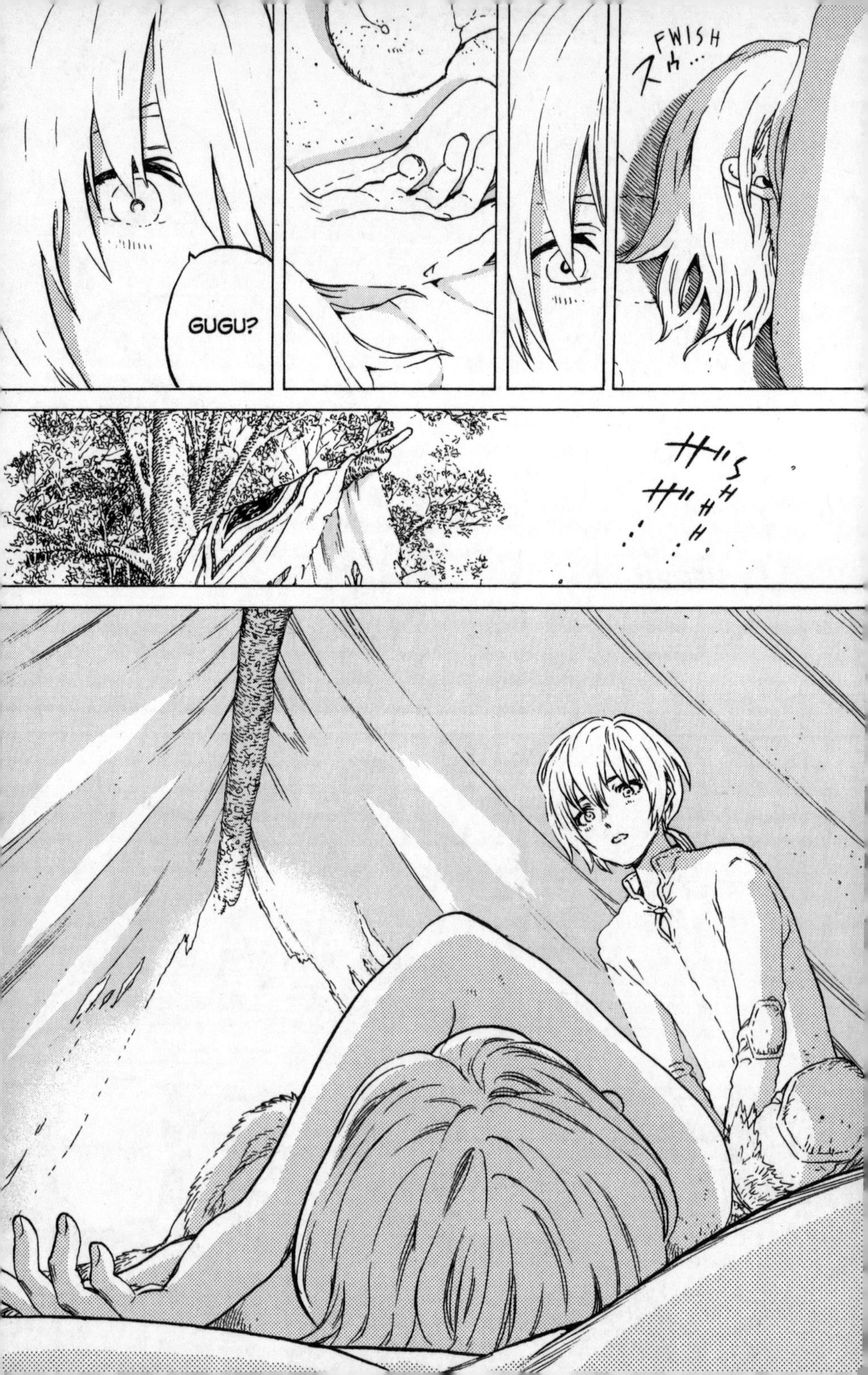
FWISH
GUGU?
SHHHH

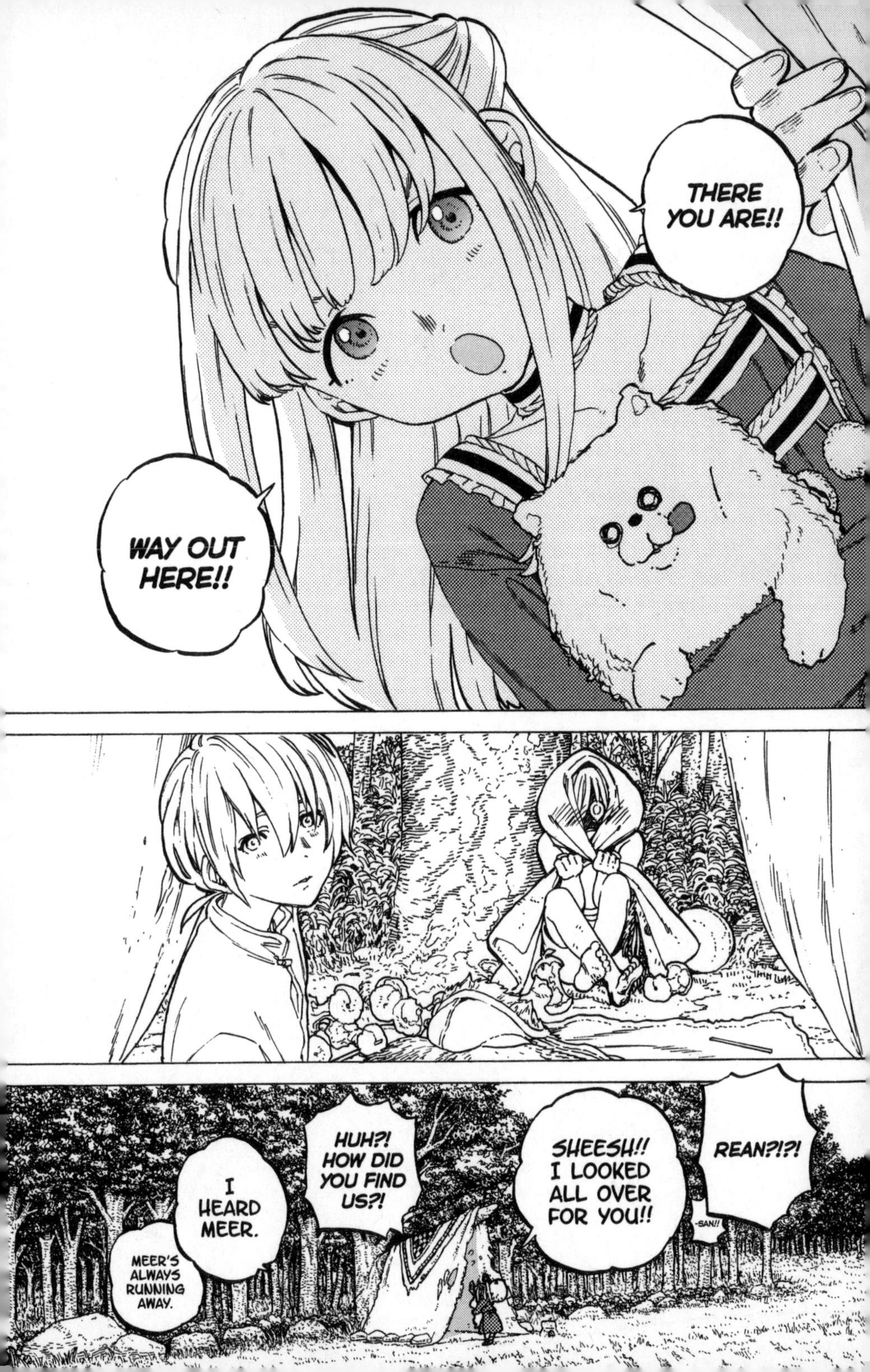
THERE YOU ARE!!
WAY OUT HERE!!
REAN?!?!
-SAN!!
SHEESH!! I LOOKED ALL OVER FOR YOU!!
HUH?! HOW DID YOU FIND US?!
I HEARD MEER.
MEER'S ALWAYS RUNNING AWAY.

#20 The Exterior of Humans and 'Monsters'

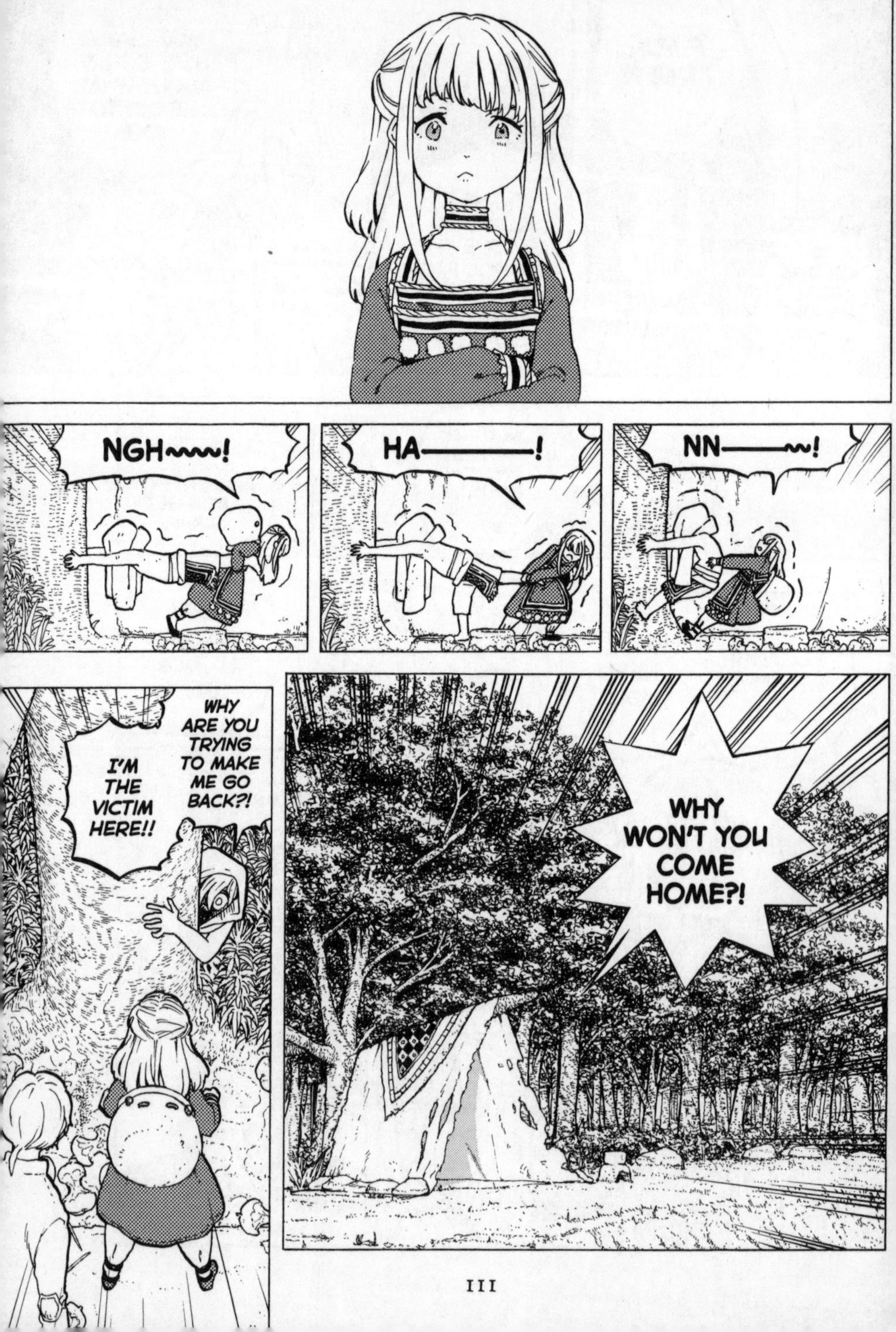
NN———~!
HA————!
NGH~~~!
WHY WON'T YOU COME HOME?!
WHY ARE YOU TRYING TO MAKE ME GO BACK?!
I'M THE VICTIM HERE!!

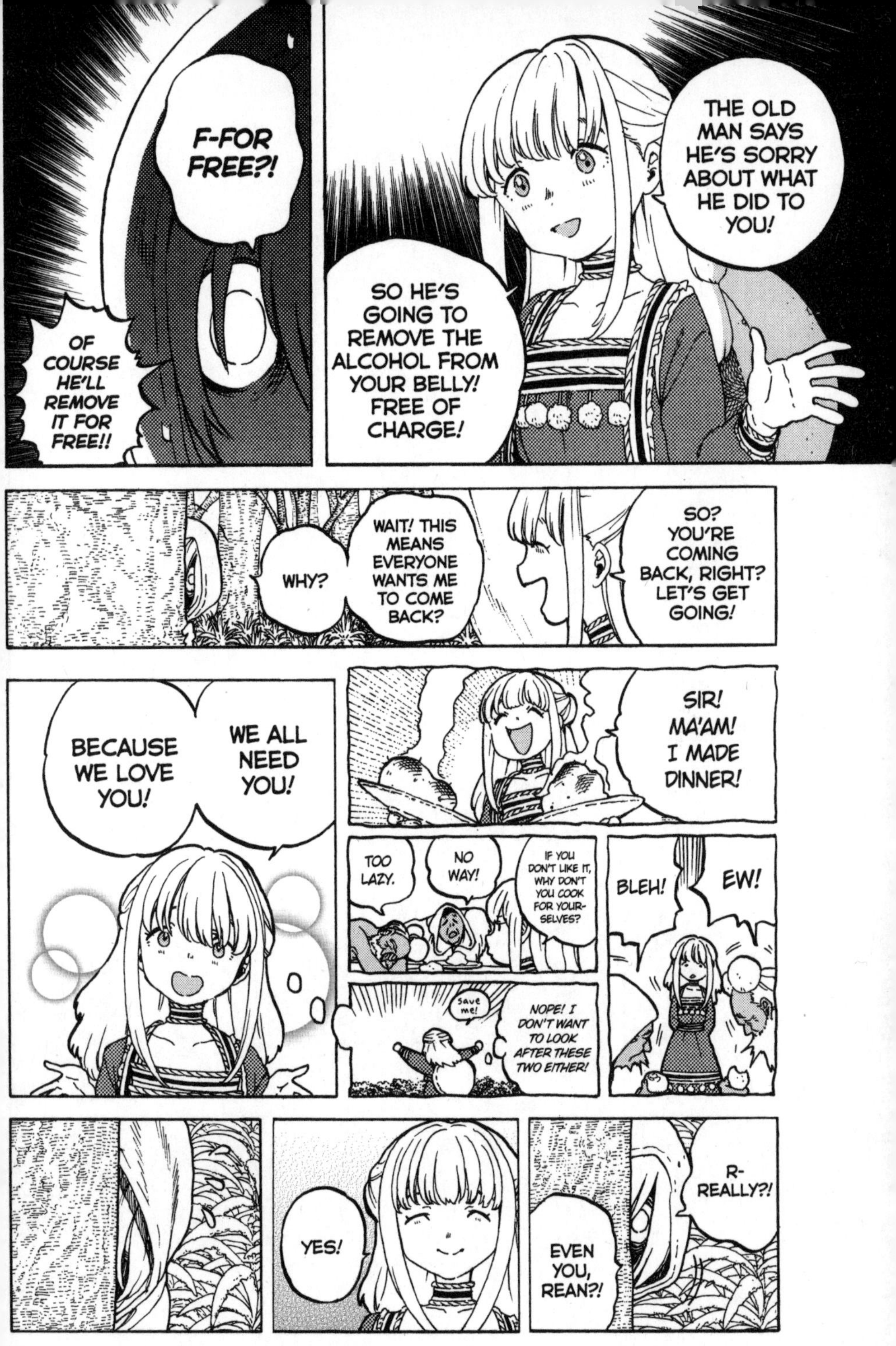
THE OLD MAN SAYS HE'S SORRY ABOUT WHAT HE DID TO YOU!
SO HE'S GOING TO REMOVE THE ALCOHOL FROM YOUR BELLY! FREE OF CHARGE!
F-FOR FREE?!
OF COURSE HE'LL REMOVE IT FOR FREE!!
SO? YOU'RE COMING BACK, RIGHT? LET'S GET GOING!
WAIT! THIS MEANS EVERYONE WANTS ME TO COME BACK?
WHY?
SIR! MA'AM! I MADE DINNER!
EW!
BLEH!
IF YOU DON'T LIKE IT, WHY DON'T YOU COOK FOR YOUR-SELVES?
NO WAY!
TOO LAZY.
NOPE! I DON'T WANT TO LOOK AFTER THESE TWO EITHER!
Save me!
WE ALL NEED YOU!
BECAUSE WE LOVE YOU!
R-REALLY?!
EVEN YOU, REAN?!
YES!

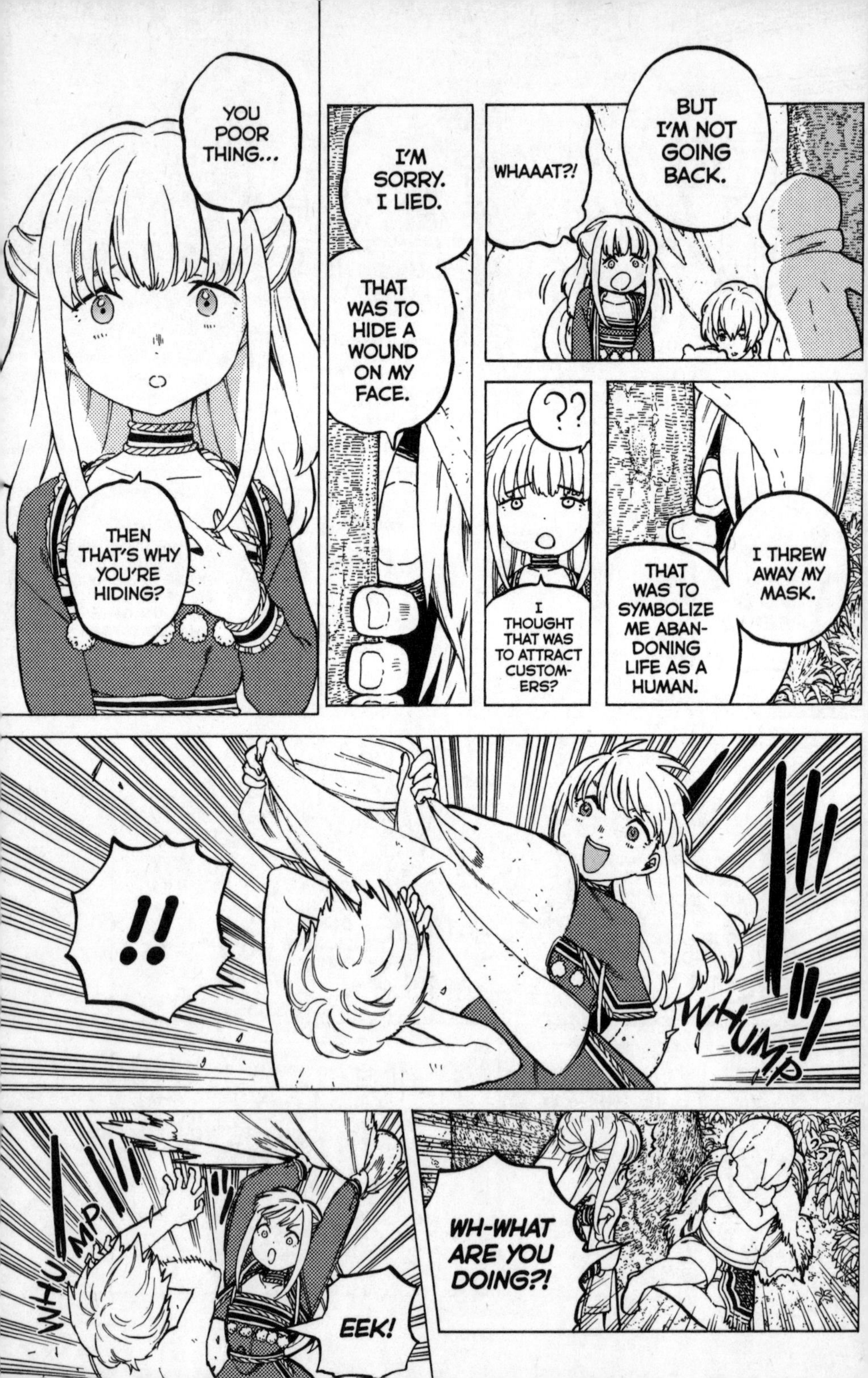
BUT I'M NOT GOING BACK.
WHAAAT?!
I THREW AWAY MY MASK.
THAT WAS TO SYMBOLIZE ME ABAN-DONING LIFE AS A HUMAN.
??
I THOUGHT THAT WAS TO ATTRACT CUSTOM-ERS?
I'M SORRY. I LIED.
THAT WAS TO HIDE A WOUND ON MY FACE.
YOU POOR THING...
THEN THAT'S WHY YOU'RE HIDING?
WHUMP
!!
WH-WHAT ARE YOU DOING?!
WHUMP
EEK!

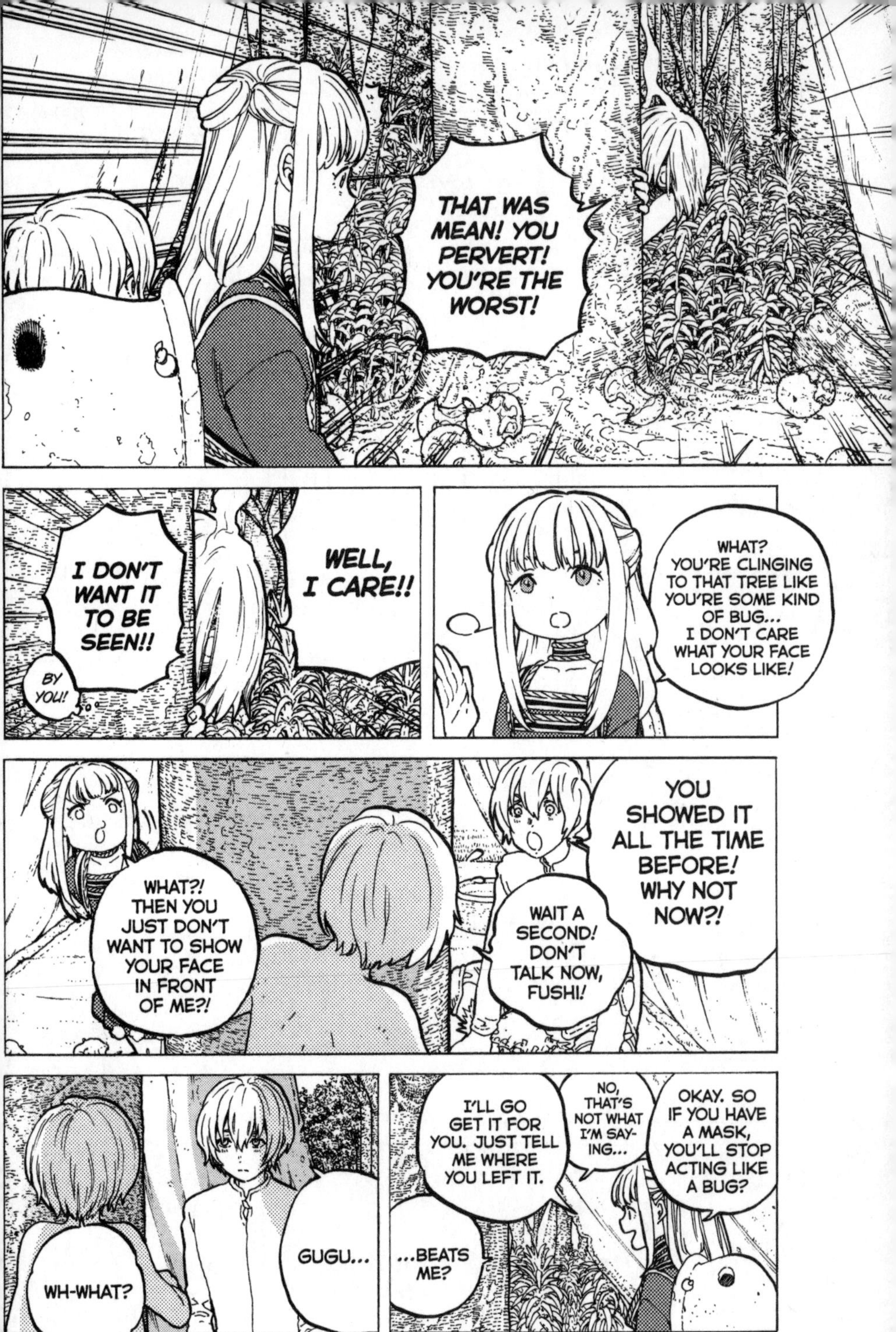
THAT WAS MEAN! YOU PERVERT! YOU'RE THE WORST!
WHAT? YOU'RE CLINGING TO THAT TREE LIKE YOU'RE SOME KIND OF BUG... I DON'T CARE WHAT YOUR FACE LOOKS LIKE!
WELL, I CARE!!
I DON'T WANT IT TO BE SEEN!!
BY YOU!
YOU SHOWED IT ALL THE TIME BEFORE! WHY NOT NOW?!
WAIT A SECOND! DON'T TALK NOW, FUSHI!
WHAT?! THEN YOU JUST DON'T WANT TO SHOW YOUR FACE IN FRONT OF ME?!
OKAY. SO IF YOU HAVE A MASK, YOU'LL STOP ACTING LIKE A BUG?
NO, THAT'S NOT WHAT I'M SAY-ING...
I'LL GO GET IT FOR YOU. JUST TELL ME WHERE YOU LEFT IT.
...BEATS ME?
GUGU...
WH-WHAT?

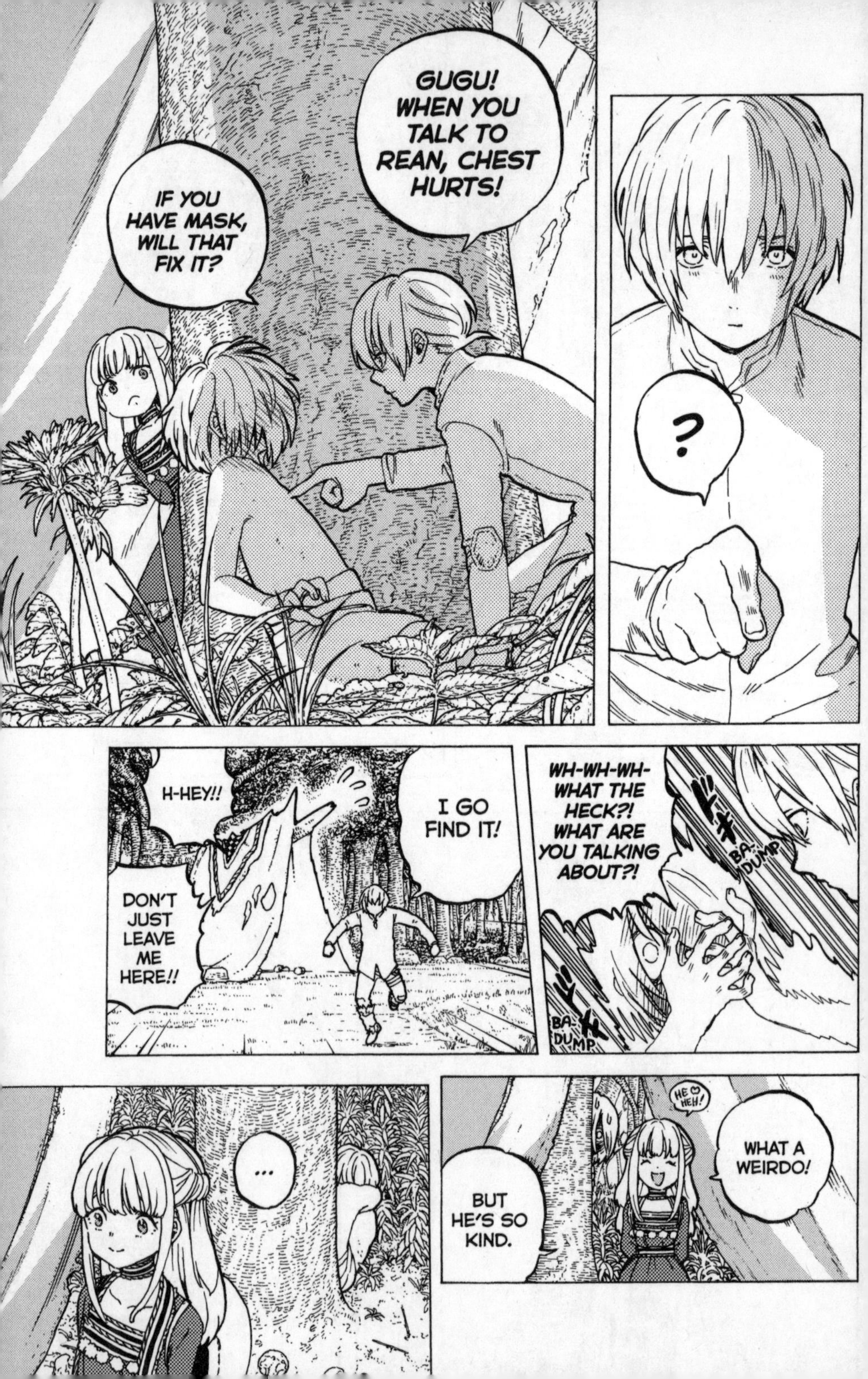
?
GUGU! WHEN YOU TALK TO REAN, CHEST HURTS!
IF YOU HAVE MASK, WILL THAT FIX IT?
WH-WH-WH-WHAT THE HECK?! WHAT ARE YOU TALKING ABOUT?!
BA-DUMP
BA-DUMP
I GO FIND IT!
H-HEY!!
DON'T JUST LEAVE ME HERE!!
HE♡ HEH!
WHAT A WEIRDO!
BUT HE'S SO KIND.
...

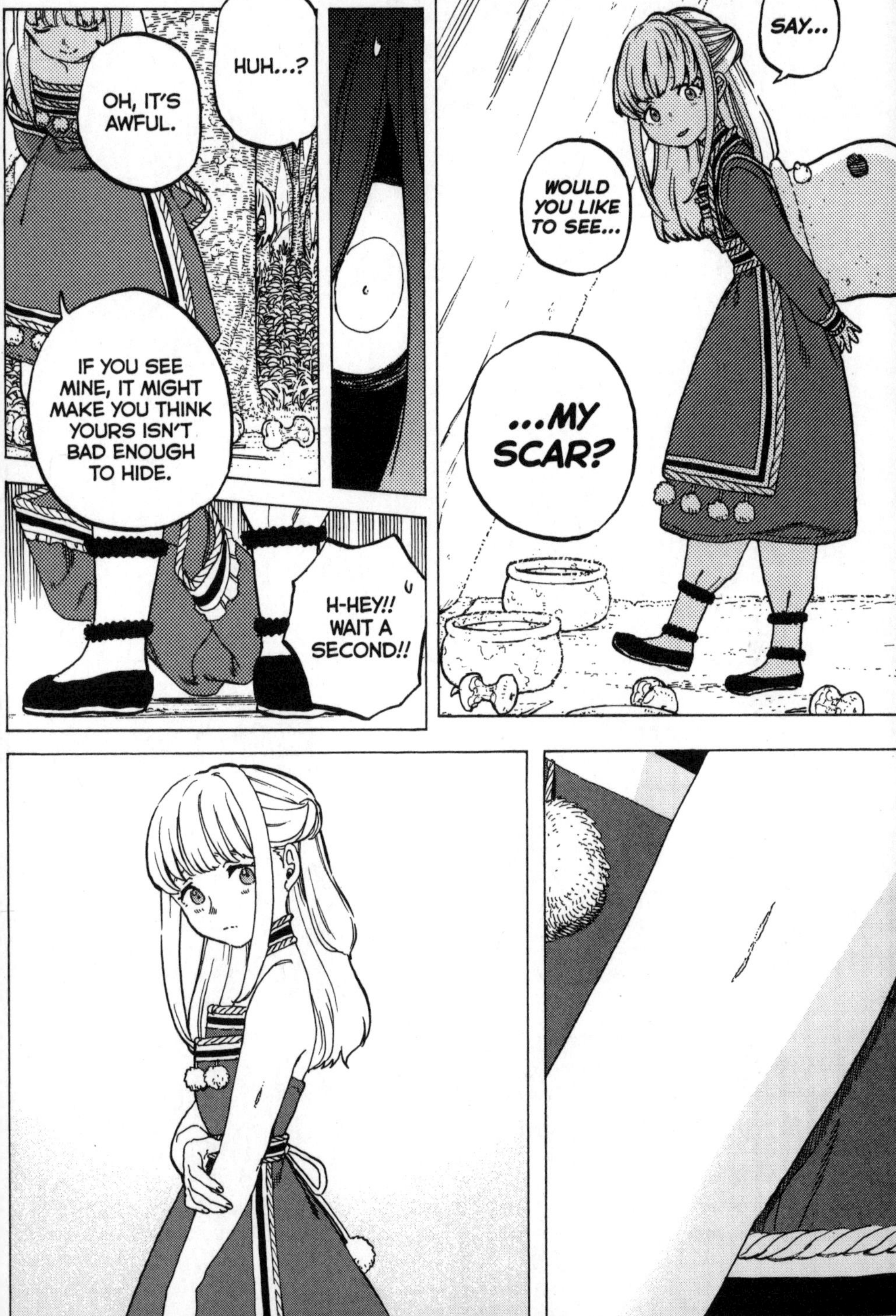
SAY...
WOULD YOU LIKE TO SEE...
...MY SCAR?
HUH...?
OH, IT'S AWFUL.
IF YOU SEE MINE, IT MIGHT MAKE YOU THINK YOURS ISN'T BAD ENOUGH TO HIDE.
H-HEY!! WAIT A SECOND!!

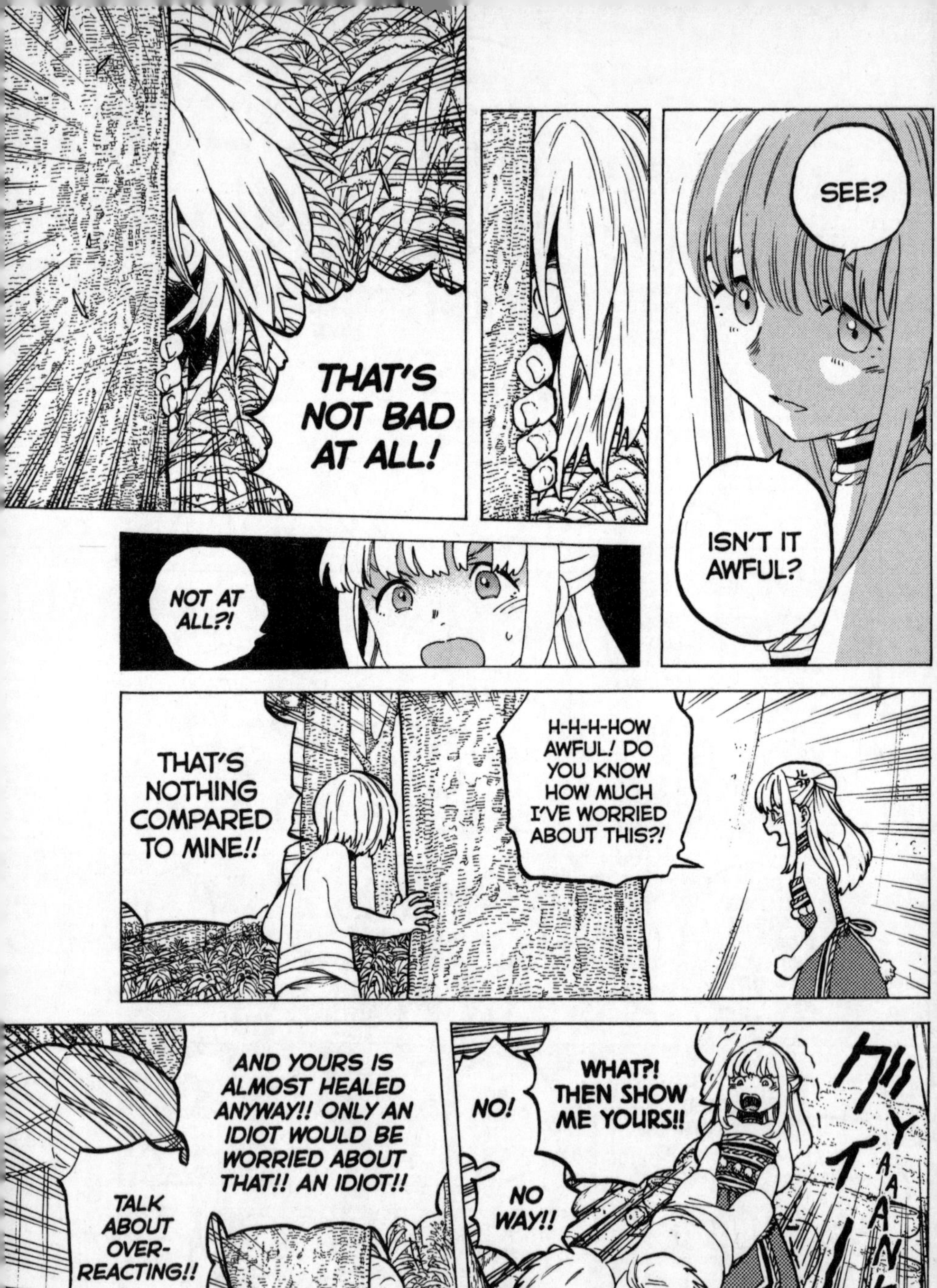
SEE?
ISN'T IT AWFUL?
THAT'S NOT BAD AT ALL!
NOT AT ALL?!
H-H-H-HOW AWFUL! DO YOU KNOW HOW MUCH I'VE WORRIED ABOUT THIS?!
THAT'S NOTHING COMPARED TO MINE!!
グイ
YAAANK!!
WHAT?! THEN SHOW ME YOURS!!
NO!
NO WAY!!
AND YOURS IS ALMOST HEALED ANYWAY!! ONLY AN IDIOT WOULD BE WORRIED ABOUT THAT!! AN IDIOT!!
TALK ABOUT OVER-REACTING!!

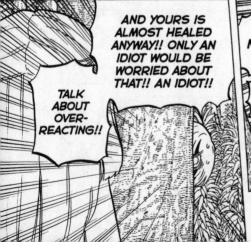

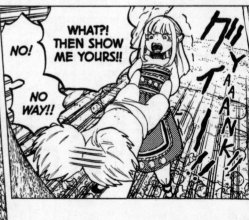

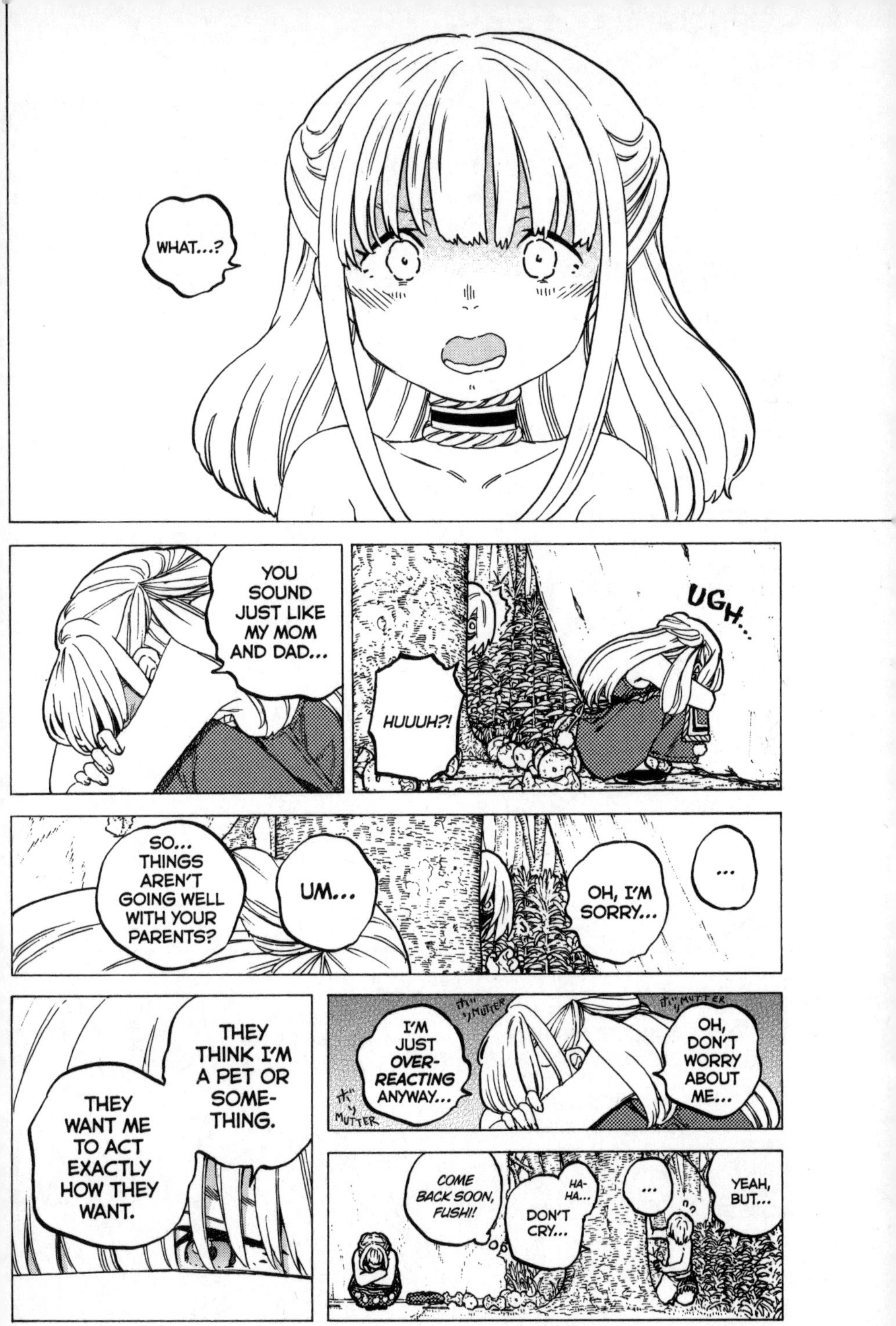
WHAT...?
UGH...
HUUUH?!
YOU SOUND JUST LIKE MY MOM AND DAD...
...
OH, I'M SORRY...
UM...
SO... THINGS AREN'T GOING WELL WITH YOUR PARENTS?
MUTTER
OH, DON'T WORRY ABOUT ME...
MUTTER
I'M JUST OVER-REACTING ANYWAY...
MUTTER
YEAH, BUT...
...
HA-HA... DON'T CRY...
COME BACK SOON, FUSHI!
THEY THINK I'M A PET OR SOME-THING.
THEY WANT ME TO ACT EXACTLY HOW THEY WANT.

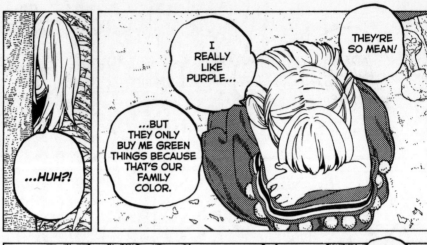

THEY'RE SO MEAN!
I REALLY LIKE PURPLE...
...BUT THEY ONLY BUY ME GREEN THINGS BECAUSE THAT'S OUR FAMILY COLOR.
...HUH?!
WHAT'S WRONG WITH GREEN?
THAT'S NOT THE ONLY THING.
AFTER SHE SAW A PICTURE I DREW, MOM HIRED AN ART INSTRUCTOR.
BUT I DIDN'T WANT A TEACHER, SO I STARTED DOING NEEDLEWORK INSTEAD. AND THIS TIME SHE HIRED A NEEDLEWORK INSTRUCTOR!!
I WANT TO DO THINGS ON MY OWN!
IN FACT, THERE WAS ALWAYS SOMEONE AROUND ME.
IF I SNEEZED, SOMEONE ALWAYS RAN UP TO CHECK ON ME.
EVEN WHEN I WASN'T HUNGRY, SOMEONE ALWAYS MADE ME EAT.
AND SOME-ONE ALWAYS BRUSHED MY HAIR FOUR TIMES A DAY.
AND EVEN WHEN I GOT FED UP WITH THAT AND WENT OUTSIDE, A MAID WOULD ALWAYS FOLLOW ME.
I THOUGHT I WOULD NEVER HAVE ANY ALONE TIME IN MY ENTIRE LIFE!

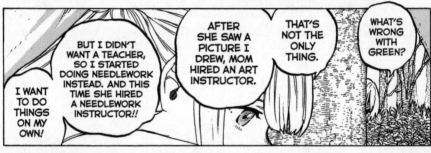

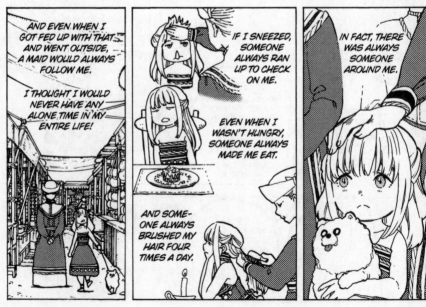

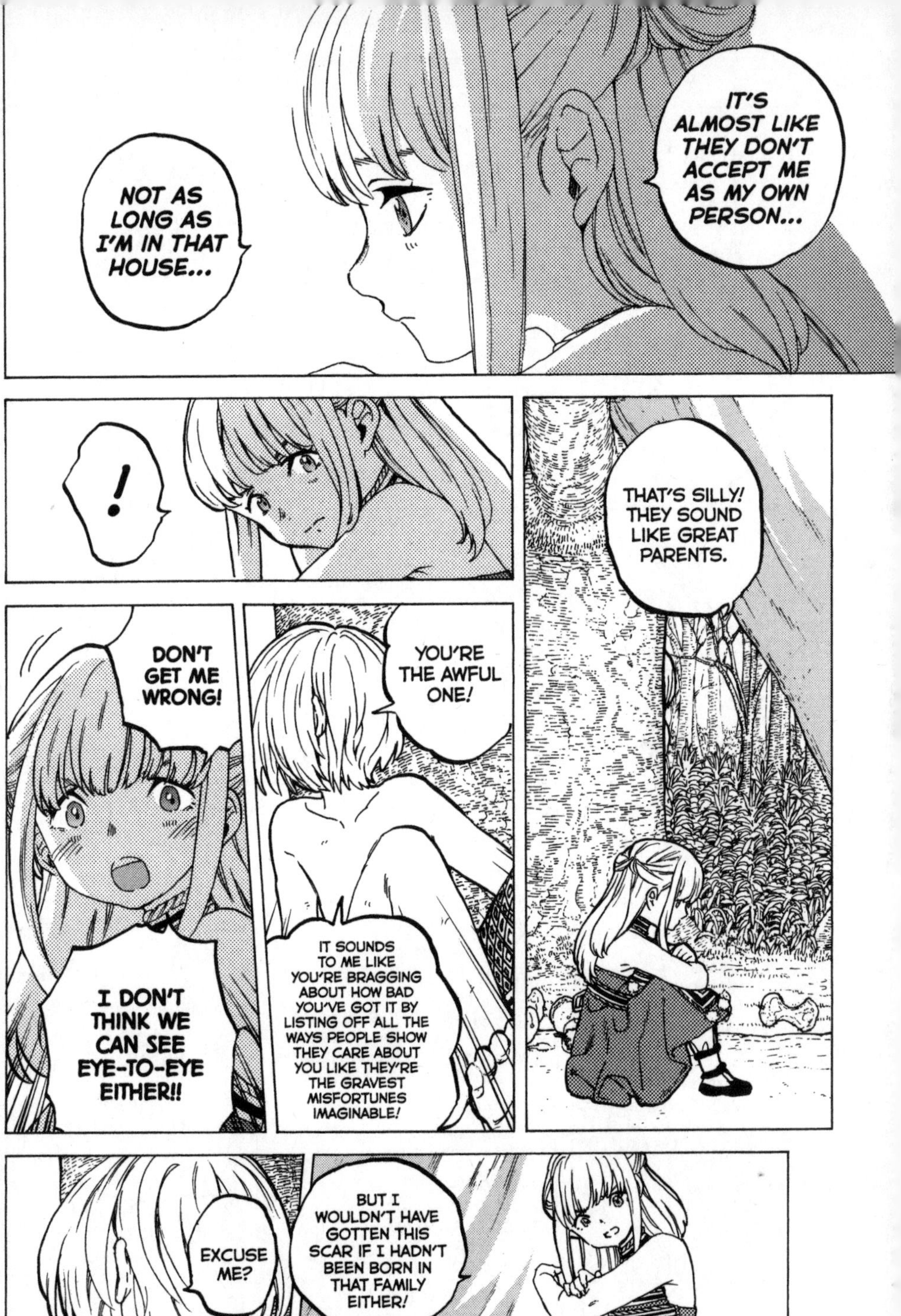
IT'S ALMOST LIKE THEY DON'T ACCEPT ME AS MY OWN PERSON...
NOT AS LONG AS I'M IN THAT HOUSE...
THAT'S SILLY! THEY SOUND LIKE GREAT PARENTS.
!
YOU'RE THE AWFUL ONE!
IT SOUNDS TO ME LIKE YOU'RE BRAGGING ABOUT HOW BAD YOU'VE GOT IT BY LISTING OFF ALL THE WAYS PEOPLE SHOW THEY CARE ABOUT YOU LIKE THEY'RE THE GRAVEST MISFORTUNES IMAGINABLE!
DON'T GET ME WRONG!
I DON'T THINK WE CAN SEE EYE-TO-EYE EITHER!!
BUT I WOULDN'T HAVE GOTTEN THIS SCAR IF I HADN'T BEEN BORN IN THAT FAMILY EITHER!
EXCUSE ME?

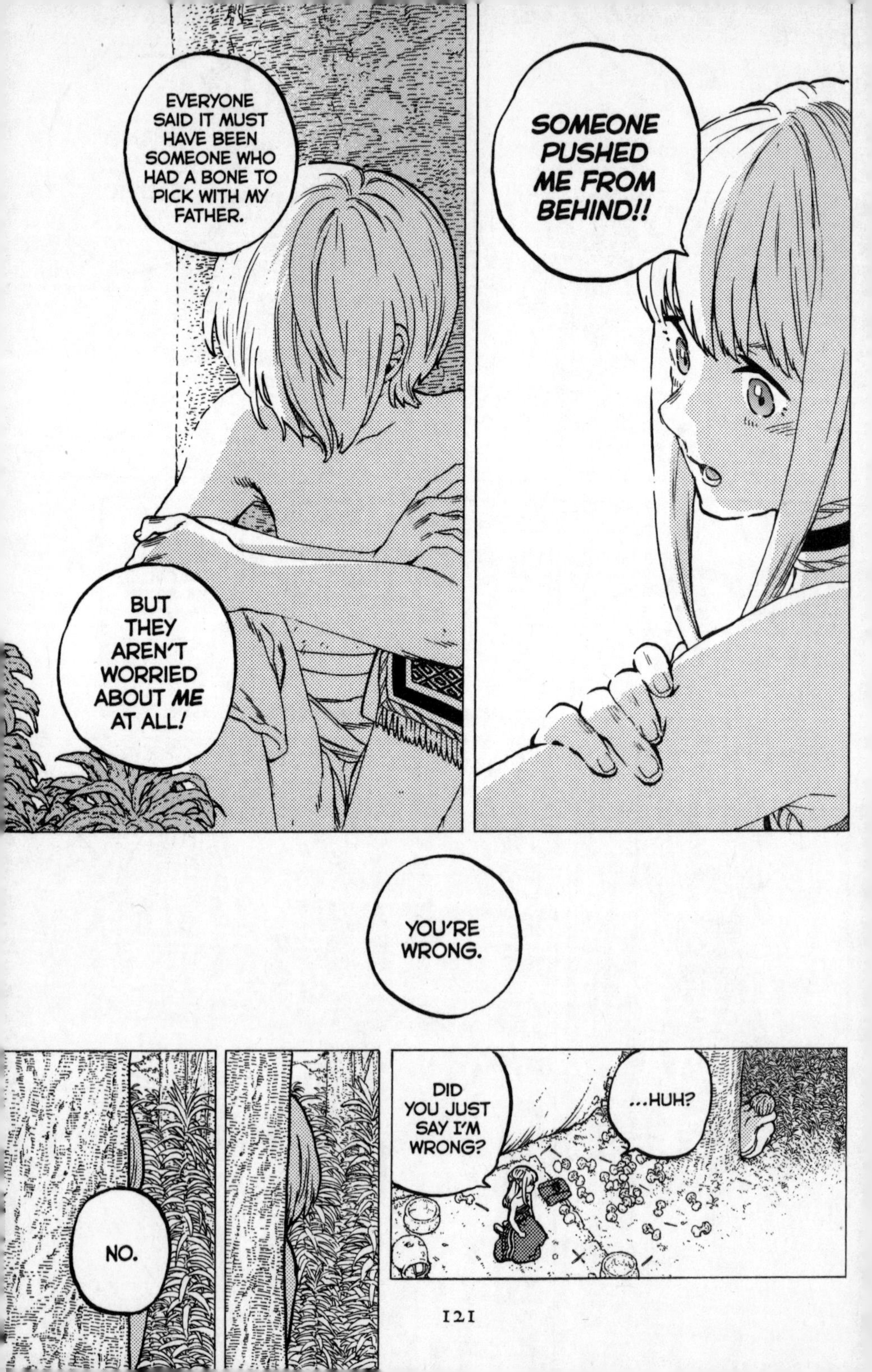
SOMEONE PUSHED ME FROM BEHIND!!
EVERYONE SAID IT MUST HAVE BEEN SOMEONE WHO HAD A BONE TO PICK WITH MY FATHER.
BUT THEY AREN'T WORRIED ABOUT *ME* AT ALL!
YOU'RE WRONG.
...HUH?
DID YOU JUST SAY I'M WRONG?
NO.

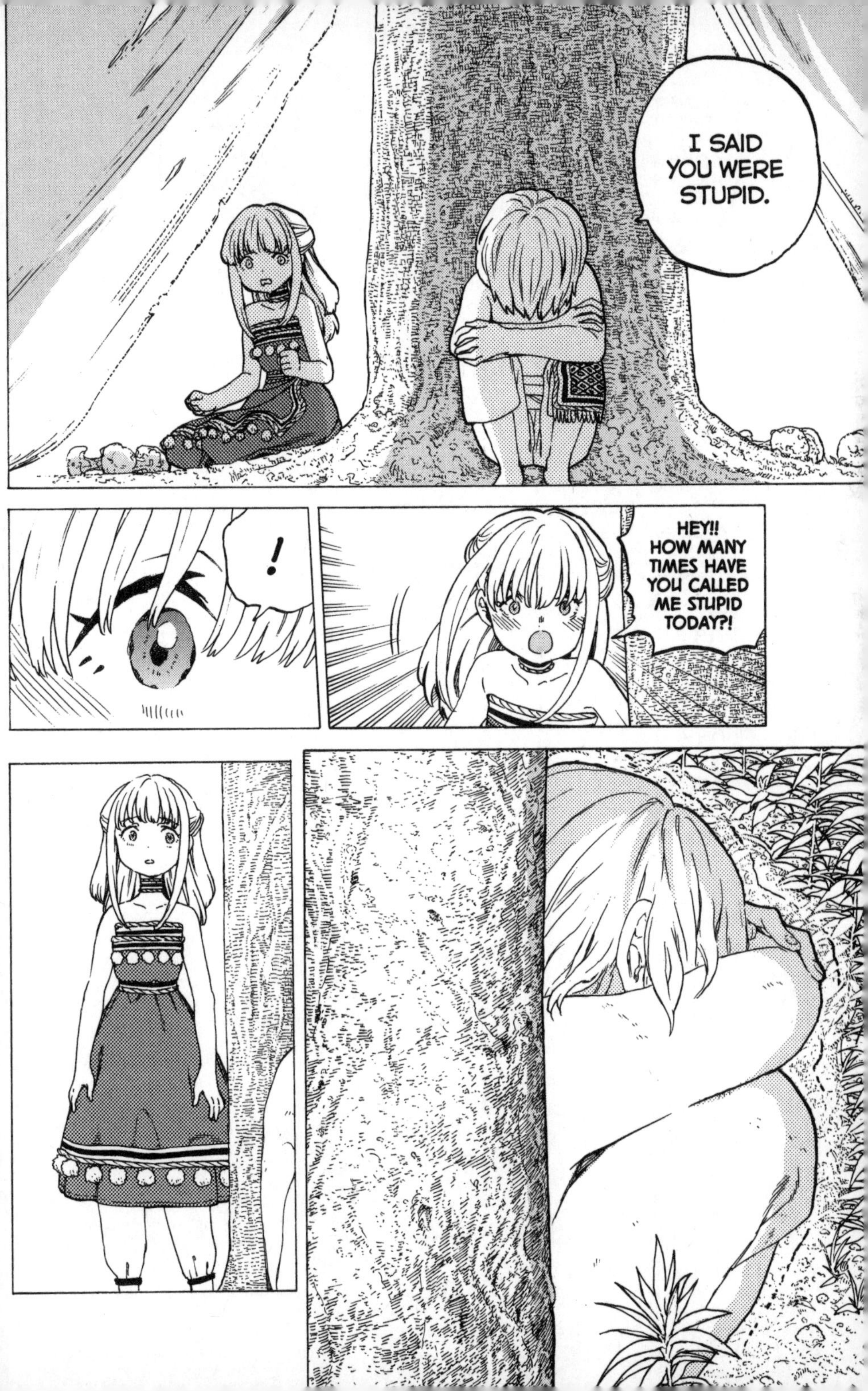
I SAID YOU WERE STUPID.
HEY!! HOW MANY TIMES HAVE YOU CALLED ME STUPID TODAY?!
!

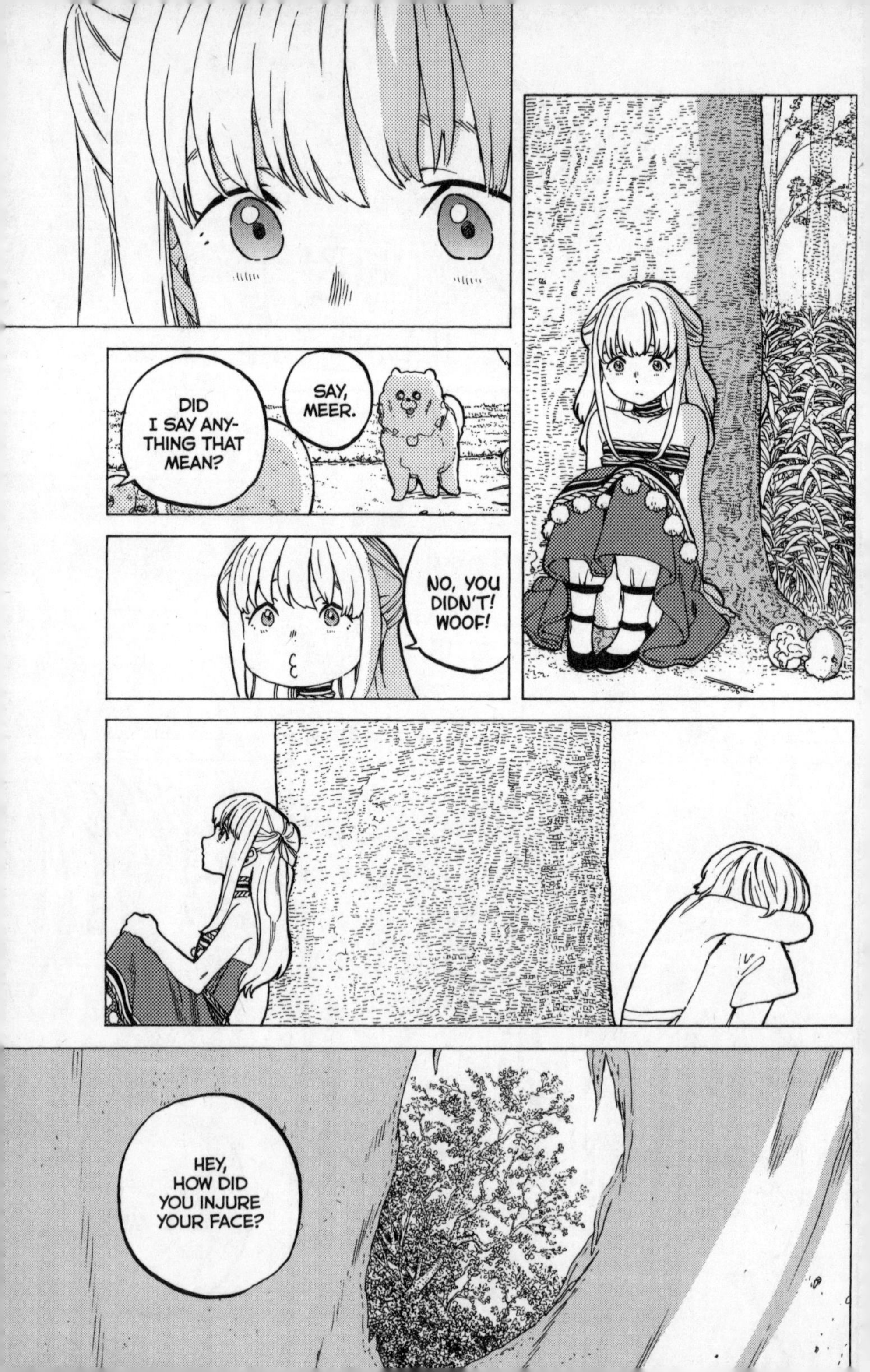
SAY, MEER.
DID I SAY ANYTHING THAT MEAN?
NO, YOU DIDN'T! WOOF!
HEY, HOW DID YOU INJURE YOUR FACE?

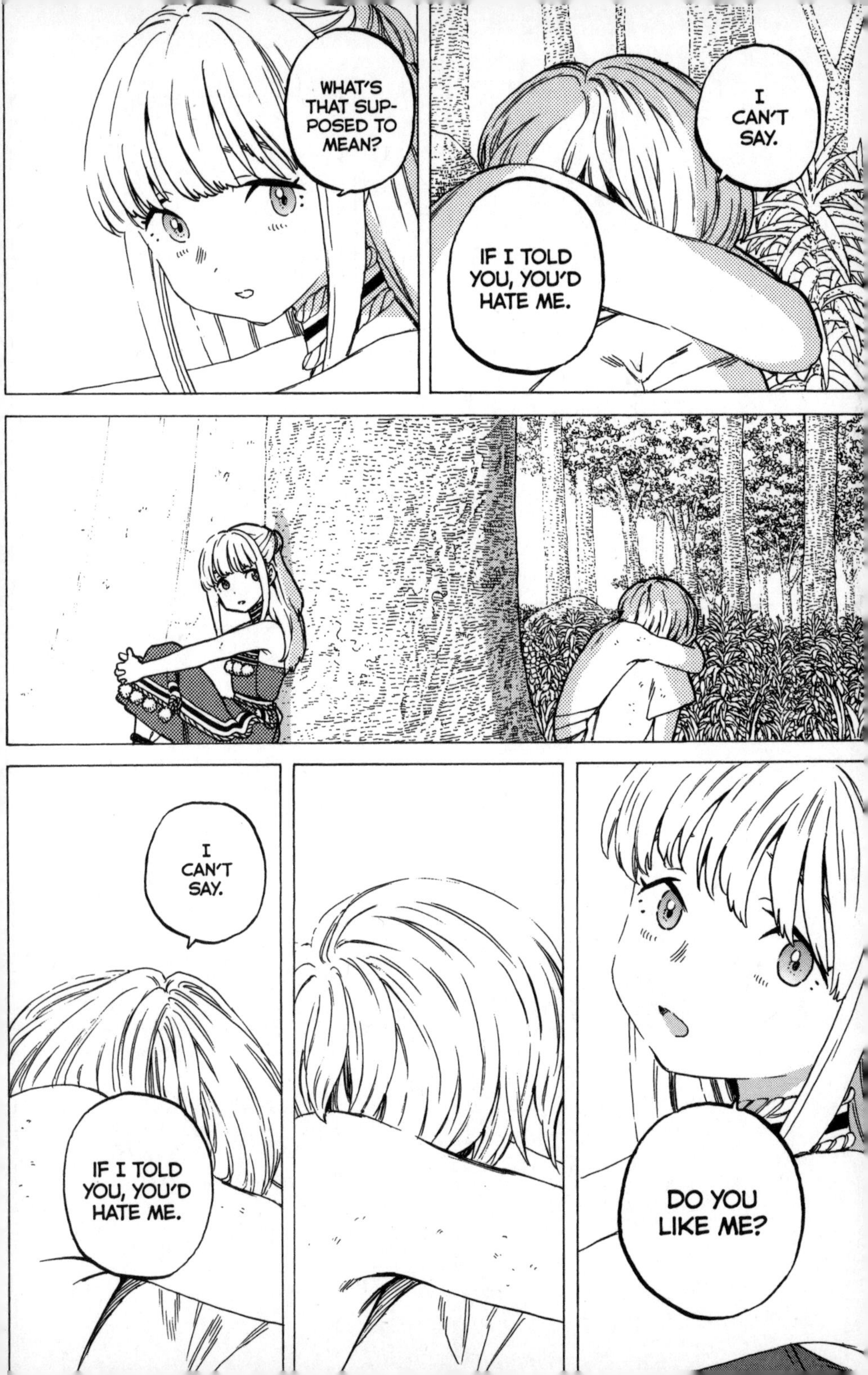
I CAN'T SAY.
IF I TOLD YOU, YOU'D HATE ME.
WHAT'S THAT SUP-POSED TO MEAN?
DO YOU LIKE ME?
I CAN'T SAY.
IF I TOLD YOU, YOU'D HATE ME.

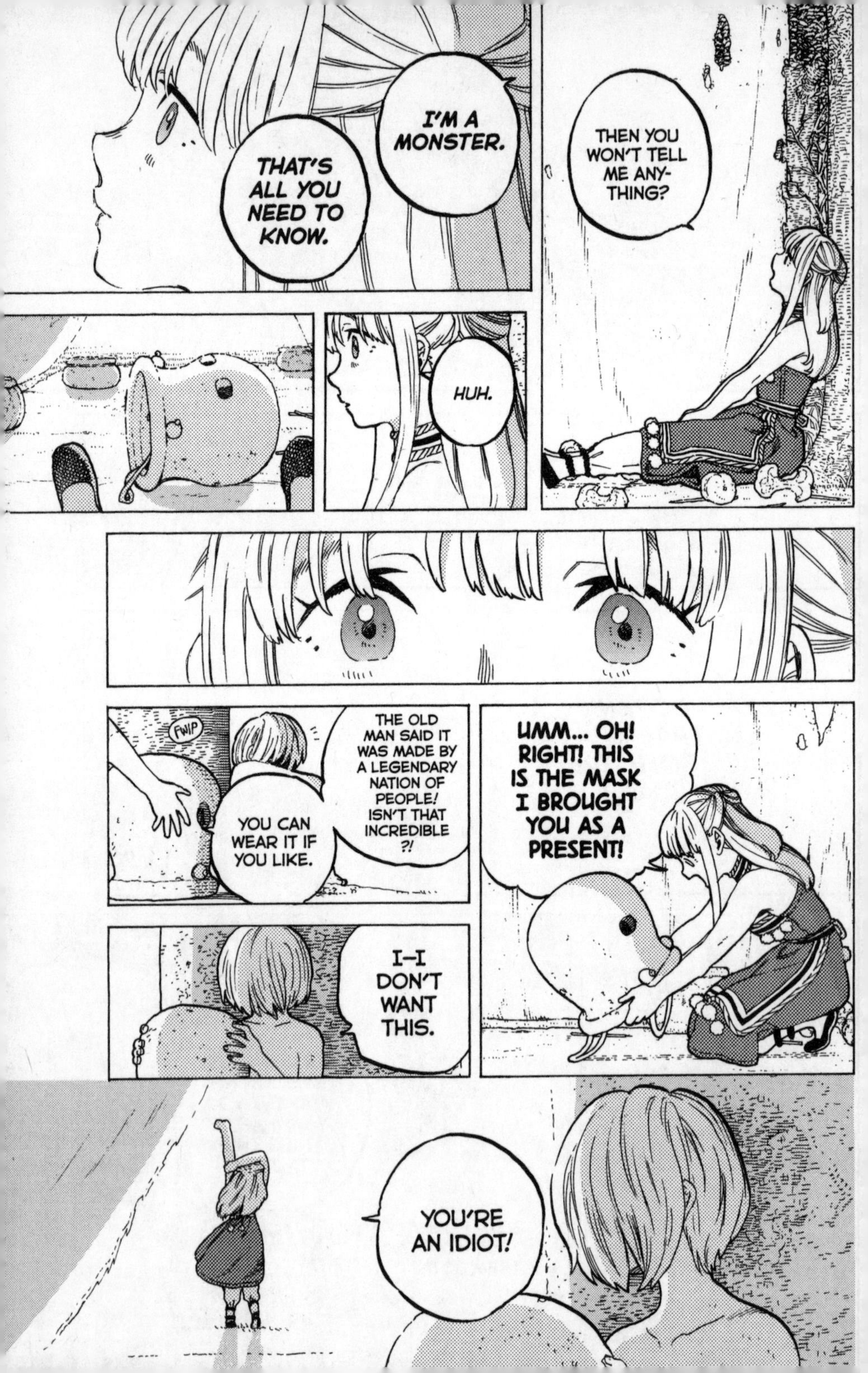
THEN YOU WON'T TELL ME ANY-THING?
I'M A MONSTER.
THAT'S ALL YOU NEED TO KNOW.
HUH.
UMM... OH! RIGHT! THIS IS THE MASK I BROUGHT YOU AS A PRESENT!
THE OLD MAN SAID IT WAS MADE BY A LEGENDARY NATION OF PEOPLE! ISN'T THAT INCREDIBLE ?!
FWIP
YOU CAN WEAR IT IF YOU LIKE.
I–I DON'T WANT THIS.
YOU'RE AN IDIOT!

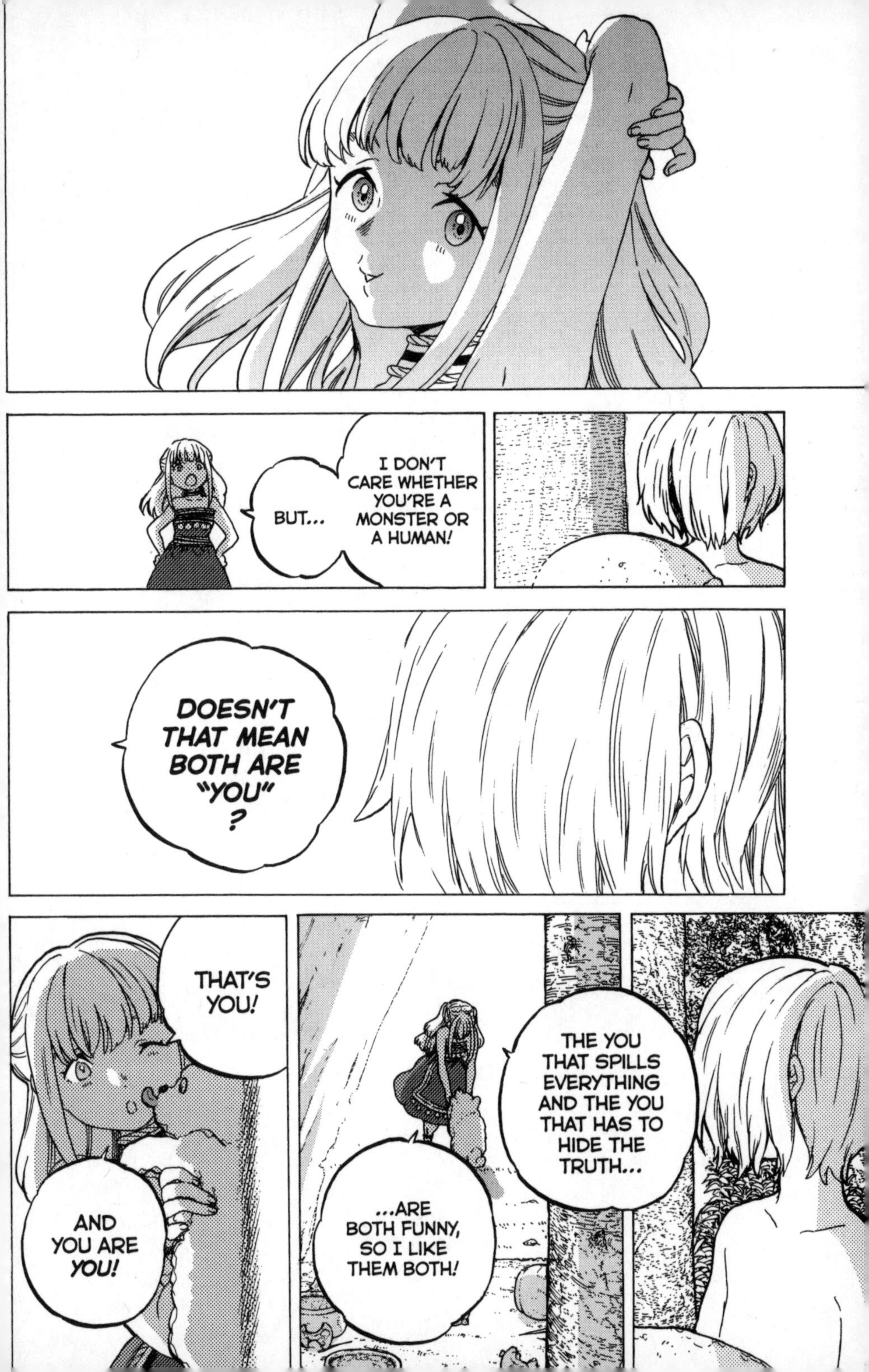
BUT...
I DON'T CARE WHETHER YOU'RE A MONSTER OR A HUMAN!
DOESN'T THAT MEAN BOTH ARE "YOU" ?
THE YOU THAT SPILLS EVERYTHING AND THE YOU THAT HAS TO HIDE THE TRUTH...
...ARE BOTH FUNNY, SO I LIKE THEM BOTH!
THAT'S YOU!
AND YOU ARE *YOU!*

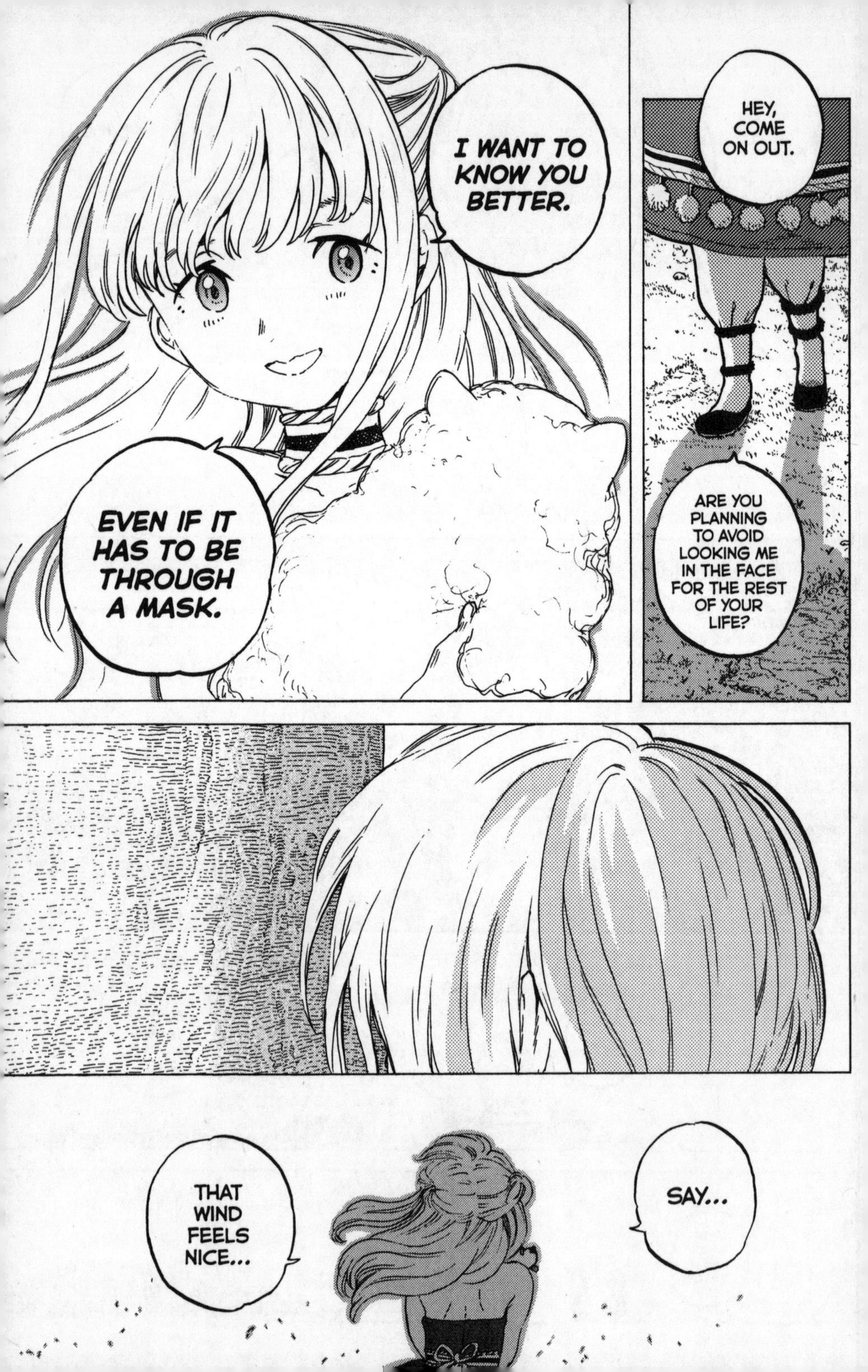
HEY, COME ON OUT.
ARE YOU PLANNING TO AVOID LOOKING ME IN THE FACE FOR THE REST OF YOUR LIFE?
I WANT TO KNOW YOU BETTER.
EVEN IF IT HAS TO BE THROUGH A MASK.
SAY...
THAT WIND FEELS NICE...

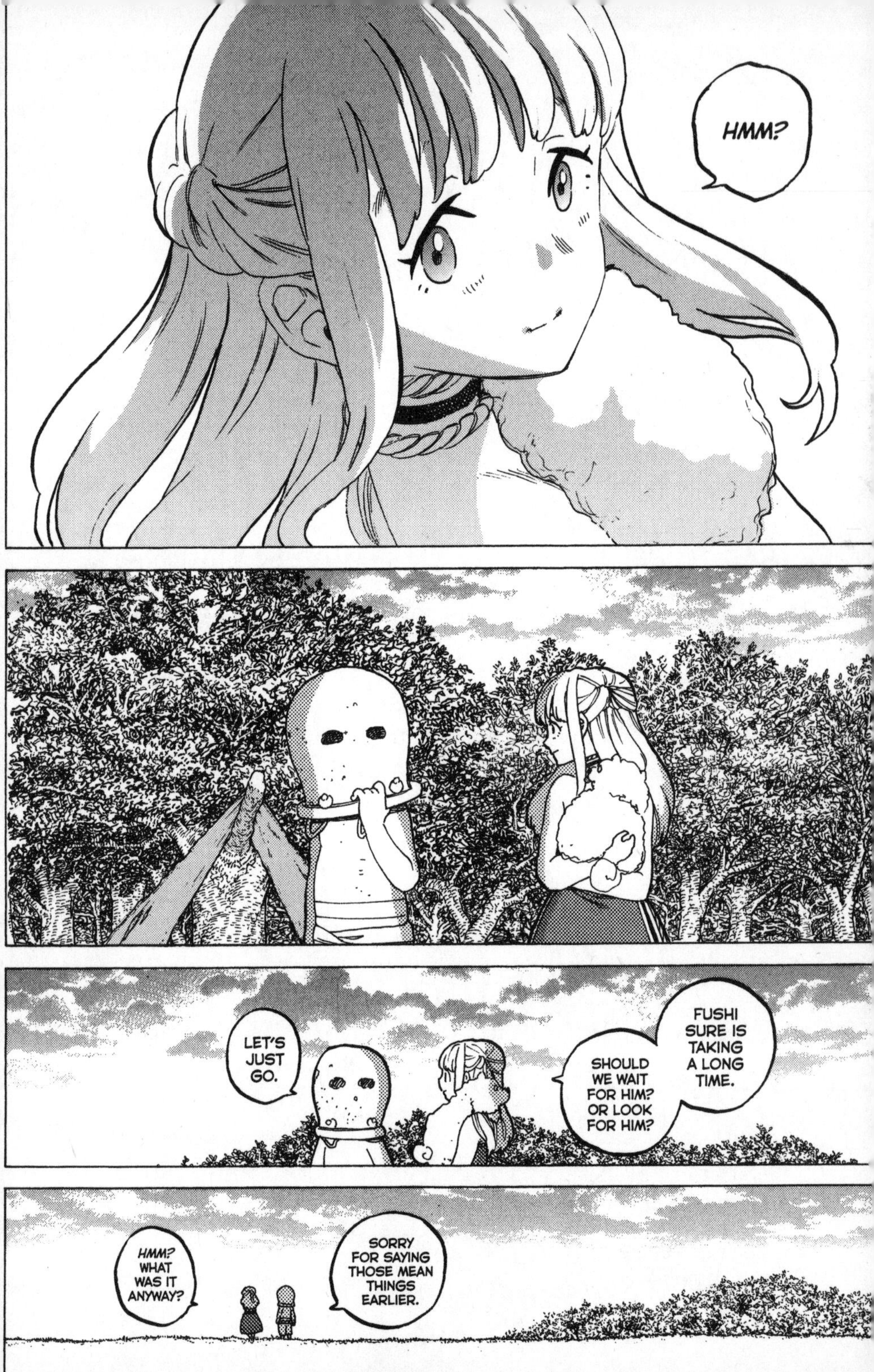
HMM?
FUSHI SURE IS TAKING A LONG TIME.
SHOULD WE WAIT FOR HIM? OR LOOK FOR HIM?
LET'S JUST GO.
SORRY FOR SAYING THOSE MEAN THINGS EARLIER.
HMM? WHAT WAS IT ANYWAY?

TO YOUR
ETERNITY

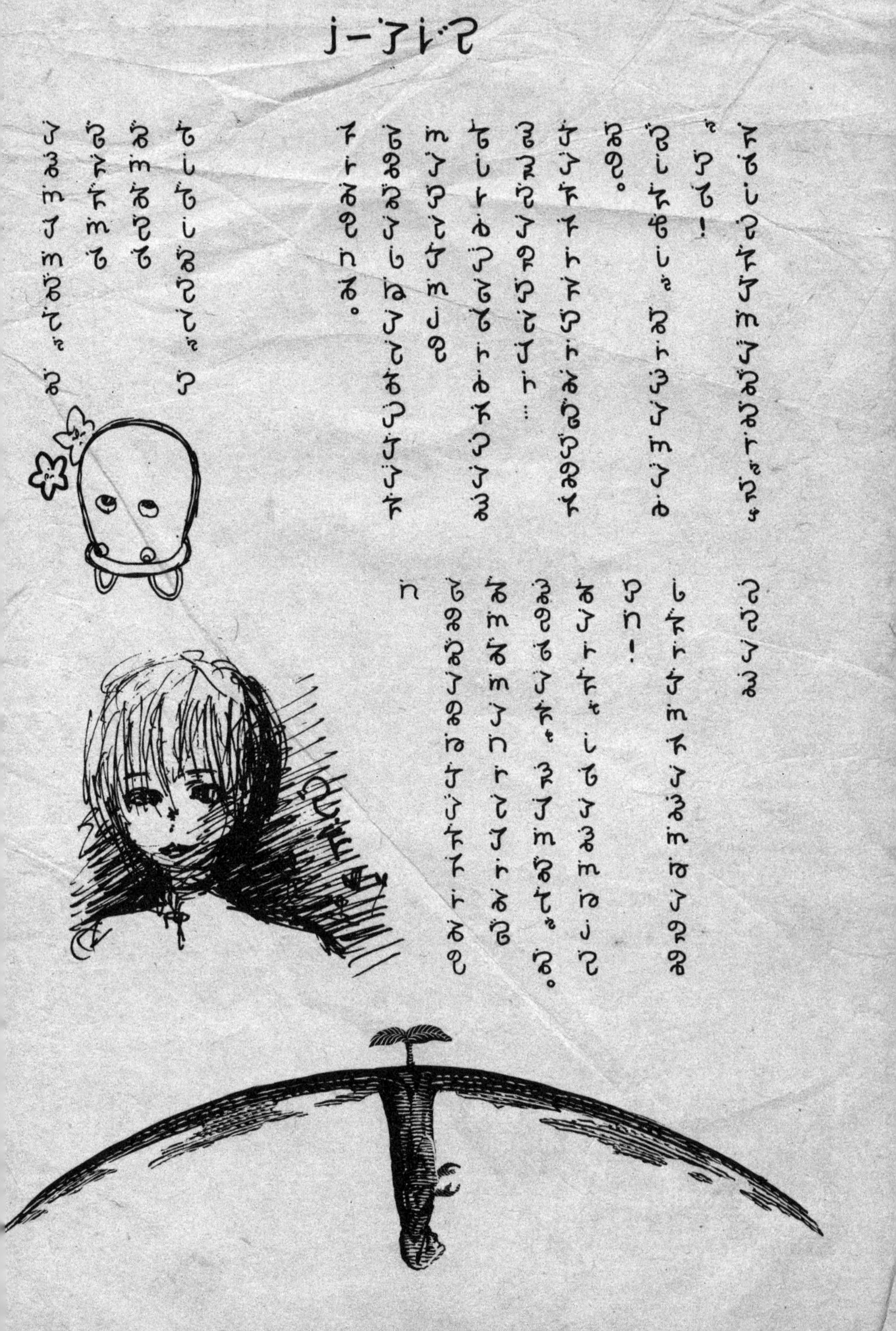

#21 An Encounter Before Returning Home

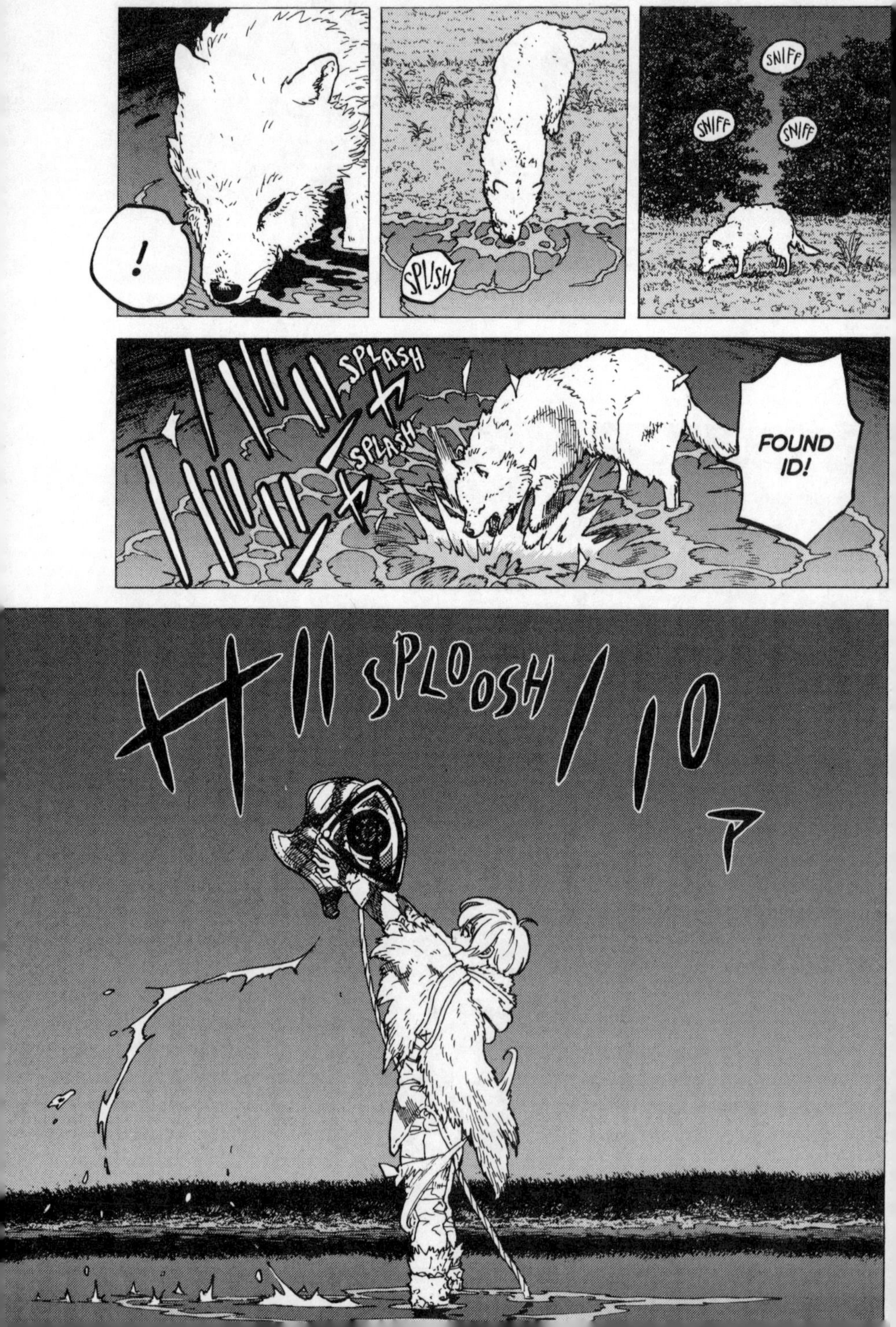
SNIFF
SNIFF
SNIFF
SPLISH
!
FOUND ID!
SPLASH
SPLASH
SPLOOSH

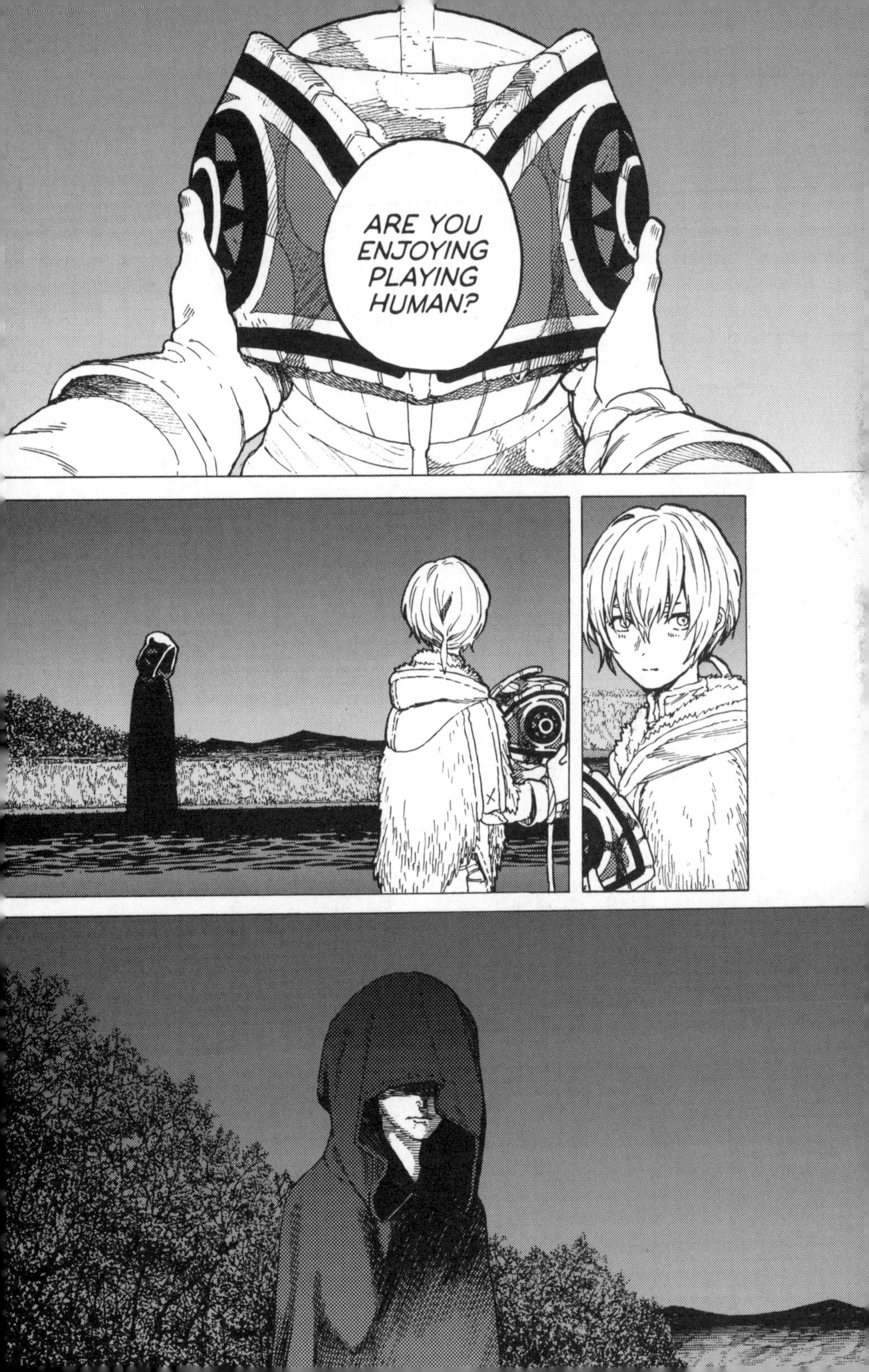
ARE YOU ENJOYING PLAYING HUMAN?

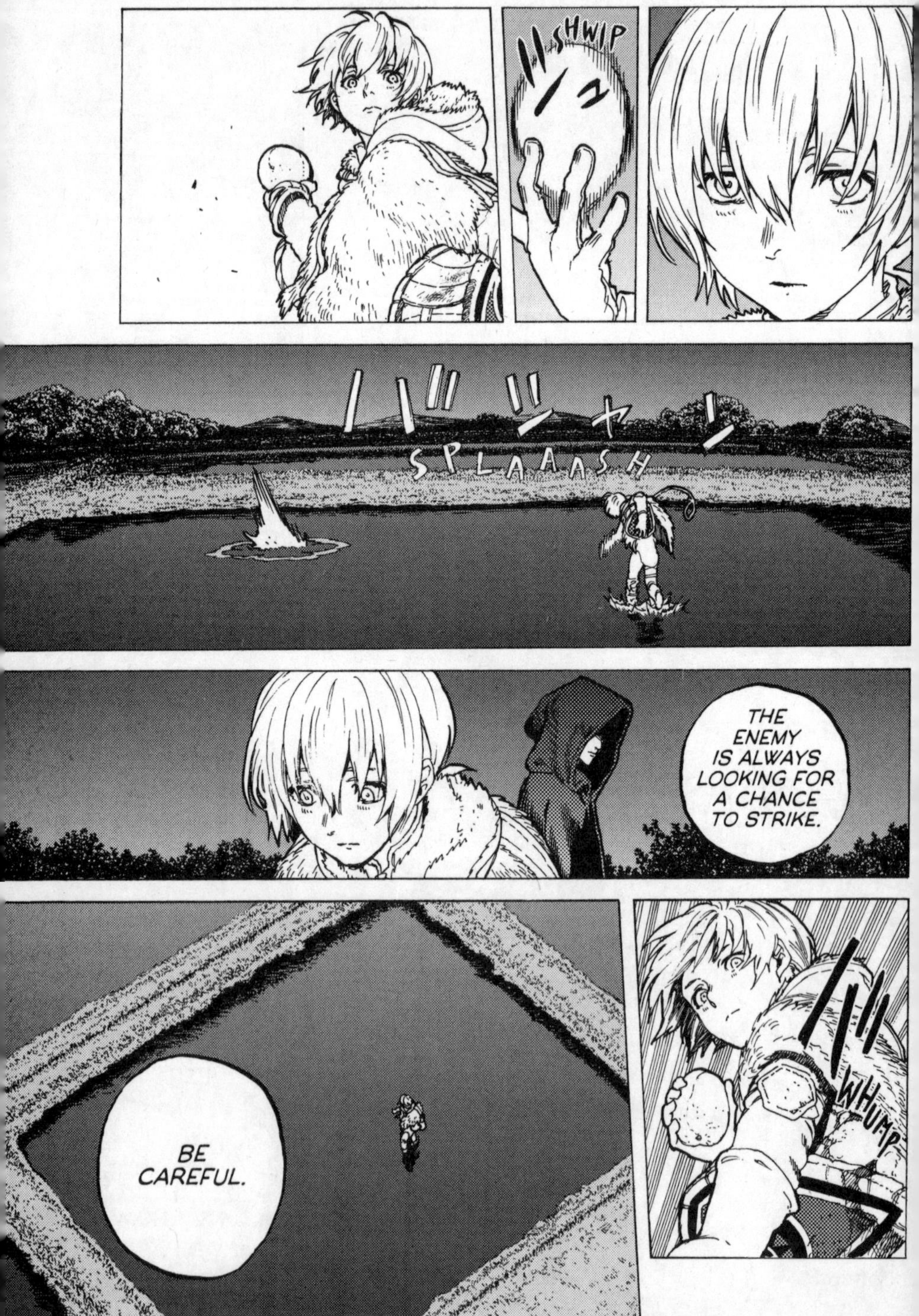
SHWIP
SPLAAASH
THE ENEMY IS ALWAYS LOOKING FOR A CHANCE TO STRIKE.
WHUMP
BE CAREFUL.

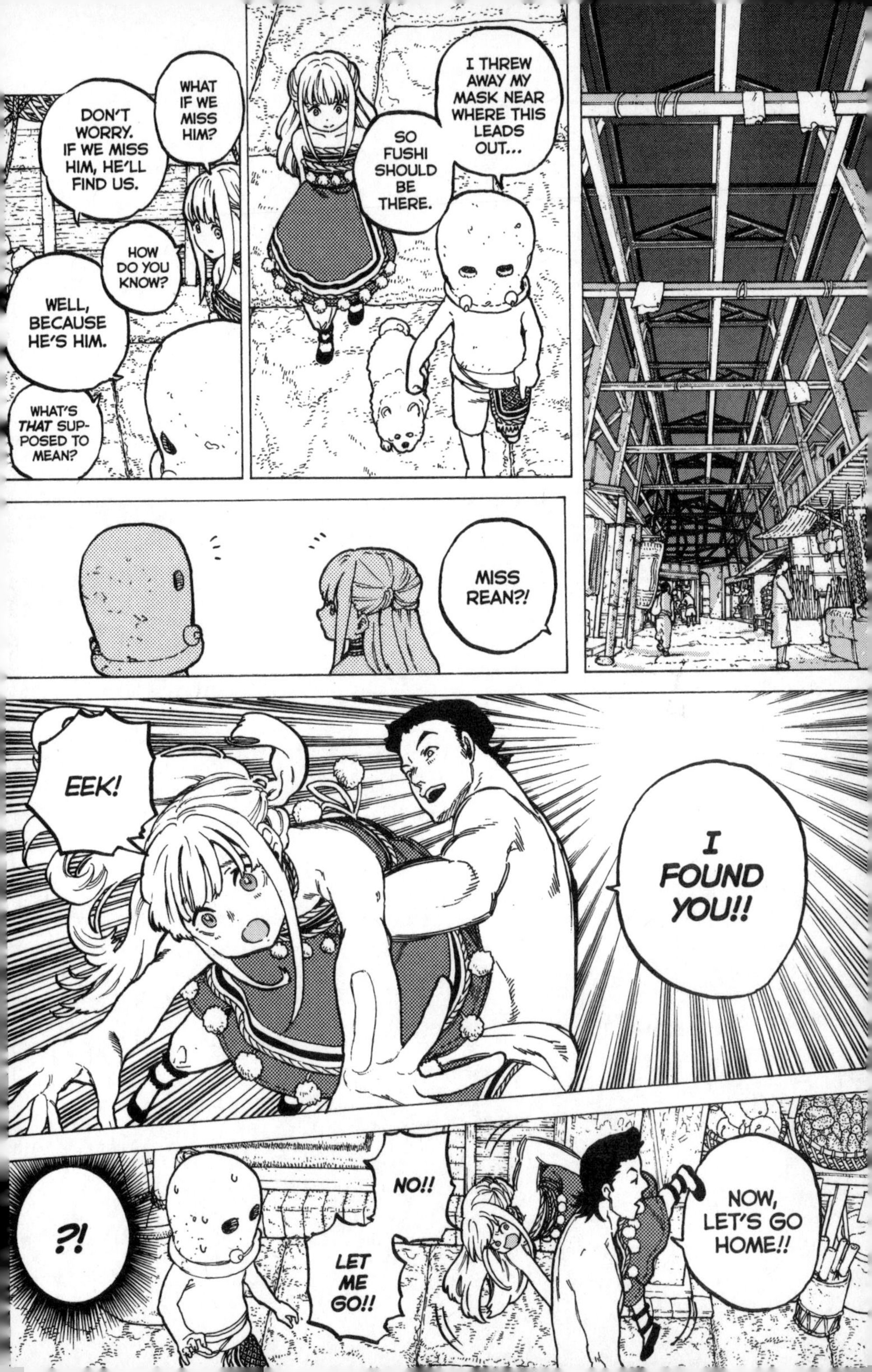
I THREW AWAY MY MASK NEAR WHERE THIS LEADS OUT...
SO FUSHI SHOULD BE THERE.
WHAT IF WE MISS HIM?
DON'T WORRY. IF WE MISS HIM, HE'LL FIND US.
HOW DO YOU KNOW?
WELL, BECAUSE HE'S HIM.
WHAT'S *THAT* SUPPOSED TO MEAN?
MISS REAN?!
I FOUND YOU!!
EEK!
NOW, LET'S GO HOME!!
NO!!
LET ME GO!!
?!

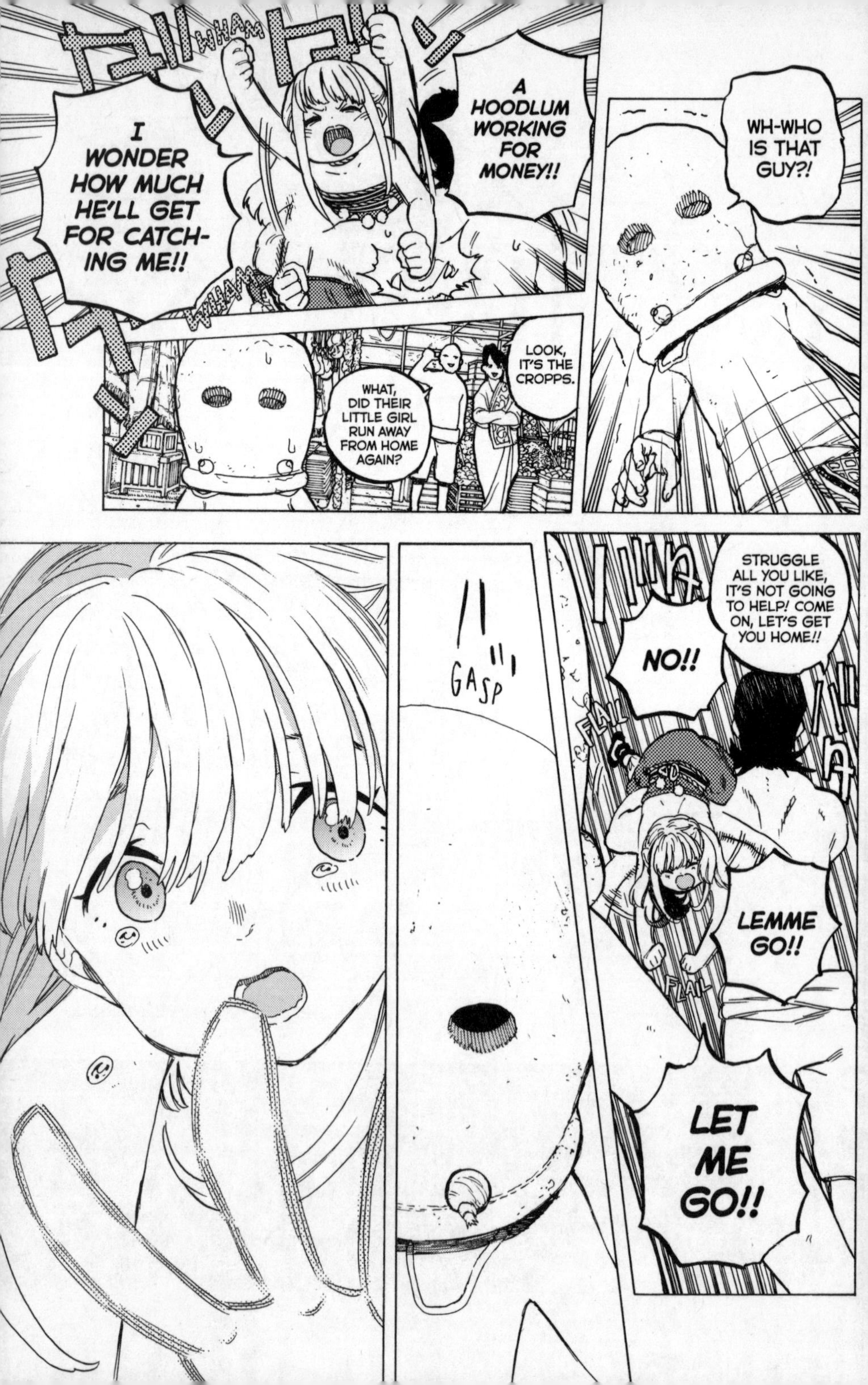
WH-WHO IS THAT GUY?!
WHAM
A HOODLUM WORKING FOR MONEY!!
I WONDER HOW MUCH HE'LL GET FOR CATCHING ME!!
WHAM
LOOK, IT'S THE CROPPS.
WHAT, DID THEIR LITTLE GIRL RUN AWAY FROM HOME AGAIN?
STRUGGLE ALL YOU LIKE, IT'S NOT GOING TO HELP! COME ON, LET'S GET YOU HOME!!
NO!!
FLAIL
LEMME GO!!
FLAIL
LET ME GO!!
GASP

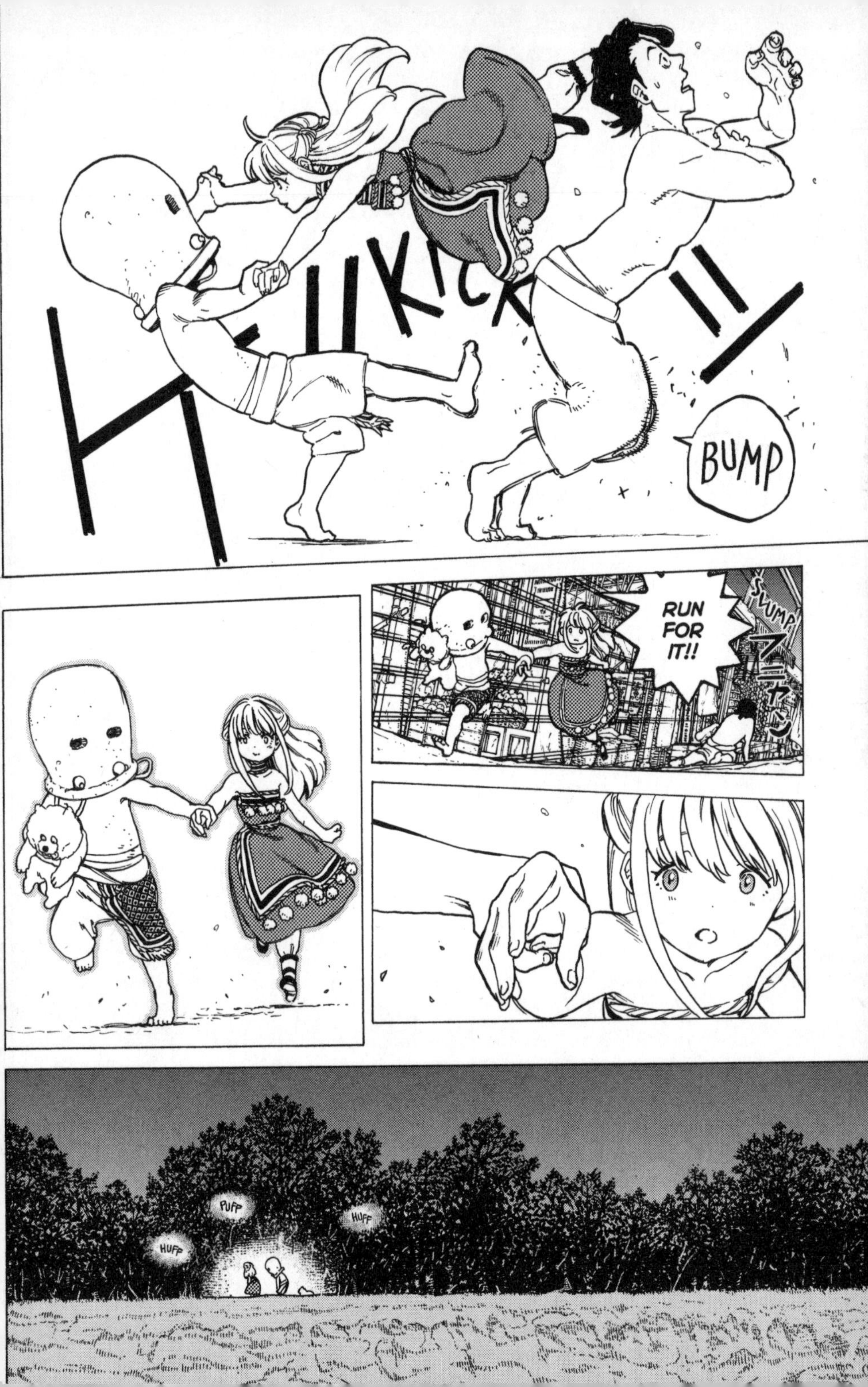
KICK
BUMP
RUN FOR IT!!
SWUMP
HUFF
PUFF
HUFF

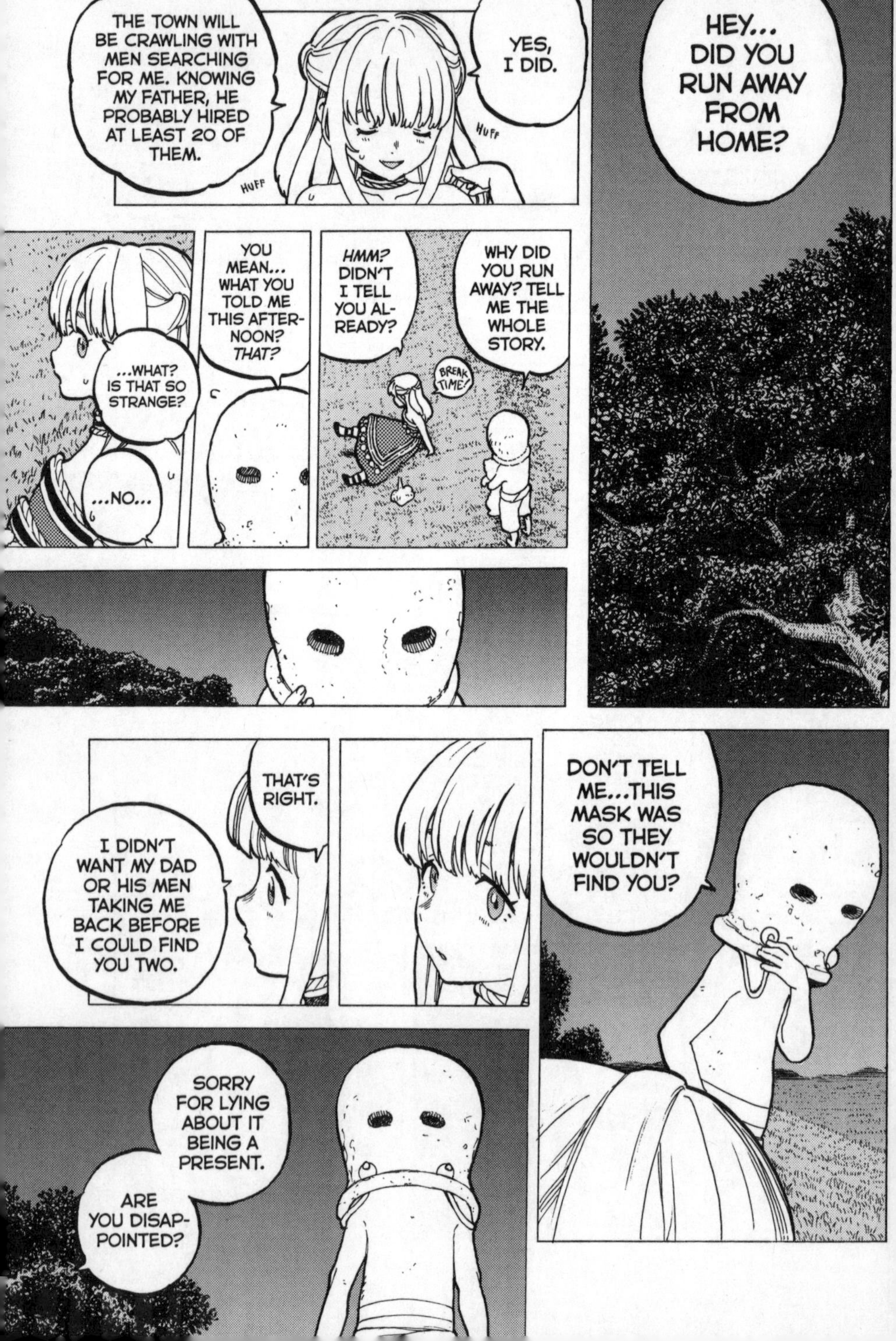
HEY... DID YOU RUN AWAY FROM HOME?
YES, I DID.
HUFF
THE TOWN WILL BE CRAWLING WITH MEN SEARCHING FOR ME. KNOWING MY FATHER, HE PROBABLY HIRED AT LEAST 20 OF THEM.
HUFF
WHY DID YOU RUN AWAY? TELL ME THE WHOLE STORY.
HMM? DIDN'T I TELL YOU AL-READY?
BREAK TIME!
YOU MEAN... WHAT YOU TOLD ME THIS AFTER-NOON? THAT?
...WHAT? IS THAT SO STRANGE?
...NO...
DON'T TELL ME...THIS MASK WAS SO THEY WOULDN'T FIND YOU?
THAT'S RIGHT.
I DIDN'T WANT MY DAD OR HIS MEN TAKING ME BACK BEFORE I COULD FIND YOU TWO.
SORRY FOR LYING ABOUT IT BEING A PRESENT.
ARE YOU DISAP-POINTED?

YOU CAN HAVE IT BACK.

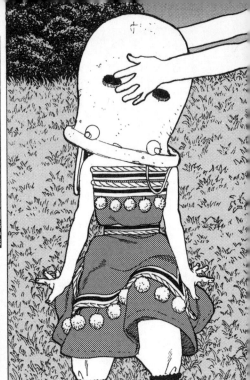

THANKS FOR LENDING ME YOUR MASK.

IF YOU HADN'T, I WOULDN'T HAVE LEARNED THAT ABOUT YOU.

...DON'T WORRY. I WON'T LOOK THAT WAY.

THANKS...

...

OH, I DON'T REALLY CARE ANY—

138

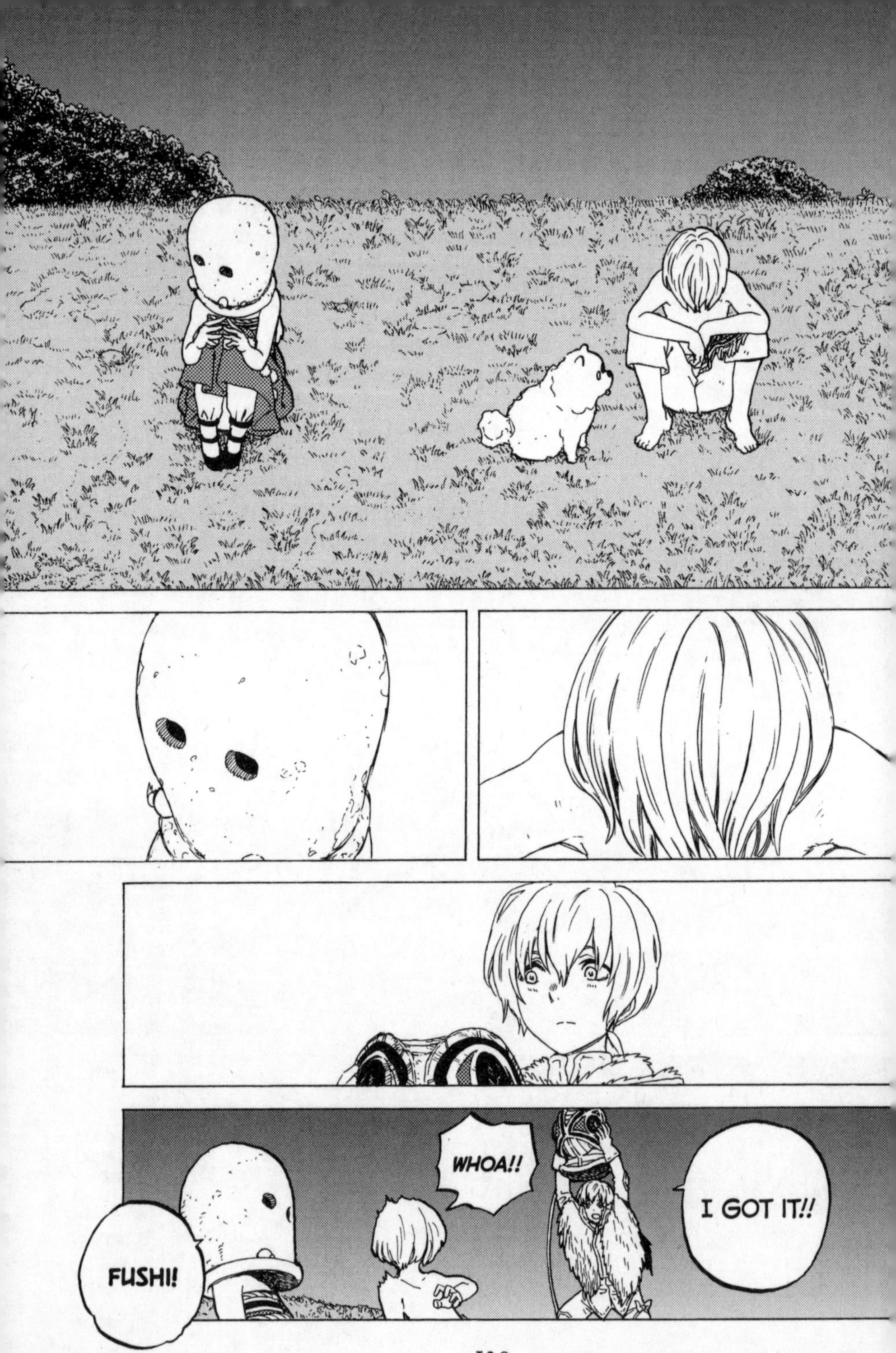
I GOT IT!!
WHOA!!
FUSHI!

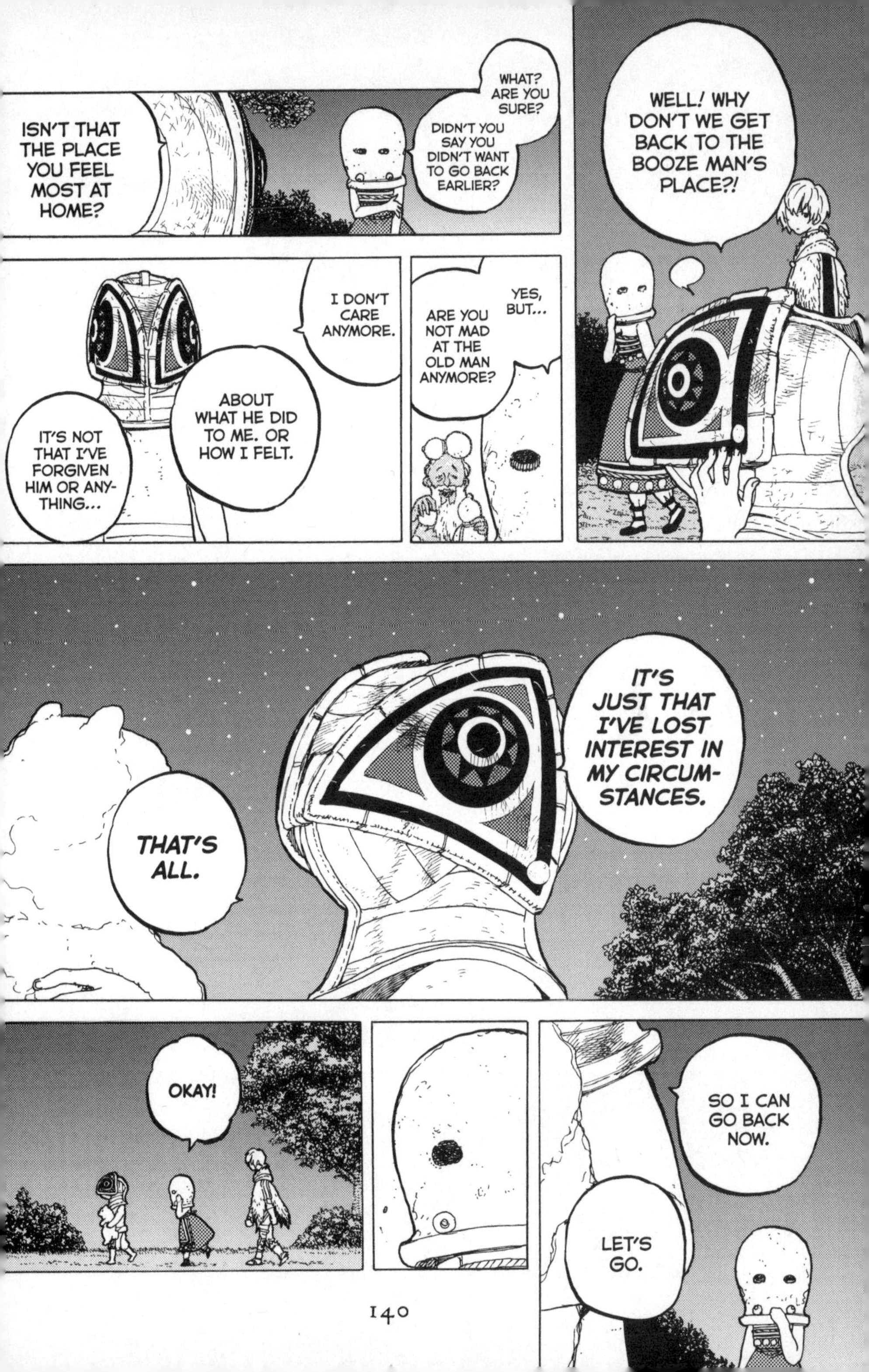
WELL! WHY DON'T WE GET BACK TO THE BOOZE MAN'S PLACE?!
WHAT? ARE YOU SURE?
DIDN'T YOU SAY YOU DIDN'T WANT TO GO BACK EARLIER?
ISN'T THAT THE PLACE YOU FEEL MOST AT HOME?
YES, BUT...
ARE YOU NOT MAD AT THE OLD MAN ANYMORE?
I DON'T CARE ANYMORE.
ABOUT WHAT HE DID TO ME. OR HOW I FELT.
IT'S NOT THAT I'VE FORGIVEN HIM OR ANY-THING...
IT'S JUST THAT I'VE LOST INTEREST IN MY CIRCUM-STANCES.
THAT'S ALL.
SO I CAN GO BACK NOW.
LET'S GO.
OKAY!

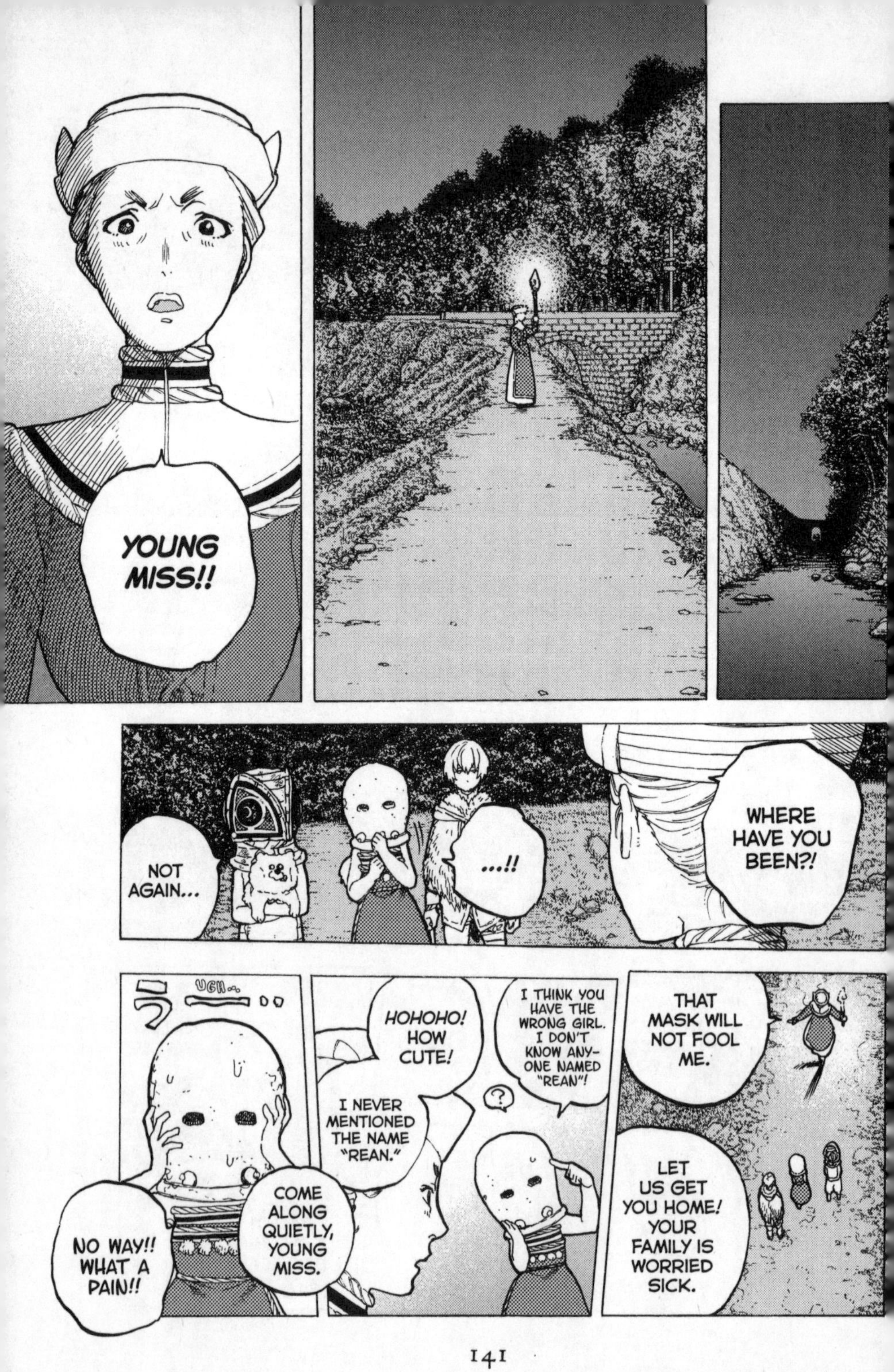
YOUNG MISS!!
WHERE HAVE YOU BEEN?!
...!!
NOT AGAIN...
THAT MASK WILL NOT FOOL ME.
LET US GET YOU HOME! YOUR FAMILY IS WORRIED SICK.
I THINK YOU HAVE THE WRONG GIRL. I DON'T KNOW ANYONE NAMED "REAN"!
HOHOHO! HOW CUTE!
?
I NEVER MENTIONED THE NAME "REAN."
UGH...
COME ALONG QUIETLY, YOUNG MISS.
NO WAY!! WHAT A PAIN!!

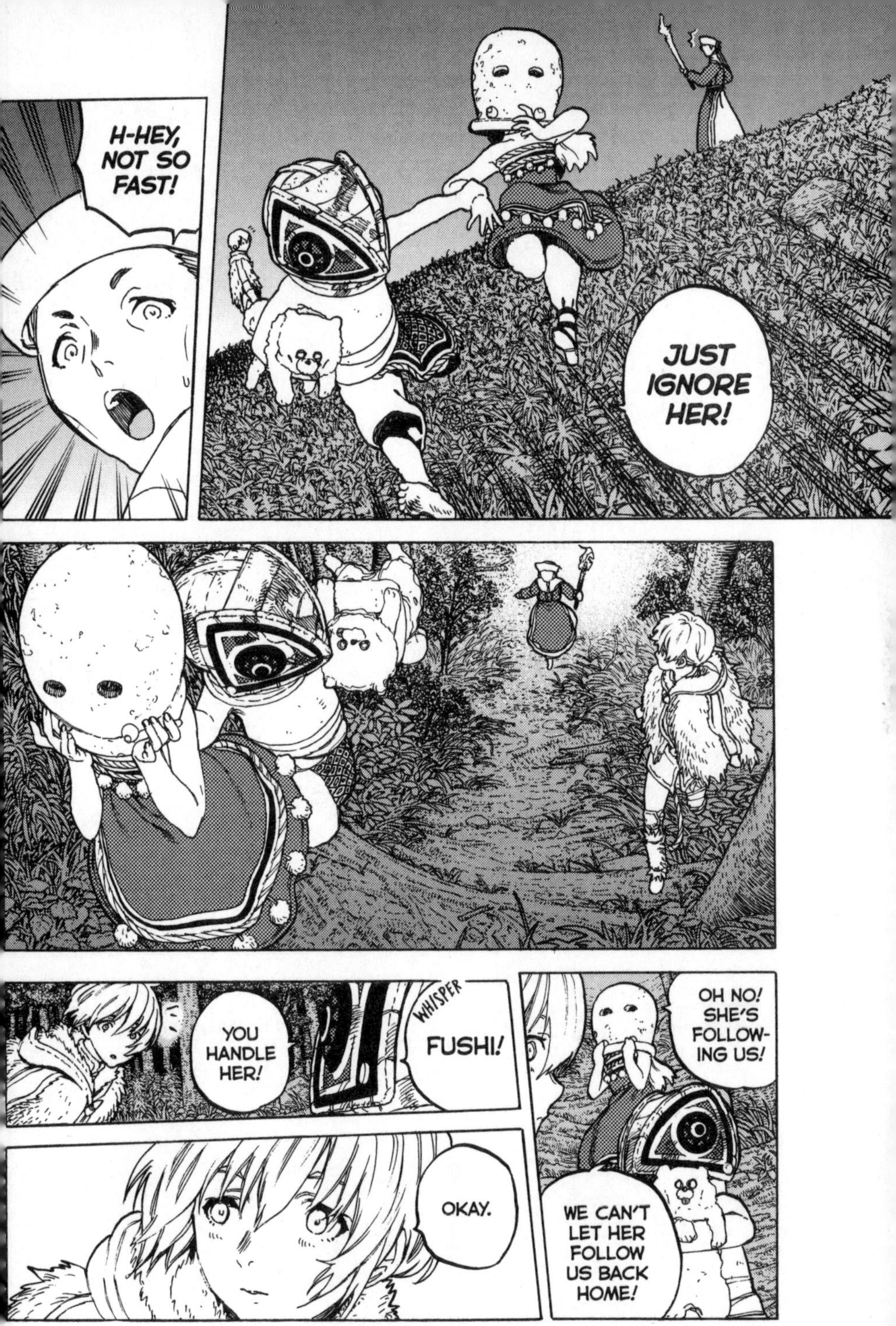
JUST IGNORE HER!
H-HEY, NOT SO FAST!
OH NO! SHE'S FOLLOWING US!
WE CAN'T LET HER FOLLOW US BACK HOME!
WHISPER
FUSHI!
YOU HANDLE HER!
OKAY.

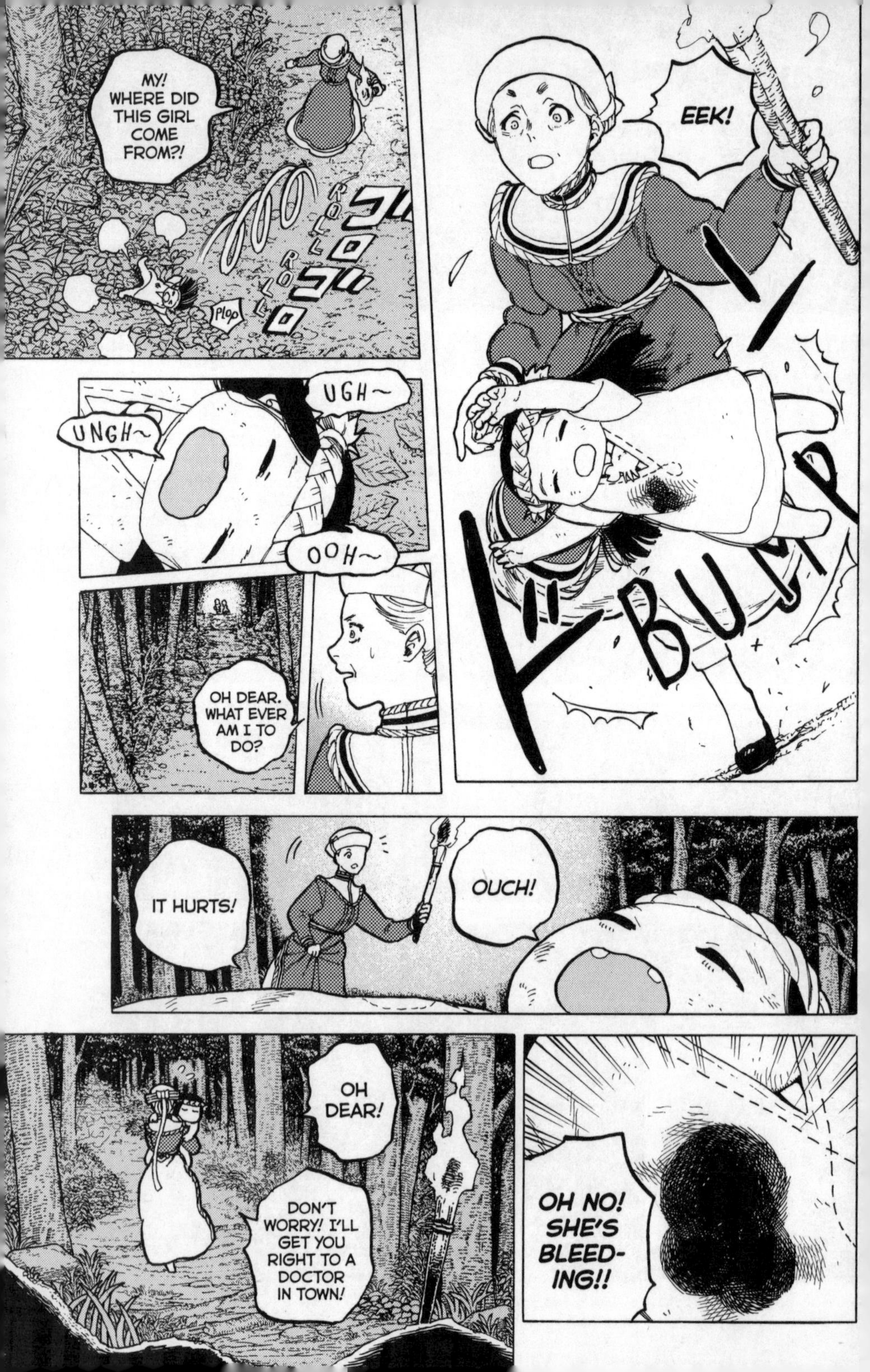
EEK!
BUMP
MY! WHERE DID THIS GIRL COME FROM?!
ROLL
ROLL
PLOP
UGH~
UNGH~
OOH~
OH DEAR. WHAT EVER AM I TO DO?
OUCH!
IT HURTS!
OH NO! SHE'S BLEEDING!!
OH DEAR!
DON'T WORRY! I'LL GET YOU RIGHT TO A DOCTOR IN TOWN!

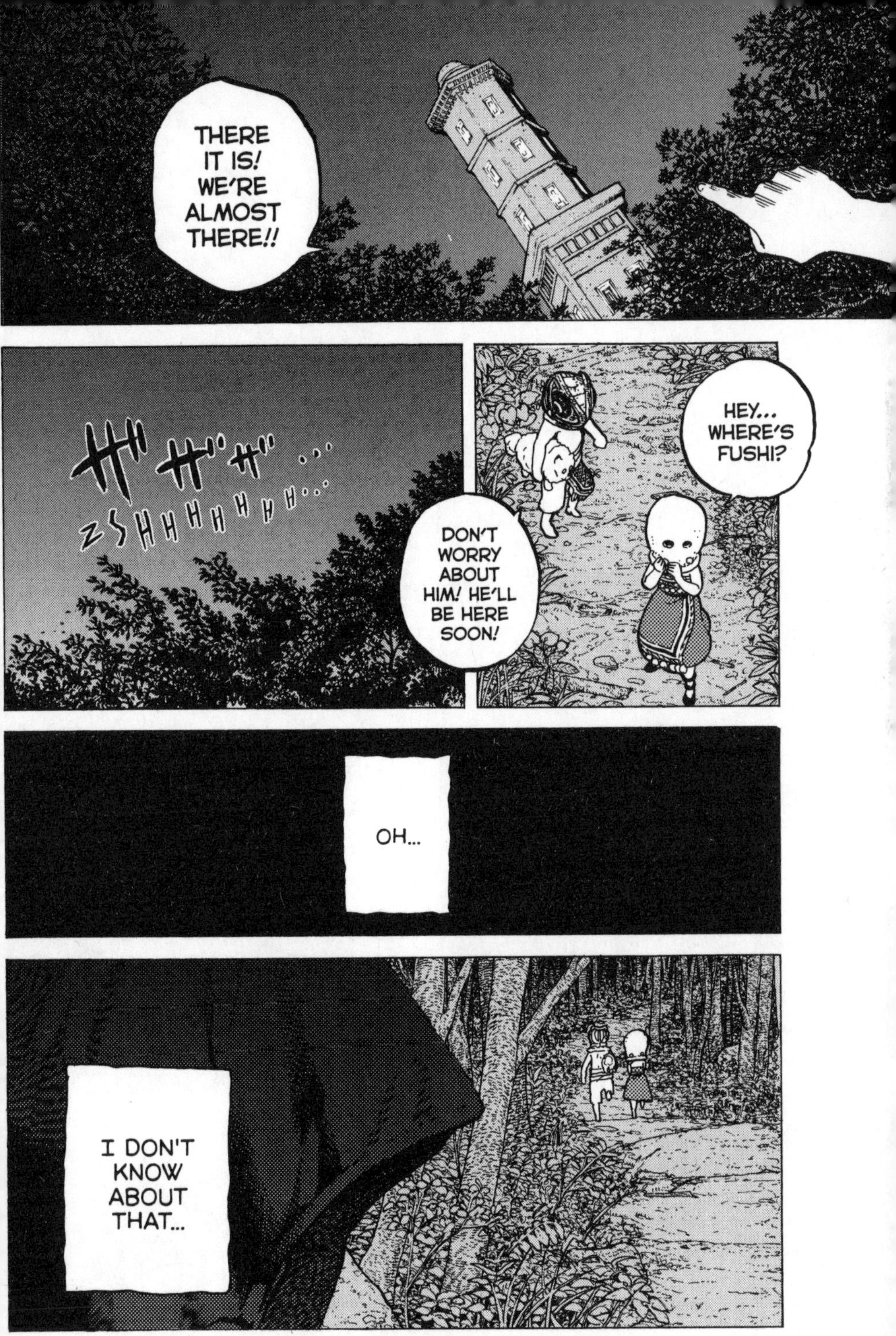
THERE IT IS! WE'RE ALMOST THERE!!
HEY... WHERE'S FUSHI?
DON'T WORRY ABOUT HIM! HE'LL BE HERE SOON!
ザザザ...
ZSHHHHHHH...
OH...
I DON'T KNOW ABOUT THAT...

HE PROBABLY WILL NOT RETURN.

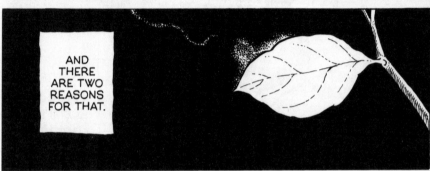

AND THERE ARE TWO REASONS FOR THAT.

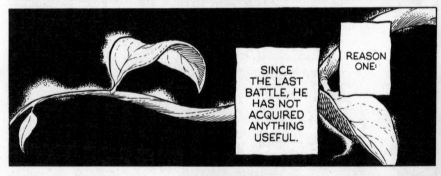

REASON ONE:

SINCE THE LAST BATTLE, HE HAS NOT ACQUIRED ANYTHING USEFUL.

REASON TWO:

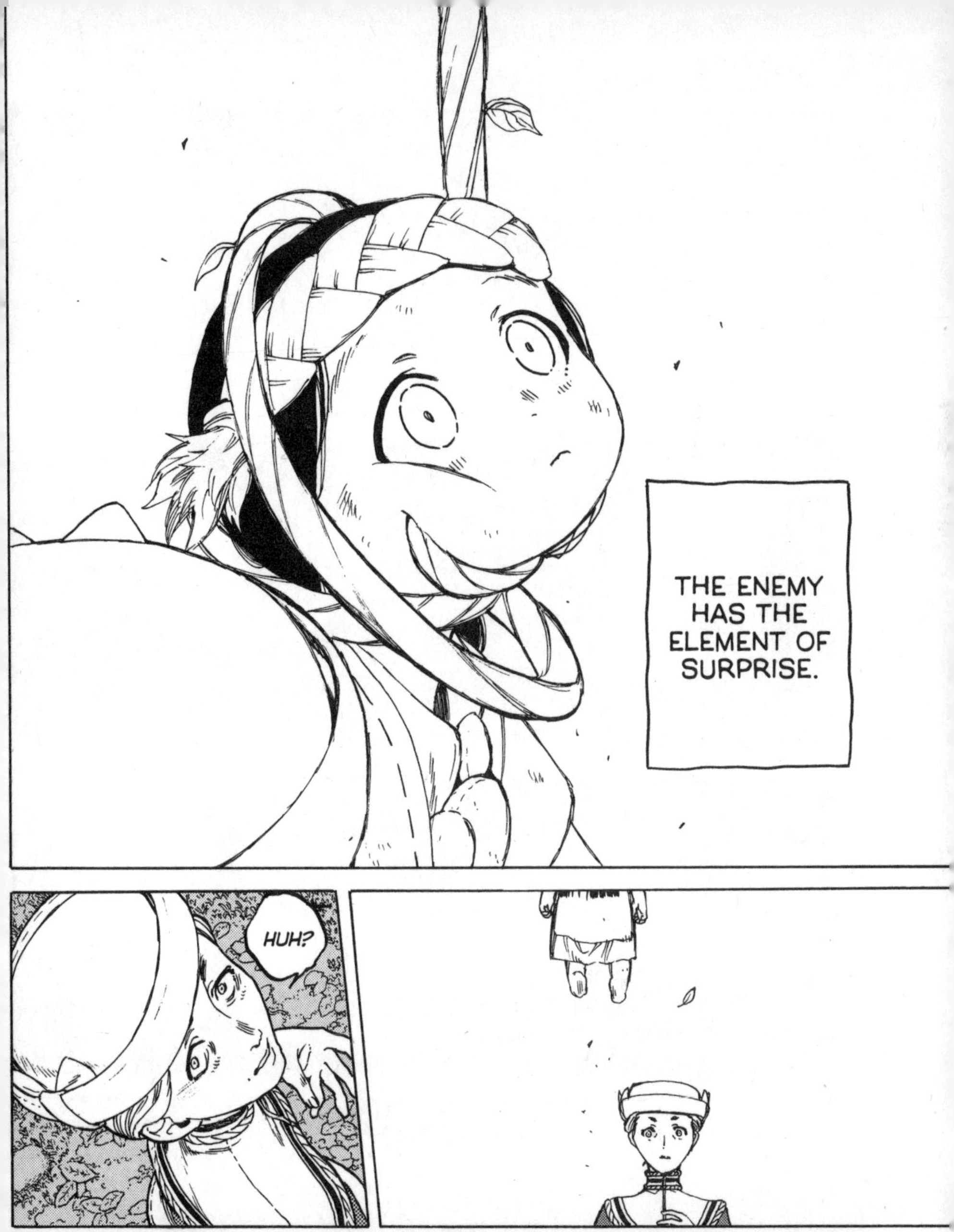
THE ENEMY HAS THE ELEMENT OF SURPRISE.
HUH?
キャアアア
EEEEEK

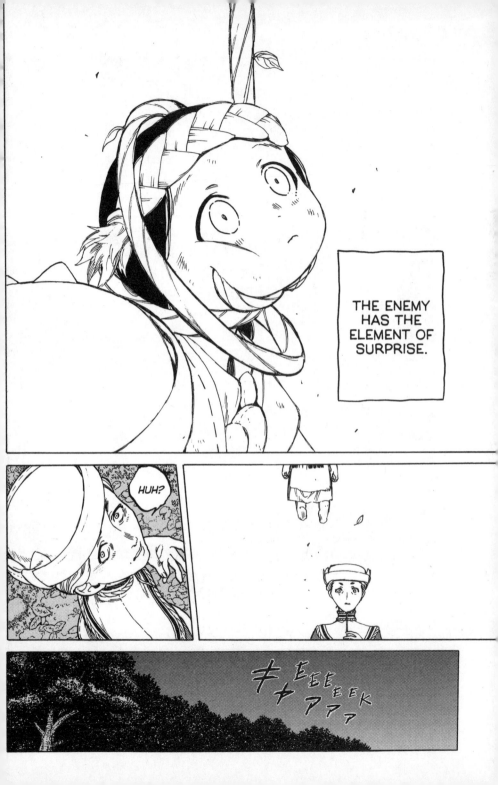

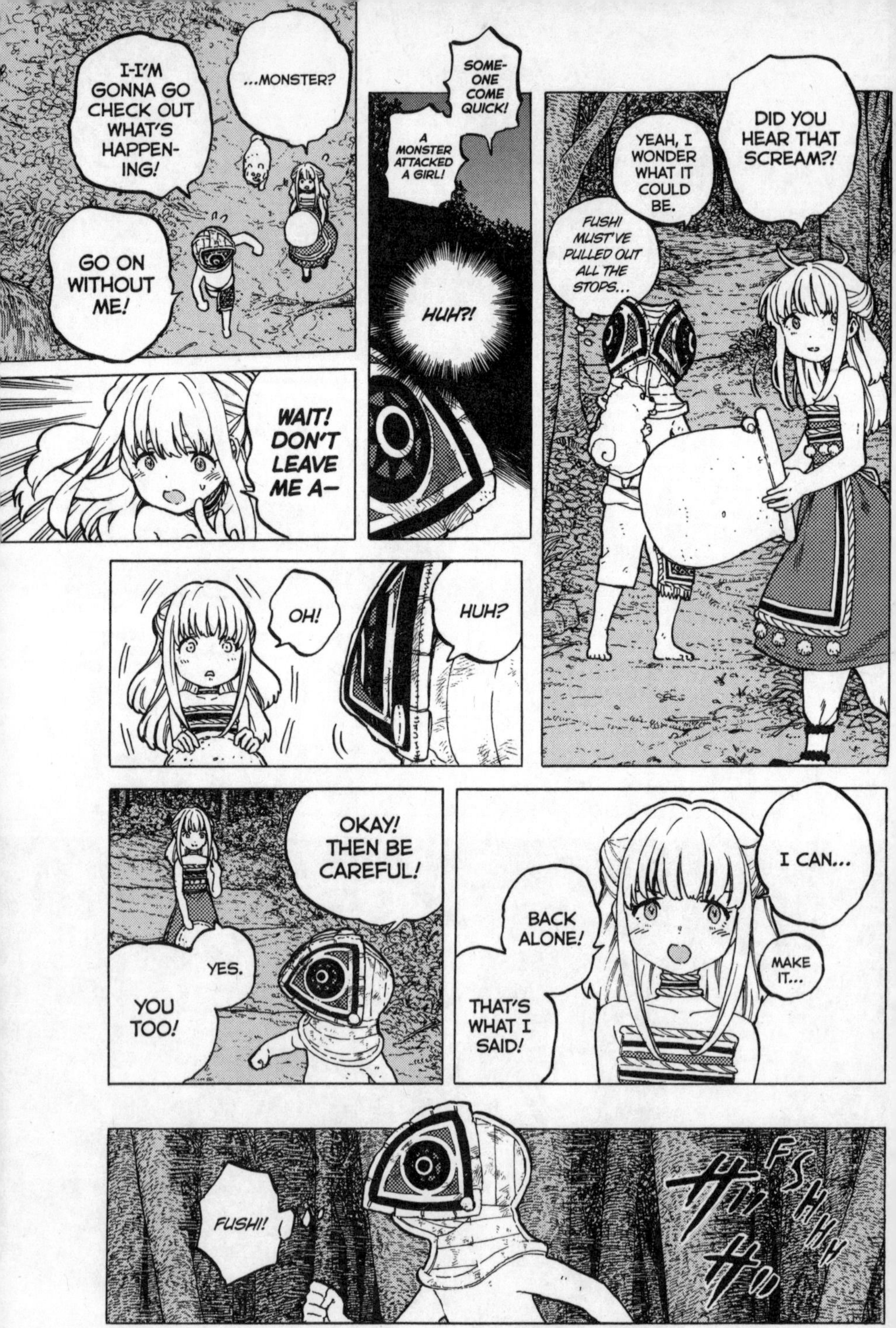
DID YOU HEAR THAT SCREAM?!
YEAH, I WONDER WHAT IT COULD BE.
FUSHI MUST'VE PULLED OUT ALL THE STOPS...
SOME-ONE COME QUICK!
A MONSTER ATTACKED A GIRL!
HUH?!
...MONSTER?
I-I'M GONNA GO CHECK OUT WHAT'S HAPPEN-ING!
GO ON WITHOUT ME!
WAIT! DON'T LEAVE ME A—
HUH?
OH!
I CAN...
MAKE IT...
BACK ALONE!
THAT'S WHAT I SAID!
OKAY! THEN BE CAREFUL!
YES.
YOU TOO!
FSHHH
FUSHI!

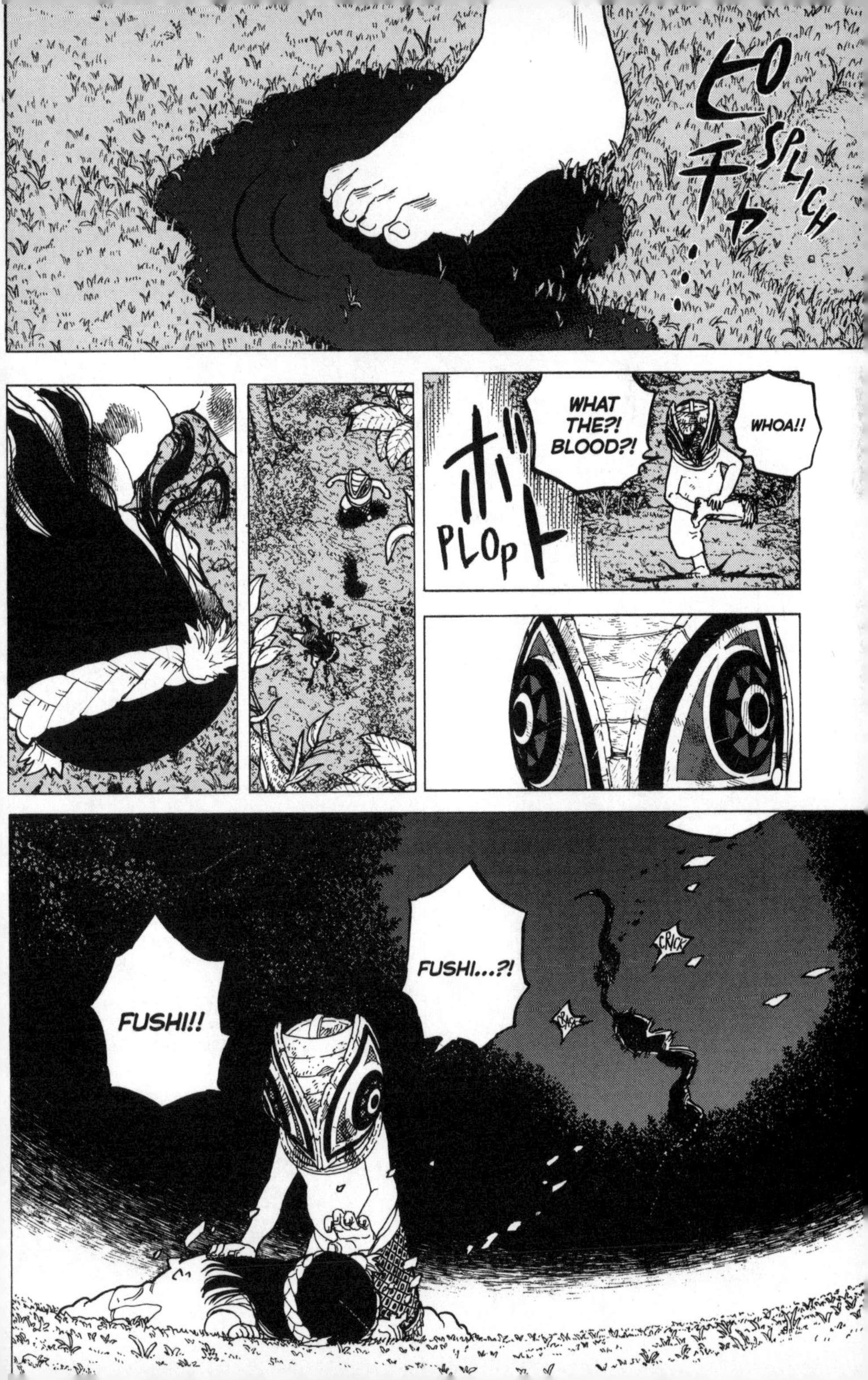
ピチャ
SPLICH
WHOA!!
WHAT THE?! BLOOD?!
ボト
PLOP
FUSHI...?!
FUSHI!!
CRICK
CRACK

TO YOUR ETERNITY

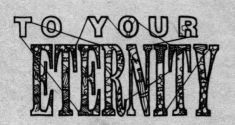

WHAT THE DEMON LEFT BEHIND

In the forest, I picked up a chunk of flesh.
I believe it is something the demon dropped.
It is spherical, and an ivy-like fiber stretches around it.
It is hard, like a tree.

The inside is soft and like a pouch.
I cut it. There is a mysterious fluid inside.
When I lick it, it is just like water.
I flip it over. It is encased in a soft flesh, similar to the offal of a pig.
It feels like the inside of a mouth.

I cut it into four parts, and grill it so I can eat it.
The outer surface is hard so I take it off. Requires some strength.

When grilled, it smells just like meat.
I scrape off the burned portions of the outer surface,
sprinkle salt on it, and eat it.
I chew thoroughly.

Delicious. Should last at least two days.

NOTES FROM PIORAN OF TAKUNAHA

#22 Fight of the Brothers

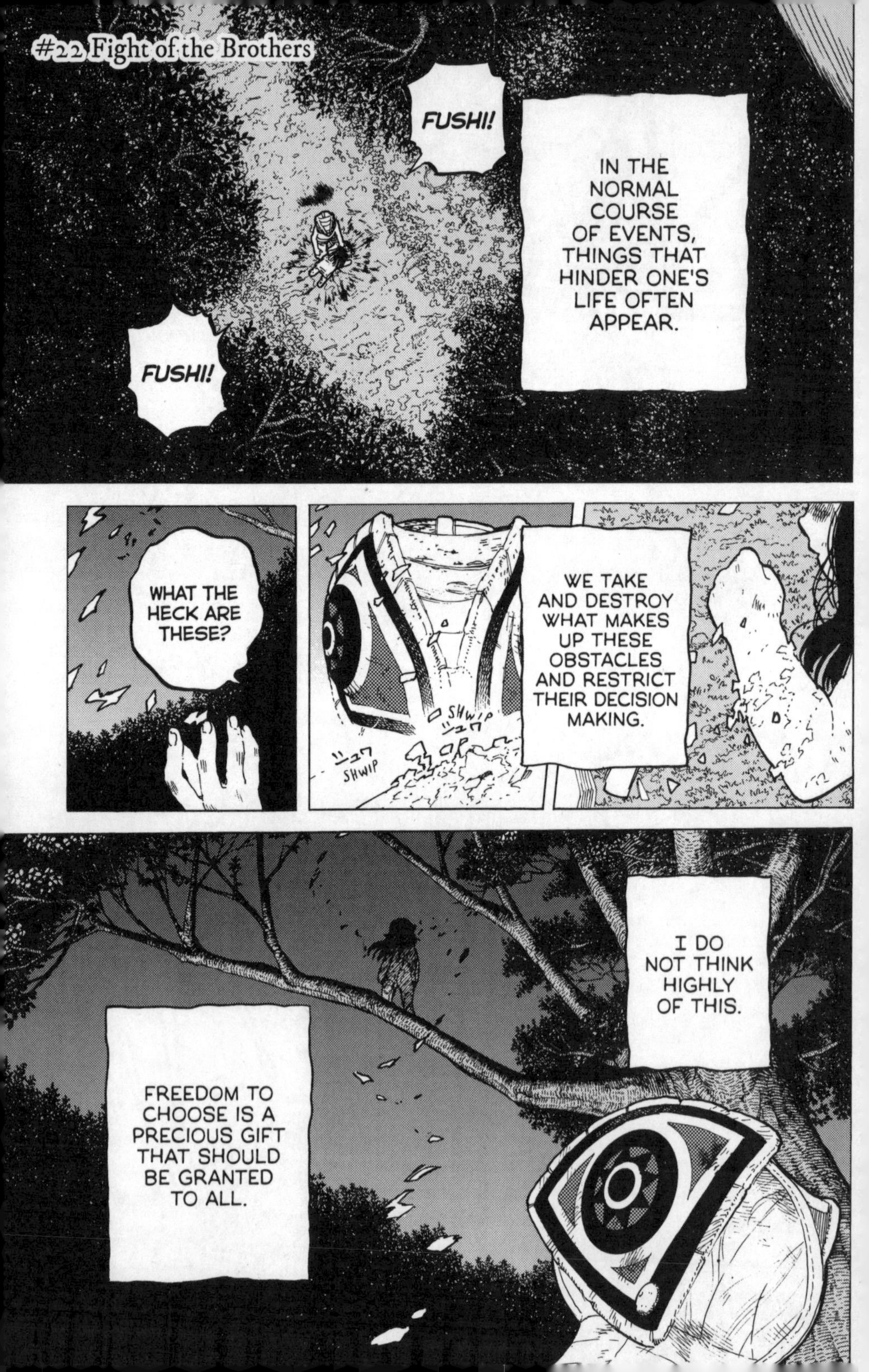

IN THE NORMAL COURSE OF EVENTS, THINGS THAT HINDER ONE'S LIFE OFTEN APPEAR.
FUSHI!
FUSHI!
WE TAKE AND DESTROY WHAT MAKES UP THESE OBSTACLES AND RESTRICT THEIR DECISION MAKING.
SHWIP
SHWIP
WHAT THE HECK ARE THESE?
I DO NOT THINK HIGHLY OF THIS.
FREEDOM TO CHOOSE IS A PRECIOUS GIFT THAT SHOULD BE GRANTED TO ALL.

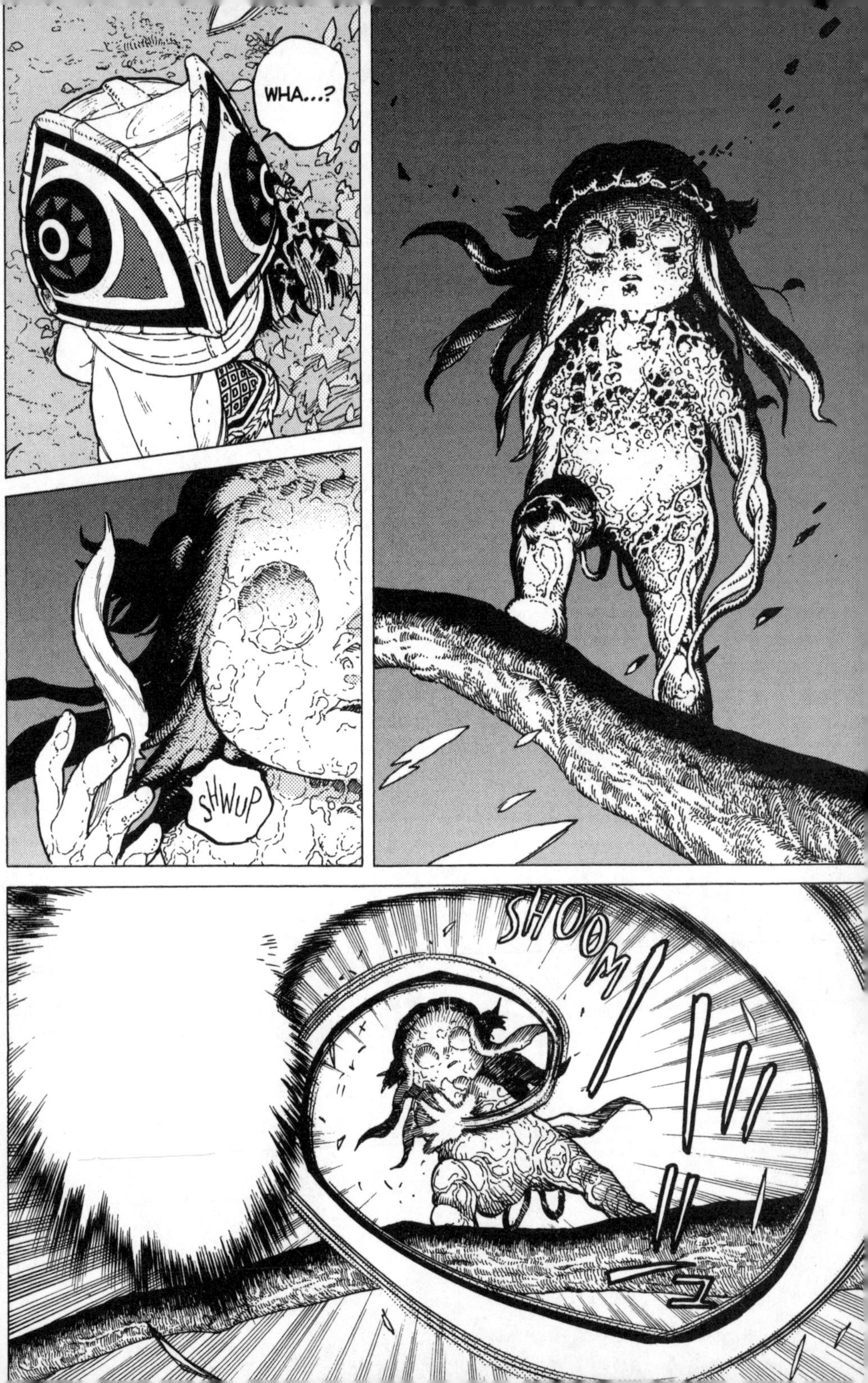
WHA...?
SHWUP
SHOOM

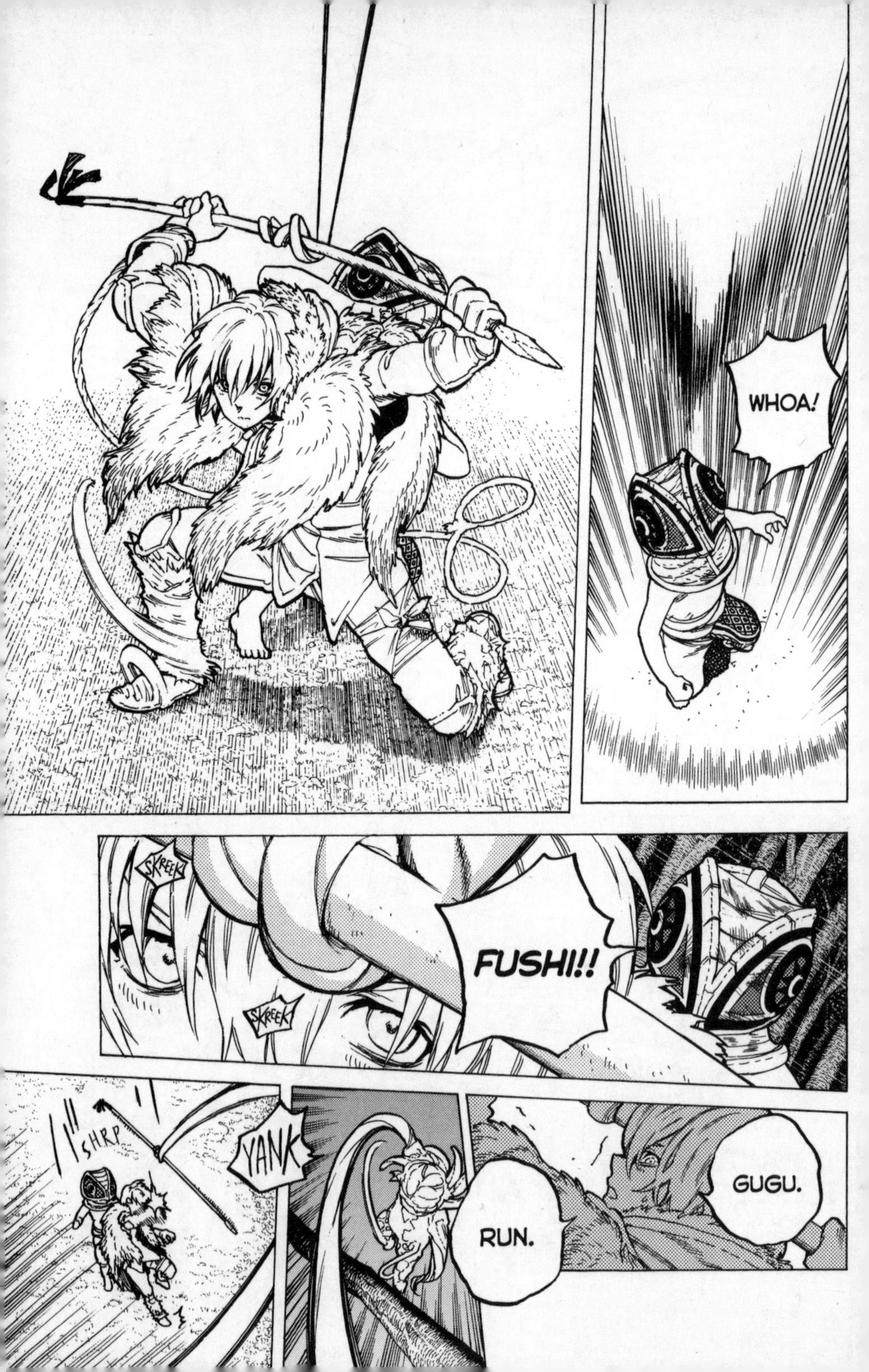
WHOA!
FUSHI!!
SKREEK
SKREEK
GUGU.
RUN.
YANK
SHRP

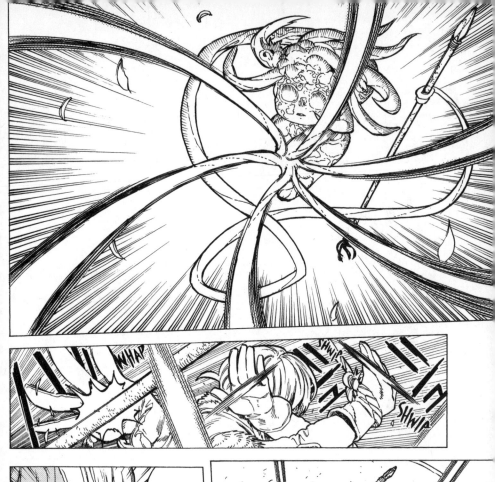

RUN!

NOW!

NO!
I WANT
TO HELP
YOU!!

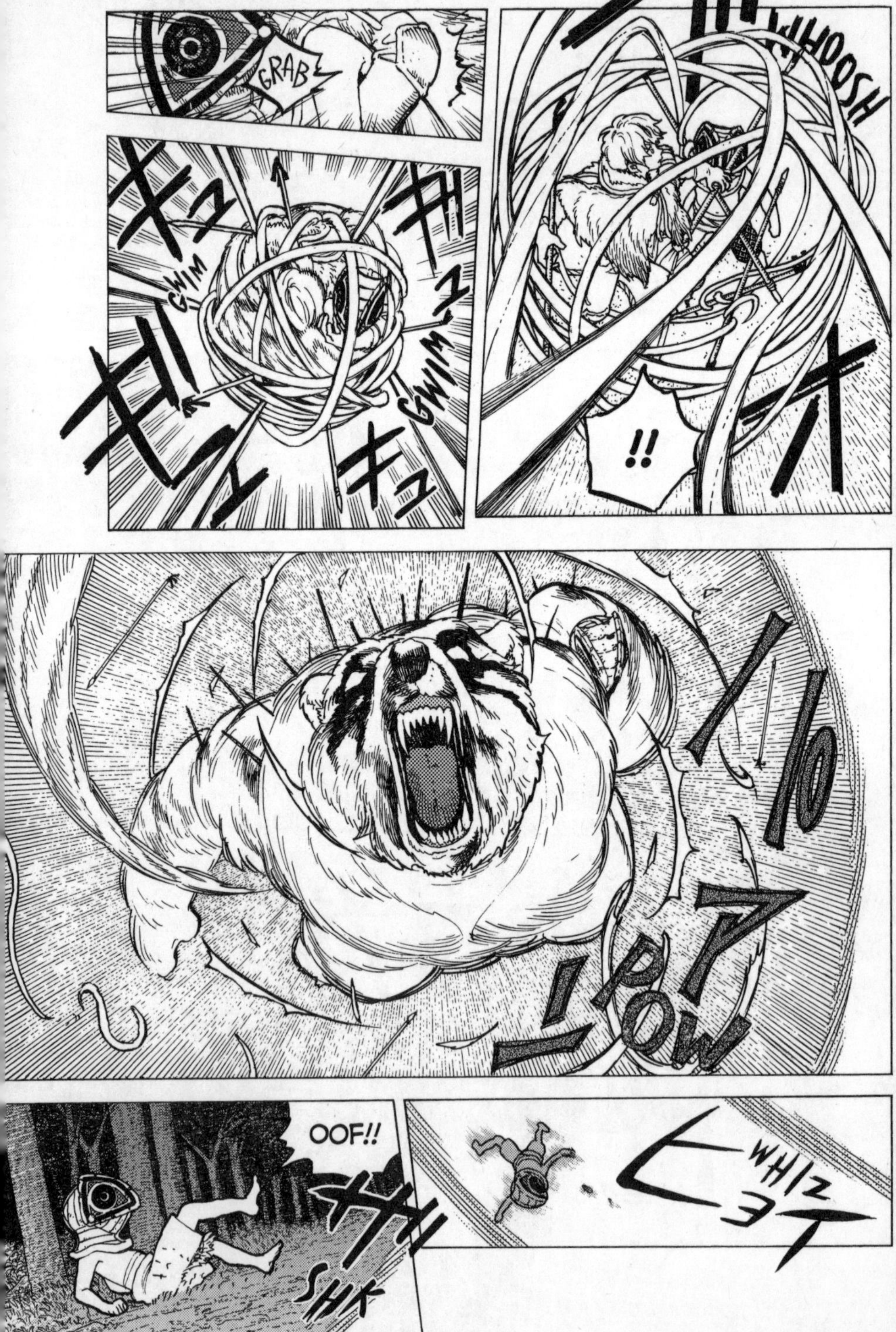
WHOOSH
!!
GRAB
GWIM
GWIM
POW
WHIZ
OOF!!
SHK

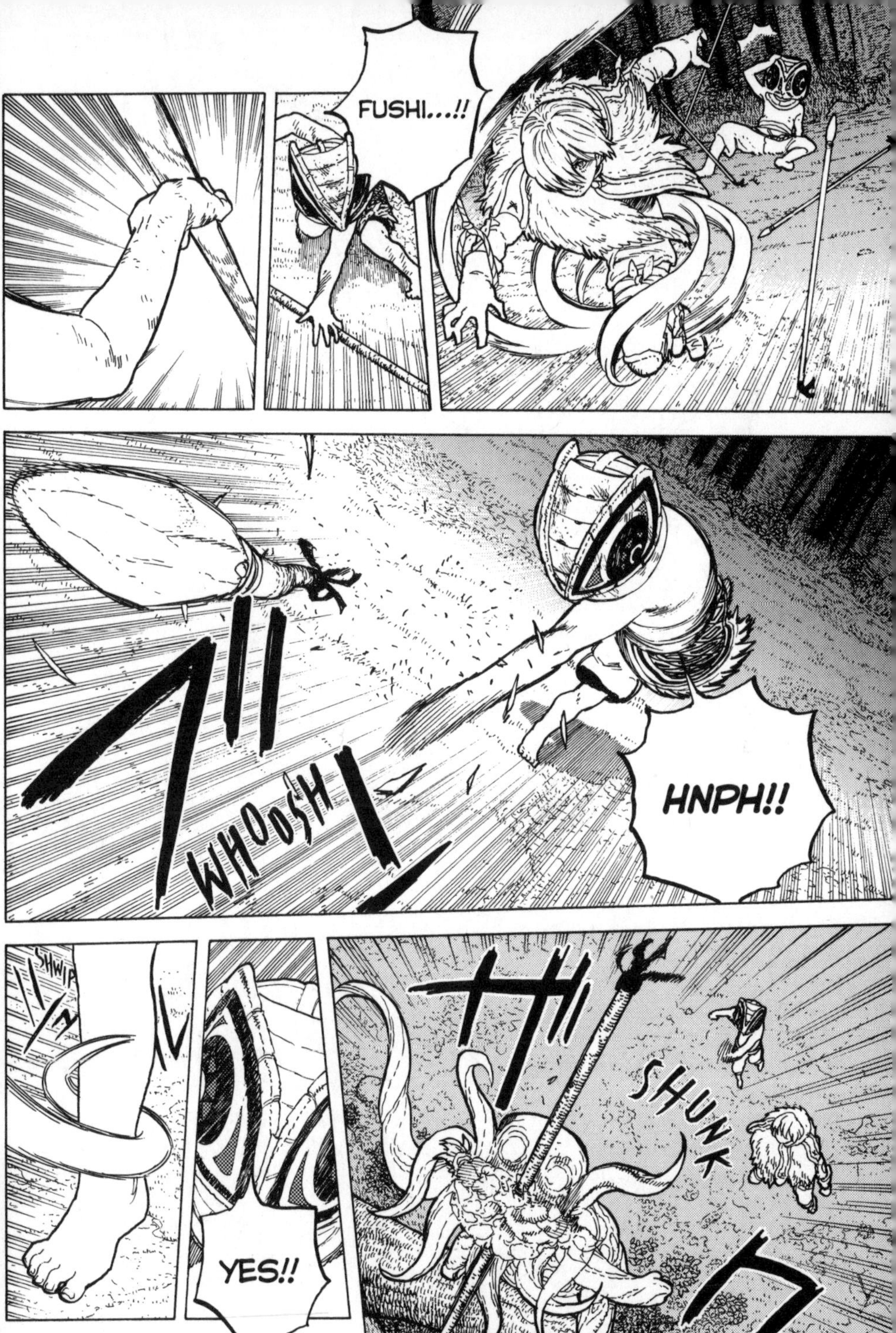
FUSHI...!!
HNPH!!
WHOOSH
SHUNK
YES!!
SHWIP

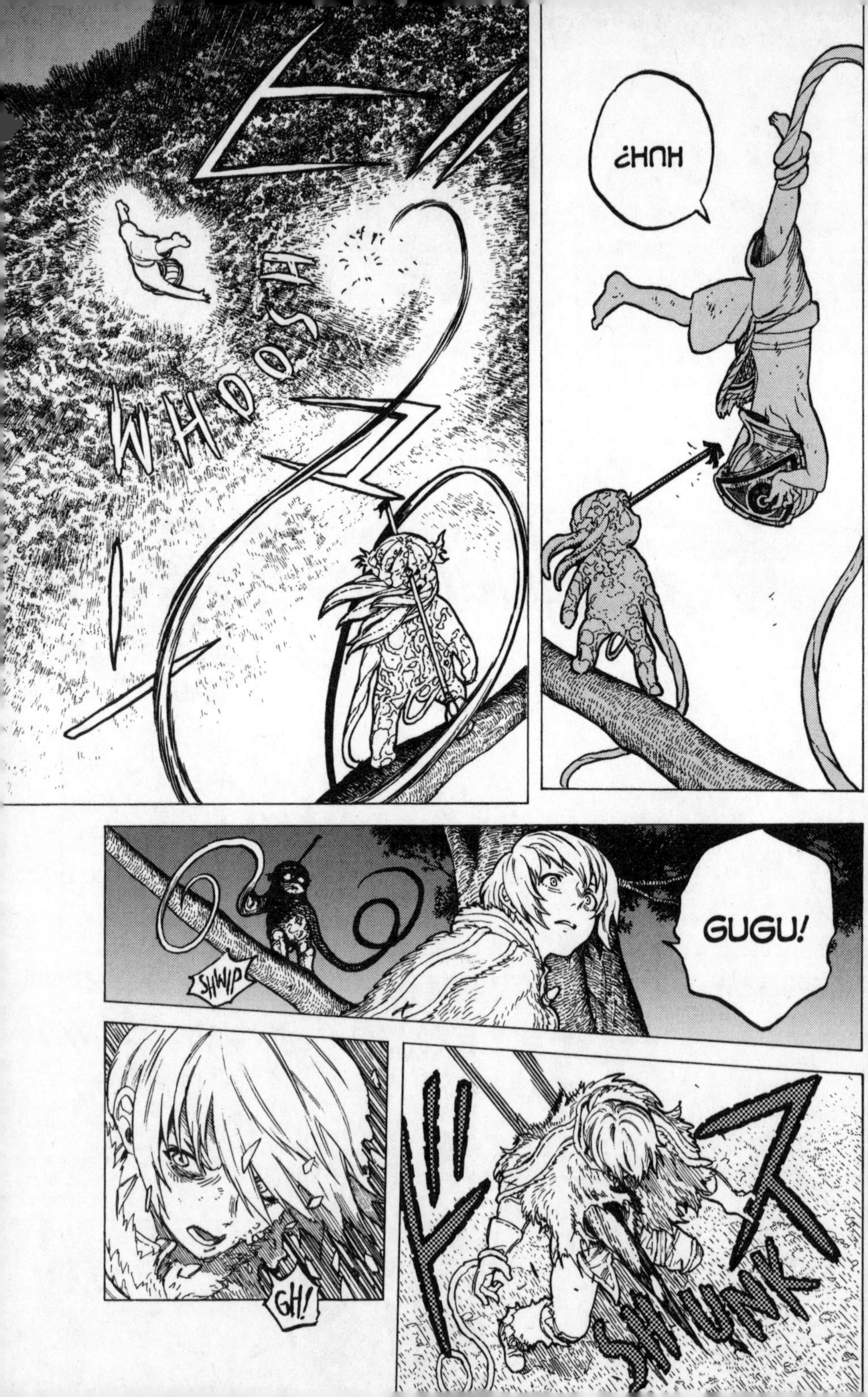
HUH?
WHOOSH
GUGU!
SHWIP
SHUNK
GH!

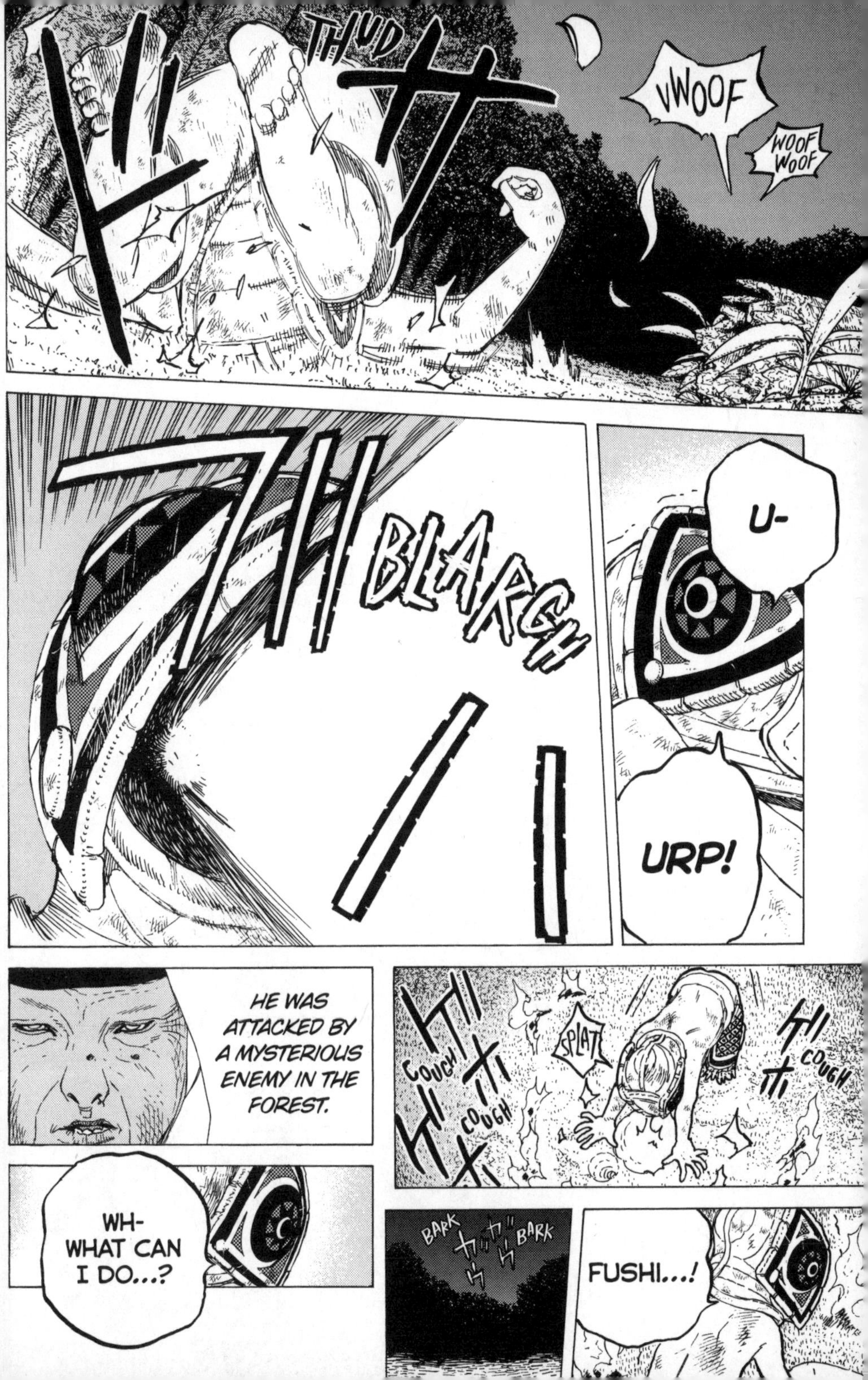
VWOOF
WOOF WOOF
THUD
U-
URP!
BLARGH
COUGH
SPLAT
COUGH
COUGH
HE WAS ATTACKED BY A MYSTERIOUS ENEMY IN THE FOREST.
FUSHI...!
BARK
BARK
WH- WHAT CAN I DO...?

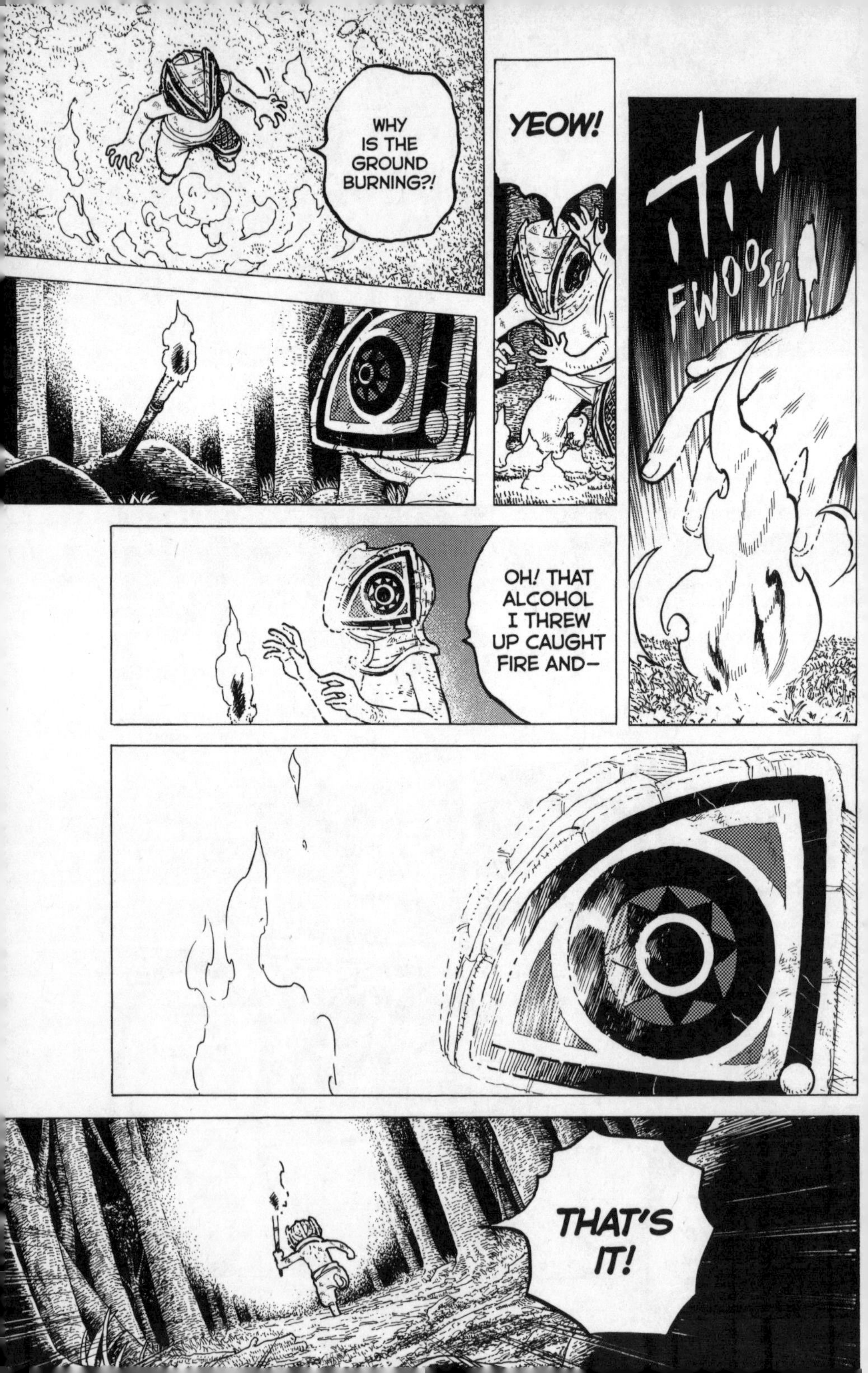
FWOOSH
YEOW!
WHY IS THE GROUND BURNING?!
OH! THAT ALCOHOL I THREW UP CAUGHT FIRE AND—
THAT'S IT!

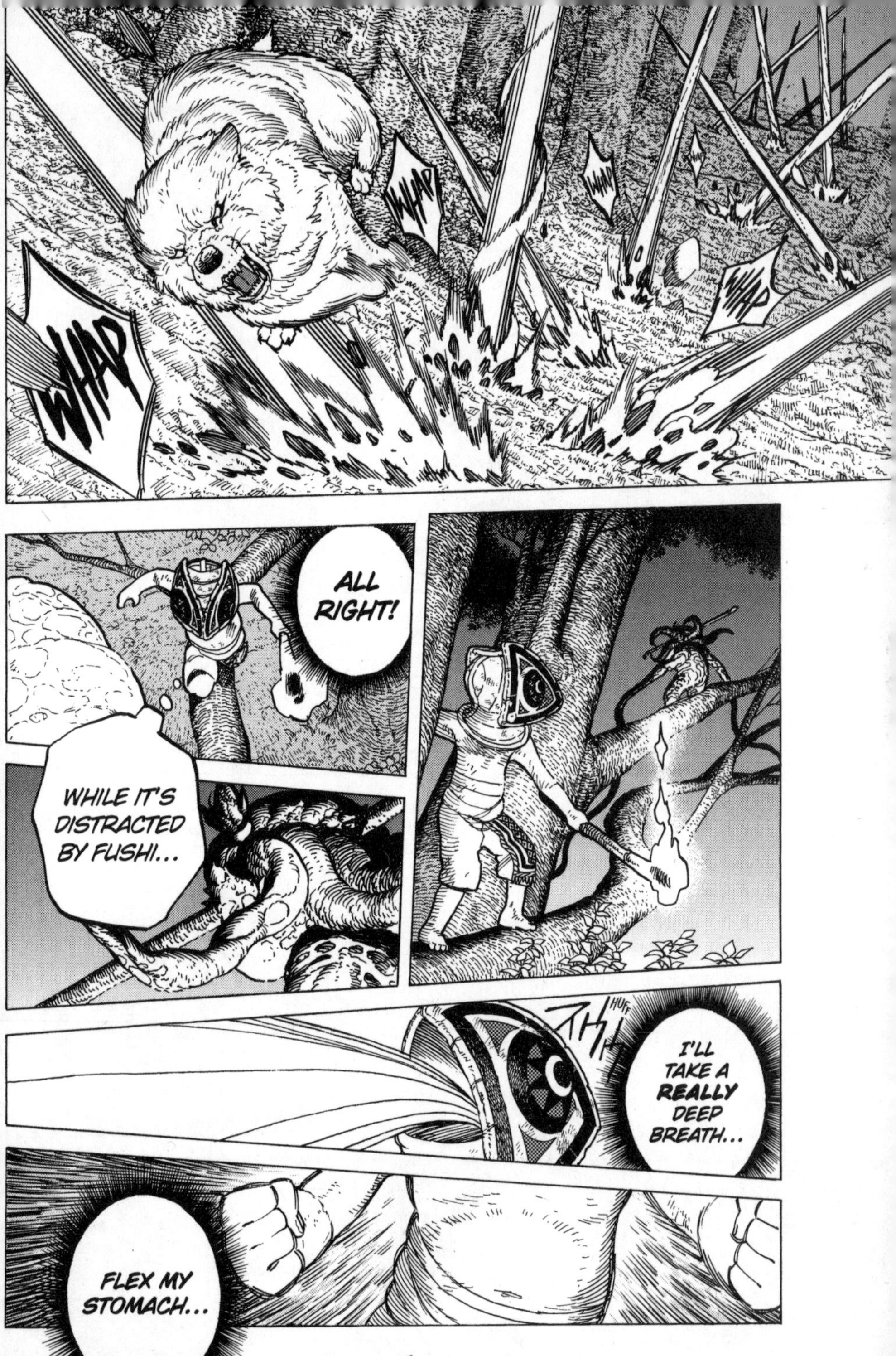
WHAP
WHAP
WHAP
WHAP
ALL RIGHT!
WHILE IT'S DISTRACTED BY FUSHI...
HUFF
I'LL TAKE A REALLY DEEP BREATH...
FLEX MY STOMACH...

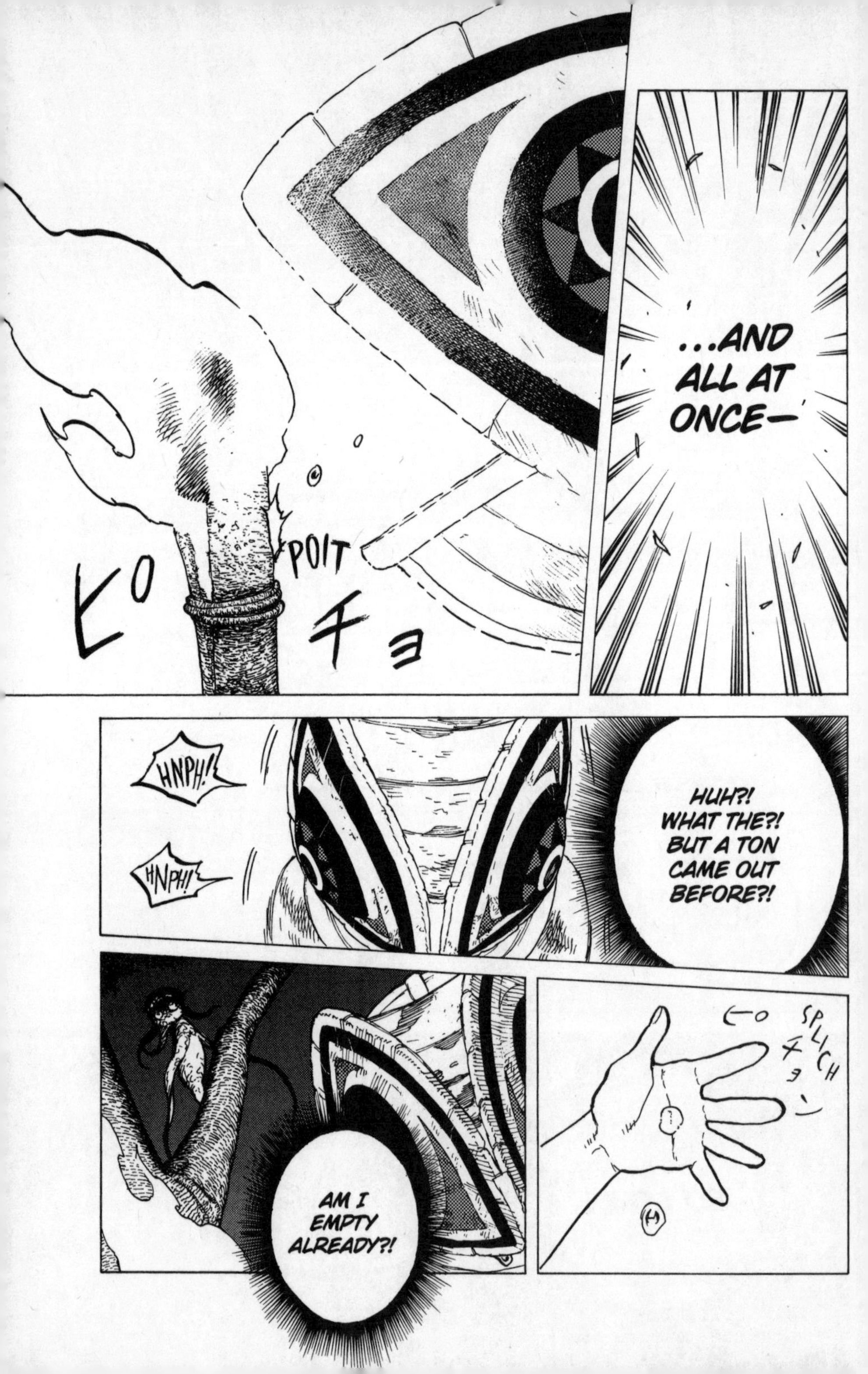
...AND ALL AT ONCE—
POIT
ピチョ
HUH?! WHAT THE?! BUT A TON CAME OUT BEFORE?!
HNPH!
HNPH!
SPLICH
ピチョ
AM I EMPTY ALREADY?!

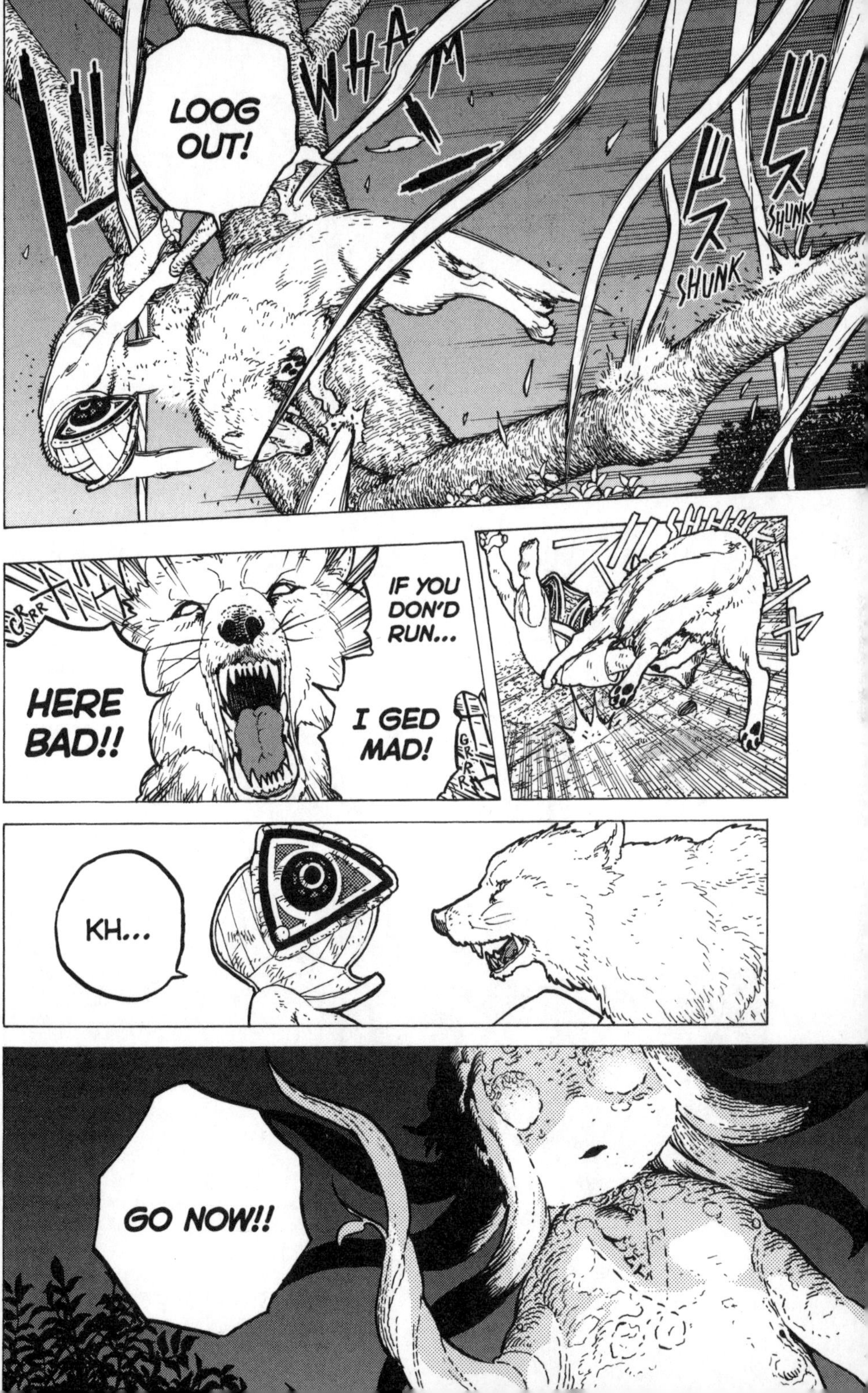
WHAM
LOOG OUT!
SHUNK
SHUNK
IF YOU DON'D RUN...
I GED MAD!
GRRR
HERE BAD!!
KH...
GO NOW!!

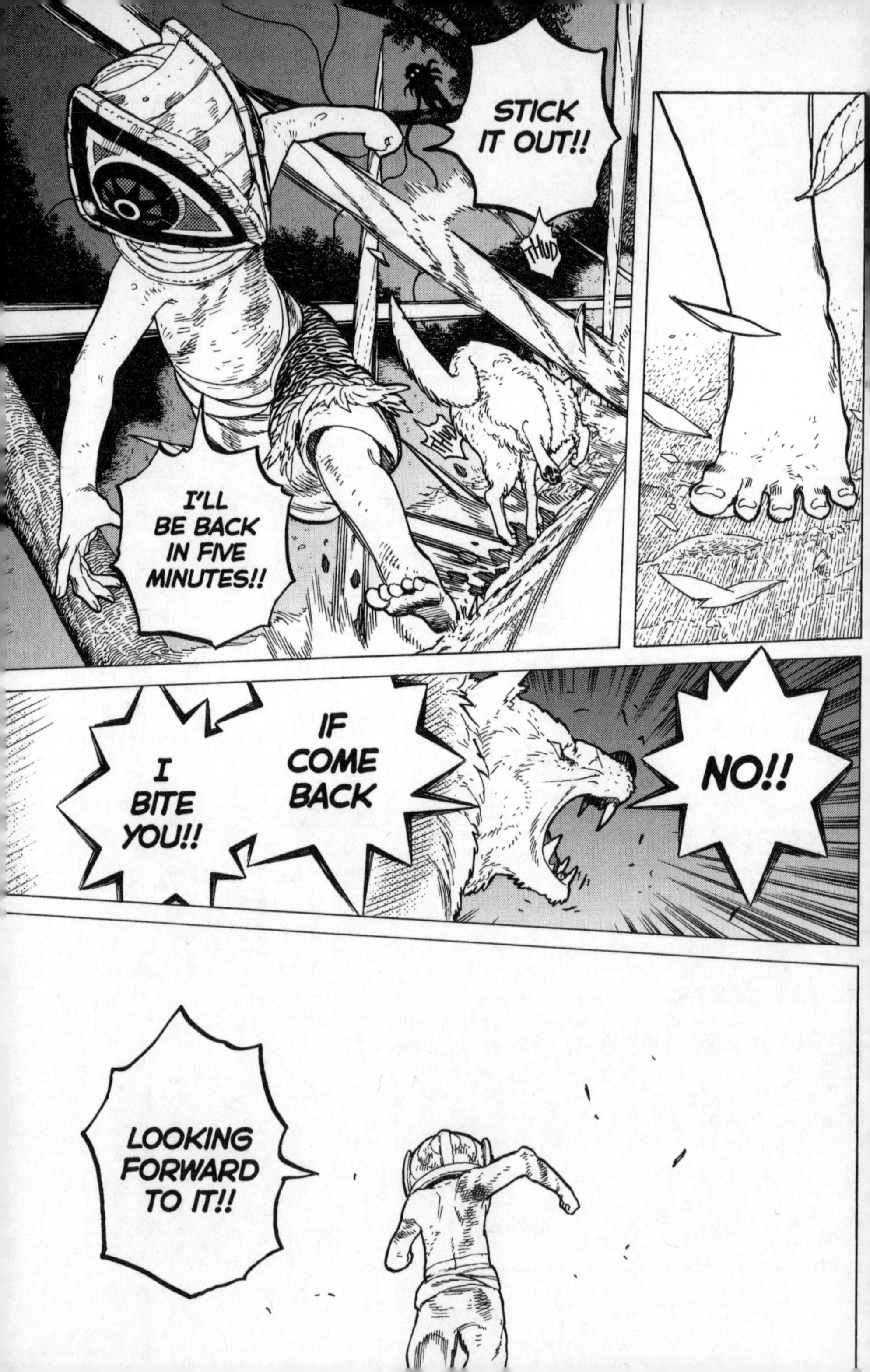
STICK IT OUT!!
THUD
THUD
I'LL BE BACK IN FIVE MINUTES!!
NO!!
IF COME BACK
I BITE YOU!!
LOOKING FORWARD TO IT!!

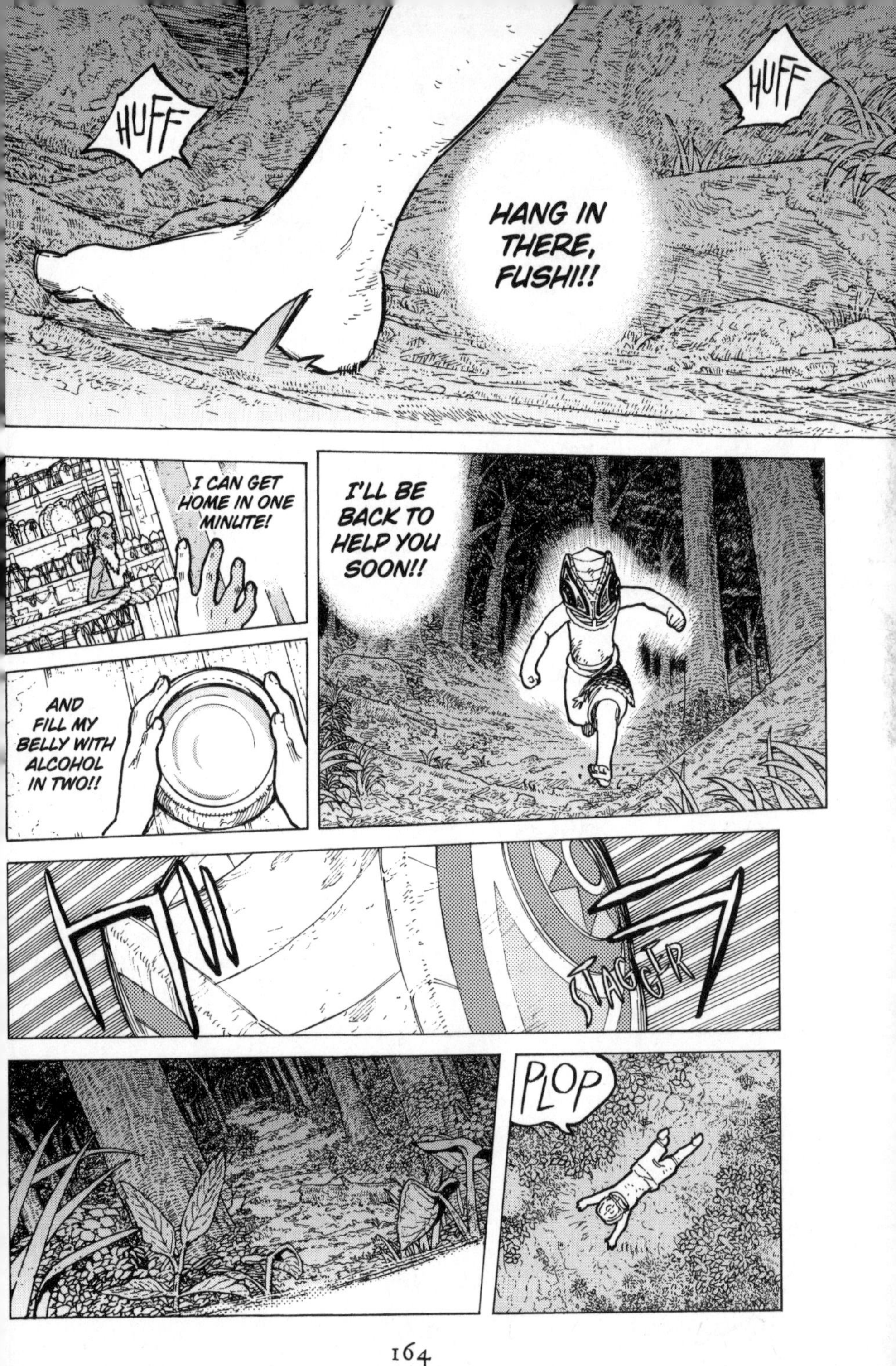
HUFF
HUFF
HANG IN THERE, FUSHI!!
I'LL BE BACK TO HELP YOU SOON!!
I CAN GET HOME IN ONE MINUTE!
AND FILL MY BELLY WITH ALCOHOL IN TWO!!
STAGGER
PLOP

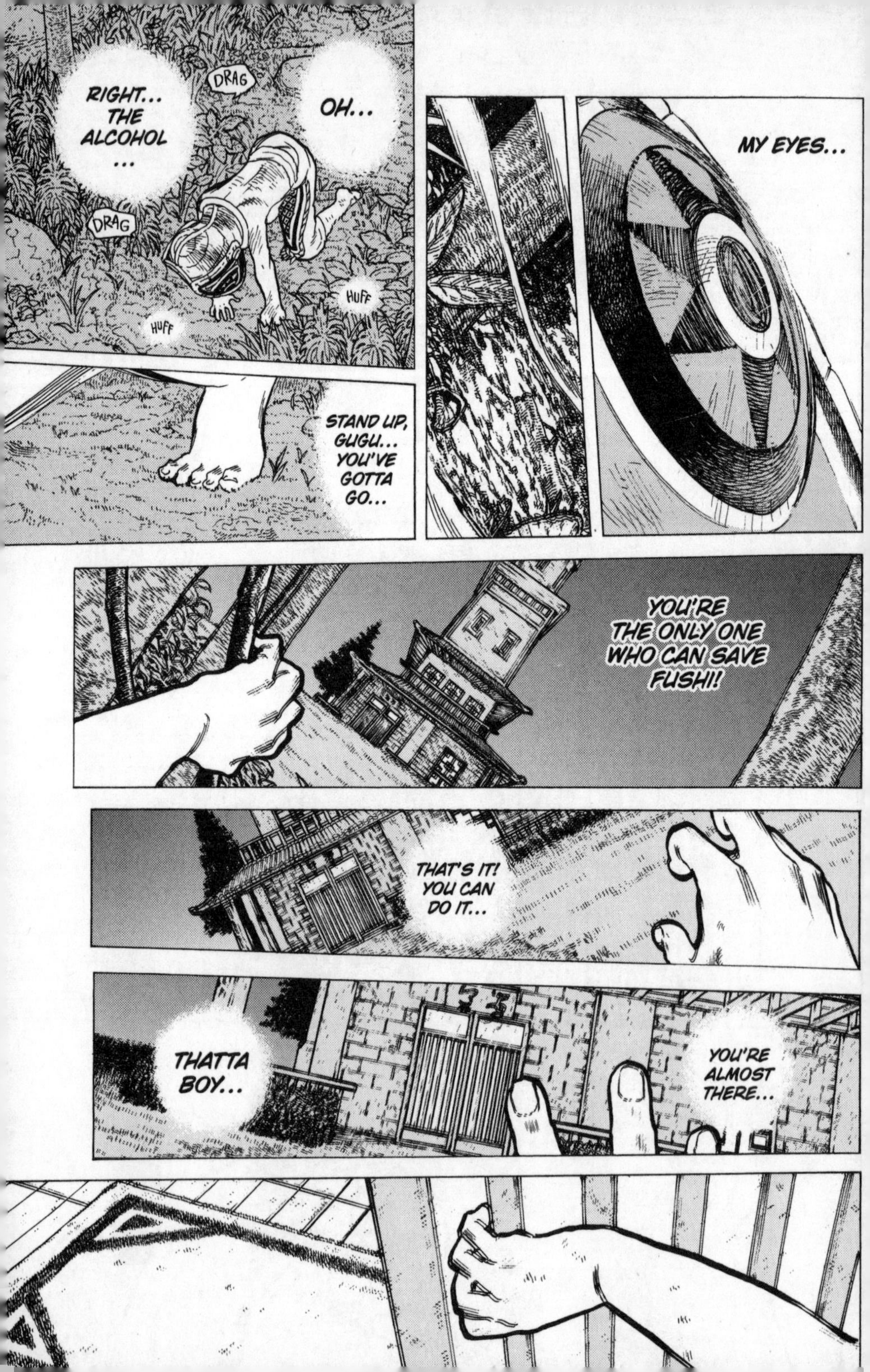
MY EYES...
OH...
DRAG
RIGHT... THE ALCOHOL ...
DRAG
HUFF
HUFF
STAND UP, GUGU... YOU'VE GOTTA GO...
YOU'RE THE ONLY ONE WHO CAN SAVE FUSHI!
THAT'S IT! YOU CAN DO IT...
YOU'RE ALMOST THERE...
THATTA BOY...

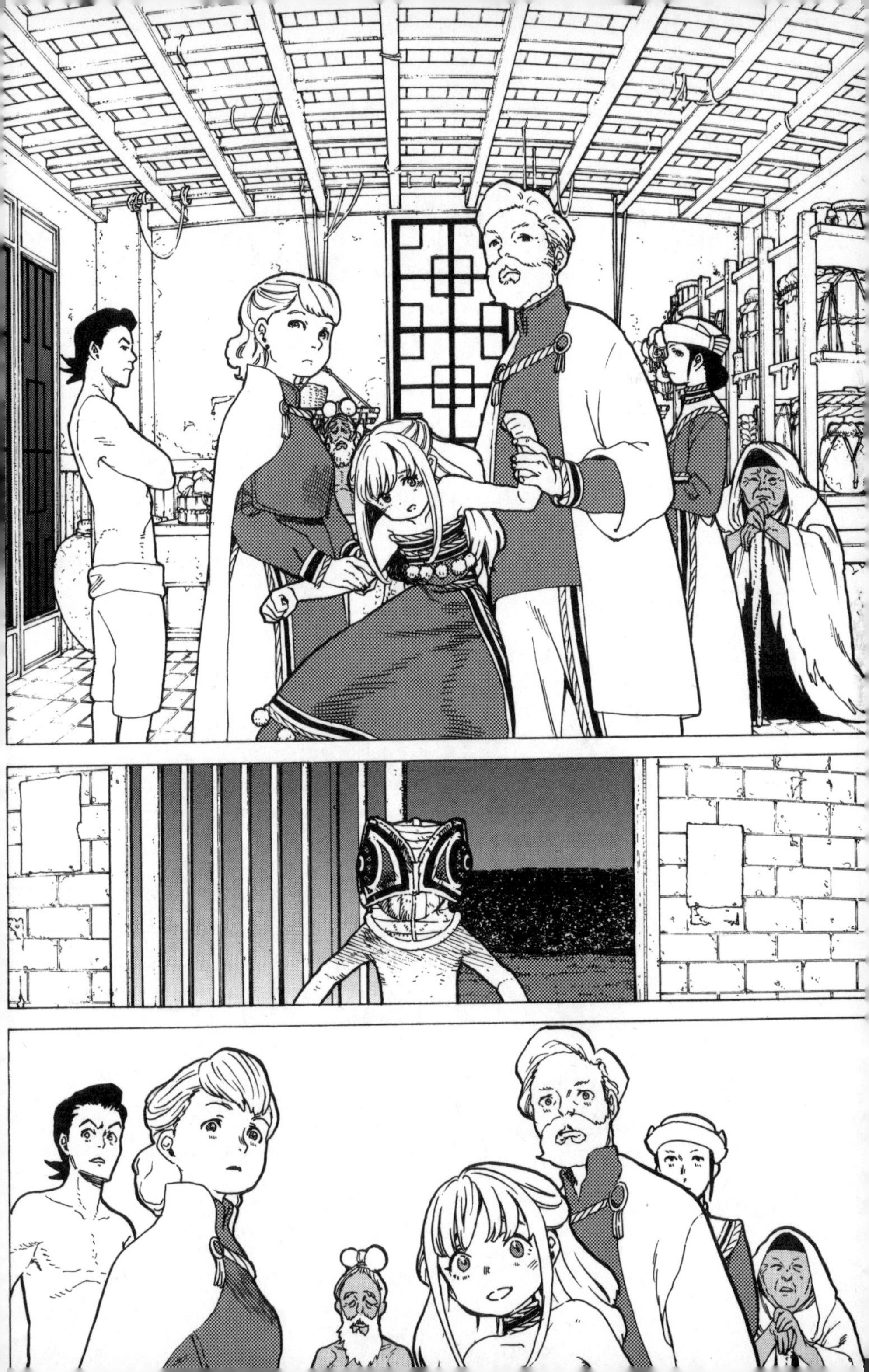

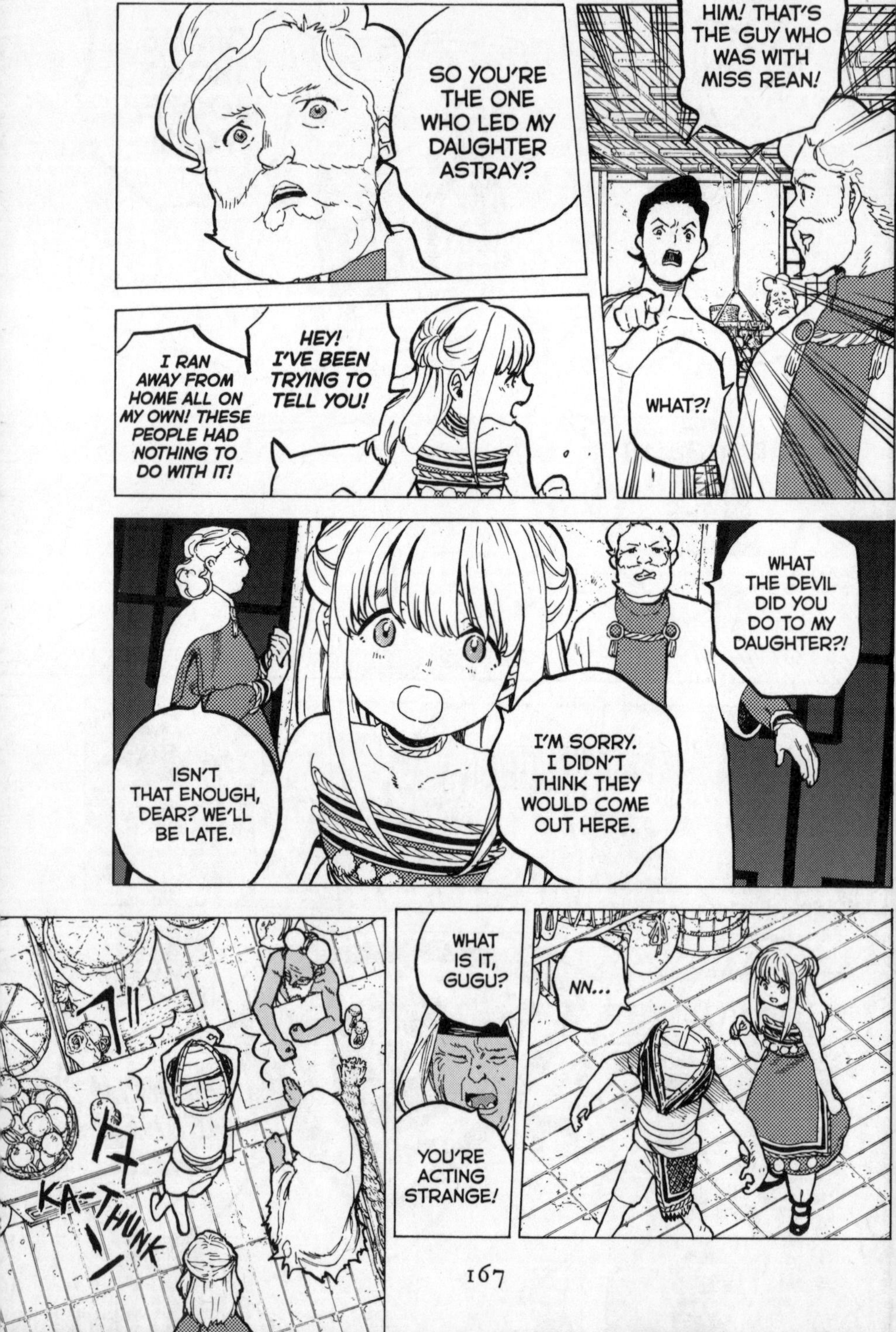
THAT'S HIM! THAT'S THE GUY WHO WAS WITH MISS REAN!
WHAT?!
SO YOU'RE THE ONE WHO LED MY DAUGHTER ASTRAY?
HEY! I'VE BEEN TRYING TO TELL YOU!
I RAN AWAY FROM HOME ALL ON MY OWN! THESE PEOPLE HAD NOTHING TO DO WITH IT!
WHAT THE DEVIL DID YOU DO TO MY DAUGHTER?!
I'M SORRY. I DIDN'T THINK THEY WOULD COME OUT HERE.
ISN'T THAT ENOUGH, DEAR? WE'LL BE LATE.
NN...
WHAT IS IT, GUGU?
YOU'RE ACTING STRANGE!
KA-THUNK

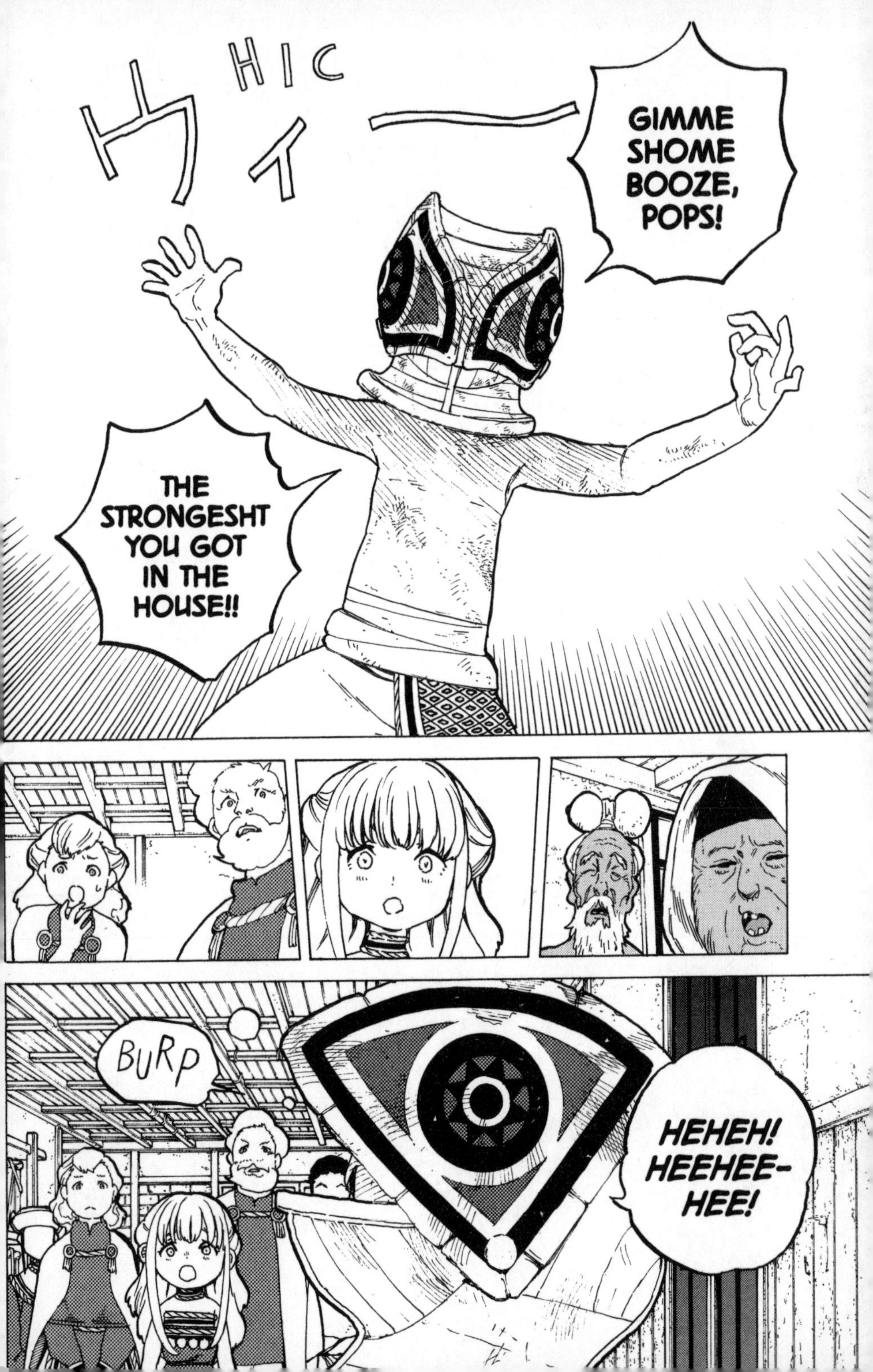
GIMME SHOME BOOZE, POPS!
HIC
ウィー
THE STRONGESHT YOU GOT IN THE HOUSE!!
HEHEH! HEEHEE-HEE!
BURP

#23 The Price of Flames

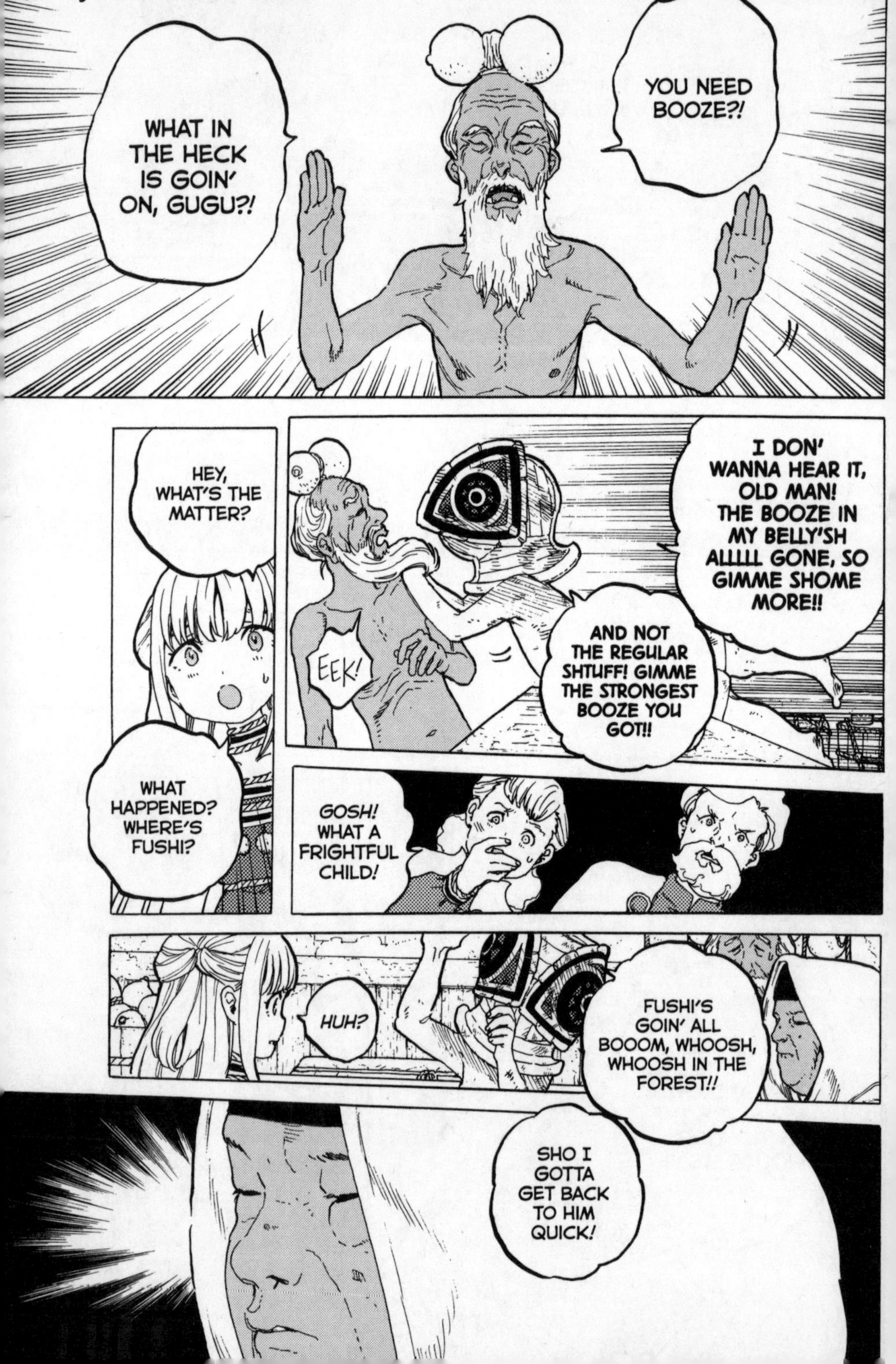
YOU NEED BOOZE?!
WHAT IN THE HECK IS GOIN' ON, GUGU?!
I DON' WANNA HEAR IT, OLD MAN! THE BOOZE IN MY BELLY'SH ALLLLL GONE, SO GIMME SHOME MORE!!
AND NOT THE REGULAR SHTUFF! GIMME THE STRONGEST BOOZE YOU GOT!!
EEK!
GOSH! WHAT A FRIGHTFUL CHILD!
HEY, WHAT'S THE MATTER?
WHAT HAPPENED? WHERE'S FUSHI?
FUSHI'S GOIN' ALL BOOOM, WHOOSH, WHOOSH IN THE FOREST!!
HUH?
SHO I GOTTA GET BACK TO HIM QUICK!

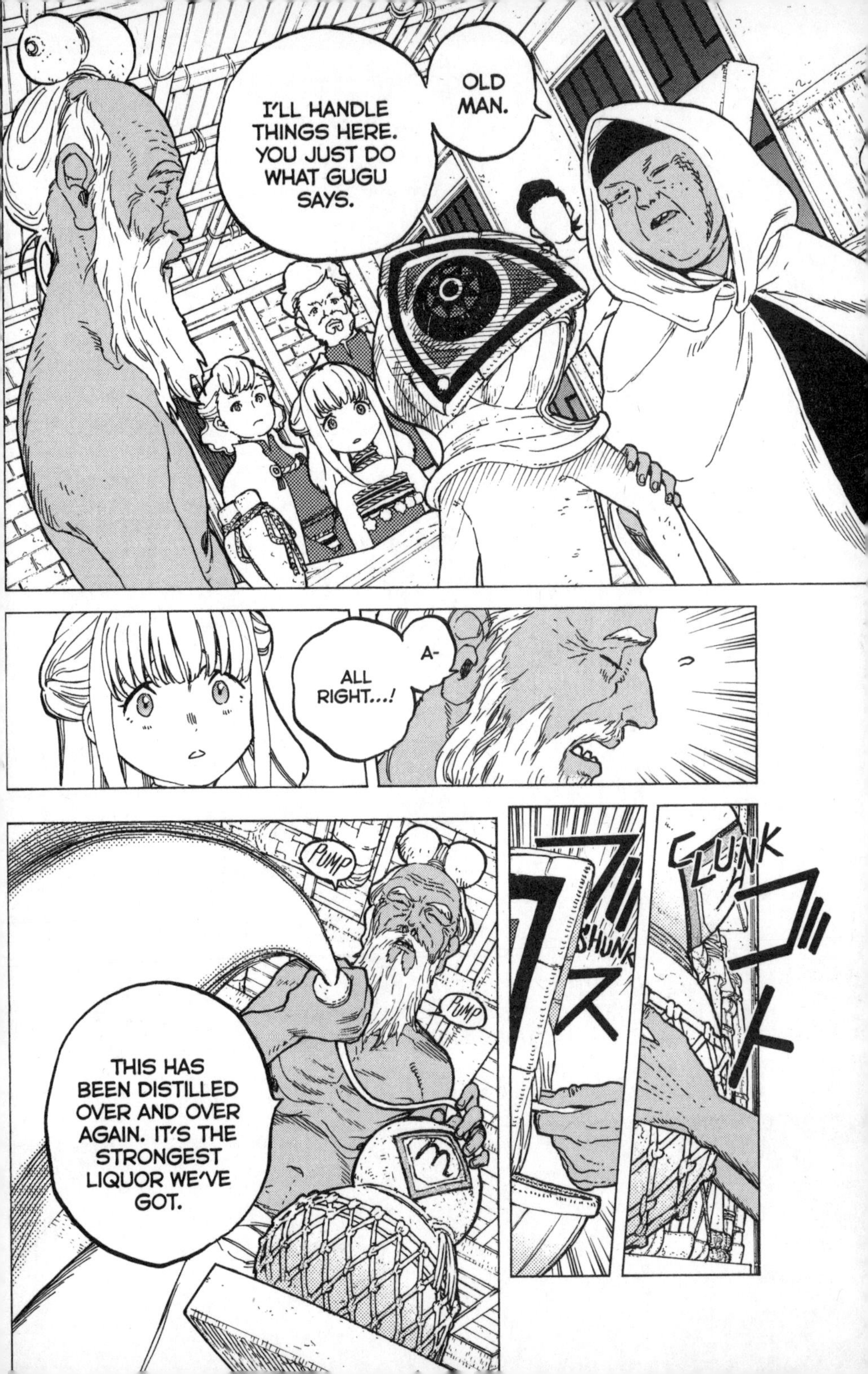
OLD MAN.
I'LL HANDLE THINGS HERE. YOU JUST DO WHAT GUGU SAYS.
A-
ALL RIGHT...!
CLUNK
SHUNK
PUMP
PUMP
THIS HAS BEEN DISTILLED OVER AND OVER AGAIN. IT'S THE STRONGEST LIQUOR WE'VE GOT.

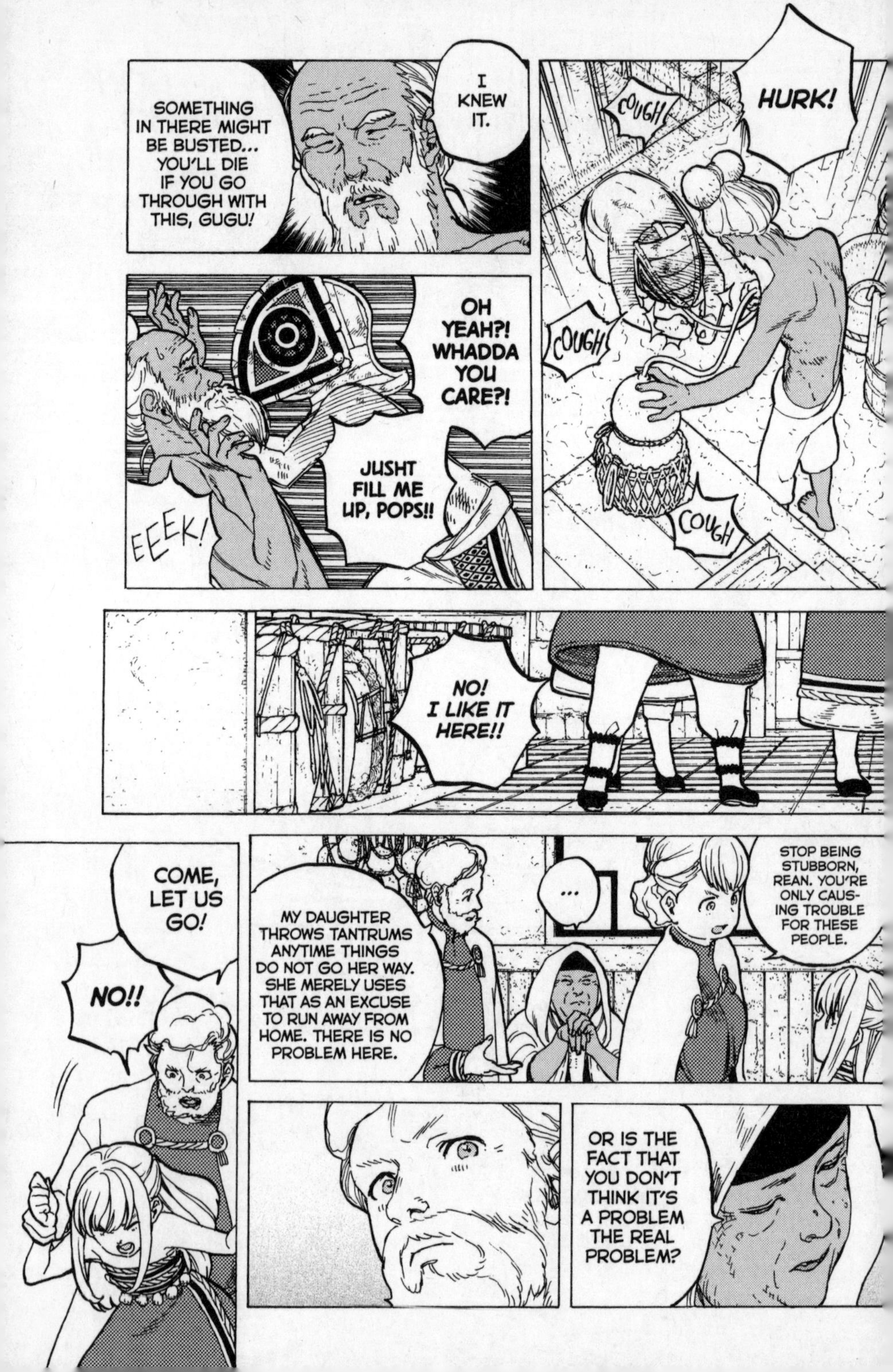
HURK!
COUGH
COUGH
COUGH
I KNEW IT.
SOMETHING IN THERE MIGHT BE BUSTED... YOU'LL DIE IF YOU GO THROUGH WITH THIS, GUGU!
OH YEAH?! WHADDA YOU CARE?!
JUSHT FILL ME UP, POPS!!
EEEK!
NO! I LIKE IT HERE!!
STOP BEING STUBBORN, REAN. YOU'RE ONLY CAUSING TROUBLE FOR THESE PEOPLE.
...
MY DAUGHTER THROWS TANTRUMS ANYTIME THINGS DO NOT GO HER WAY. SHE MERELY USES THAT AS AN EXCUSE TO RUN AWAY FROM HOME. THERE IS NO PROBLEM HERE.
OR IS THE FACT THAT YOU DON'T THINK IT'S A PROBLEM THE REAL PROBLEM?
COME, LET US GO!
NO!!

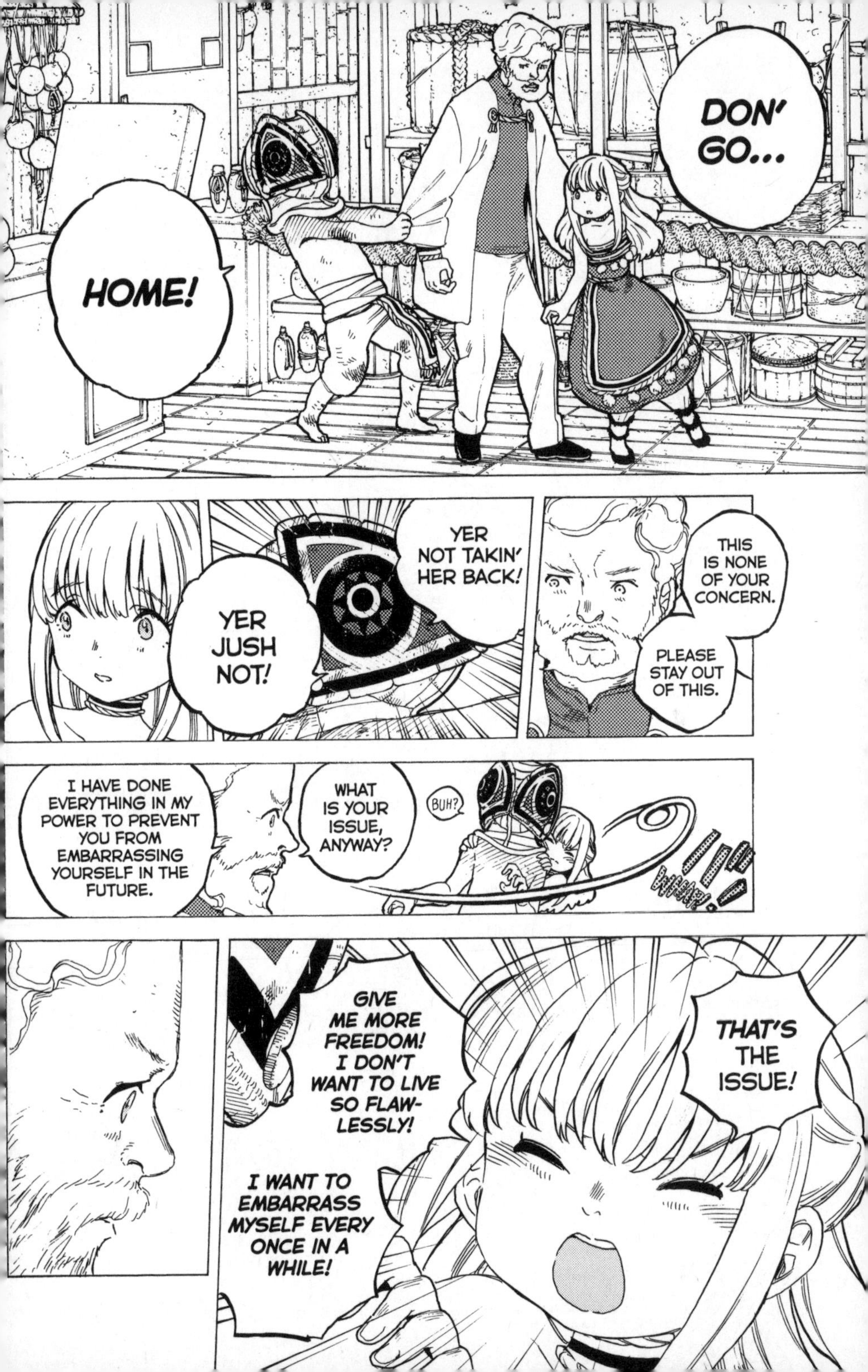
DON' GO...
HOME!
THIS IS NONE OF YOUR CONCERN.
PLEASE STAY OUT OF THIS.
YER NOT TAKIN' HER BACK!
YER JUSH NOT!
BUH?
WHAT IS YOUR ISSUE, ANYWAY?
I HAVE DONE EVERYTHING IN MY POWER TO PREVENT YOU FROM EMBARRASSING YOURSELF IN THE FUTURE.
THAT'S THE ISSUE!
GIVE ME MORE FREEDOM! I DON'T WANT TO LIVE SO FLAW-LESSLY!
I WANT TO EMBARRASS MYSELF EVERY ONCE IN A WHILE!

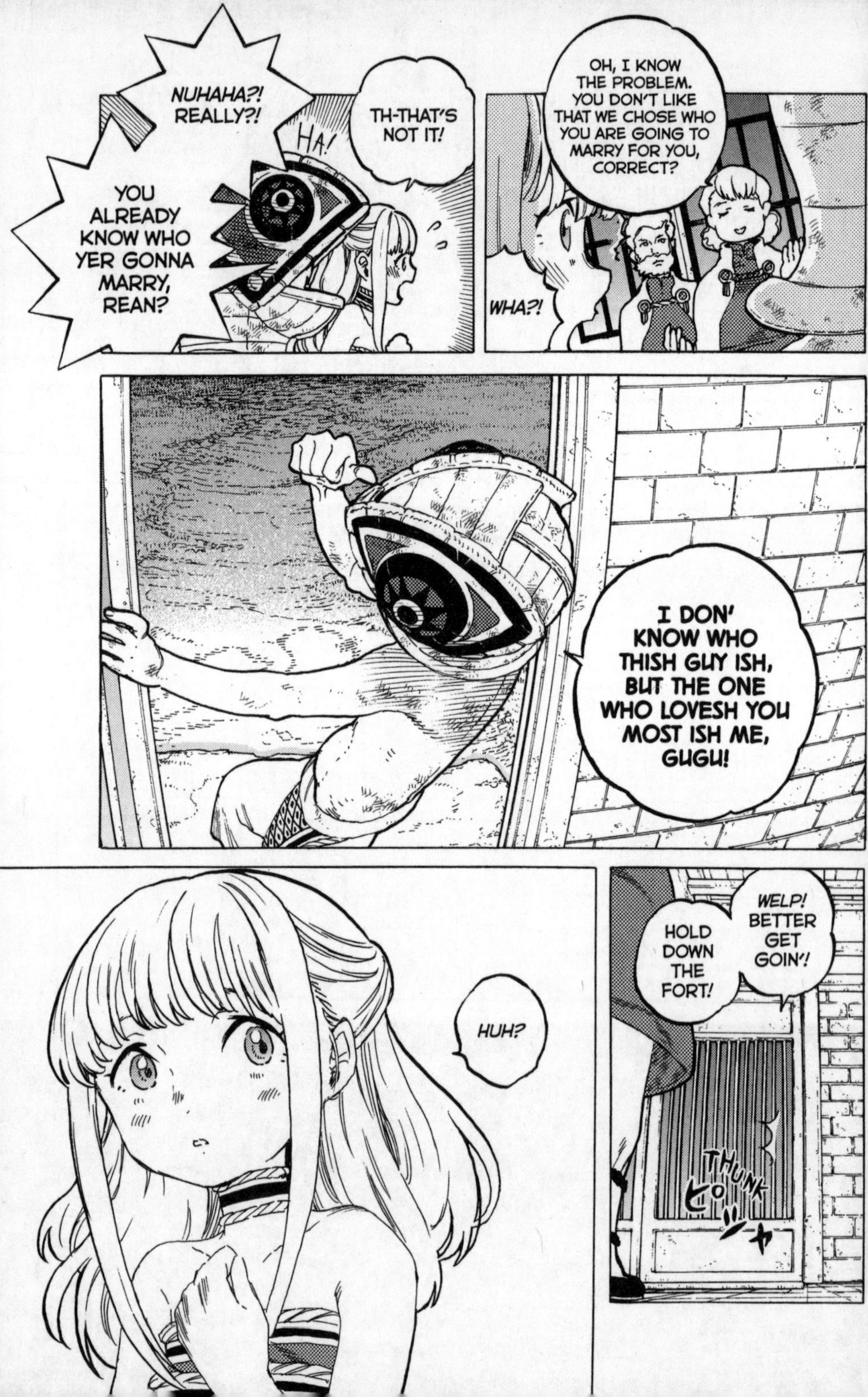
OH, I KNOW THE PROBLEM. YOU DON'T LIKE THAT WE CHOSE WHO YOU ARE GOING TO MARRY FOR YOU, CORRECT?
WHA?!
TH-THAT'S NOT IT!
NUHAHA?! REALLY?!
HA!
YOU ALREADY KNOW WHO YER GONNA MARRY, REAN?
I DON' KNOW WHO THISH GUY ISH, BUT THE ONE WHO LOVESH YOU MOST ISH ME, GUGU!
WELP! BETTER GET GOIN'!
HOLD DOWN THE FORT!
THUNK
HUH?

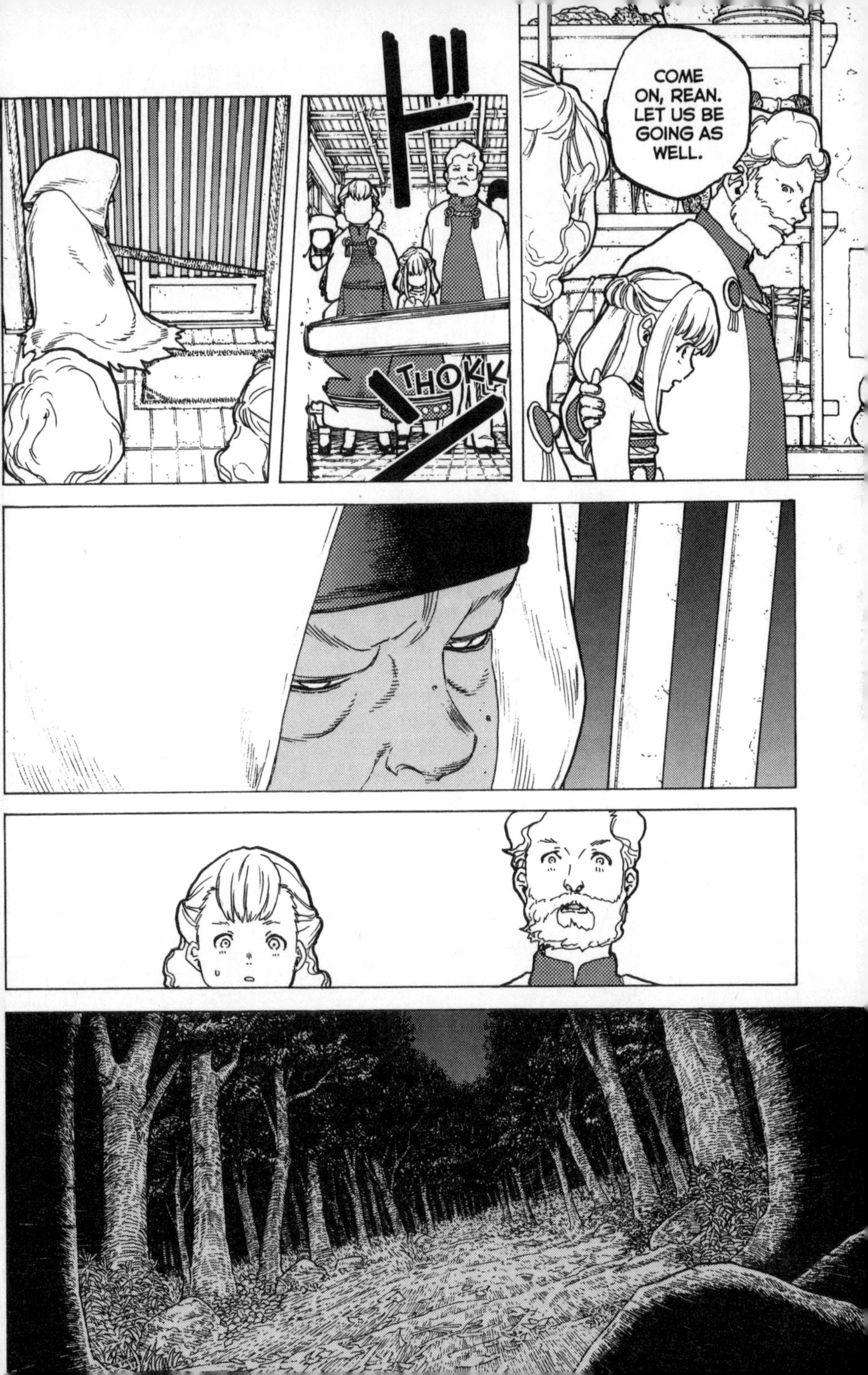
COME ON, REAN. LET US BE GOING AS WELL.
ド
THOKK

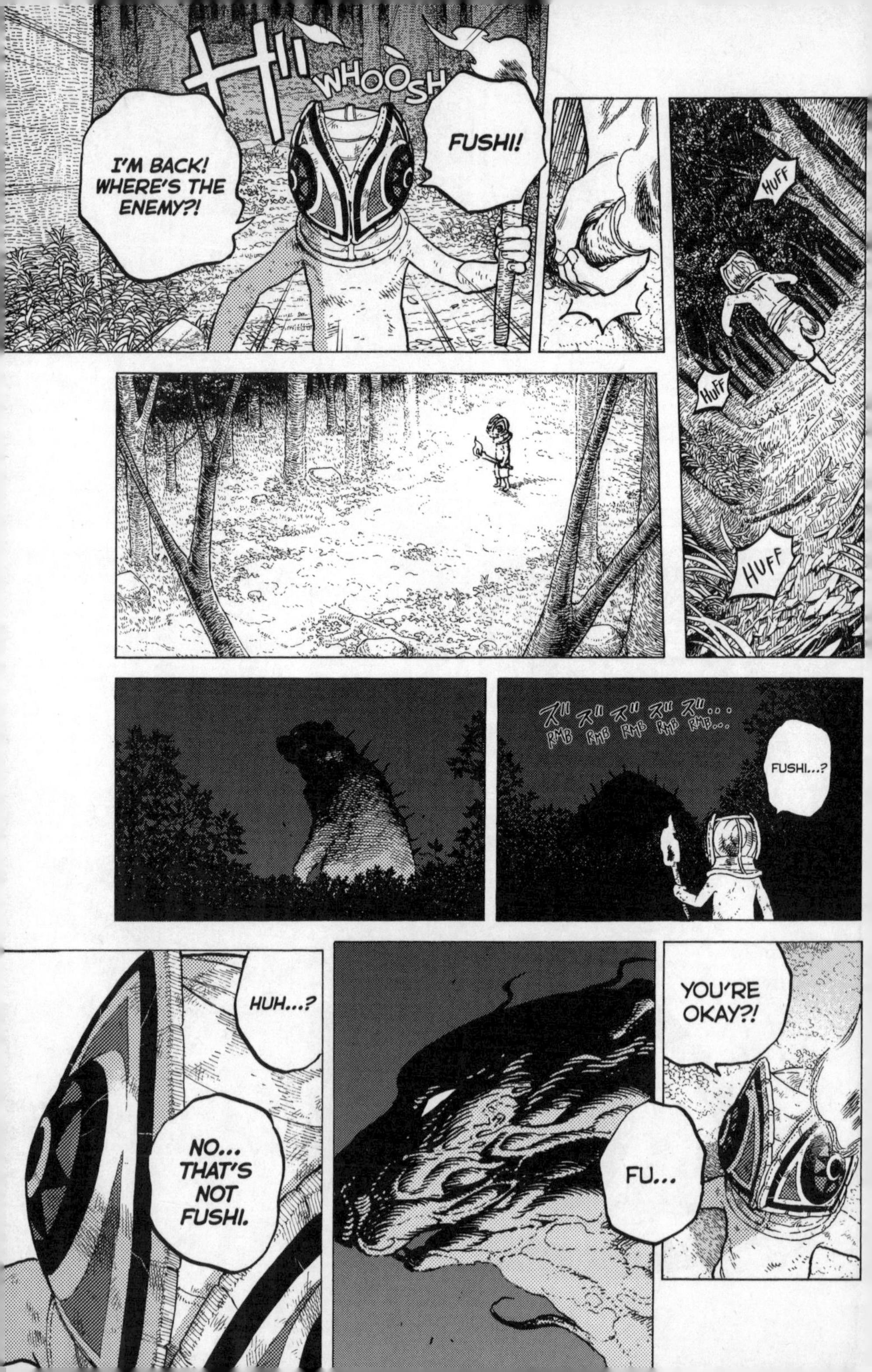
HUFF
HUFF
HUFF
FUSHI!
WHOOSH
I'M BACK! WHERE'S THE ENEMY?!
RMB RMB RMB RMB RMB...
FUSHI...?
YOU'RE OKAY?!
FU...
HUH...?
NO... THAT'S NOT FUSHI.

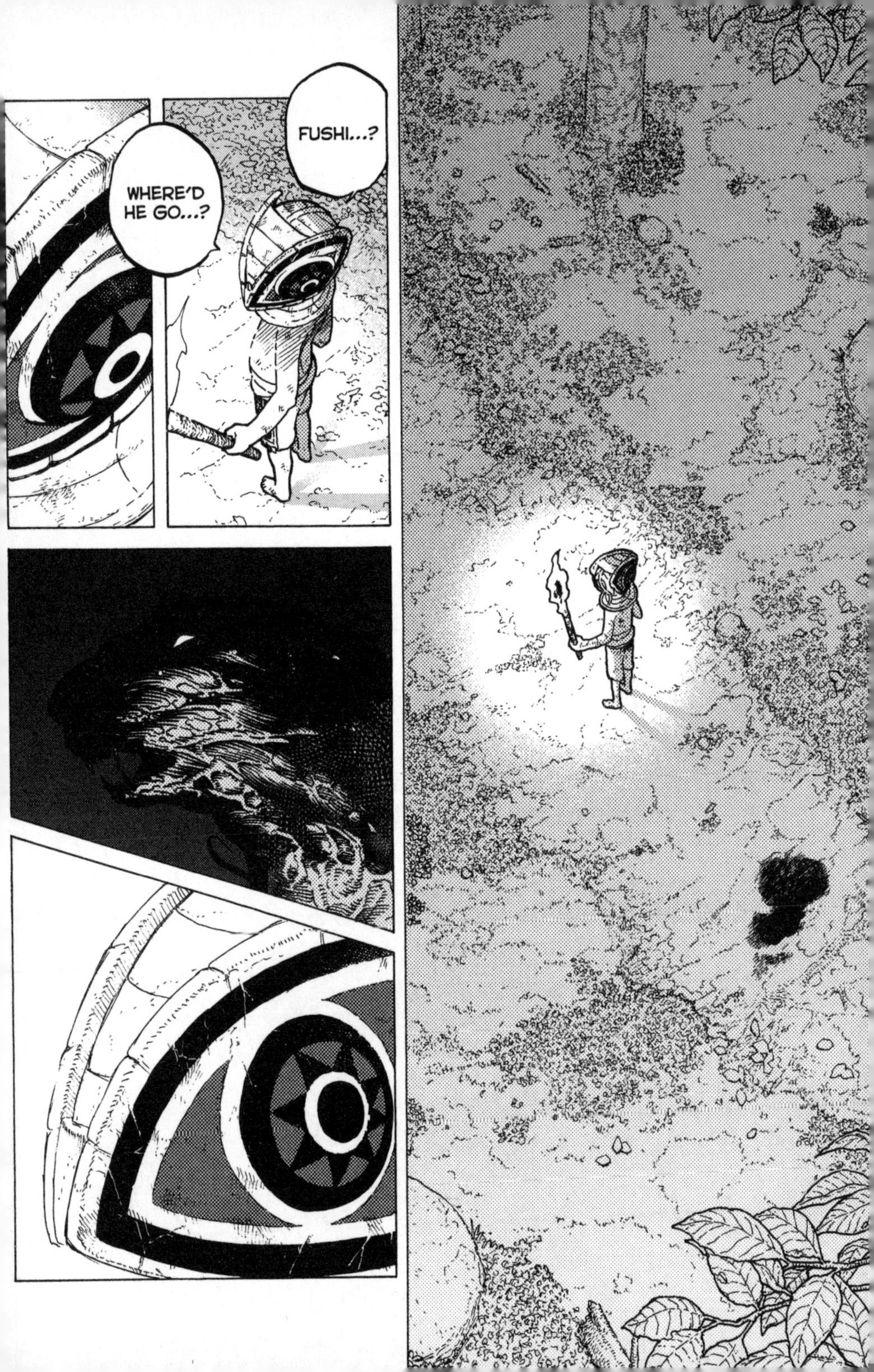
FUSHI...?
WHERE'D HE GO...?

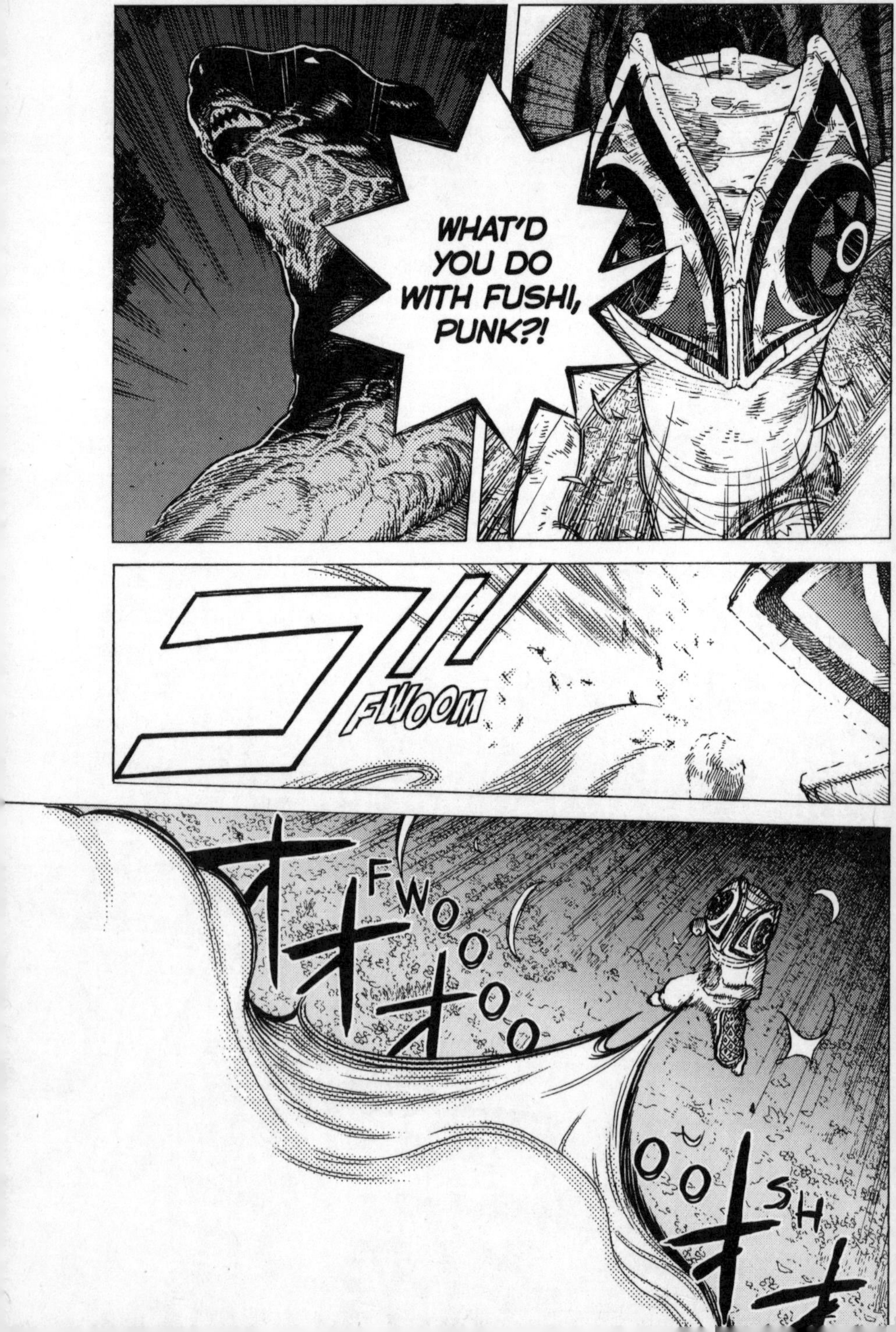
WHAT'D YOU DO WITH FUSHI, PUNK?!
FWOOM
FWOOOOO
OOSH

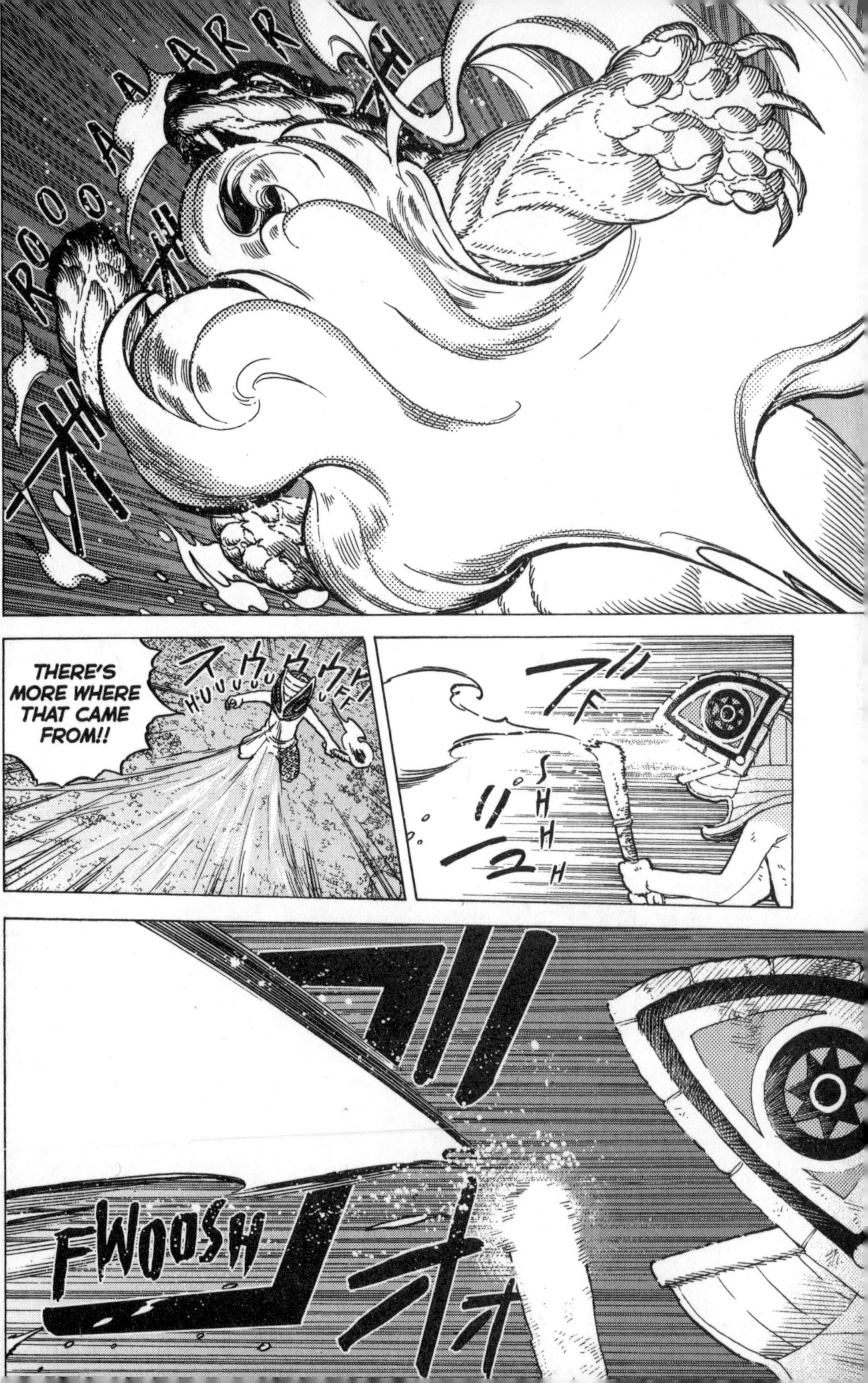
ROOOAAARRR
SHHHH
HUUUUUFF
THERE'S MORE WHERE THAT CAME FROM!!
FWOOSH

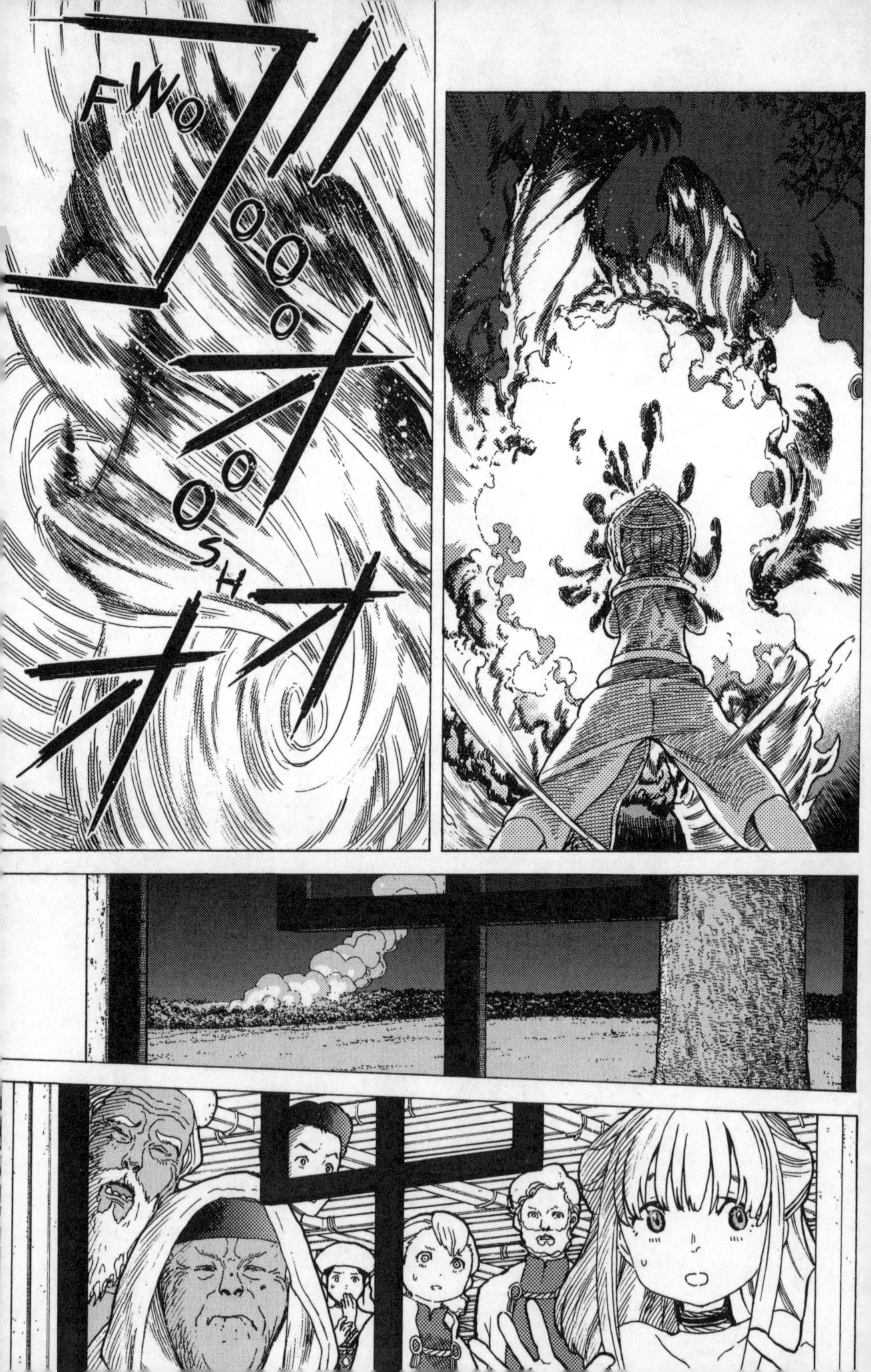
FWOOOOOOOSH

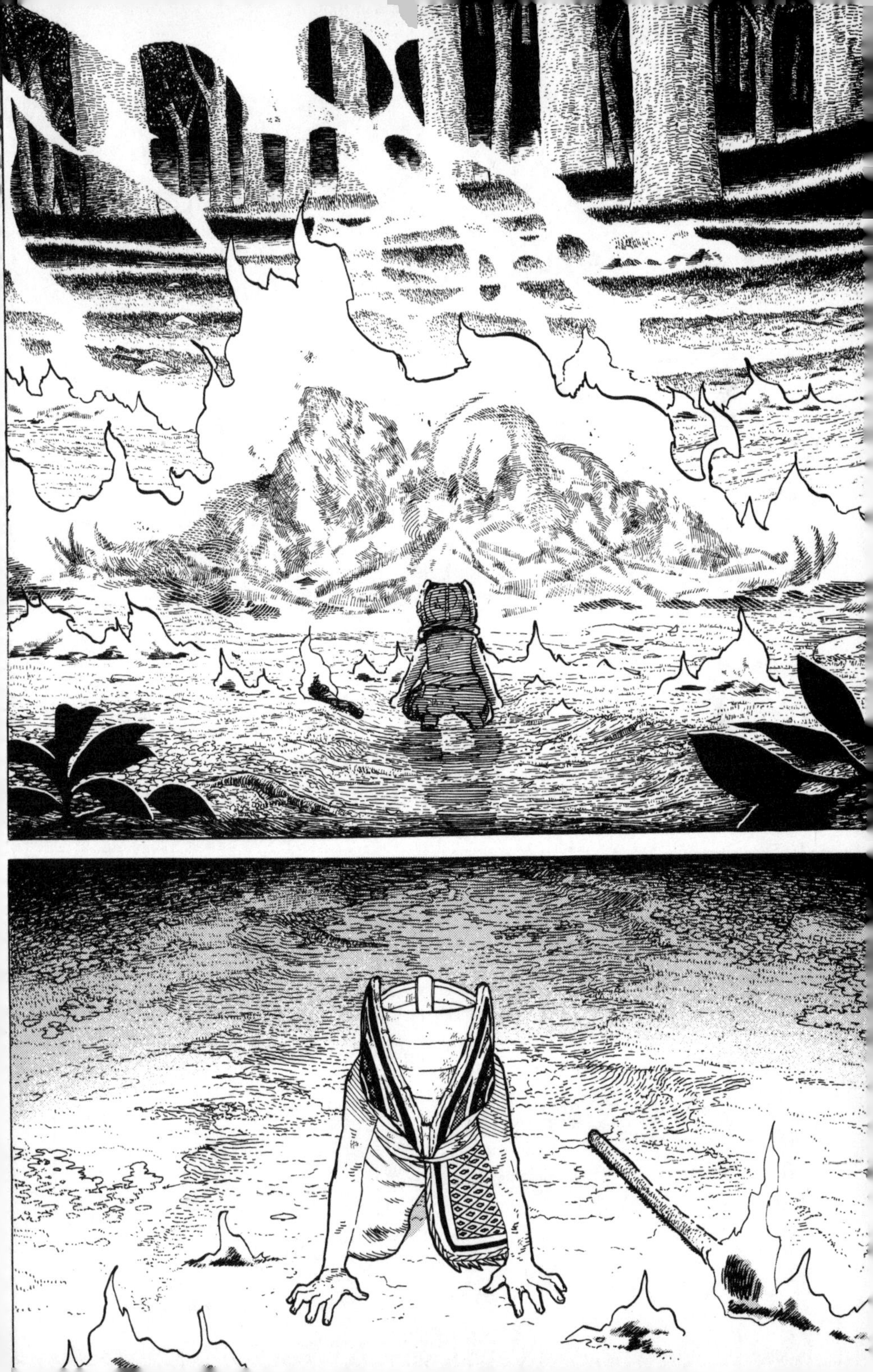

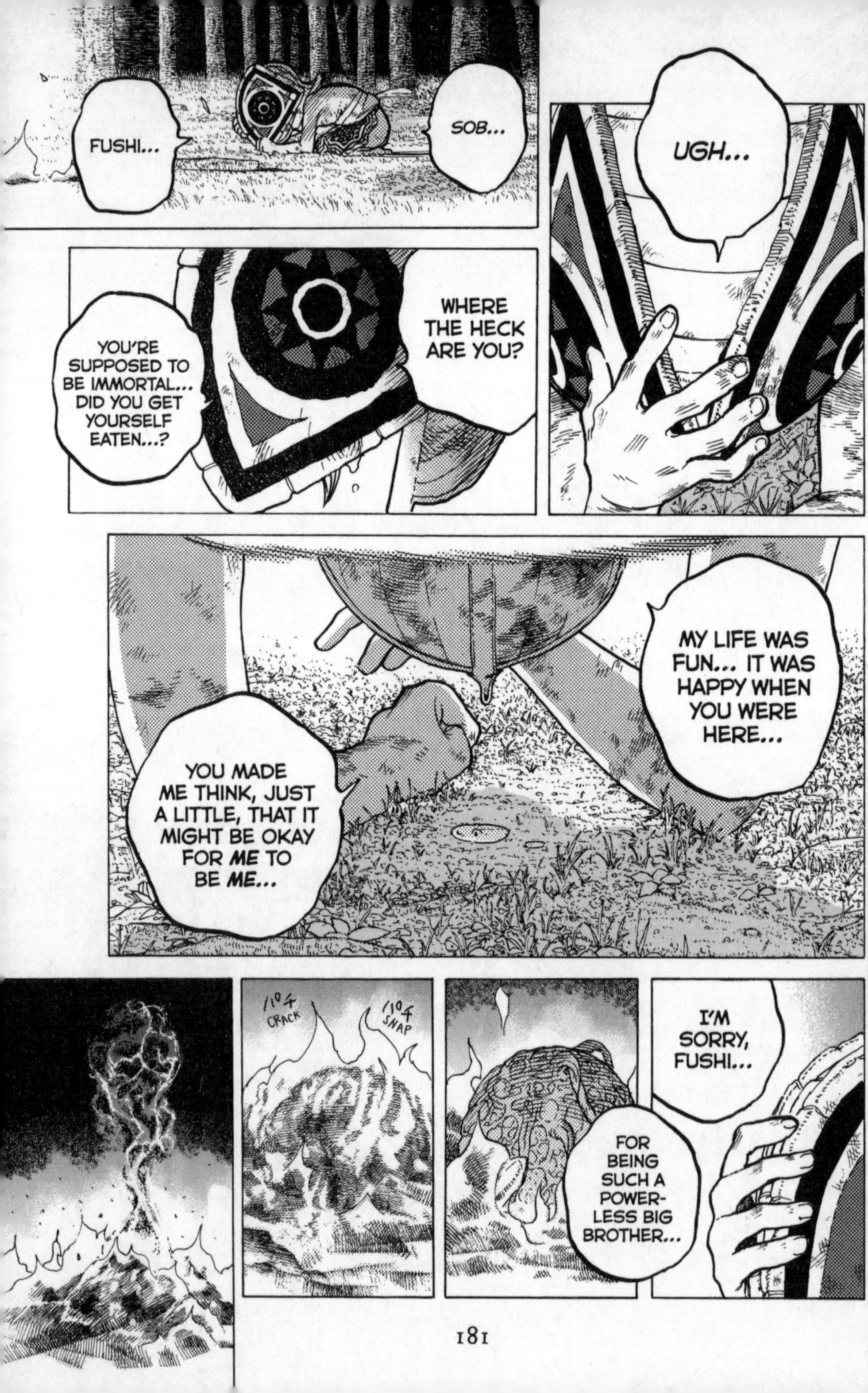
UGH...
SOB...
FUSHI...
WHERE THE HECK ARE YOU?
YOU'RE SUPPOSED TO BE IMMORTAL... DID YOU GET YOURSELF EATEN...?
MY LIFE WAS FUN... IT WAS HAPPY WHEN YOU WERE HERE...
YOU MADE ME THINK, JUST A LITTLE, THAT IT MIGHT BE OKAY FOR *ME* TO BE *ME*...
I'M SORRY, FUSHI...
FOR BEING SUCH A POWER-LESS BIG BROTHER...
SNAP
CRACK

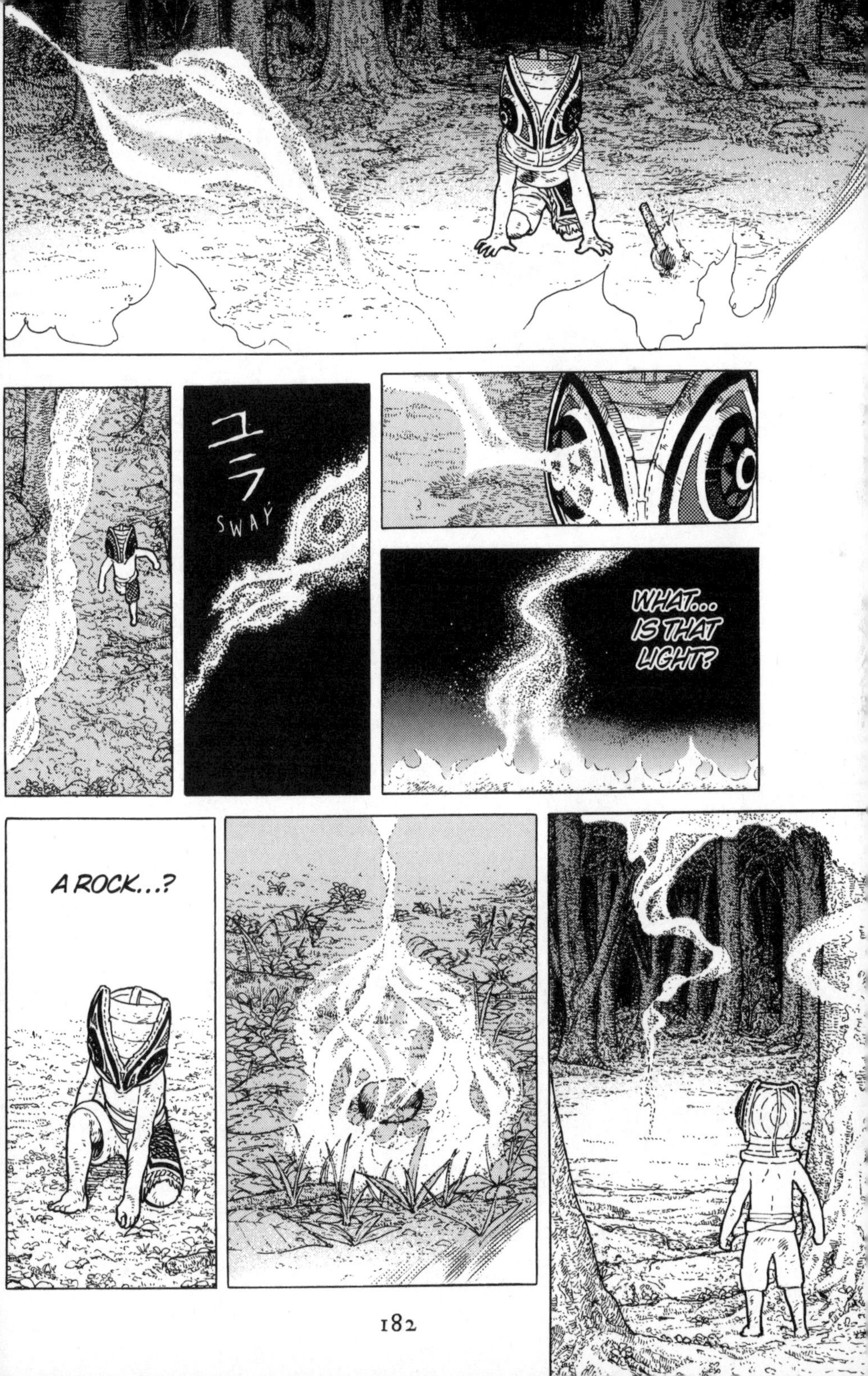
WHAT... IS THAT LIGHT?
ユラ
SWAY
A ROCK...?

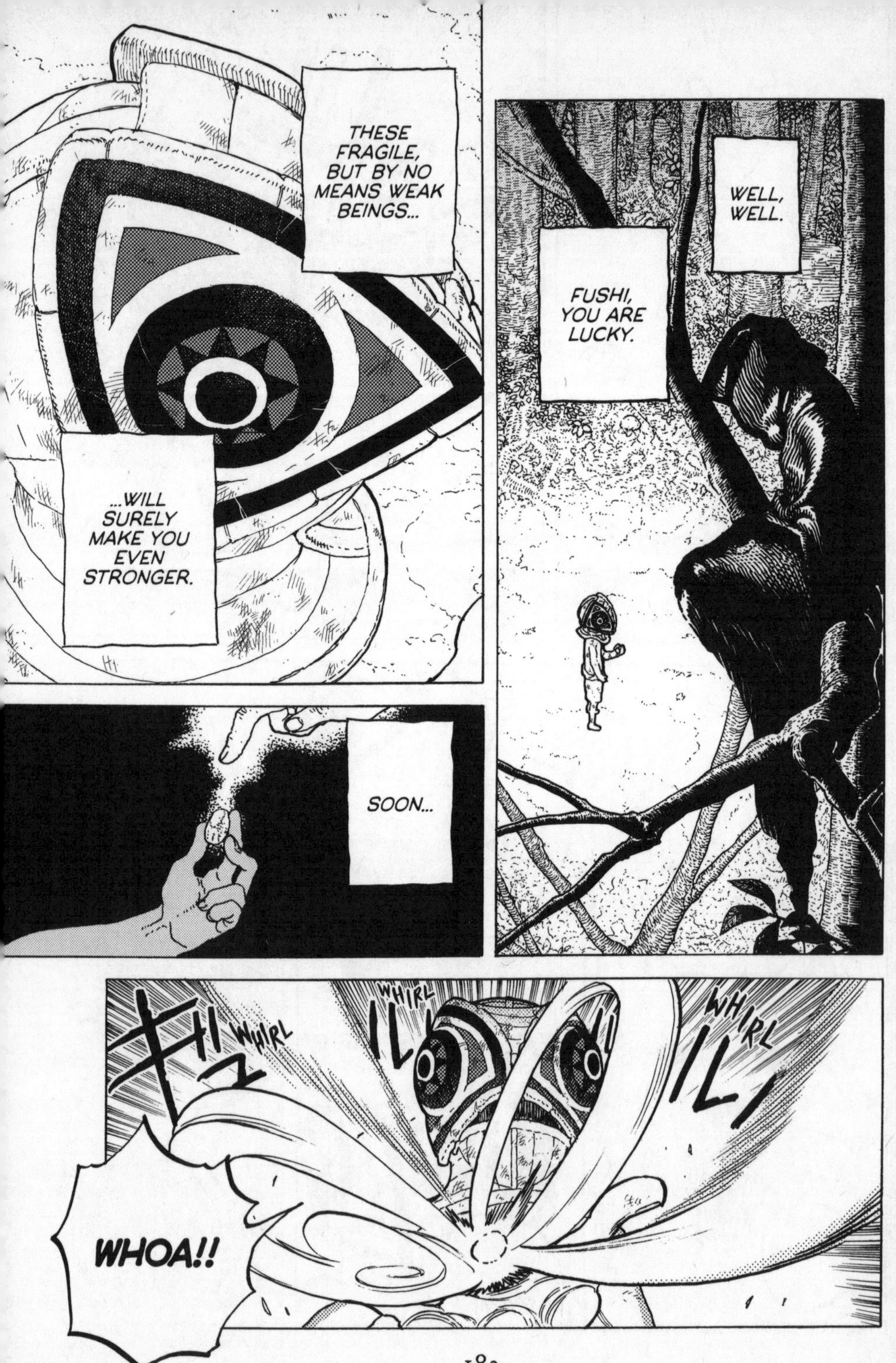
WELL, WELL.
FUSHI, YOU ARE LUCKY.
THESE FRAGILE, BUT BY NO MEANS WEAK BEINGS...
...WILL SURELY MAKE YOU EVEN STRONGER.
SOON...
WHIRL
WHIRL
WHIRL
WHOA!!

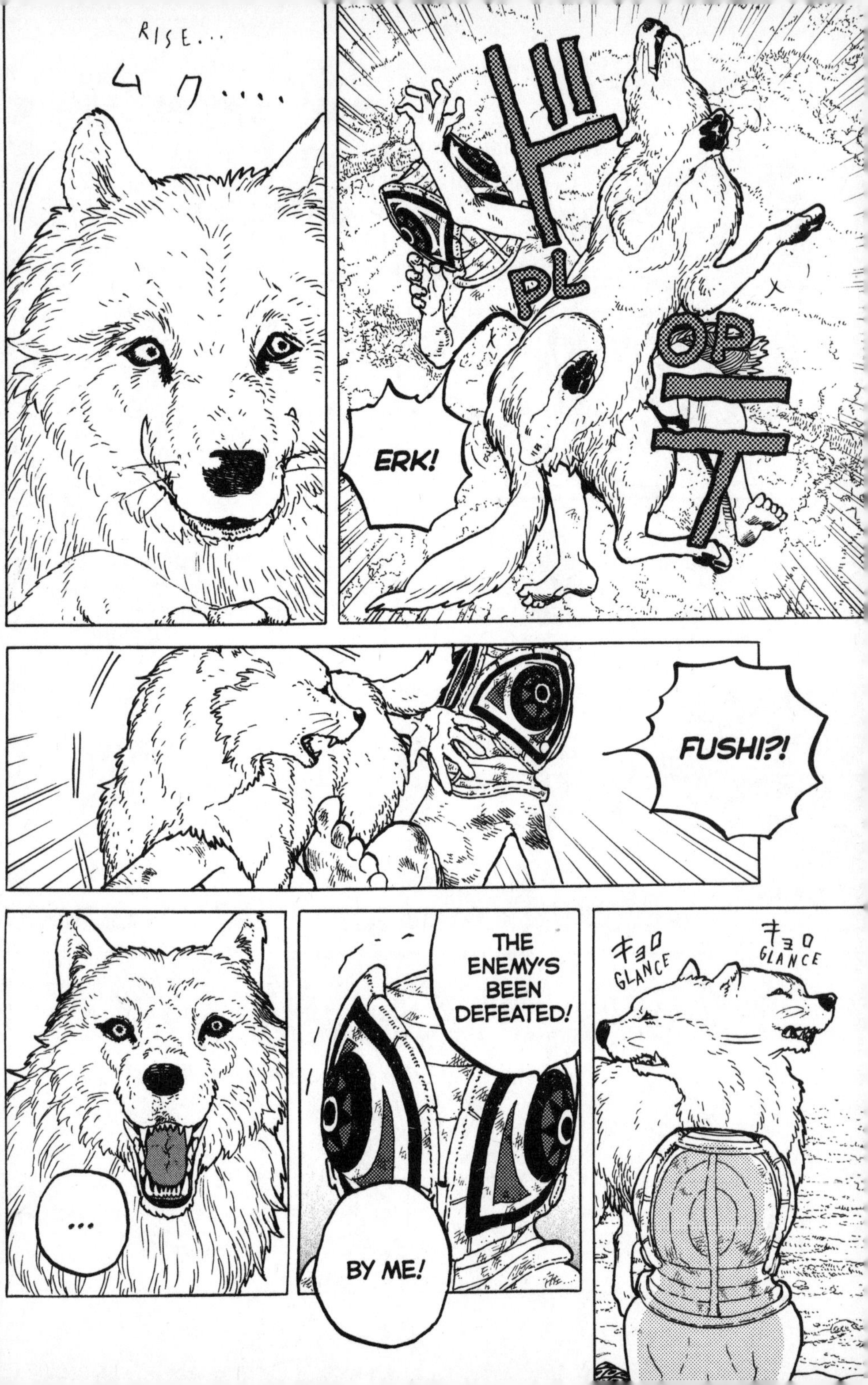
PLOP
ERK!
RISE...
ムク...
FUSHI?!
キョロ
GLANCE
キョロ
GLANCE
THE ENEMY'S BEEN DEFEATED!
BY ME!
...

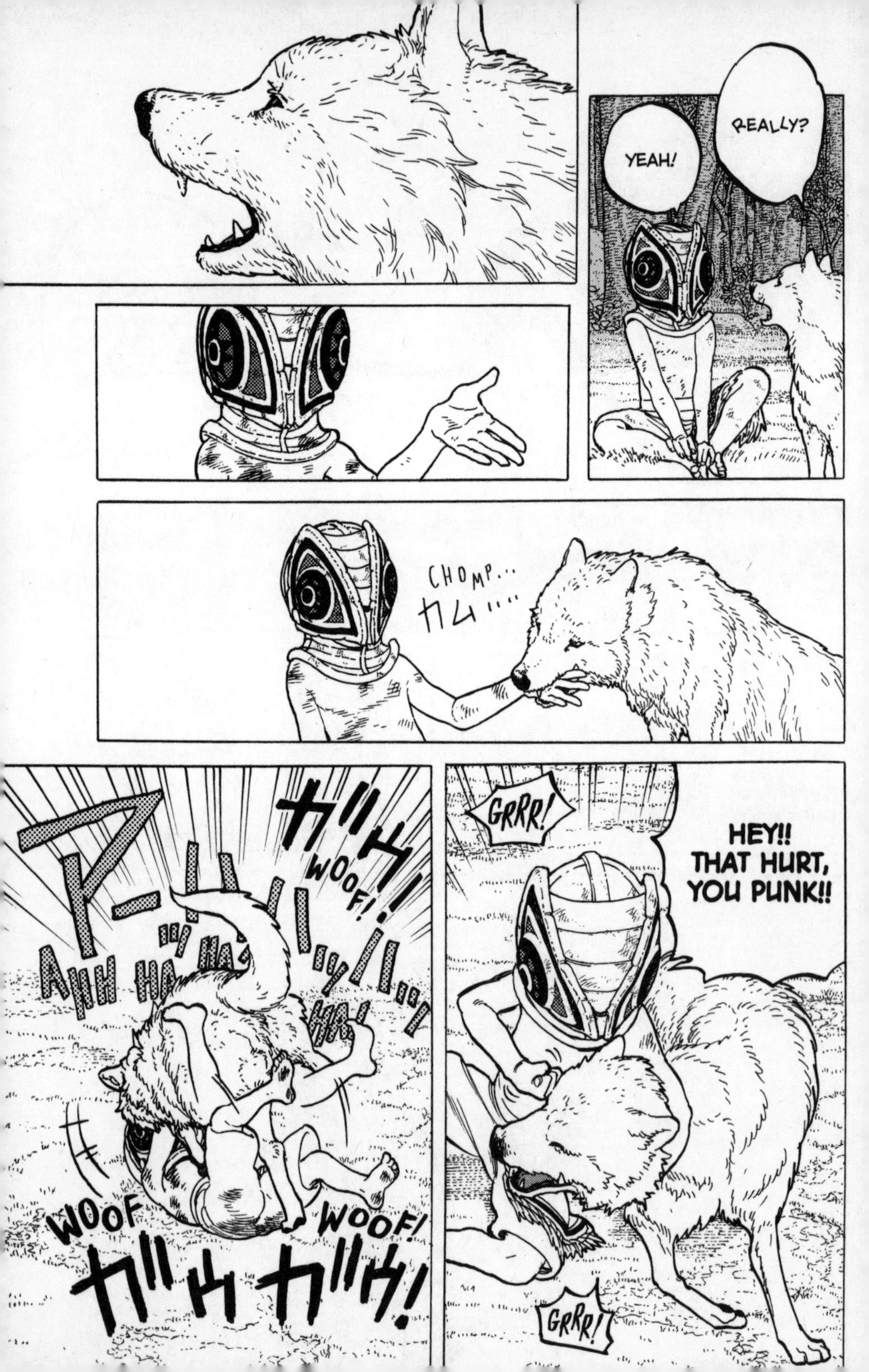
REALLY?
YEAH!
CHOMP...
カム...
GRRR!
HEY!! THAT HURT, YOU PUNK!!
GRRR!
WOOF!
AHH HA HA HA!
WOOF WOOF!

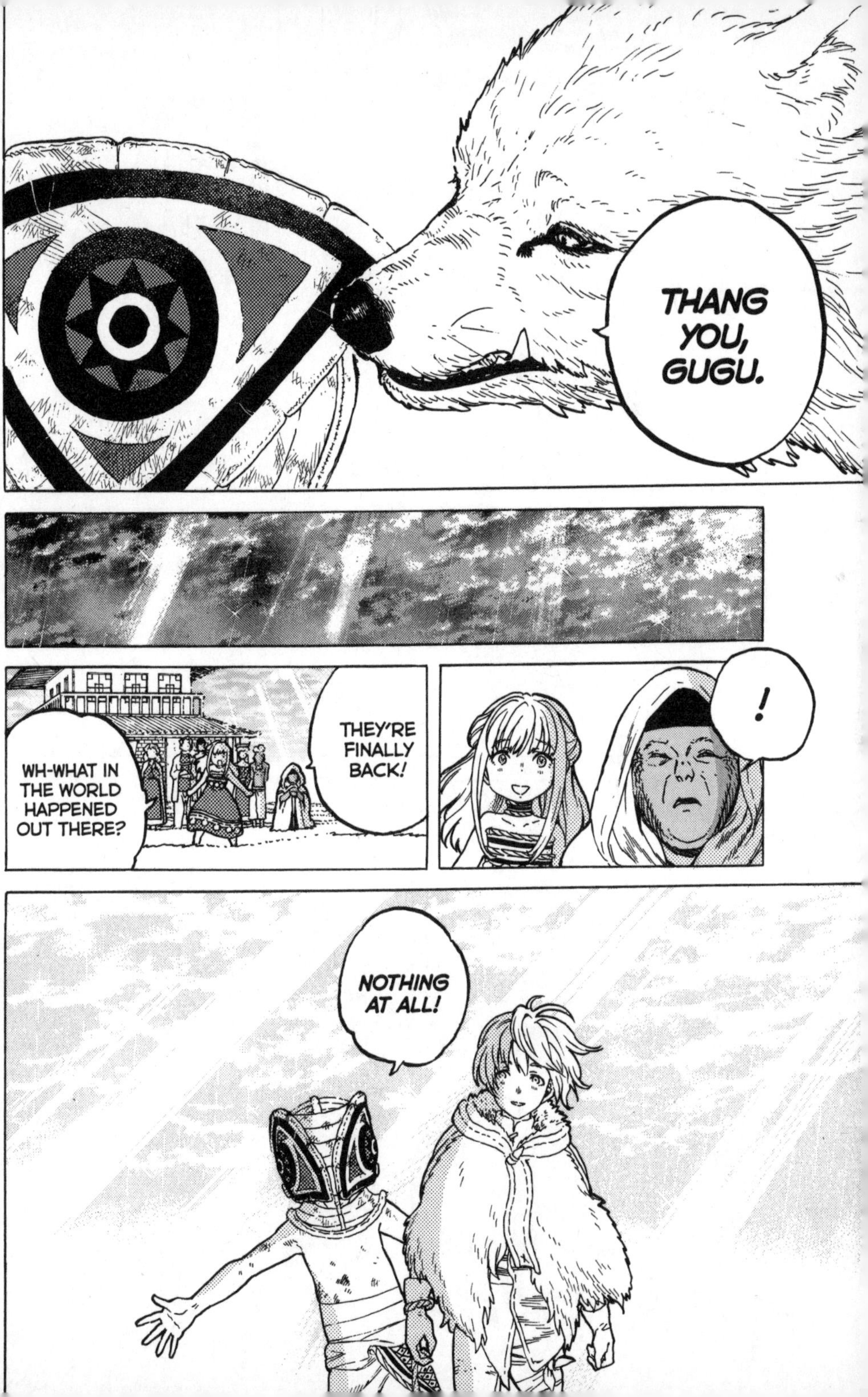
THANG YOU, GUGU.
!
THEY'RE FINALLY BACK!
WH-WHAT IN THE WORLD HAPPENED OUT THERE?
NOTHING AT ALL!

#24 New Family

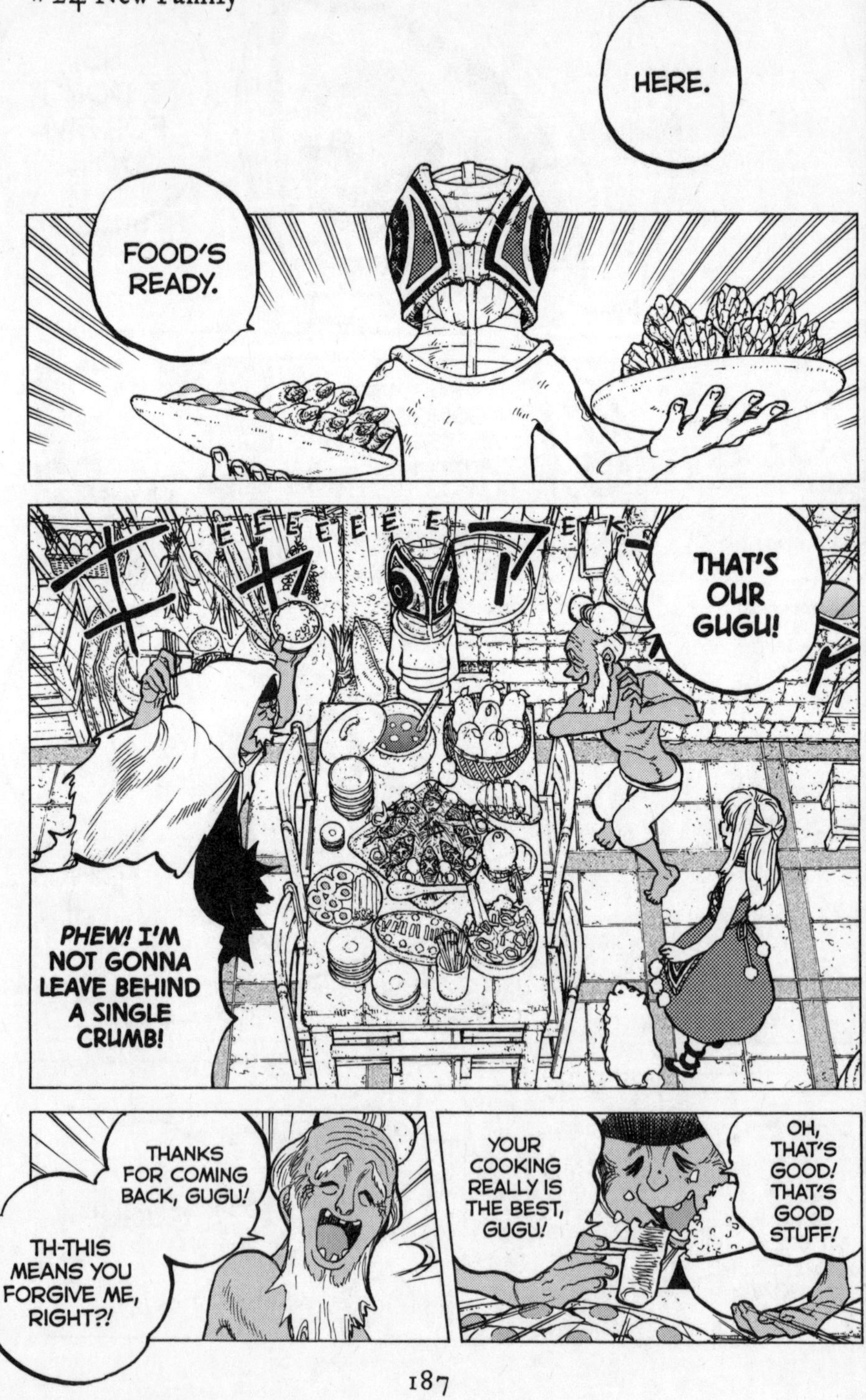
HERE.
FOOD'S READY.
THAT'S OUR GUGU!
PHEW! I'M NOT GONNA LEAVE BEHIND A SINGLE CRUMB!
OH, THAT'S GOOD! THAT'S GOOD STUFF!
YOUR COOKING REALLY IS THE BEST, GUGU!
THANKS FOR COMING BACK, GUGU!
TH-THIS MEANS YOU FORGIVE ME, RIGHT?!

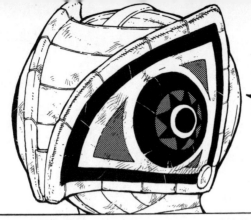

NO, I DON'T FORGIVE YOU.

SO I'M NOT GOING TO CALL YOU "BOOZE MAN" ANYMORE. FROM NOW ON, IT'S GONNA BE "ASSHOLE BOOZE MAN."

BUT YOU DID SAVE MY LIFE ONCE.

SO I'LL LEAVE OUT THE "ASSHOLE" PART AND JUST CALL YOU "BOOZE MAN."

HEY! THAT IS NO WAY TO SPEAK TO YOUR ELDERS, SON!

G—

GUGU!

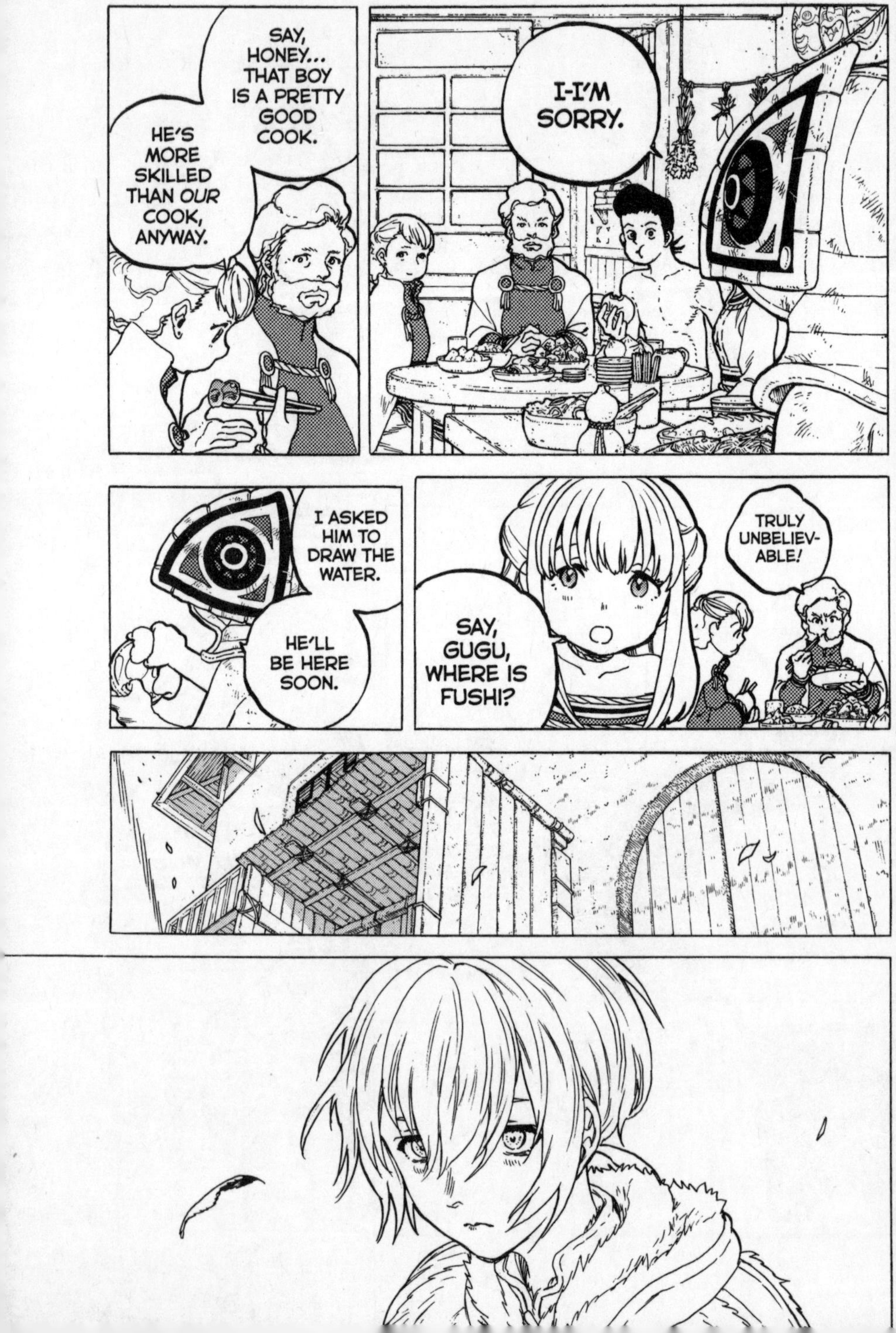
I-I'M SORRY.
SAY, HONEY... THAT BOY IS A PRETTY GOOD COOK.
HE'S MORE SKILLED THAN *OUR* COOK, ANYWAY.
TRULY UNBELIEV-ABLE!
SAY, GUGU, WHERE IS FUSHI?
I ASKED HIM TO DRAW THE WATER.
HE'LL BE HERE SOON.

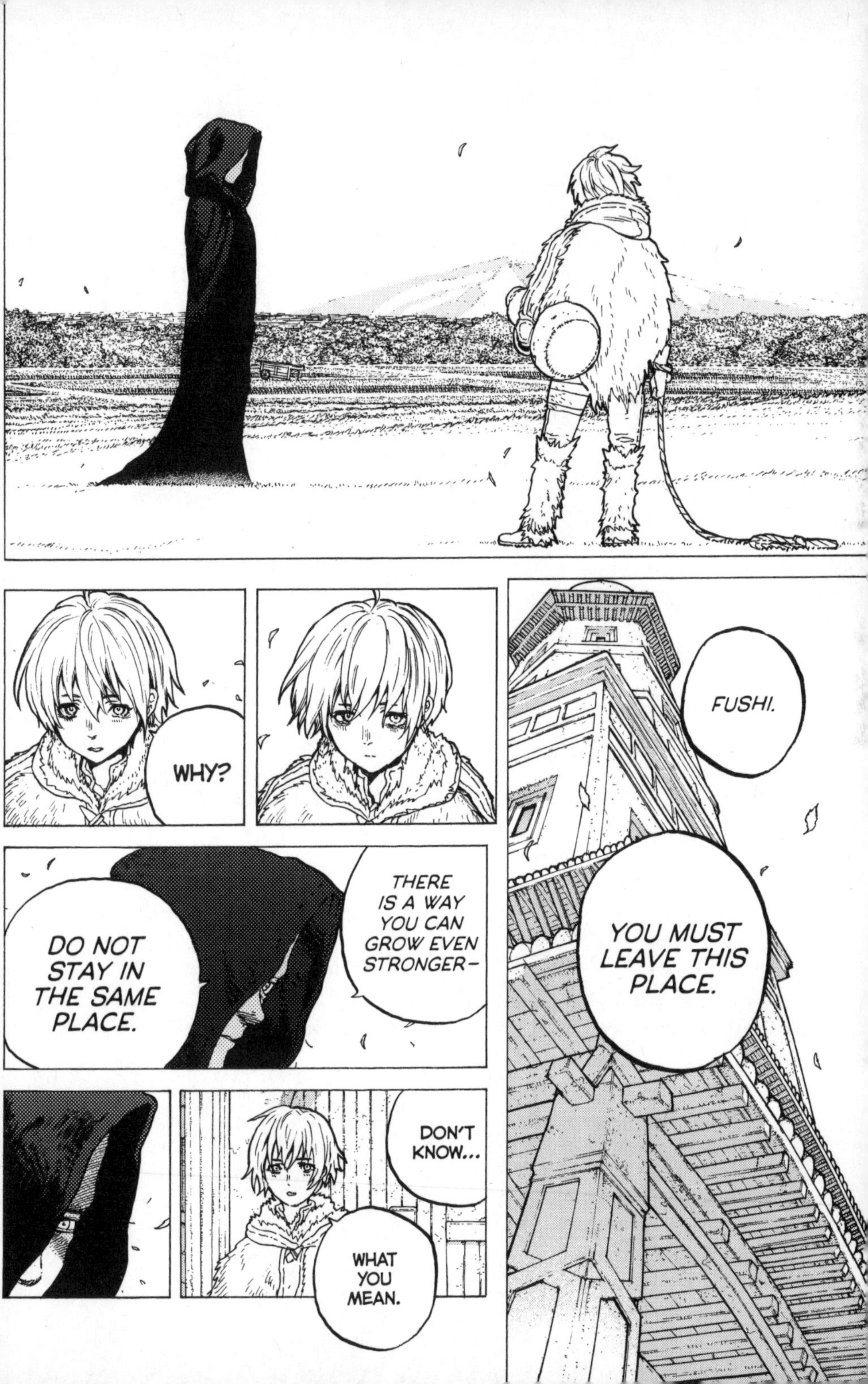
FUSHI.
YOU MUST LEAVE THIS PLACE.
WHY?
THERE IS A WAY YOU CAN GROW EVEN STRONGER–
DO NOT STAY IN THE SAME PLACE.
DON'T KNOW...
WHAT YOU MEAN.

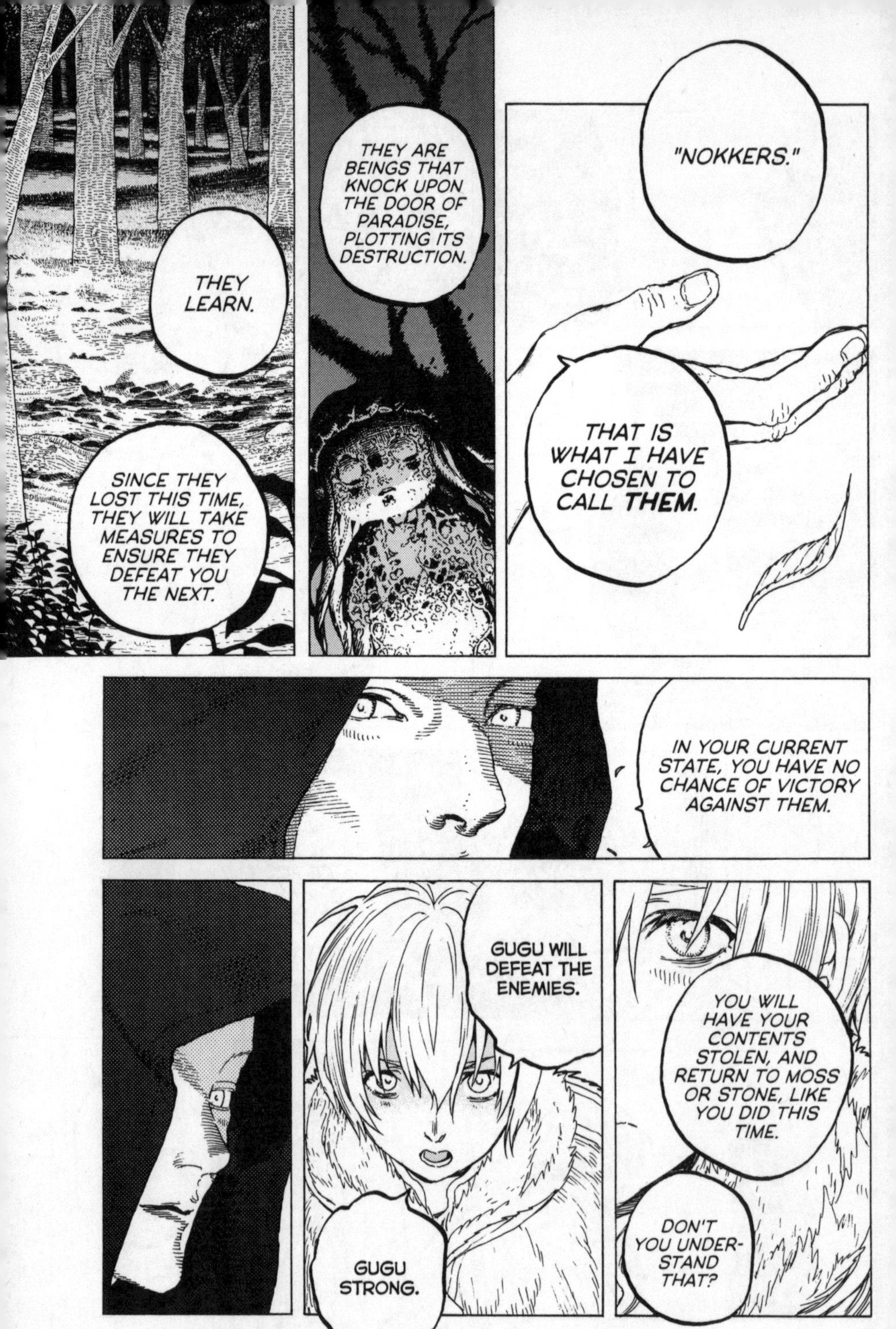
"NOKKERS."
THAT IS WHAT I HAVE CHOSEN TO CALL **THEM**.
THEY ARE BEINGS THAT KNOCK UPON THE DOOR OF PARADISE, PLOTTING ITS DESTRUCTION.
THEY LEARN.
SINCE THEY LOST THIS TIME, THEY WILL TAKE MEASURES TO ENSURE THEY DEFEAT YOU THE NEXT.
IN YOUR CURRENT STATE, YOU HAVE NO CHANCE OF VICTORY AGAINST THEM.
YOU WILL HAVE YOUR CONTENTS STOLEN, AND RETURN TO MOSS OR STONE, LIKE YOU DID THIS TIME.
DON'T YOU UNDER-STAND THAT?
GUGU WILL DEFEAT THE ENEMIES.
GUGU STRONG.

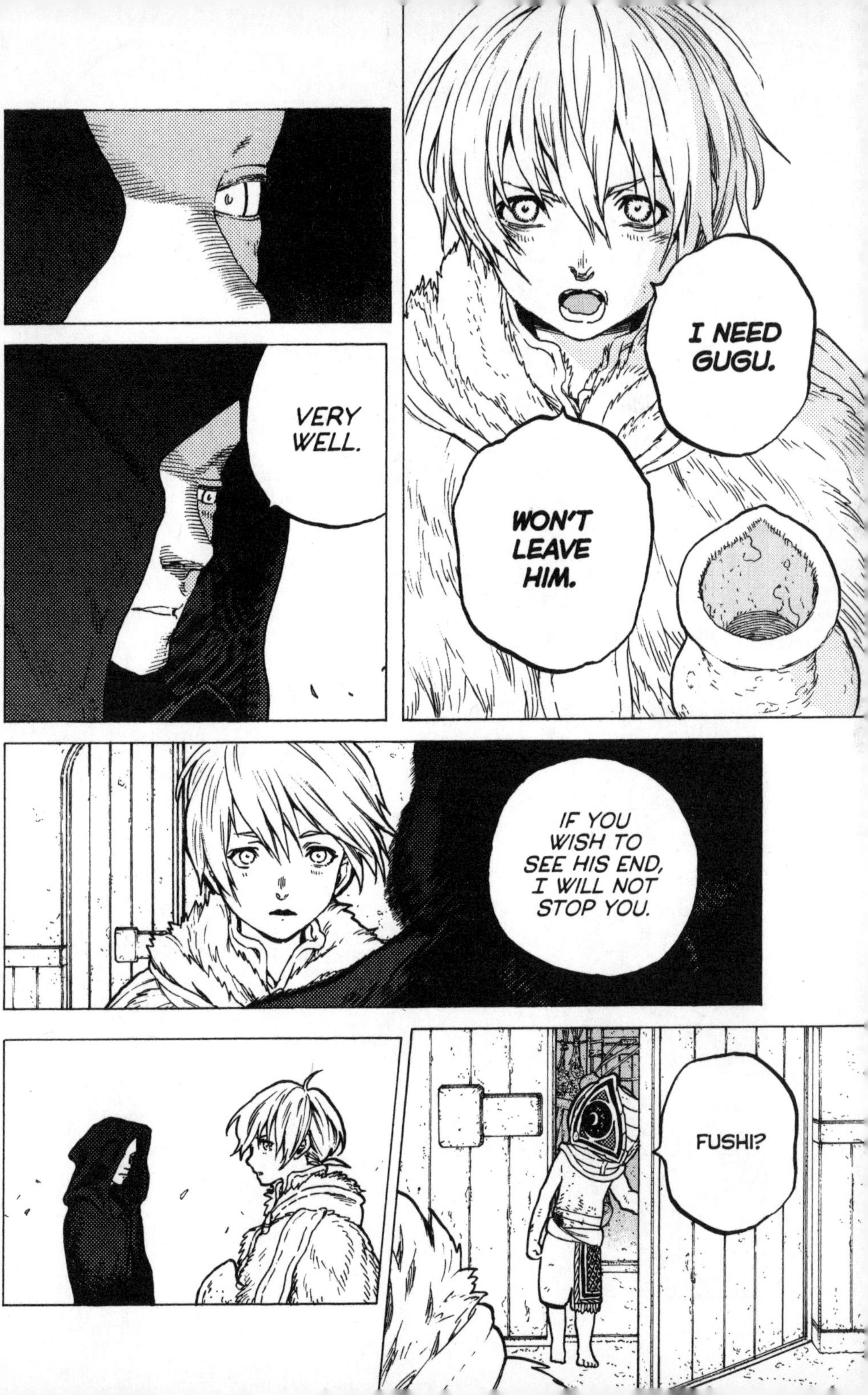
I NEED GUGU.
WON'T LEAVE HIM.
VERY WELL.
IF YOU WISH TO SEE HIS END, I WILL NOT STOP YOU.
FUSHI?

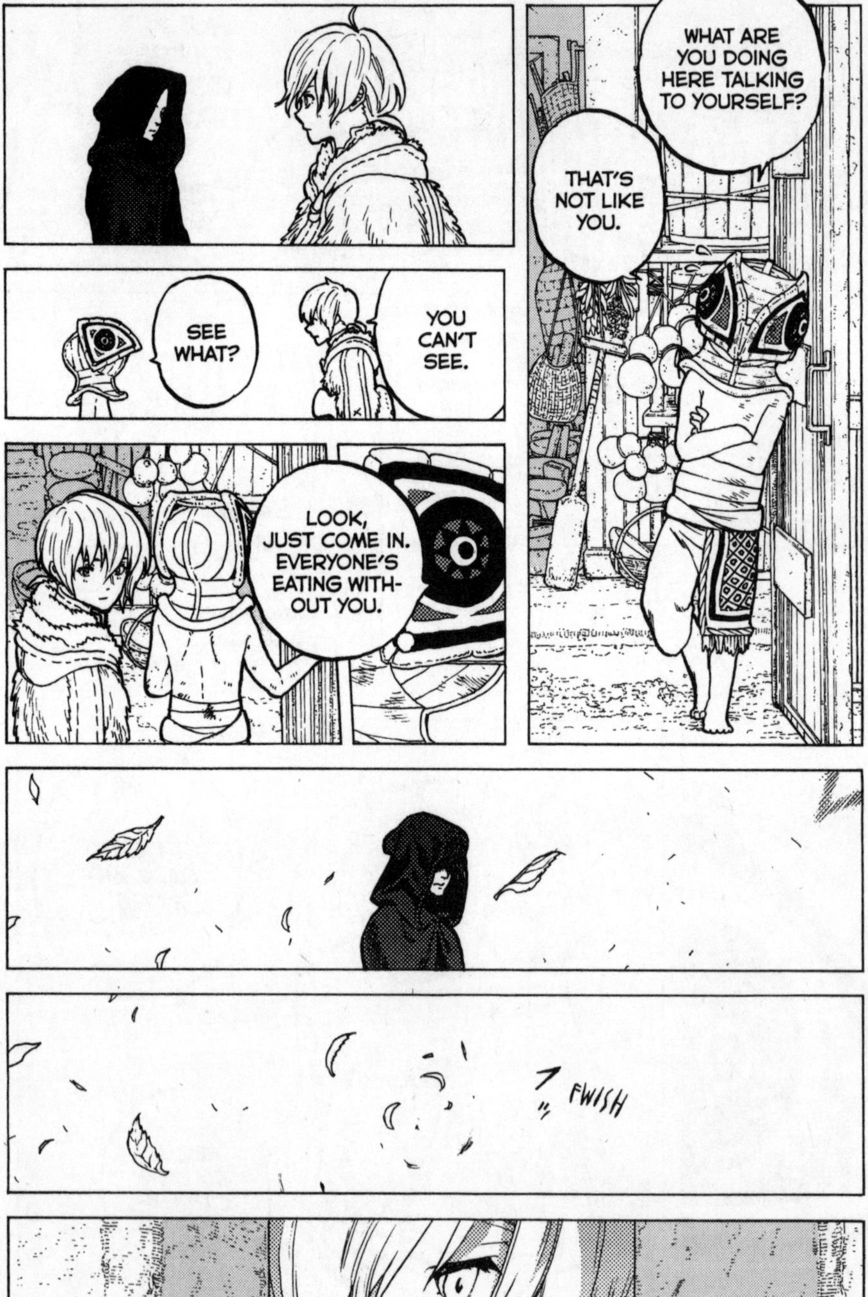
WHAT ARE YOU DOING HERE TALKING TO YOURSELF?
THAT'S NOT LIKE YOU.
YOU CAN'T SEE.
SEE WHAT?
LOOK, JUST COME IN. EVERYONE'S EATING WITH-OUT YOU.
FWISH

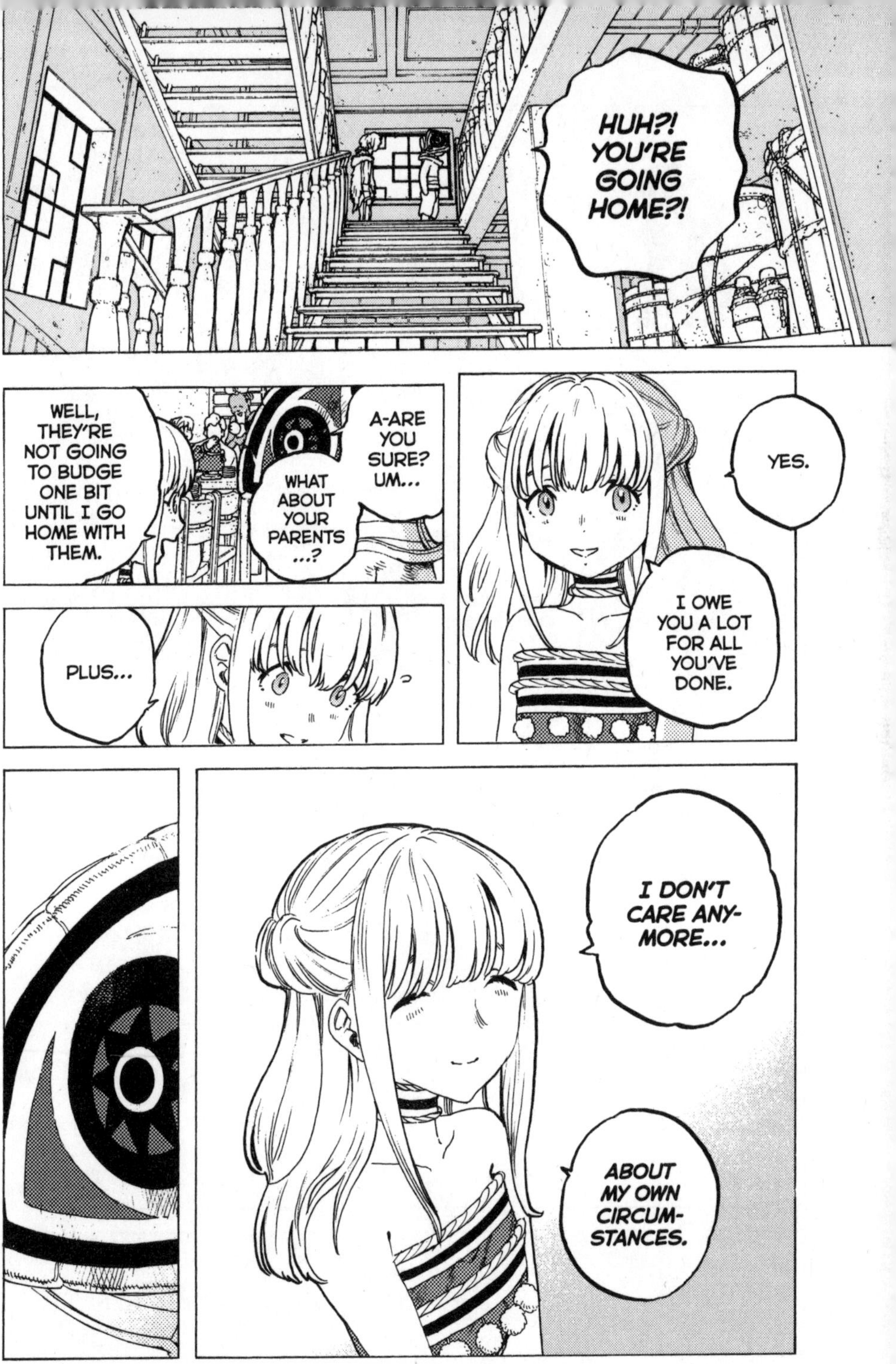
HUH?! YOU'RE GOING HOME?!
YES.
I OWE YOU A LOT FOR ALL YOU'VE DONE.
A-ARE YOU SURE? UM...
WHAT ABOUT YOUR PARENTS ...?
WELL, THEY'RE NOT GOING TO BUDGE ONE BIT UNTIL I GO HOME WITH THEM.
PLUS...
I DON'T CARE ANY-MORE...
ABOUT MY OWN CIRCUM-STANCES.

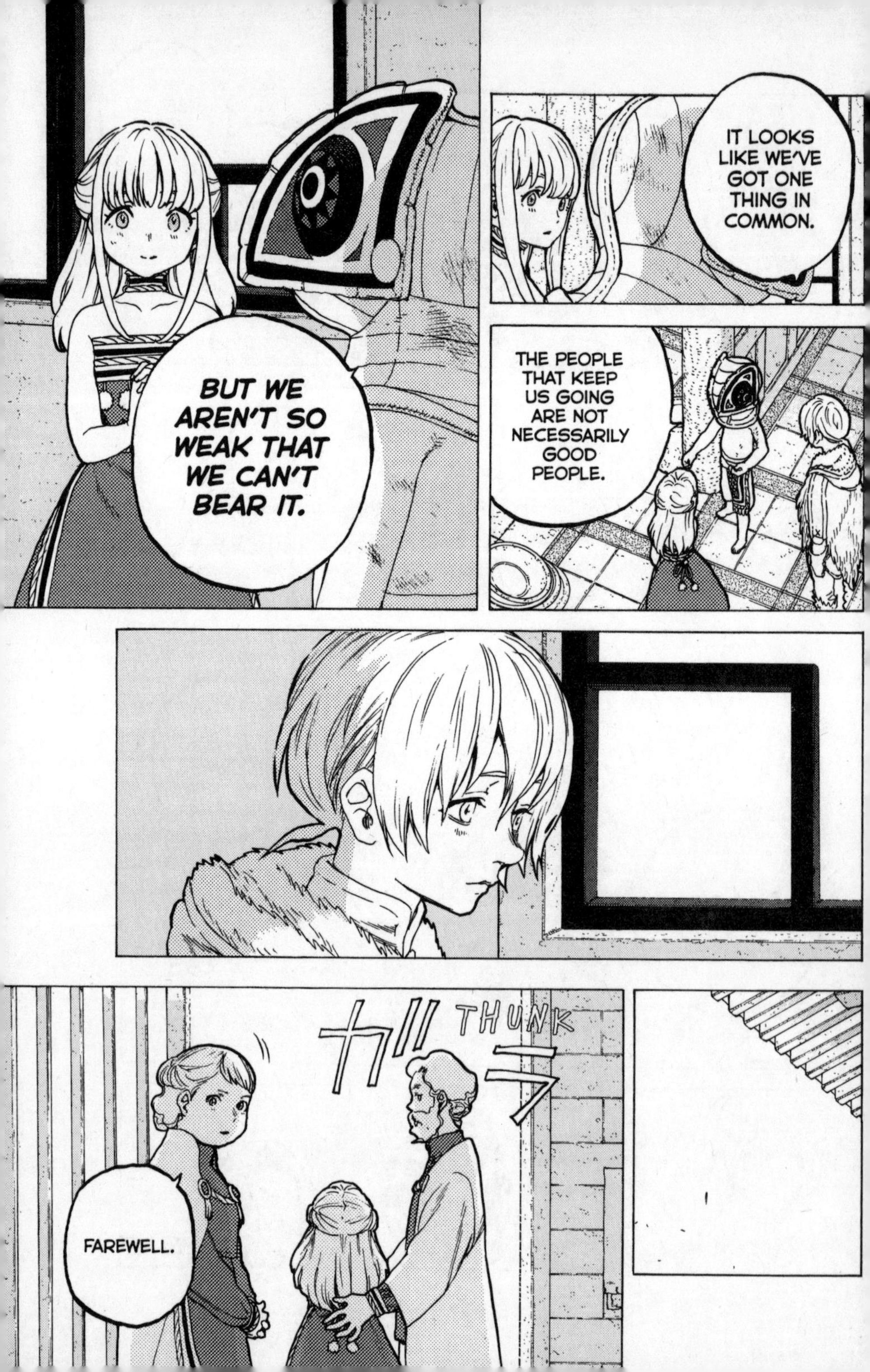
IT LOOKS LIKE WE'VE GOT ONE THING IN COMMON.
THE PEOPLE THAT KEEP US GOING ARE NOT NECESSARILY GOOD PEOPLE.
BUT WE AREN'T SO WEAK THAT WE CAN'T BEAR IT.
THUNK
FAREWELL.

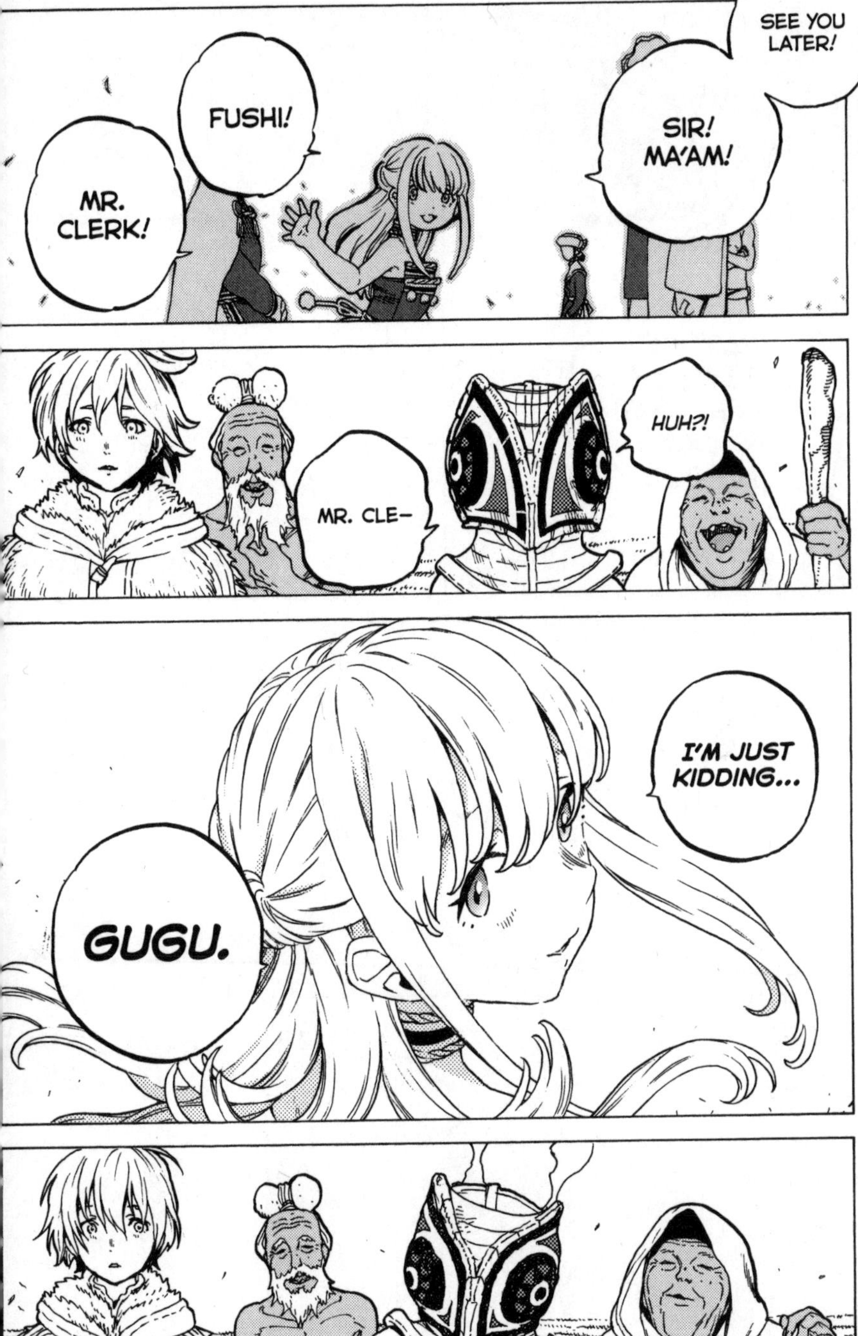
SEE YOU LATER!
SIR! MA'AM!
FUSHI!
MR. CLERK!
HUH?!
MR. CLE–
I'M JUST KIDDING...
GUGU.

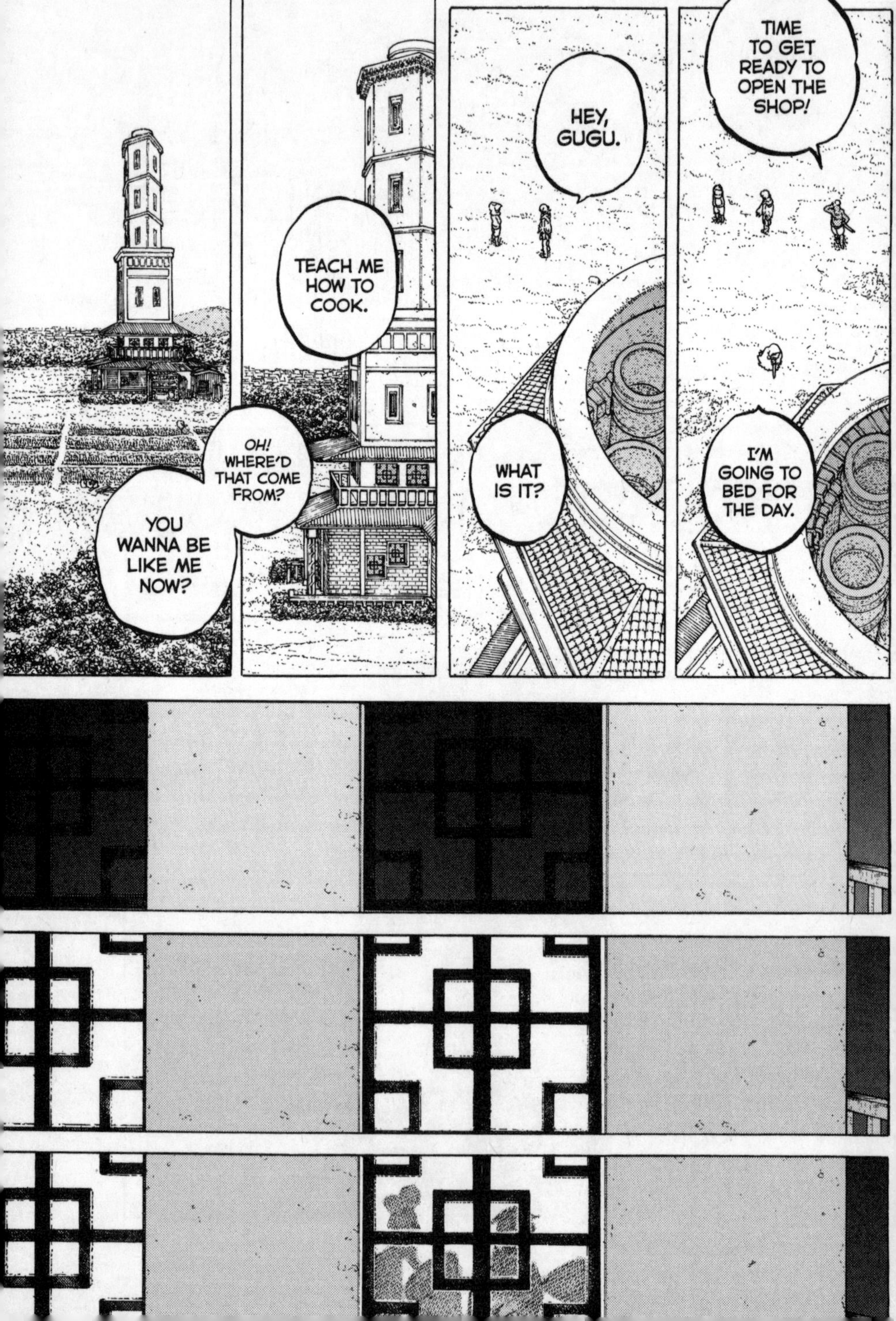
TIME TO GET READY TO OPEN THE SHOP!
I'M GOING TO BED FOR THE DAY.
HEY, GUGU.
WHAT IS IT?
TEACH ME HOW TO COOK.
OH! WHERE'D THAT COME FROM?
YOU WANNA BE LIKE ME NOW?

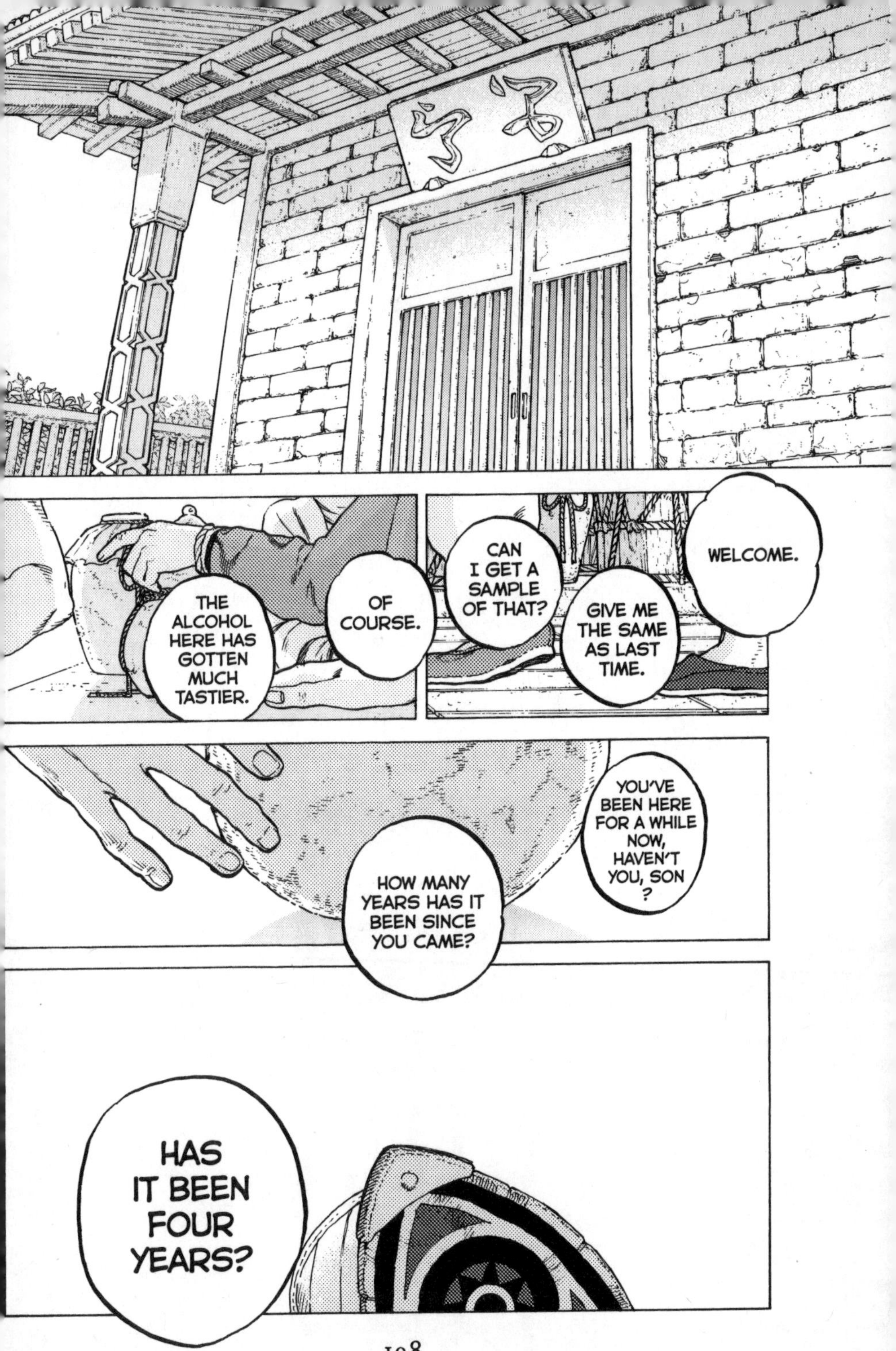
WELCOME.
GIVE ME THE SAME AS LAST TIME.
CAN I GET A SAMPLE OF THAT?
OF COURSE.
THE ALCOHOL HERE HAS GOTTEN MUCH TASTIER.
YOU'VE BEEN HERE FOR A WHILE NOW, HAVEN'T YOU, SON?
HOW MANY YEARS HAS IT BEEN SINCE YOU CAME?
HAS IT BEEN FOUR YEARS?

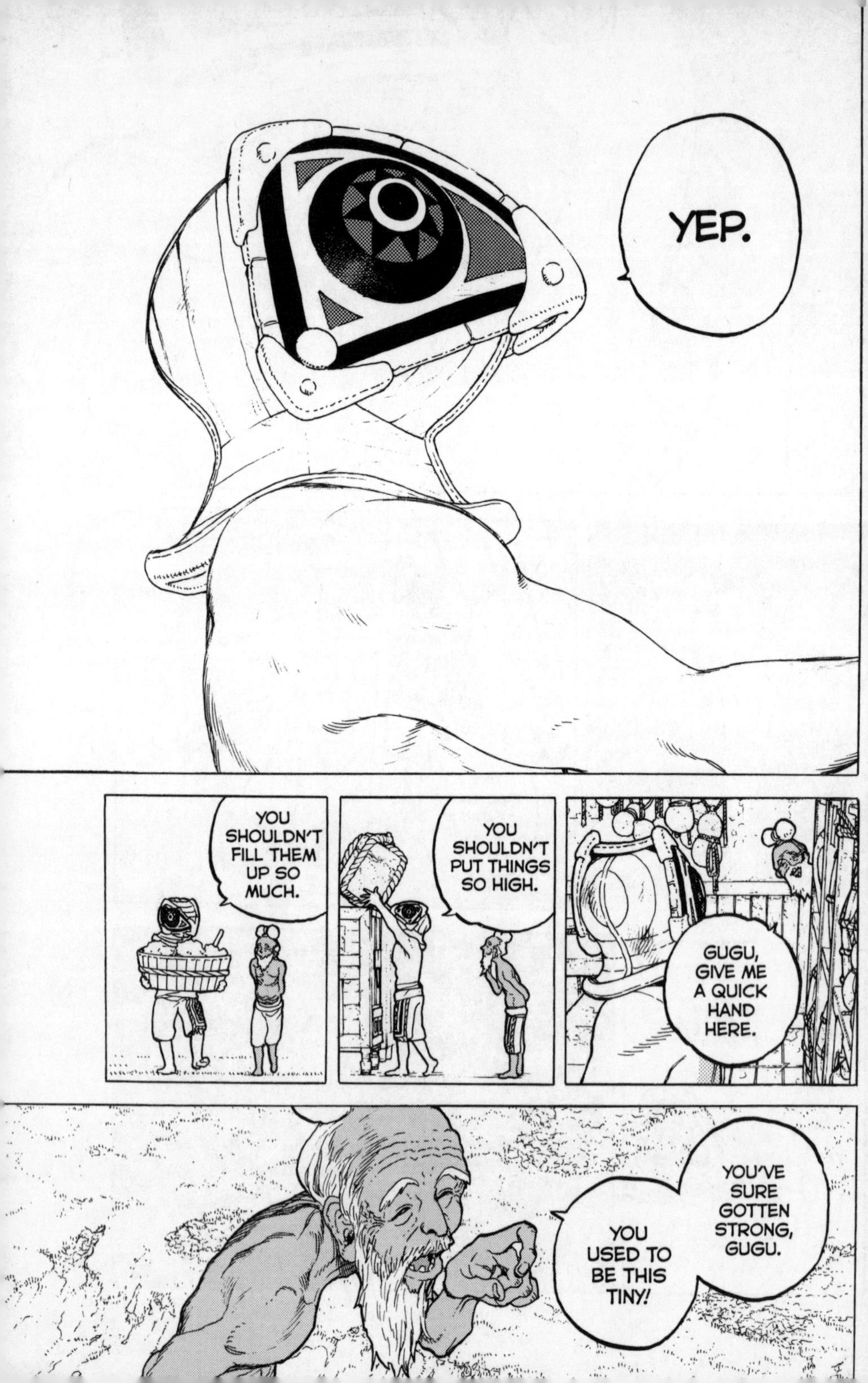
YEP.
GUGU, GIVE ME A QUICK HAND HERE.
YOU SHOULDN'T PUT THINGS SO HIGH.
YOU SHOULDN'T FILL THEM UP SO MUCH.
YOU'VE SURE GOTTEN STRONG, GUGU.
YOU USED TO BE THIS TINY!

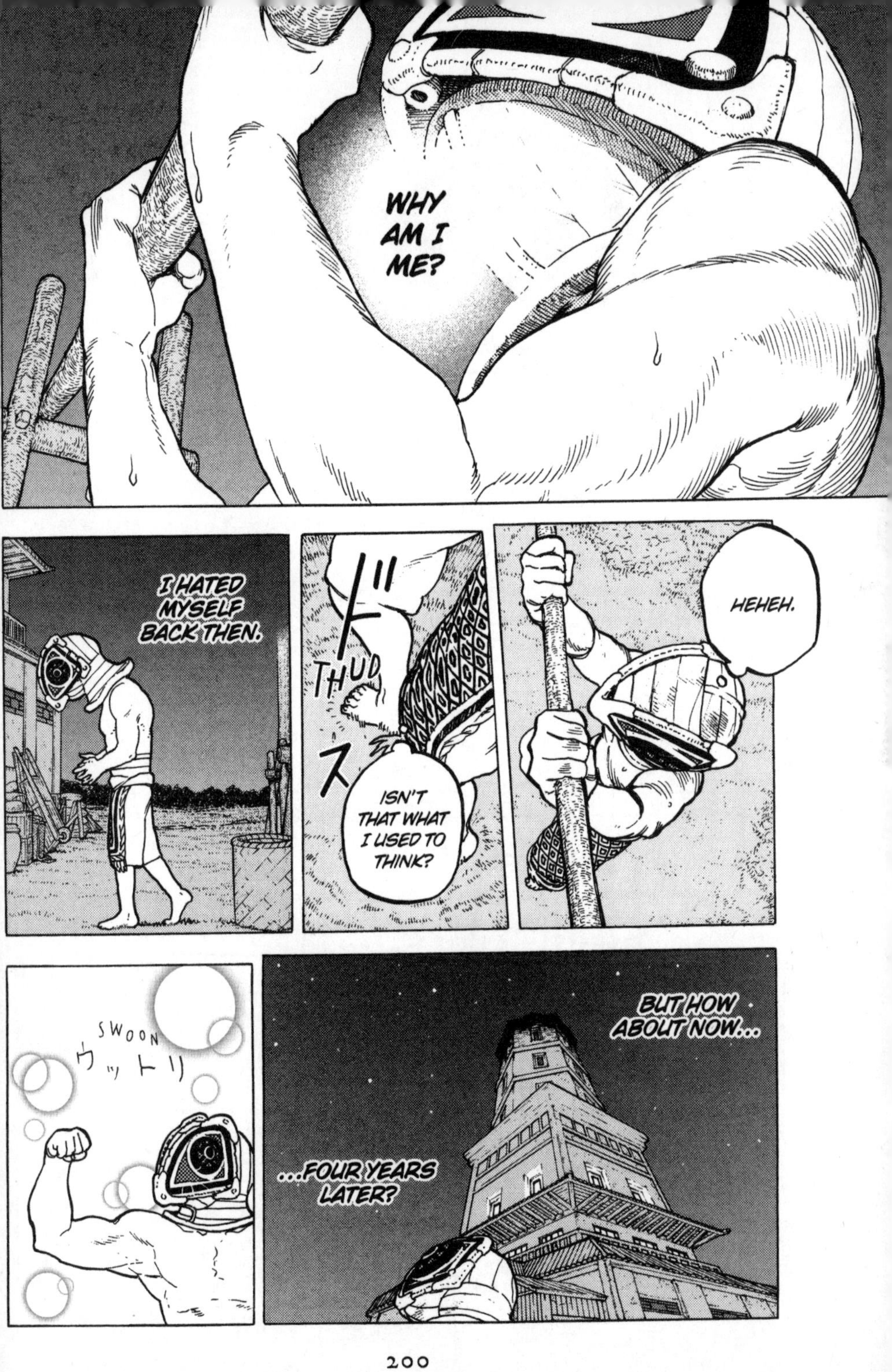
WHY AM I ME?
HEHEH.
ドス
THUD
ISN'T THAT WHAT I USED TO THINK?
I HATED MYSELF BACK THEN.
BUT HOW ABOUT NOW...
...FOUR YEARS LATER?
SWOON
ウットリ

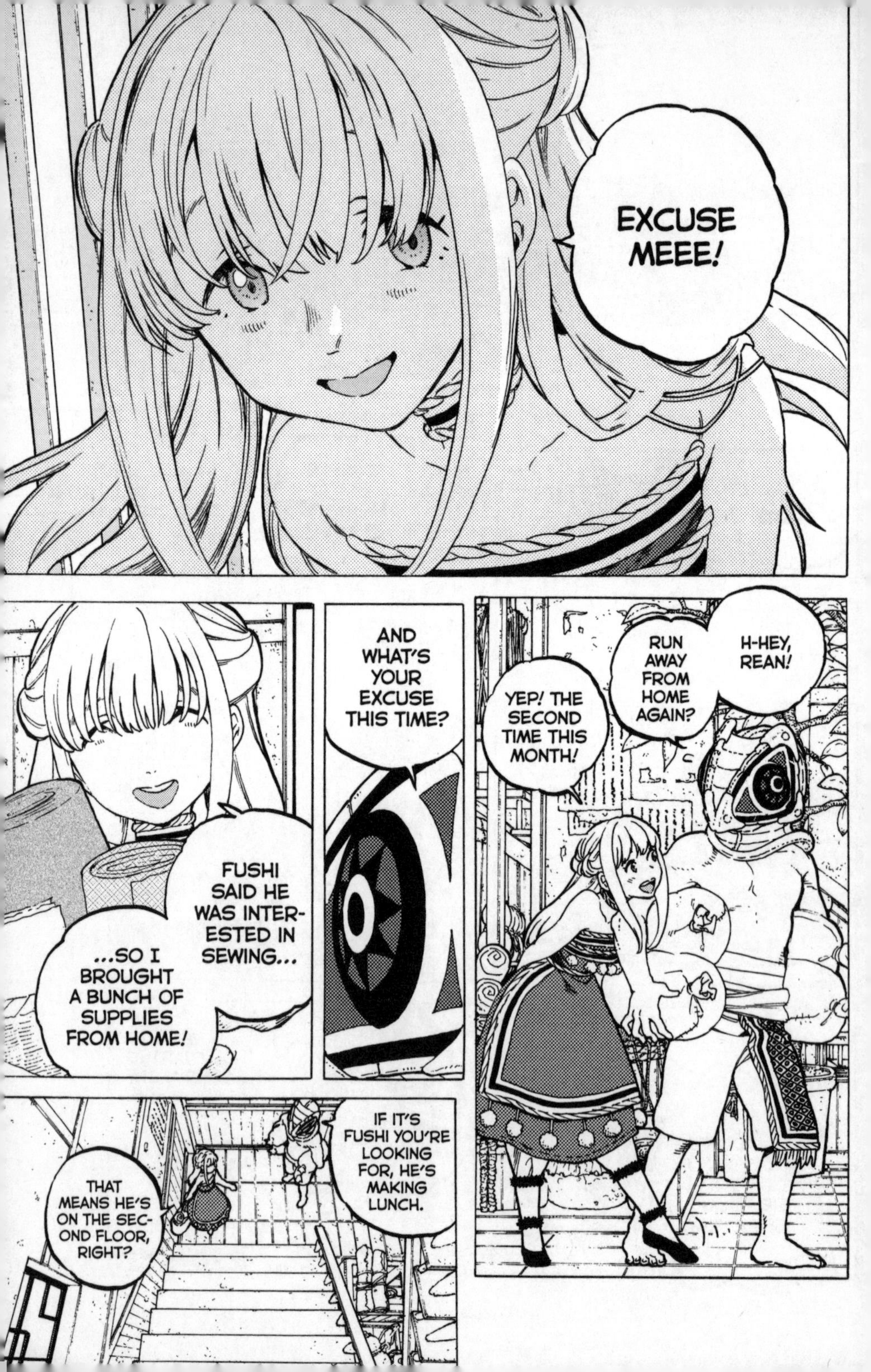
EXCUSE MEEE!
H-HEY, REAN!
RUN AWAY FROM HOME AGAIN?
YEP! THE SECOND TIME THIS MONTH!
AND WHAT'S YOUR EXCUSE THIS TIME?
FUSHI SAID HE WAS INTERESTED IN SEWING...
...SO I BROUGHT A BUNCH OF SUPPLIES FROM HOME!
IF IT'S FUSHI YOU'RE LOOKING FOR, HE'S MAKING LUNCH.
THAT MEANS HE'S ON THE SECOND FLOOR, RIGHT?

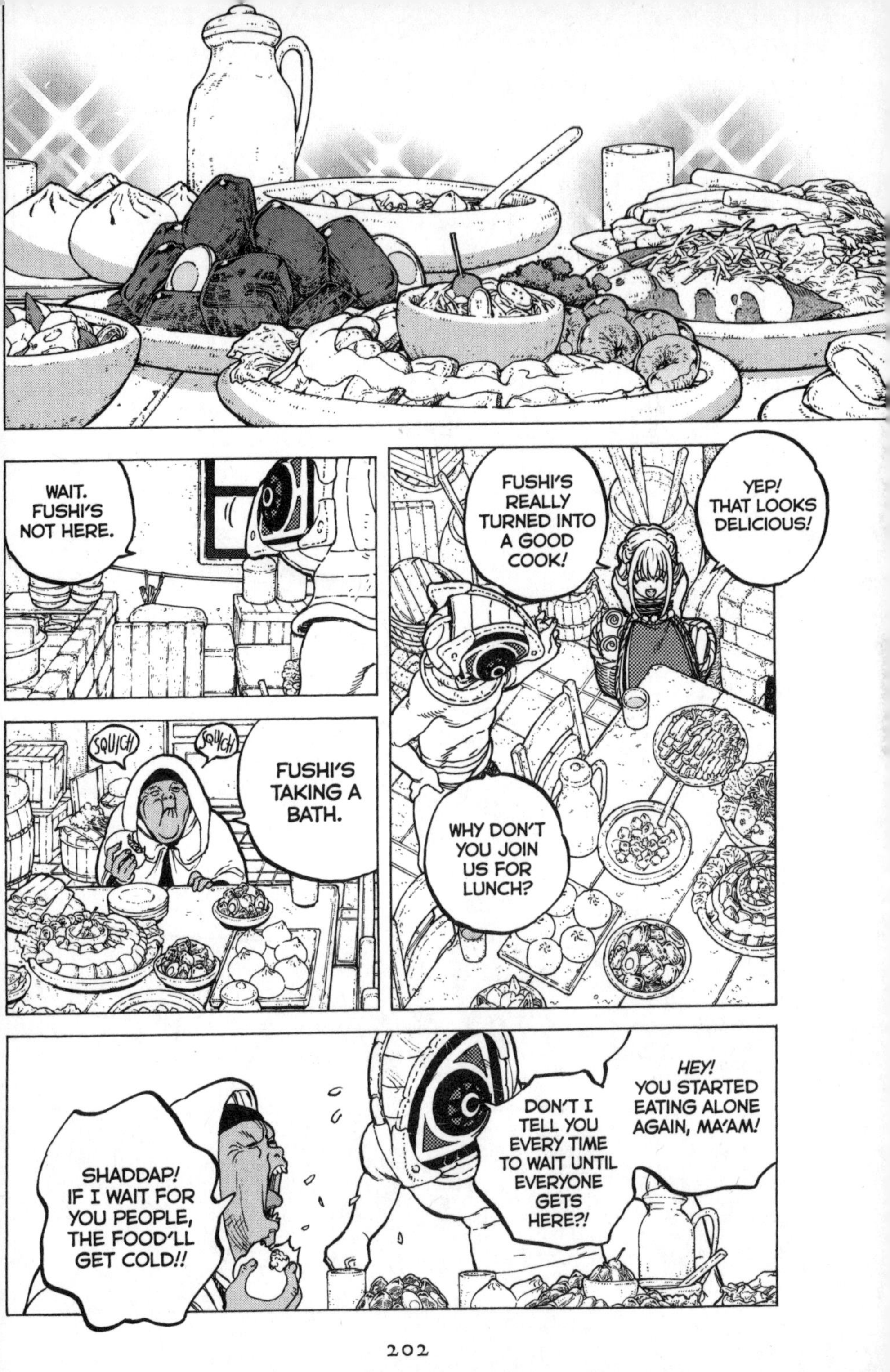
YEP! THAT LOOKS DELICIOUS!
FUSHI'S REALLY TURNED INTO A GOOD COOK!
WHY DON'T YOU JOIN US FOR LUNCH?
WAIT. FUSHI'S NOT HERE.
SQUICH
SQUICH
FUSHI'S TAKING A BATH.
HEY! YOU STARTED EATING ALONE AGAIN, MA'AM!
DON'T I TELL YOU EVERY TIME TO WAIT UNTIL EVERYONE GETS HERE?!
SHADDAP! IF I WAIT FOR YOU PEOPLE, THE FOOD'LL GET COLD!!

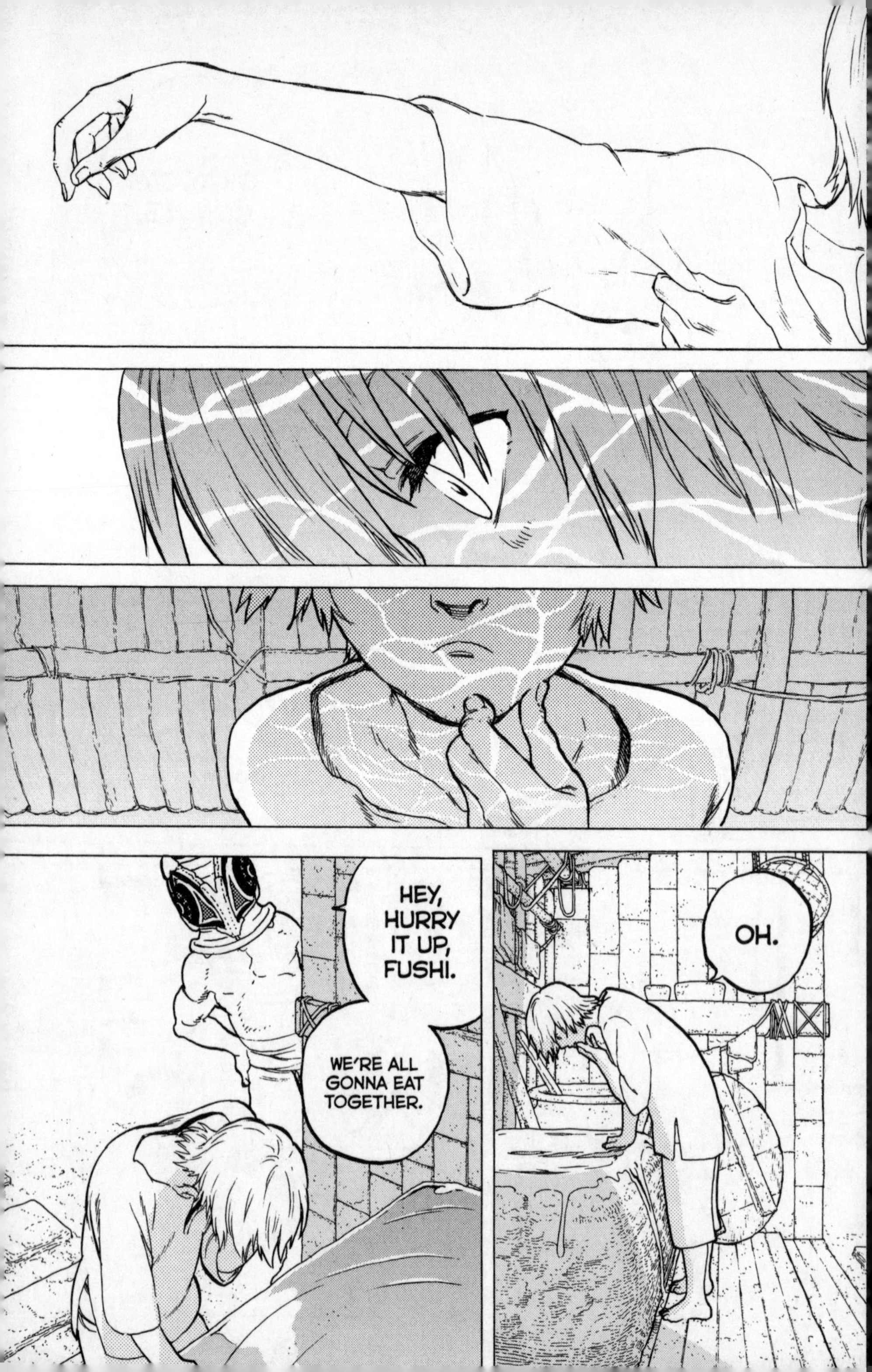
OH.
HEY, HURRY IT UP, FUSHI.
WE'RE ALL GONNA EAT TOGETHER.

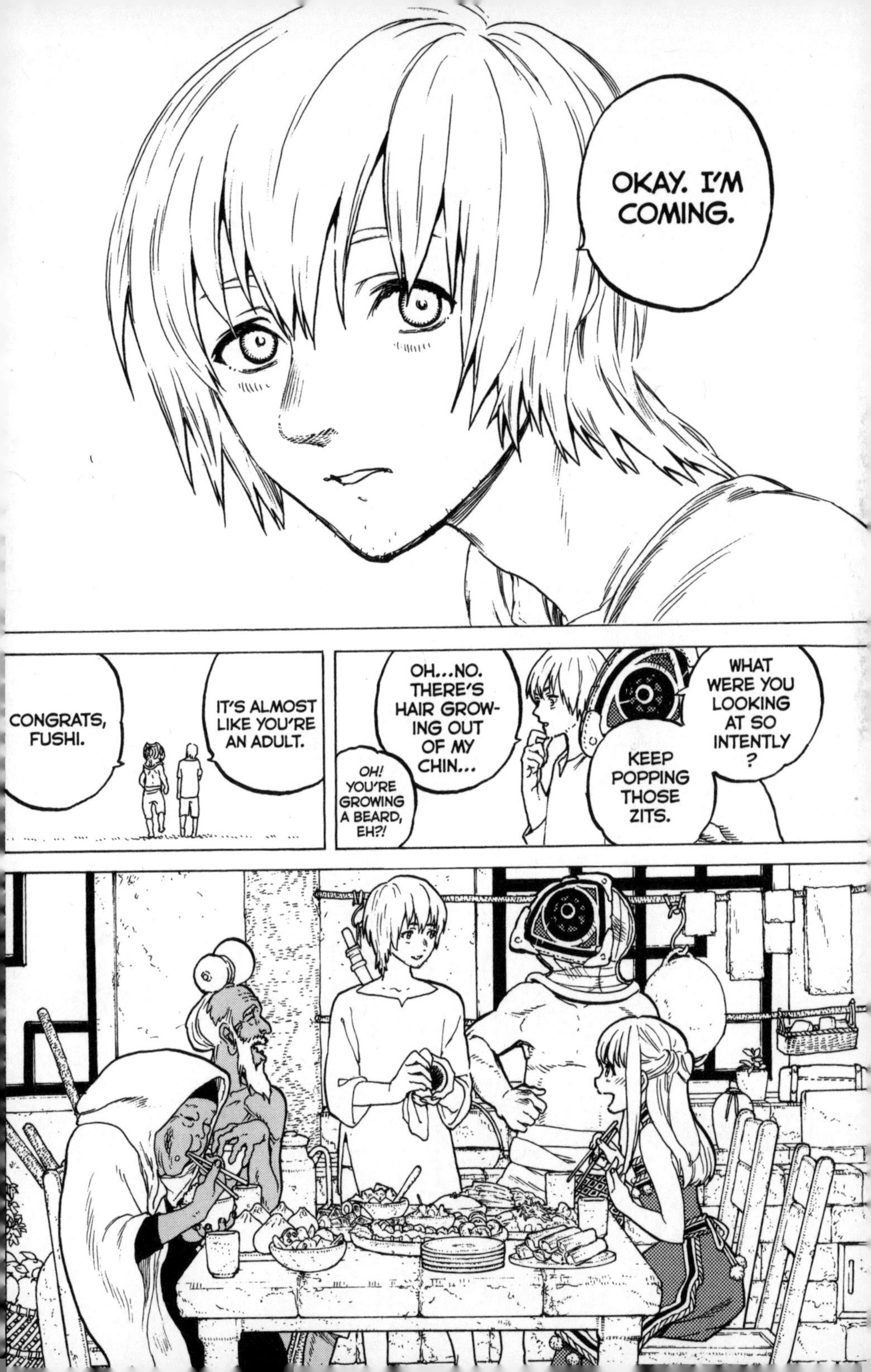
OKAY. I'M COMING.
WHAT WERE YOU LOOKING AT SO INTENTLY?
OH...NO. THERE'S HAIR GROWING OUT OF MY CHIN...
KEEP POPPING THOSE ZITS.
OH! YOU'RE GROWING A BEARD, EH?!
IT'S ALMOST LIKE YOU'RE AN ADULT.
CONGRATS, FUSHI.

TO YOUR
ETERNITY

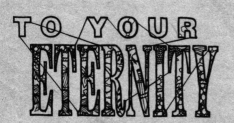

Based on the critically acclaimed classic horror manga

The first new *Parasyte* manga in over 20 years!

NEO
ParaSyte f

BY ASUMIKO NAKAMURA, EMA TOYAMA, MIKI RINNO, LALAKO KOJIMA, KAORI YUKI, BANKO KUZE, YUUKI OBATA, KASHIO, YUI KUROE, ASIA WATANABE, MIKIMAKI, HIKARU SURUGA, HAJIME SHINJO, RENJURO KINDAICHI, AND YURI NARUSHIMA

A collection of chilling new *Parasyte* stories from Japan's top shojo artists!

Parasites: shape-shifting aliens whose only purpose is to assimilate with and consume the human race... but do these monsters have a different side? A parasite becomes a prince to save his romance-obsessed female host from a dangerous stalker. Another hosts a cooking show, in which the real monsters are revealed. These and 13 more stories, from some of the greatest shojo manga artists alive today, together make up a chilling, funny, and entertaining tribute to one of manga's horror classics!

The Black Museum The Ghost and the Lady

By Kazuhiro Fujita

Deep in Scotland Yard in London sits an evidence room dedicated to the greatest mysteries of British history. In this "Black Museum" sits a misshapen hunk of lead—two bullets fused together—the key to a wartime encounter between Florence Nightingale, the mother of modern nursing, and a supernatural Man in Grey. This story is unknown to most scholars of history, but a special guest of the museum will tell the tale of The Ghost and the Lady...

Praise for Kazuhiro Fujita's *Ushio and Tora*

"A charming revival that combines a classic look with modern depth and pacing... **Essential viewing both for curmudgeons and new fans alike.**" — Anime News Network

"**GREAT!** The first episode of Ushio and Tora captures the essence of '90s anime." — IGN

"I'm pleasantly surprised to find modern shojo using cross-dressing as a dramatic device to deliver social commentary... Recommended."

-Otaku USA Magazine

The prince in his dark days

By **Hico Yamanaka**

A drunkard for a father, a household of poverty... For 17-year-old Atsuko, misfortune is all she knows and believes in. Until one day, a chance encounter with Itaru–the wealthy heir of a huge corporation–changes everything. The two look identical, uncannily so. When Itaru curiously goes missing, Atsuko is roped into being his stand-in. There, in his shoes, Atsuko must parade like a prince in a palace. She encounters many new experiences, but at what cost...?

HAPPINESS

ハピネス

By Shuzo Oshimi

From the creator of *The Flowers of Evil*

Nothing interesting is happening in Makoto Ozaki's first year of high school. His life is a series of quiet humiliations: low-grade bullies, unreliable friends, and the constant frustration of his adolescent lust. But one night, a pale, thin girl knocks him to the ground in an alley and offers him a choice. Now everything is different. Daylight is searingly bright. Food tastes awful. And worse than anything is the terrible, consuming thirst...

Praise for Shuzo Oshimi's *The Flowers of Evil*

"A shockingly readable story that vividly—one might even say queasily—evokes the fear and confusion of discovering one's own sexuality. Recommended." —The Manga Critic

"A page-turning tale of sordid middle school blackmail." —Otaku USA Magazine

"A stunning new horror manga." —Third Eye Comics

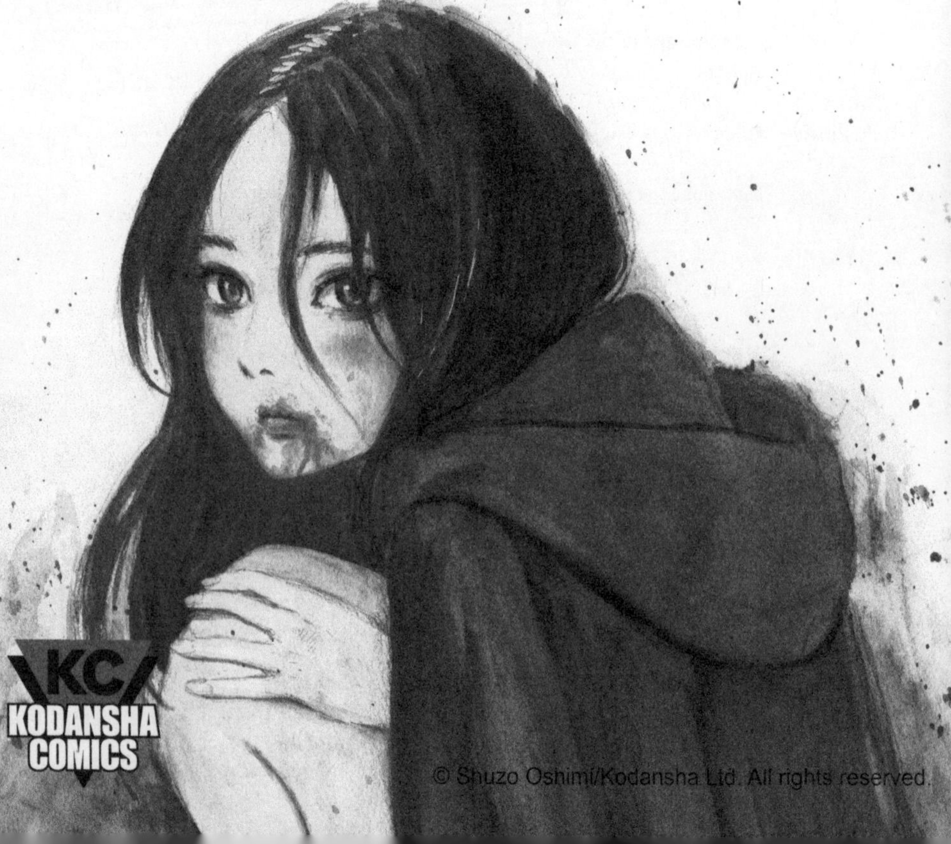

KC KODANSHA COMICS

MW00989588

To Your Eternity volume 3 is a work of fiction.
Names, characters, places, and incidents are the products of the author's imagination or are used fictitiously. Any resemblance to actual events, locales, or persons, living or dead, is entirely coincidental.

A Kodansha Comics Trade Paperback Original.

Published in the United States by Kodansha Comics,
an imprint of Kodansha USA Publishing, LLC, New York.

Publication rights for this English edition arranged through Kodansha Ltd., Tokyo.

First published in Japan in 2017 by Kodansha Ltd., Tokyo,
as *Fumetsu no Anata e* volume 3.

Cover Design: Tadashi Hisamochi (hive&co., Ltd.)
Title Logo Design: Shinobu Ohashi

ISBN 978-1-63236-573-6

Printed in the United States of America.

www.kodanshacomics.com

9 8 7 6 5 4 3

Translation: Steven LeCroy
Lettering: Darren Smith
Editing: Haruko Hashimoto, Alexandra Swanson
Editorial Assistance: YKS Services LLC/SKY Japan, INC.
Kodansha Comics Edition Cover Design: Phil Balsman